Victorians and Mystery

ALSO BY W. DAVID SHAW:

The Dialectical Temper

Tennyson's Style

The Lucid Veil

Victorians and Mystery

CRISES OF REPRESENTATION

W. David Shaw

Cornell University Press

ITHACA AND LONDON

First published 1990 by Cornell University Press.

International Standard Book Number 0-8014-2403-8
Library of Congress Catalog Card Number 89-38545
Printed in the United States of America
Librarians: Library of Congress cataloging information appears on the last page of the book.

⊛ The paper used in this publication meets the minimum requirements of the American National Standard for Permanence of Paper for Printed Library Materials Z39. 48–1984.

For my children, who restore the mystery,
and my wife, who gives it meaning

Contents

Acknowledgments   ix
Introduction: Victorians and Mystery   1

PART ONE
Mystery and the Unconscious: Can Free Will Exist?   21

1   Can We Be Conscious of Meanings That Lie outside
Consciousness?   28
2   We Know More Than We Know We Know: Repetition in
Dickens and Hardy   34
3   "It Is Unutterable": The Burden of Signs in *Wuthering
Heights* and *Villette*   53
4   "The Signless Inane": Mystery and the Unconscious in
Carlyle   72
5   Incomprehensible Certainties and Interesting
Uncertainties: Hopkins and Tennyson   88

PART TWO
Mystery and Identity: Is Self-Creation Possible?   107

6   Making up People: Are Moral Values Invented or
Described?   115
7   Estranging the Familiar: Veils of Reserve in Trollope and
James   122
8   The Dark Principle: Erosions of Identity in *Vanity Fair*   141
9   The Burden of Role-Playing: Self-Creation in Borrow and
Clough   157

10 We Make Our Truths but Cannot Speak Them: George
    Eliot and the Uses of Silence   176
11 Browning's Unheard Words: The Poetry of Silence   196

PART THREE
Mystery and Method: Is a Centerless View a True One?   221

12 Must We Explain What We Believe and Prove What We
    Explain?   228
13 Newman on Faith: A Heroic Theory of Knowledge   234
14 Meaning More Than Is Said: Sources of Mystery in
    Christina Rossetti and Arnold   251
15 The Bewitchment of Words: J. S. Mill on Saying More
    Than Is Meant   276
16 The Critic as Detective: Mystery and Method in *The
    Moonstone*   288
17 Browning and Mystery: *The Ring and the Book* and
    Modern Theory   300
    Conclusion: Crises in Representation   322

    Bibliography   349
    Index   361

Acknowledgments

As I was writing this book I became increasingly aware of my debt to F. E. L. Priestley, the teacher who introduced me to Victorian studies thirty years ago, and whose influence has grown stronger with time. Professor Priestley died before the book was finished, but his abiding legacy is a conviction that learning can sometimes be the demanding but liberating high adventure he always tried to make it.

I am grateful for the counsel and encouragement of Bernhard Kendler, editor at Cornell University Press, who has sustained a generous interest in my work over many years. Reports of two anonymous readers for the Press have been as painstaking in their queries as they have been charitable in their evaluations and expert in their criticisms. I thank Cornell University Press for permission to use revised segments of my essay "Poet of Mystery: The Art of Christina Rossetti," originally published in *The Achievement of Christina Rossetti*, ed. David A. Kent (copyright © 1987 by Cornell University), pp. 23–56. For permission to use portions of two essays that I published in special centenary issues of *Victorian Poetry* and *Texas Studies in Literature and Language*—"Browning's Murder Mystery: *The Ring and the Book* and Modern Theory," *VP* 27 (1989): 79–98, and "Incomprehensible Certainties and Interesting Uncertainties: Hopkins and Tennyson," *TSLL* (University of Texas Press) 31 (1989): 66–84—I am grateful to the editors of both journals.

I thank the Houghton Library of Harvard University and Alexander James for permission to quote an unpublished manuscript on Thomas Carlyle by William James. I am grateful, too, for the permission of the Houghton Library and the Harvard Theatre Collection to quote manuscripts of Charlotte Brontë and miscellaneous materials on Wilkie Collins and Thomas Hardy. For permission to quote from

Christina Rossetti's notebook manuscripts, I am indebted to the Bodleian Library of Oxford University and Imogen Dennis, who holds the copyright on the Bodleian manuscripts. I am grateful, finally, to the University of Toronto for the award of a Senior Connaught Research Fellowship. While allowing me to finish the book, the Connaught Fellowship has also enabled me to recover a portion of the lost Greek meaning of the word "scholastic," "a devotion to learning of one's leisure, of one's time to be wise," which in the modern university seems oddly enchanted—an oasis always on the verge of dissolving in the air.

I have had the good fortune to know colleagues and students who exemplify the qualities I value most: skepticism, generosity of temperament, and a quizzical impulse to test ideas and criticize authority. My friendship with Ekbert Faas of York University and my correspondence over the years with Avrom Fleishman of the Johns Hopkins University, Gerhard Joseph of the City College of New York, and Clyde de L. Ryals of Duke University have also taught me the value of sharing ideas, concern for the outcome of colleagues' projects, and the meaning of intellectual indebtedness.

My greatest debt is to my wife, Carol. To her I owe the idea of writing a book on mystery, the constant opportunity to discuss it, and the daily proof that a world that commands devotion by schooling the soul in mystery could never be as cold and ghostlike as my intellectual conceptions of it. By enlarging the mind and offering all the heart can wish, her love and friendship have kept me in touch with two of the greater mysteries.

W. DAVID SHAW

Toronto

Victorians and Mystery

Introduction:

Victorians and Mystery

Any study of mystery in Victorian literature must focus on crises of representation. I borrow this phrase from Michel Foucault to describe the extraordinary density and impediment to clarity that occur whenever a poet, novelist, or essayist, in boldly confronting mysteries within a subject, refuses to deny bewilderment or pretend that matters are less puzzling or unsettling than they really are. Such authors honor the uncertainty principle that distinguishes not only Keats's poetry of negative capability but also profundity itself from the enormous dogmatism of an unqualified assertion or the deep slumber of a prejudice. Just as Werner Heisenberg discovers that any observation by an atomic physicist may alter the particles he is trying to observe, so many Victorian writers find that every attempt to represent the ambiguities or solve the mysteries at the center of their world is in danger of destroying it. In *In Memoriam*, for example, the more accurately Tennyson *describes* the history of the earth, the more remorselessly he also *changes* the world he immediately perceives through the senses. The poet becomes a geological Prospero, turning hills into shadows and "solid lands" into melting mist (123.7) until, like an "insubstantial pageant faded," even "the great globe itself" assumes the shape of cloud and disappears (*The Tempest*, 4.1.153, 155).

Crises of faith and knowing send the Victorians in search of new language for their bewilderments. Like skeletons locked away in some family closet, three of these bewilderments keep coming back to haunt them. Some of their best writers are obsessed, in the first place, by the specter of the unconscious. Carlyle and the Brontës both fear and desire a repressed or subliminal form of consciousness. At times the hidden world seethes volcanically from dark foundations; at other

1

times it can be glimpsed peeping furtively from an attic window, like the madwoman of Gothic fiction. The Victorians are puzzled, in the second place, by mysteries of identity. Given an apparent excluder, Darwin's science of universal flux, how can any identity be said to endure over time? And finally, because of widely divergent starting points, many Victorian scientists and humanists are puzzled to explain how any shared knowledge is possible. T. H. Huxley knows that unless science is carried on in the spirit of the humanities it can never be experienced as the high adventure it really is. Yet he never quite grasps how the two cultures can be brought together by a common feeling for the strangeness of a world whose seemingly solid matter turns out to be a sea of atoms, where even the hardest facts have a way of dissolving overnight into new and deeper mysteries.

Crises of faith and knowing in Victorian literature come to a focus in three questions: Can free will coexist with a detached view of the self? Is self-making limited by what is given? And can the gap between beliefs and their grounds be closed? The more the Victorians lose themselves in a quest for answers, the more these three separate questions resolve themselves into a single question: Can the objective perspective, the view from outside, ever coexist with the subjective perspective, the view from here? Or must the convergence of the two points of view always result in incomprehension and mystery?

The doctrine that if something is real, it is real independent of our capacity to conceive it confronts the mind with intractable nescience. And it bequeaths to language the silence of the inexpressible. We can be nescient, as opposed to merely ignorant, of a mystery in two ways. We may have no conception of such a thing, in which case it is negatively inconceivable to us, like Carlyle's "signless Inane" (1898, 1:205). Alternatively, we may see positively, through paralogisms and antinomies, that something both infinite and absolute, like the deity invoked by Hopkins as "past all / Grasp God" ("The Wreck of the Deutschland," 32. 6–7), can never be made an object of conceptual understanding. Even if, like Tennyson's Ancient Sage, we could conceive of everything there is, this capacity would not make it real. "The Nameless of the hundred names" ("The Ancient Sage," l. 49), the inexpressible reality "unshadowable in words" (l. 238), would always exceed any definition we might be tempted to impose.

The contrary assumption of the idealists, the axiom that our capacity to conceive of something guarantees it is real, produces a more manageable form of ignorance. And it gives rise to a different form of silence—to the silence of something merely unspeakable in representational discourse. The subject of a dream or a vision, for example, may survive such a crisis of representation by disclosing its secret meanings in more presentational forms of language. From an idealist perspective, to be silent about the unknown is either to be silent about what we are at present merely ignorant of, like some article of faith still being formulated by a community of believers, or else it is to be silent about a mere fiction, a chimera, something like H. L. Mansel's absolute and infinite God, which can have no intelligible meaning except perhaps in some philosophical laboratory of ideas.

One source of puzzlement, then, is associated with the realist thesis that because the sum of truth vastly exceeds anything we can understand or say about it, only idolaters assume it is ever fully knowable or known. A second source of mystery proceeds from the counterthesis of the idealists that because our understanding of God or matter, say, is circumscribed by the often contradictory propositions we make about such things, there is never any venerable secret concealed behind the formulas that we ourselves have not inscribed there. A third source of mystery assumes the form of an antinomy or aporia. There is a way things are, the argument runs, but whether it can be strictly compassed by what we can understand or express about it or whether it vastly exceeds this condition is precisely what no one can hope to say.

In part 1 I first examine the realist doctrine that because the world extends beyond the reach of our minds, there are always truths about it that we are unconscious of. Each advance in knowledge is in danger of ignoring both inner and outer limits. On the one hand, we cannot make sense of the tragedy of Hardy's Tess by simply leaving behind her point of view as we seek the more Olympian perspective of the "President of the Immortals." On the other hand, there are inner limits to knowledge; it is easy to assume we have conceived the world as a whole when, like Carlyle's minnow in its creek, we have conceived only a small part of it. If Tess is a mere plaything of Hardy's capricious God—a perfection of absolute zero whose only law is that there is no law—then the world she inhabits, both controlled and oddly open, is forever beyond human understanding. Hardy may secretly admire divine indifference, since any alternative to a God of power devoid of feeling may generate too little humility in his interpreters.

Idealism, a legacy of the romantic movement, takes the opposite tack: it argues that the idea of something we cannot think about or imagine makes no sense. If the limits of reality are the limits of our language, then outside the dream rhetoric of *Wuthering Heights* or the visionary tropes of *Villette* there is nothing Cathy Earnshaw or Lucy Snowe can hope to know. The moment we accept an epistemological test of reality, the meaning of the word "unconscious" changes. The idealist redefines the word to mean not the representation of some notion external to language or the mind, but a presentation of notions that, like "ideas" in music, are inseparable from the forms that express them. The "unconscious" becomes a product rather than a cause of such language.

The writers I study share a view of the world most properly called bewilderment. Instead of presuming to explain everything, the best writers use tropes of reserve to hint obliquely at the secret truth, often hidden in the darkest recesses of their culture, that what passes for confidence and knowledge is often only a species of learned ignorance in disguise. In part 1, for example, I show that as the Victorian novelists honestly deploy the full resources of their language, they excite questions about the fortune of a mystery word like "fate," which may appear to mean contradictory things. On the one hand, fate is external to characters like Dickens's Pip and Hardy's Tess, because it is a force they are powerless to control. On the other hand, as a complex web of metaphors of situation—of "organization tyrannizing over character," to use Emerson's phrase—fate is also internal to the language of each fiction. For Heathcliff the meaning of Cathy's death is "unutterable," outside language altogether; but without language there is no truth for Heathcliff to express. Carlyle must wrestle with a similar paradox: truth resides in silence and unconsciousness. But how can he be conscious of this truth unless truth itself is also a product of consciousness and words? Sublime moments in the poetry of Hopkins, Tennyson, and Christina Rossetti are usually achievements of heroic and saintly wills: but they are also a result of relaxing and surrendering the will. Is a will *not* to will a contradiction in terms? Or is it one of the necessary paradoxes of religion?

The Victorian writers studied in part 2 are torn between two theories of history and character that are often confused. Is the truth about history and its agents to be equated with what is antecedently given, as scientific historiography assumed? Or is the history of a nation or a person a self-constituting process of development through time, as Strauss and the left-wing Hegelians maintained? Every novelist or poet who struggles to present the complex truth about a character confronts a version of this dilemma. On the one hand, Trollope and Henry James insist that the exact truth about Eleanor Bold or Daisy Miller can be accurately ascertained by Grantly or Winterbourne, even when they have been "booked to make a mistake." On the other hand, the greater the constraints on Grantly's or Winterbourne's freedom to interpret, the more the novelist is able to estrange the familiar by showing that any interpretation of a character is really an invention, a fiction that we, like the historians, "make up."

Realism, the doctrine that denies that historical events are limited by our capacity to create or conceive them, invites each interpreter to advance outside the self. But such advances are continually blocked by false steps. The view from outside may be excessively impersonal, like Dinah Morris's otherworldly theology at the beginning of *Adam Bede*. Moreover, if contexts confer meaning and values adhere to bounded worlds, the centrifugal pull of expanding contexts that are fully meaningful may confront the contrary pull of values. The more meaning Dinah Morris encompasses in her otherworldly theology, the fewer values she can realize in her close attachment to people. Insoluble conflicts may also arise from interior and detached accounts of the same event. In the confrontation scene between Bulstrode and Ladislaw in *Middlemarch*, we become acutely aware of the difference between the hypocritical criminal seen by the onlooker and the causist whose closeness to us has been largely a function of our own concentration on an intensely agitated state of mind. Often such crises of representation are signaled by verbal density or blur. Syntax may start to splinter or look two ways at once. George Eliot's prose rhythm may suddenly become edgy, or a stanza in a lyric by Browning may hurry us along, past parentheses, dashes, or other roadblocks, until we begin to doubt whether the sidetracked speaker can find his way back to the highroad of his thought.

In part 3 I show how the move outside the self, when pushed too fast or too far, leads to false reductions of art, faith, and culture. The more Huxley or Newman tries to justify a belief in science or religion, the more such a belief begins to diverge from its grounds. A skeptic will simply acknowledge the existence of the rift without trying to close it. A reductionist like Pater will try to scale down Plato's doctrine of Ideas to make it fit the antimetaphysical ground of his own beliefs. A religious apologist like Newman embraces a more heroic theory of knowledge. He leaps courageously across the gap, declaring that he has arrived safely on the far side. But whatever solution is preferred, the harder the Victorians try to justify their beliefs, the more crises of faith and knowledge they precipitate.

Often the meaning and comprehensibility of such complex words as "faith," "culture," "science," appear to exist in inverse proportions. Can treatises on culture and religion make sense of what seems meaningful? And can essays on nature and scientific method confer meaning on discourse that seems otherwise merely explanatory? If truth is a function of the view from nowhere and value a function of the view from here, can the two points of view ever be made to converge? Often the contrary claims of meaning and intelligibility seem to distort what Arnold or Huxley thinks he wants to say. Such betrayals of language are "kindly infelicities," as Santayana would say, because they invite the writer to evade formulas even as he tries to use them. Two-way syntax, ellipses, and oxymorons, which allow meaning to escape in several directions at once, invite the reader to honor the contradictions of his first thoughts even as they conspire to make the ideas that are intelligible more worthy of being expressed and the ideas that are most worthy of expression more fully intelligible.

When Hardy's "President of the Immortals," a blind and groping Schopenhauerian Will, poses puzzles more baffling than the enigmas Hardy has invented God to solve, we can see how obstacles to integrating the view from inside with the view from nowhere may produce crises in representation that increasingly perplex both the novelist and his readers. By contrast, a recognition of the mystery that really exists may produce more genuine illumination in nineteenth-century poetry and fiction than any of the so-called answers that are formally proposed in Mill's *System of Logic* or Sidgwick's *Methods of Ethics*. Often a problem may have less in common with a crossword puzzle than with a parable or a prophecy, whose mystery is not removed by a solution. In these circumstances many Victorians seem to think that remaining perplexed may be wiser than trying to find permanent solutions to their deepest problems. Literature, at its best, yields not a set of theories but a set of questions. Less important than the answers, which are always in danger of consolidating the mental or imaginative level on which the questions are asked, is the search for new and better questions.

Three Stages of Victorianism

Reacting against romanticism's revolutionary idea that we are all by birth and by nature artists, architects, and fashioners of worlds, Victorianism in its original phase is an effort to reestablish essentialist notions of language and truth. Instead of evolving his ideas from "experiments of living," to use Mill's phrase, the essentialist assumes that a center of truth and authority already exists: at his most extreme, he may even try to evolve the world from an idea of the world, like Plato and the Absolute Idealists. Having said this, I must hasten to add that in its nostalgia for universals and its quest for authority, Victorianism contains at its center an agnostic moment of questioning and doubt that puts at risk the very notion of a center. Out of this agnostic void there comes to birth a new existential notion of language and truth, which patiently evolves ideas from experience of the world. Influenced by Darwin's science of universal flux, many Victorians abandon their quest for permanence and fixity. They accept in its place a god or spiritual substance that has less in common with Aristotle's Unmoved Mover or the biblical God than with the evolutionary God of Aeschylus and Hegel, a deity who is always in motion, always in the process of becoming. The original Victorian belief in a center of moral and spiritual authority is celebrated in *In Memoriam*, where moral causists are exhorted to "Hold...the good, define it well; / For fear divine Philosophy / Should push beyond her mark, and be / Procuress to the Lords of Hell" (53.13–16). Evolutionary thinkers committed to unstable, existential notions of human identity may choose "from childhood [up] to shape / [their] action like the greater ape." But Tennyson's mourner insists that he "was *born* to other things" (120.10–12). His identity is given to him at birth: he is presumably created in God's image and must learn to rest in the ends, in the antecedent definitions of his essence, that determine who he is.

Contributing to Tennyson's doctrine of a preexisting moral "end" is biblical theology's commitment to an essentialist notion of deity. It is God's essence that he should combine unchanging attributes of power, knowledge, and love (Browning's "Saul"); that he should be a compassionate lover (Christina Rossetti, "Twice"); or that he should be the trinitarian God of Christian revelation (Newman). Crises in representation arise only when an unchanging biblical notion of God's essence is found in conjunction with new developmental theories of how theological understanding evolves or in conjunction with a new existential notion of faith, which sees belief as a changing product of the affective will.

An important legacy of the Victorian quest for an unchanging center of authority and truth is a prophetic understanding that knowledge not only eliminates puzzles and problems; it also reveals a mystery. This ancient Greek and biblical idea of knowledge survives in the major Victorian religious writers and even in the skeptical Carlyle and Ruskin. If knowledge reveals a mystery, then many Victorians find their most appropriate response to it is silence. For the substance of a revelation, unlike the conclusion of a proof or an explanation, cannot be stated. It must be shown wordlessly. A prophetic work like Carlyle's *Sartor Resartus* or Ruskin's sermon-lecture "The Mystery of Life and Its Arts" should be treated as a scaffold to be knocked down once it has been used to attain a vantage point.

As silences of mere reserve deepen into the silence of what is not really sayable, a hole begins to open at the center of Victorian culture. In literature itself, we are confronted with agnostic developments of romantic doctrines of ineffability. "The deep truth is imageless," says Shelley's Demogorgon, and Carlyle's Teufelsdröckh speaks darkly of a "signless Inane." The Brontës try to reverse Coleridge's account of desynonymizing some primal word. But the more they try to collapse all words back into one original synonym, the further that synonym recedes from view.

Both evangelical theology and agnostic developments in the philosophy of religion contribute to the darkening vision. The more ineffable the God of Calvinist theology becomes, the more antinomian and morally irresponsible he begins to seem. The voluntarist God of Browning's Johannes Agricola, for example, has all the disadvantages of being unintelligible without any of the advantages of being a sublimely exalted object of religious devotion, unspeakably greater than anything Johannes can say about him. Much later in the period, a blindly groping will such as Hardy ascribes to the morally stupid "President of the Immortals" in *Tess of the d'Urbervilles* dramatizes Schopenhauer's doctrine of the phenomenal will, something that is also observable in moral idiots like Tess when she allows Alec to seduce her. But by a strange twist of metaphysical logic, the phenomenal will turns out to be nomenal. This same moral idiocy is projected upon the cosmos as the most blasphemous attribute of God himself. The reasons for this bizarre move are to be found in Schopenhauer's early treatise, written under Kant's influence, *On the Four-fold Root of the Principle of Sufficient Reason*, which Hardy was reading at the time he wrote *Tess*.

But we know Hardy also read Herbert Spencer, and Spencer's treatise "The Unknowable" obviously influences Hardy's odd poetry of cosmic inquisition, especially such indictments of deity as "The Bedridden Peasant to an Unknown God," "Unknowing," and "God-Forgotten." Of course, as soon as Spencer's Unknowable becomes the subject of predicates, as it does in Hardy's poetry and fiction, it "becomes impossible," as F. H. Bradley points out in *Ethical Studies*, "for any one who cares for consistency to go on calling it the Unknowable" (1876, 323). Either the Unknowable is genuinely unknowable, in which case we can say nothing about it, or else we can qualify Spencer's agnosticism, as Hardy does, by linking his unknowable subject to a chain of shocking predicates. But then the Unknowable is no longer unknown. The logical absurdity and even blasphemy of Hardy's calling an unknowable God cruel or without logic seems to commend at times the wisdom of Clough's more thoroughgoing agnosticism, which he prefers to call a "religion of silence."

Out of such agnostic questioning and doubt there emerges the third and final phase of Victorian thought. This phase is associated with the well-known Victorian precept of salvation through work. But "work," it turns out, is a complex word, and misunderstanding of what it means is responsible for popular travesties of the Victorians as high-minded but dull. As Ruskin insists, work should be engaged in as if it were play, an expenditure of energy for the sake of self-realization, as in the pursuit of virtue or liberal education, which are often said to be their own reward. Through work, moral vocation, and what Mill, in a happy phrase, calls "experiments of living," man becomes the architect of his own humanity and values.

The doctrine of self-making is a legacy of Vico and the left-wing Hegelians, Strauss and Feuerbach, who influence George Eliot and Browning. But it can be found in its purest form in utilitarian moral theory and in the late-Victorian pragmatism and humanism of Pringle-Pattison and F. C. S. Schiller. For Kant's closed definition of what ethics consists in (duty and moral obligation), utilitarianism substitutes an open-ended theory. Its precept to maximize happiness does not determine in advance what happiness will be like. On the contrary, by conducting "experiments of living" Mill's utilitarian must develop his own conception of bliss. Instead of evolving an idea of happiness from a preexisting Kantian or biblical definition of it, the utilitarian evolves his own conception from his experience of intellectual and other pleasures in a world he is constantly making meaningful.

More than any other contemporary, Carlyle puts the doctrines of self-making and salvation through work into cultural currency for the Victorians. Indeed, the passage from transcendentalism through descendentalism to an Everlasting Yea in *Sartor Resartus* recapitulates exactly the three phases of Victorianism I have been outlining. Teufelsdröckh moves from outmoded essentialist notions of language and truth, through a revolutionary agnostic phase, into a third and final stage of experimental living. In this last phase the self-maker infuses dead or superannuated signs with life, as a new Mythus is engendered upon a world waiting, in Williams James's pregnant phrase, "to receive its final touches at our hands" (1911, 257). Of these three moments the most important for Carlyle is the third. Our America is here or nowhere; if we are not to perish in the wilderness, we must work to make it the promised land that Arnold's critic, in "The Function of Criticism at the Present Time," despairs of ever reaching.

Evangelical theology's teaching that good works may be more important than otherworldly faith is reinforced in book 2 of *Sartor Resartus* by Fichte's doctrine of moral vocation in *Die Bestimmung des Menschen* (1800). The spectral subjectivity of the ego at Fichte's second stage of Knowledge (Teufelsdröckh's Centre of Indifference) and the dominance of alien objectivity at his first stage of Doubt (the Everlasting No) are resolved only by a proper interaction of the ego and the non-ego through moral vocation and self-making at his third and final stage of Faith (the Everlasting Yea). Carlyle's fusion of evangelical and post-Kantian doctrines of moral vocation is seminal. From him the doctrine passes on to Browning, Ruskin, and Clough, where it diffuses itself into the Victorian sensibility at large.

In Browning's hands, for example, Carlyle's existential doctrine receives a decidedly pragmatic turn. For Browning's Bishop Blougram, the meaning of religious belief is its consequence for living. And contrary to Kant's categorical imperative or such landmarks of deontological ethics as the Decalogue, we can no longer define adultery as universally right or wrong. Such is the argument propounded in "The Statue and the Bust," where Browning's reluctance to impose some new essentialist definition of virtue is evident from his poem's evasive closure: "De te, fabula" (l. 250). Contrary to Tennyson's injunction in In Memoriam to "Hold . . . the good, define it well" (53.13), only an experiment in living can tell whether a particular act of adultery will produce a moral or an immoral outcome.

Spaces of Dissension

Crises of representation in Victorian literature allow us to explore what Foucault calls "the different spaces of dissension." We can study "different types of contradiction, different levels in accordance with which it can be mapped, [and] different functions that it can exercise" (1972, 152–53).

The crises of representation found during the first essentialist phase of Victorianism I have been charting tend to conceal some fundamental law or principle that is later discovered. Once the discovery is made, all the lesser mysteries can usually be accounted for. Laws of hidden identity, tragic destiny, and providential design, for example, resolve most of the minor crises in Great Expectations, Tess of the d'Urbervilles, and Apologia pro Vita Sua. By contrast, the crises of representation generated during the agnostic and existential phases often create a new law or formula out of contradiction itself. Clough's Claude in Amours de Voyage is defined by his contradictions, by his perpetual oscillation between categorical and existential options. And in Borrow's Lavengro, as in Sartor Resartus, discourse is the path from one contradiction to another. When Teufelsdröckh analyzes extrinsic and intrinsic symbols, he is always undulatingly alive to a contradictory play between agnostic and new existential theories of the word. Each surmise about language is a trembling of one truth on the brink of its opposite.

If we take Foucault's "types of contradiction" first, we can see that the crises of representation in *Great Expectations*, *Tess*, and Newman's *Apologia* all originate in a common source: in a sense of repressed or subliminal awareness. Puzzling as it first seems, Pip, Tess, and the young Newman all know more than they know they know. By contrast, the contradiction between the mysteries of unconsciousness in *Apologia pro Vita Sua* and *Wuthering Heights*, for example, is a result of different starting points. The fixity of Newman's mysteries, which are theologically definable, would be eroded by the flux of Cathy's and Heathcliff's romantic mysticism, which is indefinable or "unutterable." In Newman's dismissive view, mysticism begins in "mist" and ends in "schism." But his distrust in no way minimizes the faith he shares with Brontë in powers of divination or a common conviction that, because consciousness is a product of language rather than the other way round, it is necessary to conclude that, outside language or the sacraments of the church, God and his surrogates are not, strictly speaking, knowable.

Unlike Newman and Brontë, Trollope and Thackeray share a common starting point. Each uses double irony, the simultaneous endorsement of incompatible codes, to refine and formulate a keen sense of contradiction. The space of dissension that opens between them is due to their developing irony in contrary ways. Trollope's narrator in *Barchester Towers* uses double irony to cultivate a reputation for seeing all around an issue and appearing tolerant and fair-minded. In *Vanity Fair*, by contrast, Thackeray's narrator uses double irony to show that in a godless universe no authenticating center of moral or spiritual authority exists. Whereas Trollope's classical irony is incompatible with relativism, Thackeray's irony of pure negation is relativism's most potent means of expression.

Crises in representation also arise from a conflict between different *levels* of a concept's history or explanation. In *Signs of the Times*, for example, and in *Sartor Resartus*, Carlyle writes as an iconoclast: signs that have petrified into idols must be smashed. In his chapter titled "Symbols," by contrast, he laments the incapacity of even new signs to be intrinsic—to participate, that is, in the mystery of their referents. But elsewhere in that chapter Carlyle analyzes a third possibility: he celebrates the genius of the heroic souls who can make their whole lives an authentically intrinsic sign. Carlyle seems to be torn among conflicting iconoclastic, agnostic, and new iconic theories of the word. But the contradictions are apparent, not real. They come from isolating mere partial phases of an evolving history of the sign, which to be understood properly must be taken as a whole.

Any abrupt shift in the level or scale of an explanation may precipitate a crisis of representation. Religious apologists like Newman in his Oxford sermons or Browning's pope in *The Ring and the Book* are patiently inductive. But they also realize that understanding is partly an intuitive and divinatory process, a revelation of mystery. And they reach a stage in their arguments when this realization frees them from inductive constraints. As a heroic knower, Newman recognizes that he must grasp the whole before he can understand the parts. But as an inductive logician rigorously trained in Aristotle, he also believes that he cannot understand the whole until he has differentiated its parts. Unless the heroic knower takes a leap that allows him to grasp simultaneously the whole and its parts, the web and the filaments together, he will never understand anything.

A contradiction of levels occurs whenever a specialized use of a formula comes into conflict with its general use. The formula "God is love" is a cornerstone of biblical theology. But a crisis of representation arises when Tennyson's mourner in *In Memoriam* uses the formula to ask a subversive question. He wonders if belief in immortality and a God of love merely "Derives... from what we have / The likest God within the soul" (section 55. 3–4). Is a loving God merely the anthropomorphic projection of a godlike human attribute? If so, then a cornerstone of biblical theology is coming into conflict with a specialized anthropomorphic development of it. And as Browning's Saint John says in "A Death in the Desert," "The lamp o'er swims with oil," and the fuel that should feed the flame extinguishes it instead (ll. 512–13). Such is the effect of Feuerbach's claim that the predicate of biblical theology, "love," should become the subject of a new anthropological religion, and that what is now subject, "God," should be relegated to the predicate as a mere godlike attribute. The crisis precipitated by Feuerbach's reversal is dramatized by his English translator, George Eliot, in *Adam Bede*. Instead of using the alienating language of an otherworldly theology to harangue Hetty, as she does in the bedchamber scene, Dinah learns in her halting but loving communion with Hetty in prison to enshrine the most godlike of human attributes as subject of her new Feuerbachian religion of man.

Crises in representation can arise not just from different *types* of contradiction and from "different levels in accordance with which [contradiction] can be mapped" (Foucault 1972, 153). Foucault identifies a third source of contradiction in the "different functions" of an explanatory model: conflicts arise when we try to translate "one group of statements into another" (155).

In *The Mill on the Floss*, for example, Maggie Tulliver precipitates a crisis of representation when she misappropriates her theological model, Thomas à Kempis's *Imitation of Christ*. In passionately embracing a devotional writer who renounces all passion, Maggie subverts the model she appropriates. She makes a category mistake about the genre of Kempis's book, turning a treatise on asceticism into a form of romance. A subtler crisis takes place when J. S. Mill, in appropriating Bentham's utilitarian formula, "the greatest happiness of the greatest number," decides to assess the quality of the pleasures as well as their number. Mill's translation of utility into a form of satisfaction emblematic of bliss precipitates a conflict between individual liberty or value, on the one hand, and moral obligation, on the other. It gives rise to a clash between what Richard Wollheim calls "preliminary Utilitarianism" and "Utilitarianism proper" (1984, 223).

Less resolvable, perhaps, is the crisis of representation that arises, when, instead of being unintentionally misused, a model like Bentham's is deliberately used to organize a *different* field of thought. Augustine's teaching that God alone has total knowledge of the world, because he is its author, is a commonplace of medieval theology. But when Vico uses Augustine's "*verum/factum*" formula to describe human history in its widest sense, he revolutionizes his model. Unlike George Eliot, who replaces Augustine's theological model with a new Viconian one, mediated through the left-wing Hegelian thought of Feuerbach and Strauss, a religious poet like Browning still tries to harmonize with doctrines of God's creation through verbal fiat in Genesis the revolutionary teaching that man is an architect of a self-made world who wills his faith into being. But crises of representation are sure to arise, for a grounded performative seems to be a contradiction in terms. To the degree that David's acts of willing his beliefs into being in "Saul" are genuinely performative, they come into conflict with a theological model. Conversely, if every act of making belief is already grounded in God's "act of creation," how can any form of religious self-making be genuinely performative?

T. H. Huxley's use of a theological model precipitates an even more complicated crisis. Having used theology to help him organize his thoughts about science, Huxley then uses science to repudiate the authority of his organizing model. At first Huxley thinks with the aid of theology. Just as the essence of the higher theologies is knowledge of the unknowable, so ignorance is said to be the beginning and end of all scientific inquiry. Physics must learn to surpass the paradoxes of agnostic theology. Not only must physicists come to imitate philosophers of religion like Sir William Hamilton and H. L. Mansel, they must also learn that a truth in physics is like one of the paralogisms in agnostic thought. It is a "truth" that treats everything it encounters as an undeveloped form of itself: it never attacks, only includes. Thus as Huxley generalizes, Clerk Maxwell's "assertion that one and the same point or area of space can have different (conceivably opposite) attributes appears... to violate the principle of contradiction, which is the foundation not only of physical science, but of logic in general. It means that A can be non-A" (l: 61).

The unknowable God of Hamilton and Spencer also helps Huxley organize his thoughts about the ultimate unknowableness of the physical world. If matter does exist, it is as mysterious and unintelligible as Spencer's unknowable God, because an unbridgeable rift necessarily divides the impalpable "substratum" of matter from the properties the scientist can observe and describe. Indeed, in "The Progress of Science" the long footnote in which Huxley concedes the objections of Boscovich and Clerk Maxwell to a materialist hypothesis betrays Huxley's own anxiety (l: 60–61). Even in Huxley's day the dissolution of matter into energy fields is preparing for Einstein's discovery that matter, "the great bastion of the objectivity of the world," as Frye calls it, is only "an illusion of energy" (Frye 1982, 14). The true hypothesis may be intelligible only as a string of paradoxes that violate the law of contradiction. In other words, it may be intelligible only as a mystery.

While agnostic theology, however, is helping Huxley organize his skeptical thoughts about the fictive status of matter, it is also helping him use the authoritative rhetoric of religion to enshrine science as the new theology. Transferring the authoritative religious rhetoric from theology to science in his essay "On the Advisableness of Improving Natural Knowledge," Huxley asserts that the scientist is "justified" not "by faith, but by verification" (l: 41). Everything Huxley values in the honest inquirer, authoritarian opponents denounce as immoral or impious. But Huxley's use of religious rhetoric to demolish authoritarian arguments precipitates its own crisis of representation. For in appropriating religious rhetoric, science is in danger of becoming the new Vatican of unquestioned authority. And it is precisely such authoritarianism that science is pledged to combat wherever it is found. Why should Huxley, in rejecting "faith," retain the creedal form? Why should he employ a religious infinitive, "to believe," and even make use of the theological concept of "justification"? He apparently uses religious rhetoric to dramatize the truth that the mantle of authority has fallen on the shoulders of the scientist. Yet science owes such authority as it possesses to a vigorous repudiation of such mantles. If science is authoritative in the way Huxley's religious rhetoric proclaims, then it loses such authority as its "absolute refusal to acknowledge authority" entitles it to claim.

An equally serious crisis arises when the transfer of a model from one historical period to another produces a result opposite from what is expected. Hoping to strengthen his belief in the Anglican doctrine of the *Via Media*, Newman looks into the mirror of historical analogy and finds he is a sixteenth-century heretic, a Monophysite. Instead of being confirmed, his "theory of the *Via Media*" is "absolutely pulverized" (*Apologia pro Vita Sua*, chap. 3).

A crisis in representation is also precipitated by circular forms of reasoning. Because Aristotle organizes nature into substances and their properties, which are the very categories he uses to explain art, his famous observation that art should imitate nature is really a petitio principii in disguise: art is said to imitate a nature that is already organized as one version of itself. When Browning writes his metafiction *The Ring and the Book*, which joins the narrative world of the source book and its witnesses to the "real" world of the poet-narrator and his commentaries, he generates a similar crisis in reasoning. For the model used by the poet-narrator to organize his historical reconstruction of the Roman murder mystery—namely, Schleiermacher's and Niebuhr's model of moral empathy and dramatic impersonation—turns out to be the precise model that Browning, as the author of *The Ring and the Book*'s monologues, has been using throughout the long dramatic parts of his fiction. According to Schleiermacher, historical and other forms of interpretation are moral acts by which the interpreter "feels" himself into the sensibility of a historical agent or author. Barthold Niebuhr and his English disciples follow Schleiermacher in insisting that the good historian must empathize with historical agents like Caesar. But what else has Browning himself been doing in writing dramatic monologues? The authenticating historical model of Schleiermacher and Niebuhr turns out to be a disguised version of the very acts of dramatic impersonation that Browning is trying to organize and explain with the help of his model.

Though such crises in representation consist of a circle, it is not a vicious circle. On the contrary, it is an example of the circle that is contained in any explanatory web, in any form of knowledge that reveals a mystery, as distinct from the kind of inductive proof that consists of a logically connected chain of statements. Because all propositions in an explanatory web contain each other, an explanation as opposed to a proof always implies a circle. The mystery revealed by such a circle may become glaringly clear, but only if we take a hermeneutical leap, a leap of faith, that allows us to establish all its explanatory statements together.

Preview of the Argument

The three parts of the book explore three sources of mystery in Victorian literature: mystery and the unconscious; mystery and identity; and mysteries arising from three methods or theories of knowledge, which, borrowing Thomas Nagel's terms (1986), I call heroic, skeptical, and reductive. In each chapter I associate a particular type of mystery with a form of silence, a model of knowledge, a use of language, and a crisis of representation. Chapter 1, for example, explores the mystery of a veiled fate operating through Miss Havisham and Magwitch and through the dark design of Hardy's "President of the Immortals." Refusing to disclose the identity of Pip's benefactor, Jaggers scrupulously enforces a silence of reserve. Hardy's Angel Clare is equally reserved when pressed by Tess to say whether they will meet again on the far side of the grave. His silence proceeds from a repressed awareness of a truth that, through known to him, is too painful for him to share. The model of knowledge that each novelist uses collapses a chain of logically connected but widely separated events: in *Great Expectations* the opening scenes on the marsh converge upon Magwitch's return as a tragedy converges on its recognition scene, and as Tess's ritual of midnight entombment converges on her tragic arrest at Stonehenge. A crisis of representation also arises when Pip, half oblivious to the core of vanity in himself, has to face the pit of emptiness and mania beneath the surface of Miss Havisham's life. A similar crisis occurs when Hardy's narrator at the end of the seduction scene and in the final paragraph of the novel betrays the scurry and strain of a mind under stress, darting desperately from one half-relevant thought to another, as if trying to avoid a truth he can no longer bear to face.

Note that the progression of chapters within each of the book's three parts coincides with the general progression from essentialist, to agnostic, to existential and pragmatic theories of language and truth that I have already mapped in the section on the three stages of Victorian thought and culture. To reverse a phrase of Christopher Ricks's, the book presents "a march of chapters," not a "gathering of essays" (1987, vii). The overlapping phases to which such complex authors as Carlyle, Browning, and George Eliot belong does not, I believe, invalidate the distinctions I have drawn. On the contrary, it was an awareness in such authors of competing authoritarian, agnostic, and existential impulses that led me to distinguish among three phases of Victorianism in the first place.

At the risk of oversimplifying, I have taken the liberty of providing a list of the fourteen types of mystery the book explores and of the corresponding crises of representation that each mystery gives rise to.

Part One: Mystery and the Unconscious

(1) Mystery of a veiled fate: Dickens and Hardy. The meaning of the detached, fatalistic view, which is the view of a vengeful Miss Havisham and of Hardy's "President of the Immortals," comes into

conflict with the value of an intensely partisan perspective, which is the perspective of Pip and Hardy's narrator, who are emotionally involved in Estella's and Tess's fate.

(2) Mystery of a primal word that is not, strictly speaking, utterable: the Brontës. An intelligible but endlessly proliferating language, as in Jabes Branderham's sermon, comes into conflict with a nearly unintelligible but primal language of tautologies and equivalences, as in Cathy's declaration: "I *am* Heathcliff."

(3) Mystery of an agnostic void and of an heroic attempt to fill it with intrinsic signs whose meanings we ourselves create: Carlyle. The more intrinsic a sign is, the less anchored it is in an antecedent ground; conversely, the more anchored a sign such as the Cross already is in a historic event, the more prescriptive and less intrinsic any subsequent use of it may be.

(4) Mystery of a sublime God who is "past all / Grasp God": Hopkins and Tennyson. Since God's hiddenness is derived from his holiness, it seems difficult to speak of God without taking his name in vain. Can an ellipitcal sublime be used to preserve the hiddenness of God while an expansive sublime is used to reveal the loftiness of his nature?

Part Two: Mysteries of Identity

(1) Mysteries of a positive moral identity in Trollope and Henry James. The highest claims to our esteem on the part of such characters as Trollope's reticent Mr. Harding and James's ingenuous Daisy Miller at first sound more like disclaimers than claims.

(2) Mysteries of negative identity in Thackeray. *Vanity Fair* has the form without the expected content of a traditional allegory: in the absence of a moral or spiritual center, the only source of value becomes the search for value.

(3) Mysteries of self-knowledge in Borrow and Clough. An identity that is self-created like Lavengro's or Claude's appears to have a black hole at its center, and characters with solid cores have inauthentic identities.

(4) Mysteries of self-making that put into practice a new religion of humanity: George Eliot. The more meaningful a life is in a public and historical sense, the less valuable it is in a private, unhistorical sense, and vice versa.

(5) Mysteries of a private identity too intimate to speak about and too interior to profane with words: Browning. Can the language of faith be simultaneously grounded and ungrounded, or is a grounded performative a misnomer, a contradiction in terms?

Part Three: Mystery and Method

(1) Mysteries of faith in Newman. Until a leap into the hermeneutical circle occurs and we grasp the whole and the parts together, we can understand nothing.

(2) Mysteries of contextual definition in Christina Rossetti and Matthew Arnold. The more at-onement with Christ that Rossetti attains in the mystical sense, the less atonement she has need of in the biblical sense, and vice versa. The more inclusive Arnold tries to make culture, the less intelligible it becomes, and the more intelligible the less inclusive. Arnold fails to realize that some great goods cannot be had together: the more strictness of conscience, for example, the less spontaneity of consciousness, and vice versa.

(3) Until mystifying essentialist definitions of such words as "obligation" and "justice" are abolished, the authentic mysteries cannot be valued for what they are. Philosophy may begin in wonder, but it must end in expulsion of the wrong kinds of wonder: J. S. Mill. The claims of individual value and moral obligation (or what Richard Wollheim calls the claims of "preliminary Utilitarianism" and "Utilitarianism" proper) appear to exist in inverse proportion.

(4) Mysteries of criminal detection in Wilkie Collins. The factual methods of Bruff and the fanciful methods of Cuff seem equally helpless in entering empathetically into the psychological experience of the criminal suspects.

(5) Mysteries of historical reconstruction in *The Ring and the Book*. The more Browning's critical historian tries to "Correct the portrait by the living face, / Man's God, by God's God in the mind of man," the more he realizes that any portrait he has to correct has more in common with other portraits than with any so-called historical original that may be said to exist. Browning explores a version of F. H. Bradley's parable of the fresco painter in *The Presuppositions of Critical History*.

This study of mystery began as an experiment. I wanted to use selected Victorian poems as a laboratory in which to test theories I developed in an earlier book, *The Lucid Veil*. To make the experiment properly inclusive, however, I soon realized I would have to test the theories on a representative sample of the whole cross-section of Victorian literature, not the poetry alone. If my concentration on philosophy and theology in the earlier study seemed too skeletal and austere, my attempt in this book to load every rift with ore may seem deficient in an organizing intellectual and historical schema. Though I have tried to provide such a schema in this Introduction and in the opening section of the Conclusion, I would like to think that the deficiencies of the two books are of opposite kinds and that, if taken together, they will correct each other's imbalances.

I have looked for ways of treating mystery that would be faithful if not to the letter, then at least to the spirit, of historical studies and rhetorical analysis, the modes of scholarship in which I have been trained. But the topic of mystery encroaches on theories of knowledge, on theology and metaphysics, and cannot be treated solely within the confines of literary criticism itself. In trying to develop an appropriate scholarly method, I have been suspicious of any critical school that makes literature less mysterious than it is: the student of mystery cannot take refuge in reduced ambitions. Poststructuralist theory, when it inhibits historical scholarship, impoverishes the critical landscape. And historical interpretation, when it denies or flattens out the puzzles, problems, and recurrent crises in representation, makes it difficult to cultivate a keen eye for mystery. It has not always proved easy to write intelligibly about authors like Browning, Hopkins, and Christina Rossetti, whose parentheses may be more telling than their direct assertions, and whose unheard words may be more revealing than anything they actually say. To elaborate a coherent argument about the sometimes scornful, often difficult, lucidity of Newman and Carlyle, for example, or of George Borrow and Clough, a critic may even have to go against the spirit of reserve and indirection in their work. In writing about mystery, I have also become distressingly aware that everything I say about it is surrounded by an endless regress of other mysteries that I have not found time to explore. I hope it has been useful, however, to chart a little of the frontier territory, if only as a means of encouraging more penetrating explorations of the unknown continent that lies just across the border.

PART ONE

Mystery and the Unconscious: Can Free Will Exist?

Literature reaches a crisis of representation whenever the density of its language leads a writer into a maze, complicating or deforming what he wants to say. Words become an antagonist not because Dickens or Hardy is using language inattentively, but because he is faithful to something in language that he is not conscious of creating. The more Dickens and Hardy try to unmask a fate external to the world and its language, the more internal that fate becomes. Pip falls prey not just to the mad designs of the older generation, but to Dickens's own unconscious sacrifice of human ends to verbal means. Tess is a victim not just of a malign God, but of the organizational rigors of Hardy's fiction. The fate that is thought to be outside language and the world is found to be embodied in tropes like tmesis that delay closure even as they cause foreseen convergences to occur.

Emily Brontë and Carlyle seem betrayed by language at the very moments they are most keenly attentive to it. In *Wuthering Heights* the truth is said to be "unutterable." To speak at all is to partition words into as many fragments as Jabes Branderham's sermon. To preserve her secret meanings Brontë keeps encoding them in a complex nesting structure of narrative. Even in trying to show how truth resides in the unconscious, Carlyle, like Brontë, is forced to speak as if truth were also a product of the fall into consciousness. Since consciousness is a necessary product of the words Carlyle must use, this most declamatory writer finds himself in the odd but inescapable position of having to advocate silence and reserve. Though Hopkins, Tennyson, and Christina Rossetti must work at the height of their powers to compass the sublime, they find that some relaxation and even abandonment of will may be necessary. When these poets are using language most scrupulously, its tense, belabored densities are also bringing into momentary clarity the mysterious "trouble spots" of knowledge.

Of these "trouble spots," the one that most persistently defeats ordered inquiry is the idea of an unconscious that lies under or behind ordinary consciousness. This idea of something primary and privileged, but fugitive and evasive, just out of sight, often expresses itself as nostalgia for Utopia or a lost paradise. But what can be the origin of a loss that seems always to have existed? A vestige of this mysterious idea survives in the noun "understanding," which implies the act of standing under something, at a foundation level of experience. The repressed or subliminal forms of awareness that appear as half-recognized repetitions in the language of *Great Expectations* and *Tess of the d'Urbervilles* assume that something outside consciousness is more primary than what we are conscious of knowing. By contrast, the notion of the unconscious in *Wuthering Heights* and *Villette* denies that there is anything beneath or outside consciousness for language to reach. The Brontës put in question the very notion of underlying truth. If a deep truth exists, it is "unutterable" and imageless. The question whether to accept or reject the notion of an underlying or deep truth sounds itself like a deep question. Carlyle seems at times to accept the idea of a deep truth, only to suggest at other times that everything is superficial. There is nothing beneath the venerable concealments of language that is not already transparent—that is not there to be seen on the surface of words.

Mysteries of the unconscious are inseparable from another puzzle: the problem of free will. For if we are largely unconscious of the forces that shape our life and our language, do we not enjoy the mere illusion of free will? The schemes of Miss Havisham and Magwitch in *Great Expectations*, the caprices of fate in *Tess of the d'Urbervilles*, the juggernaut of necessity bearing down on Teufelsdröckh in "The Everlasting Nay," all seem to undercut human dignity and value. Without free will we seem diminished, a mere plaything of the gods, as Hardy suggests, who kill us for their sport. And it is sometimes hard to tell whether Hopkins, Tennyson, and Christina Rossetti are exalted or diminished by their encounters with God. Can these poets erase the boundaries between themselves and God without losing their free will and worth? Even if they *are* controlled by forces of which they are only subliminally aware, does this make the control and despotism any less diminishing?

If actions are causally determined rather than random, then free will seems impossible. But to deny casual determination altogether is equally intolerable. For an uncaused action is merely a random happening, indistinguishable from that absence of design discerned by Lucy Snowe in the closing sentences of *Villette*. In *Tess of the d'Urbervilles*, one extreme runs into the other. Does Tess live in a totally random world, where everything is underdetermined, or in an overdetermined one, where a malign fate is in charge? Random acts and caused acts alike seem to leave no room for human initiative and the invention of value.

To be human is to *lead* a life as well as merely *live* it. Even in old age Tennyson's Ulysses continues to lead his life forward. But in declining into his "twilight-piece," Andrea del Sarto manages to live his life only in retrospect, so to speak, by finding a resting place in memory from which to understand it backward. To lead as well as live a life is to be free to plan it, to shape its future course. Three answers have traditionally been given to the question, When are actions free? Locke and Hume argue that we are free unless our acts are caused by a power operating independent of our will, like Tennyson's God, the "wild poet" of *In Memoriam* (34.7–8), working "Without a conscience or an aim." Mill argues that our acts are free when they accord with a law of reason. When Heathcliff denounces Cathy in the death scene, it is because, as a free agent rationally planning her life, she cannot choose to enslave herself to Linton. To choose her destiny by marrying Heathcliff would not have constrained her. Yet for a free agent the choice was unavoidable. Cathy forfeits her freedom when she attempts the impossible: she tries to escape from the inescapable. Spinoza presents a third theory of free will: he argues that our acts are free only when they arise out of the needs of our nature. According to Spinoza, God alone is free. A desire to be unlimited like God is a desire like Cathy's *not* to be any particular creature, to be only a disembodied spirit whose marriage to Linton, for example, can never betray a prior spiritual at-onement with Heathcliff. But how is such a contempt for the body and the needs of nature distinguishable from death? There is another problem with Spinoza's theory. If women like Christina Rossetti and Lucy Snowe are stuck with stoic, repressed, and disappointed natures, or if male-dominated societies thrust these natures upon them, why should expressing such constraint count as freedom? Should these women not be free to choose identities that constrain them less?

Characters are usually freer to explain facts than to change them. In *The Wreck of the Deutschland*, disaster at sea is causally determined. But Hopkins is still free to decide what God's motive was, and so is the nun. Decision making produces the rhetorical equivalent of thrashing about, the verbal blur and density of a crisis of faith. Crisis means choice. And acts of crisis or decision are performative acts, in J. L. Austin's sense, ways of doing something new with words. In baptizing her "wild-worst / Best" (24.8–9), the nun's reasons for choosing as she does come into focus only in the act of choosing. Any explanation of why explanation A was chosen rather than explanation B will have to refer to the nun's actual choice of A.

The difference between a doing and a happening is that a doing assigns reasons. Tess insists that she murders Alec to convince Angel she is still loyal to him. Had she not murdered Alec, she would have acted as she did for a different reason. She might have spared Alec's life as a way of dramatizing to Angel the ironic truth that he has returned too late to claim her. In each case her deed would be caused, but in neither case would it be causally determined. At Stonehenge Tess even turns her surrender to the police into a doing rather than a happening by making it part of a domestic ritual, a ceremony of valediction and leave-taking. And in *The Wreck of the Deutschland* what might have been a mere *happening*—death at sea—is turned by the nun into a *doing*. Her bestowal of value and explanation is never causally determined, since other interpreters would have bestowed different values.

Anxiety about hidden causes is constantly unsettling the language of Victorian poetry and fiction, making it suddenly dense, broken, or belabored. When an act is in equilibrium, it withstands knowledge of its own causes. Pip's acts as a gentleman become unsupportable and lose their equilibrium when the cause of his good fortune is revealed to him. Angel is unable to withstand knowledge of Tess's past, and his life lacks equilibrium after Tess makes her disclosure. The barrage of non sequitur questions after Tess's seduction and after her execution dramatizes a similar crisis of knowledge in Hardy's narrator. In religious poets like Christina Rossetti and Hopkins equilibrium appears to flow from a knowledge of necessity. But how can knowledge of what we are bound by constitute freedom rather than knowledge of constraint? The puzzle is partly solved when choosing becomes self-choosing. If in choosing God Rossetti is also choosing herself, then nothing the divine nature can decree can curb her autonomy. Hopkins makes a comparable discovery in his sonnet "The Caged Skylark," where constraints arising out of acts of choice are said to bind without imprisoning.

> Man's spirit will be flesh-bound when found at best,
> But uncumberèd: meadow-down is not distressed
> For a rainbow footing it nor for his bónes rísen.
>   ("The Caged Skylark," ll. 12–14)

In the secularized theology of *Wuthering Heights*, Heathcliff is a kind of god whose essence is self-choosing. He thinks the same should be true of Cathy, since her freedom to marry him is an inalienable right. As soon as Cathy surrenders that right, she loses the only identity she has. Like the Wordsworth of "Ode to Duty," the stoical Christina Rossetti sometimes speaks as if self-choosing were a burden. Though it seems to constitute the least constraint imaginable, even the choice to be free may sometimes constrain our freedom. Tennyson's mariners in "The Lotos-Eaters" dislike unchartered freedom and prefer not to be self-choosers. But even their desire must come from somewhere. When the mariners say they "will not wander more" ("The Lotos-Eaters," l. 173), they must at least have willed their decision not to will again. Like Lucy Snowe or Christina Rossetti, they remain self-choosers still, choosers of the desire not to want self-choice.

To speak of the unconscious is to acknowledge that forces controlling our language and our life extend far beyond the margins of what we can possibly experience or know individually. In "Natural Supernaturalism" Carlyle's Teufelsdröckh discovers that a capacity to view himself from distant galaxies wipes out his autonomy by reducing him to a mere minnow in a creek. How can anything so small as a minnow be a spectator of all creation? The minnow's desire to be autonomous like God is related essentially to the agent's point of view; when looked at from outside, it becomes a desire for the impossible. Ironically, this desire is evoked by the precise view of ourselves—the view from outside—that admits only causal explanations and reveals free will to be impossible. But the more impossible free will proves, the more everyone seems to want it.

After introducing the subject of mystery and unconsciousness in chapter 1, I turn in chapter 2 to unconscious truths that are in principle recoverable. The silence surrounding the buried identity of Pip's benefactor or Estella's parents is an example of a mystery that is unspeakable for social reasons; it is not, strictly speaking, incapable of being expressed once it is known. In Dickens and Hardy I examine a fatalistic type of mystery, influenced perhaps by patterns of predestination in evangelical theology. The truths to be discovered—the avenging schemes of the older generation in *Great Expectations* and the tragic destiny of Tess—are kept buried or subliminal, partly because they are too painful for Pip or Hardy's narrator to confront directly. In each fiction the model of repressed knowledge slowly swimming into focus like the material that is dredged up from the unconscious during psychoanalysis is also the model of a slowly collapsing chain of carefully separated events. As intermediate links are removed, the chain so laboriously constructed by the conscious mind begins to fall apart. The associated rhetorical trope is tmesis, the figure of speech that sunders grammatical elements. Dickens and Hardy also use

widely separated metaphors of situation to construct a kind of generalized tmesis, spacing out events that are meant to be taken together.

In the third chapter, I show how the silence of the unspeakable
gives way to a deeper form of silence: to Heathcliff's sense that the
truth is "unutterable." This darker type of mystery, though indebted
to romantic theories of the ineffable—to the notion of Shelley's
Demogorgon that "the deep truth is imageless" (*Prometheus Unbound*,
2.4.116)—is reinforced both by evangelical teachings of an omnipotent God whose properties cannot be fathomed and by agnostic
demonstrations that God's attributes are in logical contradiction. In
Emily and Charlotte Brontë romantic and agnostic theories of language are associated not with a collapsing chain of widely separated
links, but with a collapsing pyramid of words. At the top of the
pyramid is a primal name, a near tautology like Cathy Earnshaw's "I
am Heathcliff," too holy or too primal to be uttered. All utterable and
fully intelligible language is to be found only below the apex of the
pyramid, in the ever-widening base of antonyms and metonymies that
allow the novelist to "desynonymize," as Coleridge would say, the
primal word and its equivalents. But once the process of dividing
words begins, nothing seems capable of stopping it. Only in dream
visions or hallucinatory states can Cathy Earnshaw or Lucy Snowe
begin to reverse the process. Out of three depictable objects—the
dead nun, the nun's ghost, and Paul Emmanuel's ward—Lucy Snowe
has created a fourth thing that is not graphically depictable. She has
used the proper name she overhears at the fête to create a fearful
primal word and ideogram—like the montage of cinema. Such a
sinister amalgam cannot be translated out of the visionary medium of
the dream or trance in which Brontë presents it.

Chapter 4 shows how agnostic and new Viconian theories of the
word give rise in Carlyle to a radically different form of mystery.
Carlyle is unconscious of some truths not because they are too dark
or mysterious for him to utter, but because, as William James would
say, they are still waiting "to receive" their "final touches at [his] hands"
(1911, 257). An agnostic silence descends when the old idols are
destroyed. But it is soon replaced by a silence of renewed possession
as the superannuated symbols are replenished with new descriptive
and emotive meanings. Carlyle uses prophetic fragments, oracular
questions, and aphorisms not as a language of unquestioned authority, but as a provisional language of inquiry and probation, designed
like the aphorisms of Bacon and Schiller, to involve the reader in a
personal quest for truth. As a persuasive redefiner of such key words
as "man," "clothes," "sign," and "law," Carlyle is a Victorian Vico, his
age's first and most resourceful advocate of a new existential or
pragmatic theory of language and truth: "*verum/factum*."

Whereas Carlyle is by turns a spokesman for the inexpressible and for the unspeakable, the last chapter of part 1 shows that Hopkins and Tennyson are poets of subliminal and sublime truths that are, paradoxical as it may sound, simultaneously unspeakable and inexpressible. They are unspeakable for reasons of theological reserve and incapable of being expressed because incomprehensible or uncertain. Since Hopkins's God is "past all grasp / God," He is too sublime a subject for Hopkins to name. Yet through oxymoron, paradox, and even a catachresis, Hopkins still struggles to name him. In both poets the notion of God's holiness—of his inexpressible otherness and separateness from the world—combines with a heroic theory of knowledge, which gives the sublime namer courage to attempt the impossible: to bridge the gap between human words and the Logos. This odd combination of despair and confidence, which unites the reserve of the unspeakable with the deeper mystery of the inexpressible, is linked to two contrary movements in the language of each poet. Sudden deletions and elisions, which contract meaning to the vanishing point, alternate with expansive dilations. At one moment Hopkins's sublime appositional naming collapses into agrammatical "word-heaps," which conspire to say noting about everything. At other moments his "similarity-disorder" turns into the opposite linguistic habit, a form of "continguity-disorder," to borrow Roman Jakobson's term, as Hopkins, the poet of sublime naming, seems to say everything about nothing.

CHAPTER 1

Can We Be Conscious of Meanings
That Lie outside Consciousness?

In Victorian fiction repeating words and situations prepares readers subliminally for truths that lie just outside consciousness. Either there exists an infinite chain of repeating terms, with no true end terms, as in the morally vacant world of *Vanity Fair*, or else there is a finite chain in which the end terms are either necessary truths or irreducible facts. In *Great Expectations* the end terms are the schemes of Miss Havisham and Magwitch, and then beyond them a possible blind spot of vanity or emptiness in Pip. Hardy's repressed end term in *Tess of the d'Urbervilles* is the caprice of a morally stupid God. His "President of the Immortals" is an unexplainable fact. Cathy Earnshaw's oracular equation, "I am Heathcliff," sounds more like a necessary truth. It collapses all finite terms in itself by claiming the authority of an analytic proposition or tautology.

Since end terms are veiled in secrecy and mystery, how will we know when we reach them? Anyone instructed like Christina Rossetti or Hopkins in a theology of reserve will realize that silence and proclamation are in tension: an open announcement that an ultimate principle has been reached might make an otherwise true statement false. But beyond a predilection for venerable concealment, what are the properties of such a principle? Browning often writes as if incessant motion is the desired state and rest the deviation. By contrast, Christina Rossetti, like Isaac Newton, posits rest or uniform motion as natural. When tossed back and forth as damaged merchandise, Rossetti feels that unnatural forces are acting on her body, because rest or at-oneness is the desired state. Carlyle believes that the moment we speak we have deviated from the perfection of silence. Any explanation of a deviation from silence is a further deviation from silence in what can quickly become an infinite regress of moves away from the desired state.

In *Wuthering Heights* the property of being nondual, without distinction, seems to confer ultimacy. In Hopkins's poem "Pied Beauty" ultimacy is conferred by a reversing flow of all beauty back to God. But because lack of differentiation, when "dapple is at an end," may merely be a result of eroded boundaries, the unwinding of the skein of "véined variety" alarms Hopkins in "Spelt from Sibyl's Leaves." Even when an ultimate principle, like the uses of reserve in theology, lacks a sufficient reason, there may be a sufficient reason for there not being a reason. As Browning keeps showing, were there no imperfection in the world, there could be no morality, for there must always be "broken arcs" for a moralist like Abt Vogler to connect. A mystery may be defined as an ultimate principle that does not have an explanation. In that sense, God's reasons for tormenting Job, like the laws of quantum mechanics, are a mystery. "Thou art indeed just, Lord" is a sonnet about the absence of any sufficient reason for God's apparent injustice to Hopkins. But the querulous forensic language in which Hopkins protests God's absence of sufficient reason may itself be reason enough. God may want to tutor Hopkins's heart and discipline his affections.

To reach an ultimate principle, we have to arrive at a boundary beyond which there are no further boundaries. We may not subscribe to Tennyson's doctrine of "boundless day" in section 95 of *In Memoriam.* But it is impossible not to be moved by his language, as "word by word, and line by line," he crosses boundaries. A theology of reserve like Tennyson's is fraught with secrecy. "Love's ... cry" is said to be "strange" and "dumb," and the words of the letter "silent-speaking" (95.26–27). Since the "noble letters of the dead" appear to hold a secret, their content is something Tennyson is prepared to go to great lengths to conceal. Hallam's father abetted the poet in this enterprise by destroying all the letters Tennyson wrote to his son. Tennyson flashes the fact of strange speech and contained secrets without announcing explicitly what the secrets are. At times the fault seems to lie with language: words are too full of snares to track the secret to its "inmost cell." At other times we may feel there have to be two secrets: a decoy secret and a true one. When the secrets shared with Hallam are identified as "The faith" and "vigour, bold to dwell / On doubts" (95.29–30), the disclosures seem too innocuous to qualify as the real secrets. It is as if the minor secrets in the poem were being used as successful covers for darker ones.

This first section of the book explores three theories of unconsciousness. The first theory assumes that unconscious meanings can be repossessed by a superior consciousness. In Dickens and Hardy there is usually some original secret truth to be discovered. Charlotte and Emily Brontë make the radically different assumption that unconscious meanings cannot be translated out of the dream or visionary language that is their only possible medium of presentation. The visionary medium is the message. The first theory of the unconscious is developed by Keble and Ruskin, who associate it with a system of concealments. The second theory finds expression in the critical writings of David Masson and E. S. Dallas, who treat the unconscious as an involuntary *manner* of presentation. A third theory of the unconscious, associated with Hegelian critics and Personal Idealists like F. C. S. Schiller, identifies the unconscious with a truth now out of sight, but capable of being engendered upon the world by each individual's will to create. For Hopkins and Christina Rossetti unconscious meaning is often only a latent consciousness of some purpose or design they must work to realize and make actual.

No Victorian critic more subtly expounds the mysteries of the unconscious than John Keble. Recognizing in his *Oxford Lectures* that the general condition of unconsciousness that is asserted to exist seems to invalidate any explicit consciousness of this condition, Keble argues that the clues to repressed or secret truths are often given only in digressions and asides. Only in a kind of postscript, for example, can Browning's Karshish tell Abib what he has to say. And only in his sleepwalking can Angel reveal that he is still deeply in love with Tess. Important themes are touched in passing, as if shyness or reserve is a sign of authenticity and depth. Keble's teaching that poetry gives healing relief to secret mental emotion anticipates the bringing to consciousness of painful and suppressed memories in rituals of baptism, marriage, and burial in *Tess of the d'Urbervilles*. The midnight entombment of Tess becomes a displaced and secular version of Keble's "Verbum Visibile," a symbol able to express what is otherwise unspeakable. Origen's triple sense of Scripture, which Keble expounds in *Tract 89*, differentiates the letter of a text from both the sense of the letter and its spirit. The sense of a symbol can be found only by studying it in context, as part of a metaphoric chain of ritual acts, like the baptisms, marriages, and funerals in *Tess of the d'Urbervilles*. And the spirit of the letter can be found only by studying whole chains of such metaphors.

In literature these repeating metaphors of situation provide the best example of meanings that remain just beyond the threshold of present consciousness. How do clusters of wind, rain, and fire images in *Great Expectations* relate to a pattern? When Herbert advises Pip to detach himself from Estella, Pip's involuntary association of her with the old marsh winds rising from the sea explicitly relates his longing for her to his taking leave of the forge, which takes place in similar circumstances of solemnly rising mists (chap. 30). But like any experience of déjà vu, this first association of Estella with wind coming up from the sea makes us uneasily aware of other hidden meanings. More sinister and repressed is Estella's mysterious linkage with Magwitch, who is first met under conditions of rushing wind on the marsh. Dickens's uncanny use of repeating images and metaphors of situation operates like Ruskin's account of the Imagination Associative: the writer seems to grasp unconsciously some unifying design even before he chooses the first component of that design in his opening scene on the windswept marsh.

Great Expectations is full of authority figures like Miss Havisham, Pumblechook, and even Mr. Trabb, who issue peremptory commands to their inferiors. Each new use of peremptory language requires a new rule for interpreting the series. But no rule is given. Or perhaps it is more accurate to say that too many possible rules are given: because each command might form part of many other patterns, the series in question is underdetermined. When Jaggers tells Pip after his arrival in London that he is to go to Barnard's Inn, that he is to remain with Mr. Pocket, and then go with him to his father's house, the peremptory repetitions recall too many other intimidating commands to make a reader confident that he has identified the most important item in the series. We have an uneasy feeling that the most important item—in this case, the lawyer's distant echo of the convict's order that Pip is to bring him a file and victuals and never say a word—is the precise reverberation we are most in danger of missing. It is as if the same words can function as a subset of an infinite number of different sets, and the exact set we are in search of is continually escaping us.

In *Tess of the d'Urbervilles* metaphors of situation repeat themselves like the members of a mathematical series. But nothing in a past series determines whether a new term in the series will be correctly interpreted. The sudden convergence of marriage and funeral rites in Angel's symbolic entombment of Tess appears to fit into a chain in which Tess's earlier baptism and burial of her child Sorrow form a link. Yet only the testing of this apparent linking will determine how far the pattern holds. Correctness is a matter of critical fertility. Do the ritual incantations that Angel pronounces over Tess—"Dead, dead, dead" —in chapter 37 deepen, in retrospect, the anguish of the minister's obsessive repetitions at the time of Sorrow's death: "My dear girl, . . . it will be just the same," "It will be just the same" (chap. 14)? Conversely, does the conflict in the skeptical young minister—a conflict between moral rigor and tender impulse—clarify the more complex and harrowing conflict that tears Angel apart as he carries Tess to the coffin in the later scene? Like the meanings that swim into focus during Tess's midnight burial, such metaphors of situation are most affecting when they remain subliminal or half repressed, most in danger of being missed.

Dickens fills his novels with conversations that, though wholly natural to each of his speakers, set off echoes and reverberations of which most readers are only subliminally aware. The astonished use of anaphora that anyone can hear in the casual talk of a young innocent like Pip is turned by Dickens into the exploratory design of an entire novel. On one of his late visits to Satis House in chapter 38 Pip repeats the same marveling verbs he used on his first visit: "I saw in this," "I saw in this," "I saw that," "I saw that." The phrases are more weighted than we first realize, for what Pip "sees" at the end betrays the repressed truth that on his first visit he has really "seen" nothing. Dickens's repeated use of anaphora creates significances that have far less to do with Pip's understanding at particular moments than with a larger mysterious system of proclamations and concealments. Pip's uncomprehending acts of wondering, when he first enters Satis House or Jaggers's law office, make the language dense with the irony of acts of simultaneous seeing and *not* seeing, knowing and *not* knowing. They point to a central mystery in all literature seeking to explore consciousness of the unconscious. Dickens's echoes and repetitions stir the reader with memories half evaded or repressed but still potent to seize the mind like a dream we half remember.

Like the interaction of images or semantic patterns in poetry, the metaphors of situation in fiction raise the same problem in literary theory that is raised in metaphysics by the question, How are laws possible? Is the lawlike pattern disclosed by repeating metaphors of situation merely a description of what is shown in the metaphors that compose the pattern? Or can the pattern actually explain the genesis of secret meanings? In expounding his theory of the Imagination Associative, Ruskin suggests that a predetermining design that lies just outside our present consciousness would, were it capable of being accurately discerned, provide a lawlike account of how any pattern connects its terms. But the problem of how such laws are possible is particularly difficult to solve when the laws in question must be discovered by the self-surveillance of a retrospective narrator, like Pip in *Great Expectations* or Lucy Snowe in *Villette*. However acute such self-surveillance may be, it will be necessarily incomplete, because some part of the observer must remain behind the lens if anything is to be seen.

The Pip who unmasks the "vanity of sorrow which had become a master mania" in Miss Havisham (chap. 49) will never be able to see directly the blind spot of vanity in himself. That vanity may be one of the most important meanings in the novel. But to Pip it will necessarily remain the blank space on the retina, always out of view. The blind spot of a first-person narrator, even a retrospective one, is the equivalent of that portion of the surface of England on which, in Josiah Royce's example of a self-representative system in *The World and the Individual*, the map of England is being drawn. Each step to a more complete vantage point will always add to the object to be mapped something further that cannot be included in the present mapping. Whatever in Lucy Snowe's words remains "strong" and "strange," "drawn from no well," but filled forever from a bottomless sea that generates a sense of the boundless and regressive, comes from that part of herself that does the viewing. It places part of Lucy's world beyond her capacity to know it. In a similar way, Pip can never be fully conscious of that blind spot in himself—that core of passivity, vanity, and failure to be wholly responsible for his deeds—that lies at the center of his own field of vision. The more Lucy and Pip try to study themselves objectively, as a psychoanalyst would, the more they discover that their knowledge of the unconscious includes both what they know and can express and an irreducible minimum of secrecy and mystery that they know they can never know and can never hope to express.

CHAPTER 2
_____

We Know More Than We Know We Know:

Repetition in Dickens and Hardy

Novels like *Great Expectations* and *Tess of the d'Urbervilles* have to be
read attentively, because like themes in music such repeated phrases
as Pip's astonished "I saw, . . . I saw, . . . I saw" (chaps. 8, 38) or Angel
Clare's "Dead, dead, dead" (chap. 37) keep resounding in the ear until
the unconscious meanings they intimate become uncannily clear. Such
phrases and the situations they describe are so cunningly repeated
that when they move into the foreground, they make us uneasily
aware of having always known more dark truths than we knew we
knew or perhaps than we cared to know. The power of repressed or
unconscious knowledge is dramatized in such scenes as Magwitch's
return or Tess's execution, in which all intermediate action is suddenly
collapsed in a discovery of the concealed origins and ends that matter
most. Such origins and ends, like the repeated phrases that point to
them, seem to exist prior to the narratives, as if they were riddles,
gnomic words, or oracles imposed by fate and challenging a satisfactory representation in fiction.

Once Hardy or Dickens has found a story that embodies a riddling
phrase like Angel's incantatory "Dead, dead, dead" or Pumblechook's
absurd remonstrance—" 'Take warning, boy, take warning!', as if . . . I
contemplated murdering a near relation" (chap. 15), the oracular
strangeness of these phrases is not so much absorbed by the narrative
as rendered more obsessive and acute. When fully understood,
Pumblechook's unspoken prophecy about Pip's "murdering a near
relation" brings a shocking recognition of Dickens's Oedipal displacements. For Pumblechook is obliquely linking Pip with Oedipus as the
unwitting cause of an adopted father's death and of the death of a
surrogate mother, Mrs. Joe—as well as of a putative mother by

34

adoption, Miss Havisham. In loving Estella, Pip is also courting incest with a surrogate sister, since Estella is the daughter of Pip's second father. The whole novel seems to be generated out of an unutterable seed phrase, with a tang of Oedipal redundancy to it: I am brother and lover in one, and near relations I have murdered include sisters and mothers as well as the father who adopted me. It is no wonder Pip, in telling his story, feels impelled to distance such unspeakable tautologies. *Great Expectations* keeps using a kind of generalized tmesis, the rhetorical figure that separates terms that belong together. Only by opening up a whole chain of intruded middle terms can Pip find space in which to build illusions, including the illusion that in a world where everything is fated he can act as a free agent.

The power of Magwitch's language when he returns in chapter 39 comes from its elision of Pip's carefully constructed middle terms and from its overspecification of ends. Words we have heard in chapter 1 and hear again thirty-eight chapters later collapse a chain. They make a mental bang, speeding Pip's mind by freeing it from overly confident surmises about his benefactor's identity. Once the separated identities of the secret patron and of the convict who appears to Pip on the marsh are allowed to converge, *Great Expectations* is shown to have less in common with a social novel than with a fairy tale. Pip is a male Cinderella who, after his ball in London, is faced with a transformation scene at midnight during which his fairy godmother, Miss Havisham, turns out to be a grotesque godfather instead.

Fatality in Dickens's novel is inseparable from the organizational rigor of its repeating metaphors of situation, which inexorably collapse the terms that Dickens also conspires to keep separate. The novelist's freedom is simultaneously affirmed and denied by the genius with which Dickens uses these metaphors to create an odd sense that readers know more than they know they know. These metaphors affirm his freedom by celebrating the power of his art to evoke meaning subliminally. But they also inhibit that freedom by repeating in the organizational rigor of the novel's narrative method a version of that fate which mysteriously controls the destinies of Estella and Pip. Because all the past events that slowly swim into focus are both fated and elided, even Dickens, their inventor, had to construct in his surviving manuscript notes a chronological chart to help him keep straight the exact sequence of these events and the age of each character after Magwitch's return (Dickens 1987, 321). Having spun his web, the novelist can no more escape its constraints than Pip and Estella can escape the designs of Magwitch and Miss Havisham.

Even before long-separated elements converge in chapter 39, we are made subliminally aware of them. At the end of chapter 38, the great iron ring to which the concealed end of the rope is attached in the fable of the sultan is clearly a metonymy for Magwitch, who has been associated from the beginning with a leg iron. The imminent collapse of intruded terms is even anticipated by the syntax. The repetitions of "stormy and wet, stormy and wet; and mud, mud, mud, deep in all the streets" hide as much as they reveal. Like the "vast heavy veil" that has been "driving over London" (chap. 39), the opaque words postpone disclosure even as they foretell it. Heard in one tone, these repetitions are a mere exhausted complaint, draining the words of energy. But they also compose a kind of mantra that, if pondered more attentively, may disclose secret meanings obscured or lost in memory.

The parenthesis describing Pip's thwarted opening of the windows— "(opening them ever so little was out of the question . . .)"—is itself an aperture powerless to open up a space in the language that will defer the onrush of collapsing terms. Symptomatic of this collapse is the changing function of the simile comparing the shaking wind to discharges from a cannon.

> We lived at the top of the last house, and the wind rushing up the river shook the house that night, like discharges of cannon, or breakings of a sea. When the rain came with it and dashed against the windows, I thought, raising my eyes to them as they rocked, that I might have fancied myself in a storm-beaten lighthouse . . . when I shaded my face with my hands and looked through the black windows (opening them ever so little was out of the question in the teeth of such wind and rain) I saw that the lamps in the court were blown out, and that the lamps on the bridges and the shore were shuddering, and that the coal fires in barges on the river were being carried away before the wind like red-hot splashes in the rain. (Chap. 39)

When first introduced, the simile of the discharged cannon is a mere frame around Pip's picture of his rooms at the top of the Temple, which are compared to a "storm-beaten lighthouse," But by the end of the paragraph the frame has moved in to occupy the picture space itself. Now Pip seems to be in a lighthouse whose light has blown out, surrounded by foundering barges facing shipwreck and ruin. As the fantasy of the lighthouse begins to erode distinctions between land and river, solid buildings and dissolving mist, frame and picture space switch positions. It is as if Pip, without consciously registering this sudden convergence of the story's origins and ends, were actually standing on the deck of Magwitch's convict ship, from which the cannons were discharged in the opening scenes of the novel.

Pip's impressions are curiously in and out of focus simultaneously.

Like the black window that will not be opened, the repetitions of "stormy and wet, stormy and wet" are opaquely luminous. They are luminous because they echo earlier impressions of rain, marsh, and mud, though only subliminally. And they are opaque because, in repeating words without chiastic variation, they are also singularly infantile and nonprogressive. A sense of blurred meaning is conveyed not just visually by the rain, mud, and black window, but also aurally by the failure of the church chimes to sound the hour in unison because their sound waves are flawed before they reach Pip, having been assailed and torn by the wind.

Though there is still a hole at the center of Pip's picture of foundering ships and firing cannons, Pip himself is subliminally reminded of the missing element even before it actually steps across the threshold of his room. His memory is jogged by an irrational association that "awfully connect[s]" the footstep on the stair with "the footstep of [his] dead sister." That association, however irrational, has its own unconscious logic, for Mrs. Joe's death was a direct result of a blow from Magwitch's leg iron. "Iron" is the deleted element in the scene. No sooner has it been elided than it appears in a displaced context as the intruder's iron-gray hair. Also, if the footsteps are those of his dead sister, Pip is being visited by a ghost. Everything seems slightly out of focus, as it did in Wopsle's dismal performance as Hamlet. Wopsle had trouble reading his script: now Pip, about to be confronted like Hamlet by his father's ghost, has trouble using his reading lamp to discern the ghostlike figure, his father by adoption, who addresses him "from the darkness beneath." Subliminal meanings are still very much alive: in the midst of repressed memories they are like consciousness itself.

Great Expectations sustains a slow domino effect in its collapsing of widely separated identities. No sooner have two divergent characters— the convict on the marsh and the strange visitor at the Temple—been collapsed into the same person than other even more widely separated people—Magwitch and the mysterious benefactor, presumably Miss Havisham—are similarly collapsed. But there are always other separated characters still to be merged. Among the last people to fall into a single father-daughter relation are Estella and Magwitch, although this collapse is anticipated, even in chapter 39, by Magwitch's tear-filled eyes. They recall Pip's impulse to weep when Herbert urges his friend to forget Estella in chapter 30. This grief, which is compared to the feeling that subdued Pip like a sweep of the old marsh winds when he left the forge as the mists were rising in chapter 19, also recalls his encounter with the convict in chapter 1, but now for the first time in connection with Estella. Later, in chapter 39, the discovery scene, Pip mentions Estella when Magwitch asks if he has fallen in love. There are already hints that Magwitch's adopted son wants to marry his second father's daughter, with the result that son and daughter may soon become husband and wife. Collapse enough separated terms, and the remaining identities are bound to seem incestuous and Oedipal.

Even as the atmospheric conditions of two widely separated occasions bring astonishing disclosures of identity in chapter 39, a rhetorical pattern of anaphora—"I knew him,... I knew him"—links this discovery with other scenes where comparable uses of "I saw" and "I know" remind readers that complete knowing or seeing does not come quite so readily. The first time Pip sees Satis house, a chain of incongruities linking youth with age, sumptuous decor with waste, is fixed rigidly in place by an equally astonished use of anaphora.

> It was not in the first moments that *I saw* all these things... But *I saw* that everything within my view which ought to be white, had been white long ago...*I saw* that the bride within the bridal dress had withered like the dress...*I saw* that the dress.... (Chap. 8; italics added)

In the chapter immediately preceding Magwitch's return, Pip uses the same trope to register a deeper, more searching mode of seeing.

> *I saw in this*, wretched though it made me,...—*I saw in this*, that Estella was set to wreak Miss Havisham's revenge on men,...*I saw in this*, a reason for her being beforehand assigned to me.... *I saw in this*, that I, too, was tormented by a perversion of ingenuity.... *I saw in this*, the reason for my being staved off so long.... In a word, *I saw in this*, Miss Havisham as I had her then and there before my eyes...and *I saw in this*, the distinct shadow of the darkened and unhealthy house in which her life was hidden from the sun. (Chap. 38; italics added)

Deferral of Pip's expectations in his "being staved off so long" is explicitly identified as Miss Havisham's plan. Delay is also a repeated effect of Dickens's grammar. It is created, for example, by the insertion of a past participle, "wretched," after the first use of the phrase "I saw in this," whose full meaning is only gradually disclosed in the many clauses in apposition to the pronoun, which is repeated seven times in as many sentences. "Being staved off" is also an apt description of Dickens's narrative technique of separating out and then collapsing terms. A fate that at first seems external to Pip and his world also proves internal to the ritualized use of anaphora and tmesis in Dickens's fiction.

When Magwitch cross-examines Pip about his income—"As to the first figure now, Five?" (chap. 39), a host of authority figures can be heard talking through him. We hear Pumblechook posing his arithmetic tables: "Seven times nine, boy!... Seven? And four? And eight? And six?" (chap. 8); Jaggers interrogating Pip about how much money he wants: "How much? Fifty pounds?... Five pounds?" (chap.24); and Trabb's intimidating commands to his apprentice to bring the appropriate rolls of cloth for Pip's inspection: "Give me Number Four, you!" "Are you bringing numbers five and eight?" (chap. 19). Trabb's imperious tone dramatizes to Pip the power of money to suppress and crush menials. "I saw [the boy] collapse as his master rubbed me out with his hands." The odd phrase, "to rub someone out" of a door, becomes less odd when a more awesome Mr. Trabb, the returned Magwitch of the discovery scene, engineers Pip's collapse by using comparably intimidating questions to "rub out" Pip's assurance that he, a former apprentice like Trabb's boy, is really a gentleman. Joe's purblind deciphering of the letters "J" and "O" in Pip's half-literate script had been accepted as "astonishing" proof of Pip's scholarship (chap. 7). Now in the grim ciphering of chapter 39 Pip finds equally astonishing proof that his strange visitor is a riddling scholar of mysteries: "As to the first letter of that lawyer's name now. Would it be J?" Just as the capitalized letters of Pip's youthful script substitute "U" for "you" and "B" for "be," contracting "soon" into "soN" (chap. 7), so Dickens keeps eliding the separating terms, like the consonants between Pip's vowels. With its metonymic chains and converging terms, the whole novel is like one of Pip's barely decipherable letters or like Mrs. Joe's pictograph for Orlick.

The function of Dickens's generalized tmesis, of his spacing out terms before allowing them to converge, is also assumed by a character like Jaggers, who is simultaneously the dispeller and the perpetrator of mystery. On the one hand, he is a legal Bentham, exposing the mysterious dark spots in language and the concealed poetry of everyday discourse in order to find unambigous substitutes. Even Joe's mild blasphemy, "Lord forbid," is too rhetorical for Jaggers, who takes the phrase more literally than Joe intends. "Lord forbidding is pious," Jaggers sternly chides, "but not to the purpose" (chap. 18). With his phobia of double meanings, Jaggers keeps rephrasing questions until wholly transparent answers are forthcoming. In imposing conditions that seem to Pip and Joe like no conditions, however, Jaggers leaves mysteriously open the question whether the reason for these conditions is obscurely grave or merely whimsical. And why should Jaggers insist that Pip choose his words more carefully? The substitution of the more noncommittal noun "mention" for "recommendation" implies the presence of some silent judge or invisible jury. It also implies that acceptance of the gift is almost a crime and that Jaggers wants to escape legal responsibility. Is the exaggerated precision just a lawyer's occupational obsession? Or is its enforced clarity really the opposite of clarity, a cloak of mystery designed to mask some unspeakable deed?

A reader's uncanny sense of having heard before an anaphoric use of "I saw," "I saw," or "I knew," "I knew," without being able to recall the precise place, accurately evokes the experience of déjà vu. Pip has a similar experience when he registers the strange fugitive impression of something repeated but not precisely recalled as Estella waves to him from the carriage near Newgate prison (chap. 32). "The nameless shadow" that passes before him is a subliminal recollection of Molly's hand; and the prison air Pip tries to exhale has a closer association with Estella, the convict's daughter, than his conscious mind allows him to acknowledge. Subliminal knowledge is usually the result of some fugitive memory. But sometimes an experience may bring with it such a forceful impression of what it stands for that experiencing the event the first time is like experiencing it twice. If no earlier instance of the experience has in fact ocurred, then we must invent a recurrence of it or prophesy that it will happen again sometime in the future.

In at least one such use of inverted déjà vu, Pip finds himself inventing a second occurrence of an experience and then placing it outside the novel Dickens has written. After telling us in chapter 26 that he has always associated the witchlike Molly with a face rising out of the cauldron, Pip says that years afterward he made a dreadful likeness of her pass from a bowl of spirits in a dark room. No other event in the novel quite fits this description. The closest metaphor of situation, a product of Pip's delirium, is his hallucination of Miss Havisham's being consumed in an iron furnace in a corner of the room (chap. 57). But this event does not take place "years later," and Miss Havisham's face, unlike Molly's, is not disturbed by fiery air. Another analogue can be found earlier in the novel, when Pip first enters the brewery and sees Estella holding her "pretty brown hair spread out in her two hands" as he watches her "pass among the extinguished fires" (chap. 8). In this scene we find a remote echo of "the bowl of flaming spirits" and "flaming hair" (chap. 26), but because the episode occurs in Pip's childhood, it cannot be the experience he is alluding to as a young man. It seems as if only at some unspecified future time outside the novel will Pip's conjuring of a spectral apparition from a bowl of fire confer on Molly's rising from the cauldron its truly ghostlike status as a fugitively remembered impression.

Dickens "bares the device," as Russian formalists would say, in two scenes involving Wopsle that are too often dismissed as mere comic digressions. When Wopsle recites the tragedy of George Barnwell in chapter 15, he unwittingly lays bare the whole future course of Pip's narrative. The absurdity of Pumblechook's sudden contraction of the space separating Barnwell and Pip will be matched by the collapse of other middle terms later in the novel. As Taylor Stoeher has argued (1965, 104–10), what is merely absurd in Wopsle's recitation will become truly terrifying when Barnwell's fate of going to the scaffold at Newgate threatens to become Magwitch's fate, and when other "near relations" like Mrs. Joe and Miss Havisham come to comparably violent ends. The same sudden convergence of widely separated characters takes place when the event dimly foreshadowed by Wopsle's performance as Hamlet begins to clarify in the discovery scene (chap. 39). Like the ghost of Hamlet's father, Magwitch comes back from the grave, making demands upon his adopted son that will force that son to separate himself from the world, avenging the wrong done to the father by bringing ruin on other members of the family.

The humor of incongruously conflating too many roles in the performance in which Wopsle plays Hamlet prepares for the curious combination of nightmare and absurdity in chapter 39. Who would have dreamed that an actor combining such widely separated dramatic parts as Estella's father and Pip's father by adoption, as the convict on the marsh and the long-silent benefactor, would return to haunt Pip like Hamlet's father risen from the grave? "The noble boy in the ancestral boots was inconsistent; representing himself, as it were in one breath, as an able seaman, a strolling actor, a grave-digger, a clergyman, and a person of the utmost importance at a court fencing-match" (chap. 31). The unintended comedy is a result of collapsing too many identities. The quadrupling that makes possible the noble boy's performance of five different roles in a single play humorously describes the generalized tmesis of Dickens's own narrative method, which often culminates in a sudden collapse of terms. Pip dreams that night that he is a hapless Mr. Wopsle playing Hamlet to Miss Havisham's ghost, having to perform before twenty thousand people while knowing fewer than twenty words of the play. It is as if the incongruous running together of separated entities—some in real life, some in fiction—is a direct result of an inability to command enough interposed narrative and language, enough separating middle terms.

The repetitions in *Great Expectations* are not just grounded in a fatality external to Pip's world and his language, a fatality created and imposed by the older generation. Fate is also internal to literary convention, to Dickens's willed repetition of an eighteenth-century repetition of a ballad written in the sixteenth century. *Great Expectations* repeats not only a scheme of the older generation but also a prior work of literature, a story that had several incarnations in at least two different genres before Dickens chose to present it in a third genre. *The London Merchant* by George Lillo, an eighteenth-century dramatist, is a tragedy about a middle-class hero, George Barnwell, who first appeared in an Elizabethan ballad written as an "improving" holiday amusement for apprentices like Pip.

But while Pip is telling one story about himself, Dickens is telling another story about Pip, for whom fate is also character. The mystery of Pip's proper name is a cipher for the mystery of his identity as a gentleman, whose only vocation seems to be his absence of vocation. Like his infantile writing, Pip's name runs together letters that were originally separate: it is an elision of "Philip Pirrip," which Pip contracts to "Pip" (chap. 1). To murder near relations (chap. 15) and to want to marry the daughter of one's father is to elide individual identity until one has no proper being of one's own to express. Such elisions are willed as a pretext for Pip's absence of properties, for his amorphousness, for his being nothing more distinctive than "Pip," a mispronunciation of his proper name. It is as if Pip, like one of those "self-swindlers" who cheat themselves (chap. 28), wants Pumblechook's oracle about his Oedipal murdering of near relations to rob him of any chance for freedom and responsibility he may have.

When all the terms that intrude between such apparent opposites as affection and hatred, health and disease, knowledge and ignorance are finally collapsed in chapter 49, they all come to the same annihilating end. They are all identical, and they are all a form of vanity. "And could I look upon her without compassion, seeing her punishment in the ruin she was, in her profound unfitness for this earth on which she was placed, in the vanity of sorrow which had become a master mania, like the vanity of penitence, the vanity of remorse, the vanity of unworthiness, and other monstrous vanities that have been curses in this world?" (chap. 49). The dark ground behind all the collapsing terms is briefly glimpsed in this passage, then veiled from view, as if Pip cannot bear to know the truth. The repeating word that sinks everything in an obliterating void is "vanity." But even as Pip denounces the "monstrous vanities that have been curses in this world," there seems to be a darker truth behind the story that Pip wants to tell and is conscious of telling. Is Pip not all too aware of Miss Havisham's vanity, but unaware of the equally profound vanity of his own incapacity to grow up? Pip is redundant: he is a brother instead of a husband to Estella, and a kind of infant to Biddy, who is always more his mother than the wife he wants her to be. After his fever he wakes up in Biddy's lap. Instead of marrying her, he returns to the womb that bore him, to a second mother. Mrs. Joe was always more a mother than a sister, and the second Mrs. Joe is more a mother than the wife she ought to become. Like Oedipus, Pip finds his lifeline no longer exists. If Tess's marriage bed is a deathbed, Pip's marriage bed is really a cradle. The novel is a palimpsest on which careful readers can decipher traces of other stories Pip never meant to tell.

Like *Great Expectations*, Hardy's *Tess of the d'Urbervilles* uses repetition to make the main character subliminally conscious of impending fate. Both Tess and Pip know more than they know they know. As Pip's life is circumscribed by Pumblechook's oracle about murdering a close relative, so Tess's life is limited by Angel's ritualistic pronouncement, "Dead, dead, dead" (chap. 37). When the distancing of end terms collapses and the effort to separate birth from death, baptisms from marriages and funerals can no longer be sustained, then the mysteriously fated decrees of Hardy's "President of the Immortals" (chap. 59), a blind and groping Schopenhauerian Will, slowly but remorselessly restrict its victims' freedom until they have no space left to move. Both Tess and Pip converge on their fate like a riddle on its point or a tragedy on its recognition scene.

In Hardy, as in Dickens, the end terms are given in the oracles and gnomic phrases that seem to exist prior to the fictions embodying them, and that are heard most resonantly in repeating metaphors of situation. Tess, more than most characters, lives under a suspended death sentence. Mediating terms that repress this truth suddenly collapse in the nocturnal accident that claims the life of her horse Prince (chap. 4); in the nighttime seduction scene, where sexual initiation is presented as a kind of death (chap. 11); in the burial of Tess's unbaptized child, where birth and death are harrowingly conjoined (chap. 14); and in the final execution at Stonehenge (chap. 59), which follows implacably and incongruously upon the few days of happiness Angel and Tess have known. But conflations of love and death, marriage and burial, are presented most poignantly, I think, in the sleepwalking scene (chap. 37), when Angel lays Tess in the abbot's coffin. As wedding and burial rites are bizarrely but movingly commingled, the temporal space between events that in most lives are widely separated suddenly collapses in a frightening revelation of the truth Hardy has elsewhere repressed: if we were truly awake, we would die of the roar that lies on the other side of silence. Since waking reality is the true nightmare, all life, like all art, should aspire to the condition of Angel's sleepwalking trance.

Tess's ritual interment in the stone coffin dramatizes the blind, groping, pathetically stupid fatality that makes the suffering of its victims superfluous and avoidable. That fatality is already present in

the stark, balladlike simplicity of the one-sentence paragraph opening, which is isolated in its strict autonomy like an epitaph on a
gravestone: "Midnight came and passed silently, for there was nothing
to announce it in the Valley of the Froom" (chap. 37). The absence of
the anticipated rites of love is too painful at first to mention, and so it
is elided. Only the mysteriously causal "for" marks obliquely the
graveyard of a marriage, whose expected consummation has taken a
grimly funereal turn. When Tess's fear of a ghost or an intruder
subsides into recognition of her husband, her brief surge of erotic
desire is replaced by dread of his vacant stare, then pity for the
indescribable sadness of his voice. Once before in his sleep Angel had
reenacted a combat with a man who had insulted Tess. Now he enacts
something deeply insulting to Tess herself: the burial of the woman
he thought he had married. "Indescribable" becomes a key adjective.
The real meanings are the silent ones, to be heard only in the words
behind the words that are spoken.

Angel's obsessive repetitions, "Dead, dead, dead," indicate terrible
distress of mind. He shreds the monosyllables in an agony of frustration. The words are more potent when we realize that not only are
they repeated within the sleepwalking scene itself but they also resonate subliminally with repetitions inside an earlier scene of burial.
When Tess tried to bury her unbaptized child, the kind but vacillating
minister assured her that her burial in unconsecrated ground would
make no difference. "My dear girl," he assured Tess repetitively, "it
will be just the same," "It will be just the same" (chap. 14). Ironically,
the loyalty and trust that Angel feels Tess has forfeited are proved
dramatically when Angel is too entranced to witness them. Her trust is
so deep that she experiences no fear when her husband threatens to
drown her, then lays her in a coffin. The power of the ritual burial
comes from the sudden convergence of the forlorn and hungry
longing of the wife, who wants to consummate her marriage, and the
repressed desires of the unforgiving husband. These two emotions
had been rigorously segregated during Angel's waking hours. But
now the warmth and endearment that Tess has longed for swell to
consciousness, as impulses that had been strictly censored are momentarily indulged: "My poor, poor Tess—my dearest, darling Tess! So
sweet, so good, so true." The death rites are really a kind of ghastly
fulfillment of the marriage vows. But Angel is tender only when about
to bury her. The Tess he is carrying, as if in a shroud, is not the real
Tess but an imaginary Tess who has existed only in his mind.

The pathos arises because there are really two Tesses. There is Tess
the ideal of purity, whom Angel has fallen in love with and married.
And there is the flesh-and-blood Tess, whose only consolation in the

scene of entombment comes from the desperate hope that she can be two different people at the same time. If the flesh-and-blood Tess is A and the sacrosanct Tess, the symbol of purity, is B, then it is clear that for Angel "B minus A equals nothing." That harrowing equation is echoed in the words "Dead, dead, dead," which explode powerfully upon the midnight scene, then simply disintegrate. It is the "unmeasurable woe" of both Angel and Tess that she cannot be both Tesses simultaneously.

In outward form Angel's carrying Tess in his arms across the threshold recalls the ritual of the bridegroom's carrying his bride across the door of their future home. But this crossing is painful: Angel stubs his toe and is only half-dressed. Browning's "By the Fire-Side" is quoted two chapters earlier: "The little less, and what worlds away" (chap. 35). Thin partitions divide one ritual from the other. Only slight variations in the marriage and funeral ceremonies reverse the drama of Browning's love poem, where there is no withholding, but only total giving. In both ceremonies language functions performatively. Angel's pronouncing Tess to be dead in a sense *makes* her die. She is not dead in her heart until he says she is. His funereal naming of Tess, "Dead, dead, dead," is a kind of baptism in reverse. Obsessive behavior, according to Freud, reenacts and directs events over which the performer can otherwise exercise no control. As the performer of a funereal rite, Angel is in some measure correcting the trauma that has broken his life apart and prevented the consummation of his marriage. That disorder is more manageable now as the performance of a funeral service and a burial, in which Angel as the chief mourner and celebrant can at least control what happens.

Baptisms and funerals, as the rituals of beginnings and ends, are usually widely separated. But there is a precedent in the novel for the sudden commingling of the two rituals in Angel's surprising baptism of Tess as a figure of death. We recall that Tess's improvised ritual of baptizing her child Sorrow is almost immediately followed by disputes about how the child is to be buried. Quoting Ascham's saying that "it is a marvelous pain to find out but a short way by long wandering" (chap. 15), Hardy's narrator identifies one of the novel's most important structural devices: the deferral or delay of events fated to occur. Such delays, which are a condition of every life, may be painful, but were it not for the "long wandering[s]" and detours around the straightest path, the journey itself might be unendurable. Characters and readers need the spacing out and detours, however arduous they may be, to mute the even greater pain of a sudden merging of beginnings and ends. Such a collapse of interposed terms produces the unbearable anguish of scenes in which baptisms and burials shockingly converge. What is elided for little Sorrow is nothing less than life itself.

Tess's erotic fantasy of being carried by Angel to her marriage bed is repeated in the stream crossing, when she thinks of falling to their deaths together (chap. 37). The earlier Keatsian fantasy of swooning to erotic and literal death in a luxury of sensation is now repeated in the Keatsian fantasy of going out of the world "almost painlessly." The drama of repressed or subliminal awareness splits into a reflected image of itself, like the moon on the water, in these Keatsian allusions, which run subterraneously like another swift but silent stream. Even the placing of Tess in the abbot's tomb repeats an earlier action. First the lugubrious stretching of tourists in the tomb intrudes a note of grim humor. When Tess is laid out in the same coffin a moment later the potential absurdity of the act has been effectively isolated and drawn off. Tess's bolting up in the tomb to find Angel lifeless beside her is a repetition of Juliet's awakening in the crypt to find Romeo dead beside her. In the return to the house, roles are reversed. The rite of Angel's bearing Tess out of the house, in a kind of funeral procession, is balanced now by the rite of Tess's carrying Angel back, as the love she is not allowed to show in life translates itself into the solicitude of a guardian angel, escorting him to heaven.

This apocalyptic drama of reunion and forgiveness recalls the reunion scene in *King Lear*, where the king mistakes the returned Cordelia for a spirit. The more brutal side of *Lear*, recalled in Hardy's later allusion to the gods' killing men for their sport (chap. 59), is balanced in this scene by one of the most ethereal moments in nineteenth-century fiction, an instant of life-giving illumination and insight. Again, as in the oblique use of Keats, the Shakespearean allusions are more affecting for being subliminal and repressed.

In *Great Expectations* the repressed materials are brought into focus in the discovery scene and bring Pip a measure of self-knowledge. But Angel struggles in vain to remember what happened during the night. The simile "deep as annihilation," which the narrator applies to Angel's sleep (chap. 37), is a shocking one. It has the force of one of Wordsworth's similes: "Heavy as frost, and deep almost as life" ("Ode on the Intimations of Immortality," l. 129). There are contradictory senses in which the puzzling equation of sleep with annihilation may be said to apply. Hardy may mean that in his sleepwalking Angel has buried Tess figuratively and nothing can be so annihilating as her death. And yet burial is not synonymous with annihilation. Angel's nocturnal burial has also removed from his love for Tess the pain of his having to suffer from her supposed infidelity. It is as if the infidelities of language deform what Hardy wants to say; they unexpectedly touch upon some undiscovered paradox or hidden nerve at the center of his fiction. Is sleep "deep as annihilation" because it has banished pain and preserved only clarity of judgment? Sleep may annihilate the complicating motions of the affective will and memory, retaining only the starkness of rational judgment. And Hardy knows that this second kind of annihilation can be more devastating in the end. Bare bones produce clarity of outline only at the inadmissible price of stripping away the warm and breathing passion of the heart that Angel found so delightful. Angel's cold resolve to quell scorching passion and searing will is compared to the operation of Kant's Pure Reason. But in abstracting from the whole, is Reason's pursuit of a transcendent thing-in-itself not synonymous with a quest for nothingness? Analogously, is the Will that Schopenhauer posits beyond all phenomenal wills only an empty fiction? The annihilation that collapses ends and beginnings, funerals and marriages, eliding all the complex, humanizing middle terms, leaves in its wake only a skeleton, or at best the illusion of some abstracting veil, some ghostly thing-in-itself, placed dangerously over the void.

In chapters 13 and 14, in passages of exceptional density and contradiction even for Hardy, the narrator asks if the world is a projection of the perceiver or a manifestation of some noumenal thing-in-itself. In his book *On the Four-fold Root of the Principle of Sufficient Reason*, which we know Hardy read and studied in 1889 or 1890 (Miller 1985, 305), Schopenhauer paradoxically asserts that the world must be both of these things—a projection *and* a noumenal manifestation—simultaneously. Schopenhauer's first principle of sufficient reason is the presentation of the world as an object for a subject: "the world is my idea." But if the world is only Tess's idea of it, a mere "psychological phenomenon," as Hardy calls it (chap. 13), how can she become aware of anything outside her present consciousness? Either there is no noumenal world, or Tess tragically misreads it. Surprisingly enough, Hardy and Schopenhauer both opt for the second alternative. They can logically reach this conclusion only if they insist that the proposition "the world is my idea" is true only in the world of appearances: it does not apply to the thing-in-itself. And yet once Hardy accepts Schopenhauer's doctrine that the world is only a psychological phenomenon, it is difficult to see how any access to the thing-in-itself is possible. He can think about a metaphysical Will, even about a mentally weak Will. But insofar as mindless Mind or volitionless Will is thought about, it must be an object for a subject and so, as Schopenhauer argues, merely phenomenal.

It is one thing to founder on a metaphysical paradox and another thing to realize like Tess that the full meaning of what she knows subliminally can never quite swim into focus for her. Tess's end has a sense of fulfilled expectation, yet in the scenes preceding her arrest at Stonehenge it is the opposite of obvious. "I don't know how" and "I don't know" are the two phrases that keep echoing through the sequence (chap. 57). In comparison with Tess's victories of moral imagination and consciousness, the murder is so dimly realized that Angel does "not know" whether it has actually taken place. In slowly collapsing a chain of intermediate events, the ending dramatizes potent and affecting reversals of earlier scenes. Alec had tried to lose his way with Tess the night of the seduction; now Angel plunges farther and farther into the fir forest in order to find his way out of the maze by getting thoroughly lost. The motives of the two men are entirely different. Angel wants to save and protect Tess, not ruin her. The repeated phrase, "I don't know," dramatizes the logical inconsequence and impracticality of Tess's and Angel's plans. Childlike lucidity and tenderness are permeated by a sense of waywardness and errancy. There are certain sanctities of phrase, "Ah, happy house," "So now I am at home" (chap. 58), learned as if by instinct, by rote and repetition, that have nothing to do with the moral reasoning that leads Tess to rue her deed as "madly wicked." Without any resolute will to escape, Tess and Angel only halfheartedly play at escape, like two children. They turn the deserted mansion into a kind of playhouse, where they can have their long-deferred honeymoon in Eden. But like most honeymoons, their time together is pathetically brief. This holiday interlude is a final deferral of an end that is half known and accepted. The slight deferrals in the last chapters merely serve to make the anxiety of leave-taking more harrowing.

Murder, which seems so banal and anticlimactic, might well have jeopardized the reader's intimacy with Tess. But because the thought of being loyal to Angel is truer than the reality of murder, our intimacy with Tess is never put at risk. Tess's imagination of a new beginning with Angel is a speculation of such wonderfully renovating power and appeal that it all but cancels the deed she must perform in order to make the idea valid. Closeness to Tess is always a function of Hardy's concentration on a state of mind. When she is on the edge of sleep, or close to oblivion, so are we. There is a sense of heartbreaking waste and loss in the sleepwalking scene because the reader is experiencing and becoming intimate with an Angel he has not known. How can people as much "like ourselves" as Tess and Angel do the deeds they do? There is a gap between the kind of moral idiot who would allow herself to be raped by Alec or commit murder and the kind of Tess, capable in her feelings for Angel of a deep and backward-reaching intimacy, that we come to know intimately ourselves.

Tess has a passionate sense for ordinary life, for the joys of nature and the priorities of domestic routine. The thought of being at home, domesticated, of entering into the kind of family life she ought to have had, makes Tess protest most poignantly and bitterly against her murderous destiny. Her home at Stonehenge is not the home it might have been. Tess's fate seems unnatural and unhomely just because she has so clear an idea what is due to home and nature. She has a desire for domesticity at the heart of strangeness, and indeed has murdered for its sake. Tess's last words to Angel—and to the reader—are practical, domestic, just the kind of reflection that would come to her in a husband's presence. She is mistress of an unhomely home, and she moves with promptness and dispatch. She has a sense of the fitness of the hour at which she is asked to leave, and she is punctual and ready when the time comes. Tess sees more clearly than her husband that he might have come to despise her had she lived. But Angel now displays a fine sense of propriety, persuading the officers to defer the arrest until his wife wakes up. Angel and his wife are now acting as partners who ease the pain of leave-taking by turning it into a contest in courtesy and tact. They remain intimate, even at the moment of separation, protected against the outside world even when they must allow that world to enter.

Tess's odd phrasing in the penultimate chapter, "I am not going to think outside of now," prepares for a curious reversal of outsides and insides. The unrented mansion had provided the unexpected refuge of a safe inside. But at Stonehenge they come to a second edifice in which the inside is also an outside. It is a Temple of the Winds with no obvious interior to protect them. As a fitting dwelling place for a sphinx without a secret, whose interior may be all an outside after all—a mere facade of mystery, this enigmatic Temple of the Winds is to Coleridge's aeolian harp what Hardy's darkling thrush is to Shelley's skylark. The wind plays upon this monstrous edifice as if it were not an aeolian lyre, but some gigantic one-stringed harp capable of emitting only an unsubtle monotone. And so in this temple of some curiously withdrawing deity, it seems appropriate that when Tess asks if their love for each other will survive her death, Angel merely kisses her but does not speak. Again she asks, and he remains silent. Nobody knows what death means. To the critical question at the critical time Angel can give no answer. Even the landscape turns taciturn, as if all creation bears witness to the justness of Angel's silence and to the logic of some vast and inscrutable theology of reserve.

In the final paragraph the agitation of mind in Angel and Liza-Lu involuntarily transfers itself to Hardy's narrator. The blur, density, and non sequitur quality of his comments betrays the same instability as the half-irrelevant questions that Hardy poses after the seduction (chap. 11). It is as if Hardy's mind, like the reader's, now grasps at incongruities that link up unexpected possibilities in a desperate effort to find explanations for what cannot be explained. Sequences become inconsequential, and language can trace only the scurry and strain of a mind under stress, darting desperately from one fugitive idea to another.[1]

Tess is destroyed by the very project she nurses on Angel's behalf. In murdering Alec, she does something out of character, and in that role Angel cannot recognize Tess any more than the reader can. And yet she has played the murderess for Angel's sake. She has taken the part, the role of avenging wife, and must die because of it. What Tess loses is in some sense Angel's and the reader's gain. We know Tess most intimately, as Angel does, when she has nowhere to go but into oblivion. Neither Hardy nor Angel can assure Tess that anything will speak to her across the nothingness of her own death. All we can see of her at the end is the raised flag.

Great Expectations and *Tess of the d'Urbervilles* show how reiterated oracles and gnomic words may be sibylline in opposite ways. They say either too much or too little. Angel's ritual pronouncement, "Dead, dead, dead," seems to say too much, and Pumblechook's absurd remonstrance, "Take warning boy, take warning," seems to say too little. The one is a miraculous collision of widely separated acts— marriage rituals and burials, baptisms and funerals—so packed with meaning that it skirts the oracular. The other is so inane and gratuitous that it seems comically stupid or obtuse. Pumblechook's windy rhetoric has too much sound for the sense; Angel's cryptic one-word pronouncements have too much sense or disguised meaning for the sound. Pumblechook is merely inexpressive, but Angel approaches the

1. Such vagaries and instabilities are the substance of Hardy's writing. In a typed memorandum of instructions to Roman Atkins, who played the part of Alec in a 1924 dramatic adaptation of *Tess of the d'Urbervilles*, Hardy makes it clear that Alec's changing voices, instead of referring to a stable moral or psychological self, are meant to experiment with their own dramatic possibilities (Houghton Rare Book Library MS Thr. 301 *72M-93). To sustain the mystery of Alec's motives, Hardy prescribes a whole range of changing tones for Alec in his quarrel with Tess at the Sandbourne lodging house. He is to begin their conversation in a tone of irony and reserve, mounting only at the end of the exchange to outright recrimination and abuse. Hardy calls for more restraint and controlled animus in Alec's delivery and even underlines the adjective "repressed." To leave ambiguous the precise nature of their earlier affair, which could be either a rape or a seduction, Hardy also deletes Alec's original reference to their "intimacy," which implies that Tess was a willing partner. Other deletions seem dictated by Hardy's fear that he has given Alec too plausible an argument. In case Alec's casuistry should persuade some audiences, Hardy removes Alec's boast that Tess is "morally [his] little property" and that "by the law of Nature" he is "the father of [Tess's] child, whatever [she might] think of this contract."

inexpressible. His lament that Tess is dead voices the truth that language itself, like the bride he must bury, is only a ghost of departed quantities.

I do not mean to imply that the sudden convergence of widely separated identities or the psychological paradox of knowing more than one knows one knows is limited to Gothic fictions by Dickens and Hardy. In fact, even in social novelists like Jane Austen, a character such as Emma Woodhouse may suddenly start talking like a host of widely different characters, revealing that she knows far more than she knows she knows. Subliminally, Emma is in love with Mr. Knightley long before she admits it to herself. To dramatize a subliminal consciousness of truths that lie outside consciousness, Austen makes Emma deviate from her normal forthright way of speaking. Verbally bewitched by Mr. Elton when he praises her skill in delineating Harriet Smith's character ("Skilful has been the hand"—*Emma*, 1, chap. 6), she produces an equally mannered response, "Great has been the pleasure." Hyperbaton, the wrenching of word order, is usually a symptom of other forms of wrenching, including deviations from a moral norm. When Emma is verbally seduced by Frank Churchill at Box Hill, she uncharacteristically insults Miss Bates and earns the well-deserved censure of Mr. Knightley. Her apparent overreaction to that censure makes readers conscious of a truth that still lies outside Emma's consciousness: her love for Mr. Knightley. If Emma thought less highly of Knightley, she would be less stung and mortified by his rebuke.

The consciousness of repressed truths is clearest in the remarkable exchange between Emma and Mrs. Weston at the Coles' dinner party (2, chap. 8), where Emma's violation of her normal way of speaking is so protracted and intense that she sounds a little like Magwitch returning after years of absence and talking with the intimidating authority of a Miss Havisham, a Mr. Jaggers, and a Pumblechook, all blending incongruously together. Emma sounds as comically frightening to us as Magwitch does to Pip, because her voice collapses many imperious and irrational tones into one fearful synonym for loss of self-control.

Emma's first response to Mrs. Weston's suggestion of a possible match between Knightley and Jane Fairfax is uncomprehending, a mere incredulous repetition of what her friend has already said, as if Emma cannot be hearing accurately. Disbelief is followed by rebuke: "How could you think of such a thing?" and then by intimidating formality ("Dear Mrs. Weston"), as if Emma were addressing a public meeting instead of a close friend and former governess. The illogical use of verbs of decree—"must not marry," "I cannot at all consent to it"—recalls her father's selfish desire to keep Emma at home. There is an obsessive quality in the dialogue as Emma repeats her implausible idée fixe, the idea of little Henry's being supplanted as his uncle's heir. She talks like her father, a petrified vegetable, unable to entertain any new ideas, and speaks ungenerously of Jane in a tone more characteristic of a small-minded gossip like Mrs. Elton or an unctuous playactor like Frank.

Emma insists it would be "mad" for Mr. Knightley to marry into a family like Jane's, acquiring Miss Bates as a relative. But madness has been more a feature of her own disjointed rhetoric than of Mrs. Weston's. All predominance of imagination over reason is a degree of insanity, Dr. Johnson says. And the imagination that makes Emma sound half-mad is an imagination of Mr. Knightley's being married to someone other than herself. Emma talks as if she knows Mr. Knightley's mind as well as Mr. Knightley does. But she can claim to know this only if Knightley fills up his time and his heart with her. And the condition that must exist if what she claims is true is inconsistent with the claim she makes. The rhetoric is at once oddly luminous and stubbornly opaque. In fact it approaches that curiously transparent opacity that is the most humorously striking feature of the speech she now proceeds to parody. I am referring to the speech of the scatterbrained Miss Bates, whose half-finished clauses keep detaching themselves from the beheaded trunks of sentences. The non sequiturs of Miss Bates's language, as it jolts crookedly and irrelevantly from one half-finished sentence to another, are mercilessly parodied by Emma in the one passage of this exchange in which the mimic is conscious of her mimicry. Earlier, the parody of authoritarian characters like Mr. Woodhouse and the Eltons is totally unconscious. This contrast between conscious and unconscious parody alerts the reader to the irony of the mimic's being all too proudly aware of her parody of Miss Bates while unaware of the profounder irony of her unwittingly imitating most of the characters in the novel whom we least admire.

CHAPTER 3

"It Is Unutterable": The Burden of Signs in *Wuthering Heights* and *Villette*

In *Great Expectations* and *Tess of the d'Urbervilles* repressed or subliminal knowledge is in principle recoverable. But in *Wuthering Heights* and *Villette* Heathcliff and Lucy Snowe are aware of a plenitude of emptiness. What is outside their consciousness is an empty space or void, or a fullness that is now irrecoverable. Because Dickens and Hardy assume that language is a product of consciousness, they show how repeating words may make subliminal awareness intelligible. But Charlotte and Emily Brontë often make the opposite assumption. They assume that because consciousness itself is a product of language, a meaning that lies outside consciousness is also a meaning that lies outside language and the burden of its signs: in Heathcliff's phrase, "it is unutterable" (chap. 16).

Consciousness in *Wuthering Heights* is a product of the fall into language. In paradise there would be no language: only music or silence. The more disjunction there is between the sign and what it signifies, the more intense but falsifying is the self-consciousness that language generates. If Heathcliff's feeling for Cathy were indeed unutterable, could he utter anything about it, including his utterance that it is unutterable? If the sign were truly intrinsic, it would be the thing-in-itself, and there would be no need of language. That is what paradise or death would be like. And paradise and death are hard to distinguish in this novel. Total unconsciousness would dispense with signs, and it would be either to reenter Eden or to descend into hell. To be Mrs. Edgar Linton is to be consigned to limbo. But to be merged with Heathcliff, ostensibly a very different fate, appears to come in the end to the same thing. To generate an alternative fate as the faithful catalyst of heightened consciousness, Cathy must betray

Heathcliff, and life must interpose delay after delay between Cathy's death at the middle of the novel and Heathcliff's at the end. If everything is a sign, then nothing is a sign. There is an empty god term at the center of *Wuthering Heights*, or at least no god term we can compass in words, and hence no paradisal state of primal identity and unconsciousness we can aspire to or be conscious of.

Originally despised and dismissed as a mere demonic supplement to the civilized norms, Heathcliff soon reverses these priorities. Not only does he move into the center of the picture, but he also erodes the boundaries between picture space and frame. Once divisions between light and dark, heaven and hell, love and hate are allowed to appear, they generate a process of atomic fission, of dismemberment or desynonymizing, as futile and regressive as Jabes Branderham's division of his sermon into 490 parts (chap. 3). Heathcliff forgets, however, that without such partitioning there can be no definition (from *finis*, a limit or end). Only by making boundaries and assigning limits can the nameless be named. The alternative is Heathcliff's Nietzschean desire to stand beyond good and evil, annihilating every division of words in a black hole or void.

The scribes and reporters in *Wuthering Heights* are usually low-energy transformers like Nelly and Lockwood who tame the voltage that threatens to strike down the real centers of energy. The great exception to that statement is the sequence of events culminating in Cathy's death, where Cathy and Heathcliff are finally allowed to speak for themselves. To help them say what is otherwise not strictly sayable, Brontë carefully contrasts Heathcliff's division from Cathy with Edgar's division from Isabella. Linton, who refuses to answer his sister's letter in chapter 14, will do nothing to mend the division caused by her marriage. Though Heathcliff finds the division Cathy has placed between them just as intolerable, he is passionate in its denunciation, whereas Edgar is icily aloof. Even Edgar's anger is geared down into a decorous, civilized "sorry." Like his deficient fraternal affection for Isabella, his love for Cathy seems sisterly and weak.

When Heathcliff and Nelly talk, they do not really use words in the same sense: they talk past each other (chap. 14). "Cathy's life is spared," she reports, then warns Heathcliff that he must "shun crossing her way again." In fact, Heathcliff will help falsify the first statement by ignoring the second. To cross Cathy's way is not just to appear on her path but also to vex her, to cross her will. In playing verbal tennis with Nelly, Heathcliff picks up her phrase "humanity and duty," then in two italicized passages throws the words back at her with a curve, repeating them in reverse order. As if to cross Nelly's will, Heathcliff uses the cross trope, chiasmus, to mock the dull shape of Edgar's weak "humanity," "duty," "duty," "humanity." What is left out of the chiastic vise is passion, the quantity Heathcliff resolves to establish as the primary term. Common humanity and duty must be made weakly specialized uses of passion rather than the other way round.

An incorrigible parasite, Heathcliff feeds remorselessly on what is prior, only to reverse the priorities and break down the divisions that the idea of priority assumes. To define what Catherine means to him, Heathcliff must first define what Isabella can never mean. His wife is a mere unruly child, whom he sends upstairs for punishment. Her simpering pretense of loving Heathcliff is a more degrading form of her brother's love for Catherine. True love is excluded from such shameless performances: it is their missing supplement, which Heathcliff and Cathy can alone supply. Heathcliff is a little like Browning's duke of Ferrara, with Nelly as Linton's envoy, sent over from the Grange. Before this captive auditor he must assimilate the word "pity" and its conventional opposite, "cruelty," into some larger unit of meaning where normal divisions cease to apply. Though what has to be uttered is never fully utterable, it can at least be gestured at through nonnaming tropes like oxymoron and catachresis, the tropes traditionally used to cancel divisions in an effort to restore inclusive categories. "'I have no pity! I have no pity! The worms writhe, the more I yearn to crush out their entrails! It is a moral teething, and I grind with greater energy, in proportion to the increase of pain'" (chap. 14). Does Heathcliff mean that the more his victims writhe like worms, the more he yearns to crush them? Or does he mean that the more he yearns to destroy, the more the worms inside himself writhe? The odd transfer across the comma of the comparative adverb "more," which might more logically modify "writhe" than "yearn," erodes the boundary between Heathcliff's internal and external enemies. And few phrases could be more oxymoronic than "moral teething." Morality generally entails control and mastery. "Teething," by contrast, is a painful process we suffer passively. The control implicit in "moral" is half canceled by the passivity implicit in "teething." Moreover, to "grind" is generally to impede efficiency. But here the grinding increases energy, in apparent defiance of Newton's laws. Heathcliff's paradoxes invite us to construct a totally novel universe—one where laws of motion cease to apply, even metaphorically.

In chapter 15, the deathbed scene itself, Heathcliff takes all his cues from Cathy, as in the previous scene he had picked up Nelly's words and thrown them back at her. As Cathy's rhetoric breaks apart, the silent spaces between the dashes circumscribe the true center of meaning, which cannot be translated into words. "'You have killed me—and thriven on it, I think...Will you forget me—will you be happy when I am in the earth?' " (chap. 15). Though the concessive "I think" mutes the force of the words that follow the dash, the first break mimes the wrenching of her soul, as one unspeakable aftermath of Cathy's death is forced into words. Will Heathcliff live to say, "I've loved many others since—my children are dearer to me than she was"? The silence of this third dash is a pause in which to gather up strength, as if to say the unsayable. As the anaphora "Will you," hurled at Heathcliff four times, is used as a club to beat him into submission, each dash is like a knife wound, enacting the sharp breaks and thrusts of her words. Now Cathy assumes the part played by Nelly in the preceding scene. Taunting Heathcliff with forgetting her, Cathy describes exactly what Heathcliff can never do. In setting the terms of Heathcliff's own response, she does the opposite of what she thinks: she writes the script that Heathcliff will act out to his dying day.

As Heathcliff overwhelms Cathy with a barrage of short questions, made more emphatic by anaphora, it is clear that Cathy not only has taught him how to be cruel and false, she has also taught him the use of words, the use of morally charged words like "murder" to describe her betrayal. Heathcliff is morally superior to Cathy, since he can love his own murderer but not *her* murderer. He loves the one Cathy, the victim, so much that he must hate the other Cathy, the murderess. His culminating paradox is that he hates her *because* he loves her. He would be less cruel were he not so loving. Only oxymorons that cancel each other out can begin to express the paradox that great love and great hate are inseparable. Heathcliff's play on words is really shredding them to bits in an agony of despair. Even in breaking down distinctions that normally apply between pity and cruelty, love and hate, Heathcliff uses oxymoron to express terrible distress of mind.

In Heathcliff's and Nelly's vocabularies the words "good" and "evil" have different meanings. Their incommensurability becomes explicit in Heathcliff's cruel play upon Nelly's use of the verb "lies." Her benedictory phrase, "she lies with a sweet smile on her face" (chap. 16), modulates by way of an elided pun into the bitter exclamation, "Why, she's a liar to the end!" The alarming multiplication of dashes in Heathcliff's speech fittingly culminates in his discovery that what he has to say is "unutterable." The knives and spears with which Nelly says Heathcliff is goading himself to death are also knives and spears of elision. His lament that he *"cannot* live without [his] life" comes perilously close to tautology, the most reserved and withholding of tropes. As his words begin to reach into silence, the worst torment he can conceive is the torment of existing in an abyss emptied of meaning. The unconscious is literally the "unutterable," the plentitude or void that exists on the far side of silence. To the degree that Cathy agitates and torments Heathcliff, she keeps eroding and destabilizing all the falsifying divisions that Heathcliff's language is tempted to place between them. But without divisions there can be no consciousness or speech.

The experience of reading *Wuthering Heights* is often the experience of discovering that what we had taken for an accepted norm or center is a mere margin. The frame or supplement to one picture turns out to be the center of the next one. What is excluded, for example, from the first picture of Heathcliff's throwing himself on Cathy's grave, like a crazed Hamlet, becomes the subject at the center of a second picture. In chapter 17 everything is seen from the peripheral perspectives of Isabella and Nelly. Isabella's narrative of Heathcliff's demented praying like a Methodist, full of directionless enthusiasm, incites more grim humor than tragic pity. Heathcliff's madness is that of a ruffian, physically violent, dashing his head repeatedly against the flagstones. This last detail recalls its omitted supplement: the desire to dash Hareton's infant skull against the steps when Heathcliff saves him from possible death in chapter 9. What Heathcliff has experienced at Cathy's grave is not yet told. Even in chapter 29, which provides the supplement to the potential crudities of chapter 17, the marginal experience is given first. The opening of Cathy's coffin and the discovery that her face is still recognizable are mildly horrific. Having experienced the shock, we are prepared for something more subtle and compelling, first in Heathcliff's dream of sleeping the last sleep beside Cathy, and then in a disclosure of Heathcliff's being strangely elated at the time of Cathy's burial.

His extraordinary experience at her grave is one of the novel's most striking reversals of insides and outsides, of picture spaces and margins. Instead of being inside the coffin, Cathy is outside, looking down at Heathcliff from the edge of the grave. If Heathcliff is physically outside the coffin, he is spiritually inside it. And if Cathy is physically entombed, she is also spiritually outside, wandering the earth as a disembodied ghost. There could be few more arresting metaphors for the failure of bodies to incarnate spirits or for the failure of words to incarnate their meanings. Heathcliff is willing in this scene to entertain any wild surmise to validate the fantasy of holding Cathy alive again in his arms. If she is cold, he will blame the north wind; if she is motionless, he will indulge the pathetic fallacy that she sleeps. But the truth turns out to be stranger than any of these desperate fictions. Instead of being under him and inside the coffin, she is standing on the earth outside the coffin, breathing in his ear. As Heathcliff turns "consoled at once, unspeakably consoled" (chap. 29), the weighted adverb, coming between the repeated past participle, reminds us, like his earlier use of the adjective "unutterable," that what is most worth saying cannot be said. To be told that laughter is a possible reaction at precisely the moment it becomes an inappropriate and impossible response is to be alerted to the distance we have unknowingly traveled. Though Heathcliff is talking to a spirit, no reader now considers him mad. His most irrational and absurd convictions belong to an order of things that matter more than ordinary reality and that therefore ought to exist.

Wuthering Heights threatens to become a tragedy without a catharsis, a tragedy in which Heathcliff's vision of something noble, speaking to him across his death in the grave scene, is smothered under stifling revenge codes. But toward the end of the novel Heathcliff speaks enigmatically of the approach of some "strange change" (chap. 33), which he himself only partly understands. Heathcliff's unmotivated elation, which translates itself inadequately as "a strange joyful glitter" (chap. 34), is a mark of the "unutterable." The rhetoric is a glorious failure, illustrative of Brontë's inability to incarnate a truth that is signless. One way to intimate such a truth is to use animal similes that are at once strange and familiar, like Heathcliff's inhuman, feline breathing, "fast as a cat['s]" (chap. 34), which recalls the earlier warm breathing Heathcliff felt when standing in Cathy's grave (chap. 29). Temporal dislocations place these two accounts of breathing closer together in Brontë's narration than they occurred in the actual chronology. The flashback in chapter 29 to an event first described in chapter 17 is a way of narrowing the space between Cathy and Heathcliff just before it disappears altogether.

This sense of contracting space is confirmed by Heathcliff's declaration that he is "within sight" of his "heaven." "I have my eyes on it—hardly three feet to sever me!" (chap. 34). Heathcliff may be referring either to the few feet of earth thrown over Cathy's coffin in chapter 29 or to the few feet of space separating him from Cathy's apparition, which a few moments later in chapter 34 he claims to see only two yards away. At first we think of the earth, but after Heathcliff gazes at the apparition, visible to no one but himself, we may surmise that he has actually communicated with the dead. It adds greatly to the sense of mystery that we cannot tell with certainty what Heathcliff means. The whole concluding sequence resonates mysteriously with subliminal recollections of earlier scenes. In particular, the sound of the murmuring valley stream, audible only at certain times of the year, recalls the sound that was heard at the time of Cathy's death. The space and time intervals between the events described in chapters 15 and 34 are already in a state of rapid collapse as Heathcliff prepares to cross the last divide himself.

To speak at all is to use the language of partition and division. But once the process begins, can it ever be stopped? Lockwood's odd use of the word "divide" alerts us to the dangers in the opening paragraph. "A perfect misanthropist's heaven," he observes, "and Mr. Heathcliff and I are such a suitable pair to divide the desolation between us" (chap. 1). How can one divide something so empty of content as desolation? To divide in this case is to multiply, to divide up the emptiness so it can proliferate without end. Moreover, no two people could be more divided: any division of solitude, far from drawing them together, is only going to increase the distance that separates them. Even Lockwood protests against the brainless divisions of Jabes Branderham's sermon on the forgiveness of trespasses, which are themselves a trespass on the listener's patience. In Matthew 12:25, as one commentator has observed, the unforgivable sin entails another instance of division: the division of a house against itself (Parker, 1983, 54). Because Branderham's replication of the Gospel's injunction to forgive until seventy times seven in a discourse divided into 490 parts is itself a dreamlike replication of the book-length sermon on the Gospel text that catches Lockwood's eye before he falls asleep, its partitioned discourse is also a further partitioning of experience into waking events and dream. When Lockwood in his nightmare rises to protest against the method, the irate preacher brands him as the ultimate transgressor, "The First of the Seventy-First," who would arrest the process of dividing up language by trying to collapse all words back into a primal word or synonym.

Such a synonym is Cathy's bold equation, "I *am* Heathcliff" (chap. 9), which, if valid, reverses the mindless partitioning of the sermon. Desynonymizing also yields to the recovery of one primal name as the three Cathys inscribed in the diary Lockwood has been reading—Catherine Earnshaw, Catherine Linton, and Catherine Heathcliff—are collapsed into a single identity. What is the common root, the matrix, from which Catherine and Heathcliff have sprung? They seem to belong to that small, queer margin at the very apex of the pyramid that cannot be housed inside the walls of language. Their names compose some primal word that has fallen into syntax. And only through dream vision and analogy can Cathy begin to clarify the mysteries that lie beyond the frontier of language. To be homesick in heaven, she tells Nelly, is to be estranged from her earthly home with Heathcliff (chap. 9). Linton is to Heathcliff what the moonbeam is to lightning and frost is to fire. But in heaven we expect to find the very elements that Cathy ascribes to earth and Heathcliff. What she calls heaven is really hell or the fallen world, and what she calls earth is heaven, whatever the angry angels may say. She has to use Nelly's biblical vocabulary to express reversals that profoundly alter Nelly's values. Her verbal confusion comes from the need to express revolutionary moral insights in a language inherited from the very culture and code that the insights are designed to subvert.

Ironically, the speech that most movingly attests to Cathy's at-onement with Heathcliff leads Heathcliff to think she means to divide herself from him. He stays to the point where he hears her say that to marry Heathcliff would degrade her. But it is not really Cathy who betrays Heathcliff. It is her language that betrays him—the burden of the endlessly dividing signs she must use to gesture beyond them in a retreat from the word toward ever deepening silence. Public divisions of any kind, including Cathy's removal from Heathcliff, which is really a division of herself from herself, are acts of desynonymizing, of making different, what should remain one indivisible identity. There are three Cathys who collapse into two people; and Catherine and Heathcliff are said to have a single nature. But who *is* Heathcliff? As we approach the one primal word, language falls back into untranslatable tautology. Because Heathcliff's origin like his end is a mystery, there is no fitting gravestone inscription for him. Part of his inscrutability is his lack of any surname. In its fragmentary state, his proper name is suitably improper. And yet no proper name can escape the pathos of the capital letter, which must divest even a word like "Heathcliff" of its indeterminate properties. By the time the novel's most important equation, "I *am* Heathcliff," has managed to restore a measure of intrinsic symbolism, language is already in a state of rapid retreat from the world. We are moving from definition to tautology, from rhetoric to equation. Indeed, in obliterating all sustaining difference, "I *am* Heathcliff" is no definition at all, but a return to silence and mystery.

Analysis is a kind of murder, because it breaks apart the primal language of equivalence. To divide such a language is to suffer the fate of Milo, who was devoured by beasts for splitting a tree (chap. 9). Jabes Branderham is a kind of theological Milo (chap.3), and so is every author who carries the process of desynonymizing language to its logical conclusion. As a marital Milo, dividing his wife from her true husband, Linton, according to Cathy, can no more break her at-onement with Heathcliff than winter can change the trees or erode "the eternal rocks" beneath the earth (chap. 9). If no marriage to another can annihilate their at-onement, then no atonement in the biblical sense is necessary. Unfortunately, Heathcliff labors under the burden of a more extrinsic symbolism. Imprisoned by language and trapped by its antinomies, he can never allow Cathy to use the word "marriage" in both of these contrasting senses. He feels that Cathy's betrayal of their at-onement requires something like atonement in the biblical sense, even though he rejects biblical values elsewhere. Who is being inconsistent, Heathcliff or Cathy? Each is inconsistent, because each uses ideas like at-onement and marriage both in the limited extrinsic sense of their adversaries and in the more primary intrinsic sense that represents their own truest understanding of such concepts.

To be intelligible and "utterable" at all is to be partitioned. But to be endlessly partitioned by self-replicating signs, in the kind of infinite regress that Kant associates with the mathematical sublime, is to slide further and further down the slope of words. To be sublime is to remain at the apex of the pyramid. But it is also to be nameless or "unutterable." To understand *Wuthering Heights* one has to play Wagner. Music, according to Susanne Langer, is an unconsummated form of symbolism, because its sounds lack specific denotations. The unity that Brontë celebrates between Catherine and Heathcliff is necessarily unconsummated in words, "unconsummated" in Langer's sense of the word, just as their spiritual at-onement is never consummated physically.

Heathcliff and Catherine can say what they have to say only in a dreamlike language of dark synonyms and tautologies. Similarly, Lucy Snowe in *Villette* can express her darkest fears and imaginings only by surrendering to the whirl of events and images, the phantasmagoria, in which she is always on the point of being engulfed. At the Villette carnival, for example, every sensory detail is weirdly and intimately connected with every other fragment. And during her mental break-down, Lucy creates out of separate hieroglyphs—out of the black cup she is forced to drink from, and out of the cup of the priest's ear into which she pours her words of pain a moment later (chap. 15)—a pellucid ideogram like the montage of cinema. She combines sensory impressions and half-formed thoughts to fashion out of two depictable objects the representation of a third thing that is not graphically depictable. Like the optical effects of the carnival, which possess an oddly muted radiance, Lucy's language often yields only a further receding image of itself: it composes a queer, entrancing tautology, like the house of mirrors on a midway. But when Lucy tries to break out of the spirals of her language and its gallery of self-reflecting mirrors, she finds that what she gains in clarity she loses in precision. For in the more discursive sections of her narrative, language is more often a wall than a window. Nothing turns out to be quite what it seems. It is as if Lucy must even keep experimenting with the genre of her story and cannot decide what kind of narrative she is writing until she leaves England for the Continent in chapter 6.

At the beginning Lucy Snowe is the favored child in the household of her godmother, Mrs. Bretton. But in the ninth paragraph of the novel Lucy is pushed aside by the arrival of the more favored Polly, who will displace Lucy in Graham's affections. In the first three chapters Polly seems to be the main character, then she moves out of the novel. Lucy's employment with Miss Marchmont terminates almost as soon as it begins. Until Lucy leaves for Villette, it seems as if the novel is all margin with no center. With Lucy's arrival at Mme Beck's academy, even the genre seems to switch. Conventions of the social novel are pushed to the margin, along with the English setting, and continental Gothic elements take over. But nothing is ever quite displaced, even when we think it is. The odd return at the carnival of people dead or departed on sea voyages is merely the culminating example of dreamlike reappearances that occur throughout the novel.

Lucy even constructs two very dissimilar pictures of Graham Bretton. First one seems marginal, then the other. Though the excluded attributes of the first picture, Graham's self-importance and egoism, become the principal attributes of the second, Lucy insists that "both portraits are correct" (chap. 19). But if both are correct, can either be correct? What is marginal or repressed in Lucy's affection for Mr. Paul moves gradually to center stage. Yet at times even love and life are treated as mere supplements or picture frames, to be replaced by something more sinister, like black pieces on a chessboard, at the time of Lucy's mental breakdown during the long vacation or in her final imagination of disaster and loss.

Imagination is always seducing Lucy into consciousness of what she wants to repress. First she had repressed the sensuous side of her nature, and so she has to discover and acknowledge her passionate side. But later Lucy wants to repress the pain and suffering, the still sad music of humanity, and so imagination must prepare her for a deep distress. This is the function of the carnival scene, where imagination begins to assimilate some of the darkest fears that Lucy's earlier apostrophes to imagination have tried to contain within the daylight world of reason.

In Lucy's first apostrophe, reason tries to repress false hope. Is it rational for Lucy to write letters to Graham Bretton? Her prudential reserve censors the idea. To write is to endow her feeling for Graham with the wrong kind of permanence. So the victory in chapter 21 is all on the side of a personified reason, which holds feeling in check. And yet Lucy's use of personification is a way of defeating reason in the very act of seeming to submit. For once reason is personified, its adversary must have its say. It is only a matter of time before the marginal or repressed element works its way to the center, if only for a "truant hour." In this first effusive passage of personified antagonism, inversion of grammatical subject and object makes the rhetoric mannered and factitious: "My hunger has this good angel appeased with food" (chap. 21). Such wrenching of word order, which would be mannered even in an epic poem, makes Lucy's words too portentous for their subject, which is, after all, only her modest hope that her friend Graham will continue writing to her.

The second time reason and imagination are presented in personified conflict (chap. 23), imagination has diminished into mere intensity of feeling, and the division between them is now so extreme that Lucy is forced to speak two different languages and so compose two letters. Expressed with great precision in the long sentence beginning "When we had done—when two sheets were covered," the language of feeling refuses to terminate. Dashes, interpolations in parentheses, reiterated subordinate conjunctions, copious appositions and amplification, all defer closure. When reason finally intrudes, its indecorous assaults are dramatized as rude and uncivil. "—then, just at that moment, the doors of my heart would shake, bolt bar would yield, Reason would leap in vigorous and revengeful, snatch the full sheets, read, sneer, erase, tear up, re-write, fold, seal, direct, and send a terse, curt missive of a page" (chap. 23). The incivility is as much a result of the sharp, incisive breaks in the grammar as of reason's dismissive deeds. The apodosis consists of three separate clauses, unconnected by conjunctions. Reason's culminating deeds are presented in the last and most extended of these three clauses, where the succession of eight short verbs, jammed together by asyndeton, makes the breaks sharpest, most disruptive, like so many knives thrust into the heart of the sentence.

What Lucy experiences under heightened imaginative stimulus during the Villette carnival breaks down the barriers between vindictive reason and a sweet, appeasing imagination of hope. In her imagination of betrayal and disaster during the carnival, as in her later premonitions of Paul's death at sea, Lucy finds that the dark world she has tried to banish from imagination will no longer retreat submissively to the margins. The vindictiveness she would confine to the domain of reason returns to the center of her own picture, proving that her earlier partitions are false and that to foster such divisions is to live "in a dream," as Wordsworth says, "at distance from the Kind" ("Elegiac Stanzas," l. 54).

The unveiling of mysteries in *Villette* assumes two distinct forms. Most simply, it may bring to consciousness repressed feelings such as Lucy's affection for Dr. John. Alternatively, unveiling may expose unconscious truths that cannot be translated out of the dreamlike medium in which they appear. The unconscious is then no longer a repressed meaning that lies outside consciousness, because such a meaning would lie outside language as well, and in Heathcliff's phrase it would be "unutterable." Instead, the unconscious now becomes an involuntary manner of presenting something that cannot be expressed in any other medium. During the Villette carnival, for example, Lucy becomes the oracle in whom visions happen to take place. She can exercise no voluntary control over what she sees. One hopes that forces that are mysteriously beyond the capacity of reason to dominate or subdue will bring fulfillment and peace. But what if they bring darkness and unrest? An uncontrolled imagination may possess all the disadvantages of an envenomed reason without any of reason's advantage of being tractable and subject to human design.

An extreme form of the innocuous mode of unveiling is Lucy's discovery that the enchantment of the Villette carnival is engineered out of pasteboard and wood. Like any form of anti-Gothic, this disclosure eliminates mystery by offering a rational explanation. The "new Gothic" presents unveiling in the second mode: it exposes psychological truths that may defy paraphrase and that can be expressed in no other way, since their meaning is neither literal nor figurative. But the "new Gothic" in *Villette* raises a disturbing third possibility. If an involuntary presentation is a form of unconsummated symbolism, marked by oxymoron and catachresis, then perhaps there is no meaning to unveil beyond the involuntary presentation itself. Any meaning outside language and consciousness would be unutterable, and so hard to distinguish from the void. Language itself may be only one of the mind's "amazing feats of distortion to avoid facing" what Paul de Man calls "the nothingness of human matters" (1983, 18). Even the discovery that the nun's ghost is a mere prank or practical joke hints that involuntary presentations elsewhere in the novel are a result not just of the absence of something, but of the presence of a mere emptiness or blank.

In the carnival scene imagination has to be obeyed not as something simply gratifying, but as something both feared and desired like sexual passion. The couched sphinx at the close of "the deep, torch-lit perspective of an avenue" (chap. 38) presides over an infinite regress of mysteries. Everything definite seems to be dissolved and swallowed up "like a group of apparitions." Meaning has not yet been freed from the burden of these ponderous, though strangely evanescent, signs. The ibis and sphinx would be grotesque were they not so surreal and phantomlike. A sense of dream and spectral unreality is also a feature of Brontë's grammar. "Paulina and her friends being gone," Lucy observes, "I scarce could avouch that I had really seen them" (chap. 38). Her detachment is heightened by the absolute grammar, which severs the grammatical subject of the sentence, Lucy, from the subjects of the nominative absolute construction. Can the happiness and hope that Lucy has up to now identified with her imaginative life continue to exclude the quiet desperation and despair that reason has enjoined? "As to Happiness or Hope, they and I had shaken hands, but just now—I scorned Despair" (chap. 38). The syntax looks two ways at once. Does Lucy mean that happiness and she have made each other's acquaintance "just now," for the first time? Or does "just now" modify "scorned"? The conjunction "but" may signal a fluctuation of emotion, as she veers toward the very despair she professes to scorn. Lucy's emotional states seem as unstable as her syntax and as the carnival figures who materialize and then vanish like phantoms.

The refraction of vision and the reflection of one sense impression off another make the experience surreal. First, Lucy sees the moon's image reflected in the stone water basin's "circular mirror of crystal." Even the bridal light of Paulina, as she is whisked by in her carriage, is a reflected light that repeats "in her eyes" a brilliance that "beamed first" in Graham. The streets themselves become a maze, an architectural version of deflection, preventing Lucy's direct pursuit of the basin. When she finally glimpses the basin, which she describes as a tremulous and rippled glass, it is framed by thickly planted trees. But these framing trees move in to occupy the picture space before the basin can be reached. As the song that begins to choir out of one of these framing glades shatters the picture, Lucy's attention is caught by rippled waves of tremulous sound, which displace the liquid ripples on the circular mirror of crystal. Just when we assume the basin at the center of the picture has been pushed completely to the margins, its liquid shimmerings return, though in a transformed state. For the tremulous water in the basin transfers its motion to the sound, which now reaches a crescendo in the storm of harmonies that break forth and make Lucy stagger against a tree. Ripples on the mirror of water turn into a swaying tide—a veritable sea of sound: "The effect was as a sea breaking into song with all its waves" (chap. 38). The blasts of music recall the nerve-dissolving melodies of Tennyson's surreal masterpiece, "The Vision of Sin." The two passages draw upon similar effects of synesthesia and sudden transformations of liquid light into actual water, whose liquidity then assumes the form of liquid sound. Brontë, like Tennyson, is a master of the wavering moment and the hovering emotion, poised somewhere between elation and dread. Every elation seems fluctuating on a knife edge, about to dissolve into disenchantment and despair.

Most threatening is the "strange," "dead-disturbing," "Witch-of-Endor" query posed by the haglike Madame Walravens. "'Messieurs et mesdames,' said she, 'où donc est Justine Marie?'" (chap. 39). The return from the grave of the woman Paul had loved threatens to put

Lucy's own heart in the grave. But what ghost can come out of its grave to put Lucy there instead? To cross the grave is to perform a ghastly act of chiasmus fit only for ghost stories. Even in censoring this crossing, "*You* shall go to *her*, but *she* shall not come to *you*" (chap. 39; italics added), Lucy unwittingly affirms the possibility of returning from a grave by using a chiasmus herself. The matter-of-fact response that the dead nun is on her way throws Lucy into a panic. In the confused limpidity of the overheard gossip, Lucy can find no clue to the labyrinth.

Everything is now self-replicating, a mirror image of some earlier reflection. The drama of feared exclusion from the favors of loved ones repeats a pattern that Brontë has been establishing since the opening chapters. Near the beginning Polly is torn away from the Brettons to rejoin her father, trembling life a leaf but exercising self-control (chap. 3). Later Dr. John is rejected by Ginevra Fanshawe, and Lucy is painfully excluded from the love of Dr. John. The bitter psychology of exclusion and rejection is a kind of dark Penelope's web that keeps unraveling the brighter hopes of the characters' daytime lives. At the nocturnal fête the mirrorings are most complex, and the repetitions of earlier rejection and loss are at their most unbearable and intense. Most harrowing of all, the repetitions seem to be ungrounded, like images in a nightmare. Baseless repetitions address a deep, at times unspeakable, fear that everything we repeat and say merely draws a veil across some black hole or void.

The moment of truth is preceded by a fragmentation of grammar that mimes the breakdown of Lucy's composure. "With solemn force pressed on my heart, the expectation of mystery breaking up: hitherto I had seen this spectre only through a glass darkly; now was I to behold it face to face. I leaned forward; I looked" (chap. 39). So disconnected from every prior expectation is the apparition of a ghost returned from the grave that Lucy can render its shock effect only by introducing an absolute construction that severs itself syntactically from the rest of the paragraph: "the expectation of mystery breaking up." If there is an ellipsis after "heart," and if "expectation" is meant to function as an object of the omitted preposition, why does Brontë use a colon to divide the adverbial phrase from the principal verb? The grammatical dislocations duplicate Lucy's own sense of rupture. And the odd use of a colon after two phrases, before the introduction of any principal clauses, further disorients us. Lucy tries to regain composure by offering rapid notations and simple jottings. The sentences are hurried and paratactic, as if any ordinary observation, once committed to paper or memory, will provide some stay against confusion. Anaphora also becomes a steadying device: "She is very comely... She looks well-nourished... She is not alone... She laughs, she chats" (chap. 39). Lucy's verbal play on "homely" also helps stabilize what is otherwise unstable in the quick flow of images and impressions. The web of truth that is spun in stark contradiction to the fantasies of risen ghosts is said to be "homely." And yet the girl called Justine Marie scarcely qualifies as "homely" in the sense of plain. The altered meanings of "homely" allow Lucy to reinstate the intellect, turning over different implications of the adjective.

The current of emotion is an alternating one, as relief turns to new despair, then back to desperate hope. "I liked seeing the goddess in her temple," Lucy confesses, "and handling the veil, and daring the dread glance" (chap. 39). This image of the veil of Isis modulates into the image of the veiled nun. If the unveiling of the second Justine Marie holds no terrors for Lucy, then perhaps no unveiling will. The Titaness invoked is a sublime divinity, but the true sublimity is of the viewer's making. The goddess is an image of the self-reliance Lucy has been seeking. The unconscious loses its terror when Lucy confronts in it an image of herself. To know the worst about the feared object is to take from fear its main advantage. Like the earth uplifted in a quake, the shaken heart has swallowed strength, and is now able to confront whatever meaning—or absence of meaning—the unveiling may disclose.

Racing ahead and jumping to false surmises, Lucy writes a script in which Mr. Paul will return from the Indies with a rich inheritance to claim Justine Marie as his young bride. She soon discovers that imaginations of loss and disaster are misconceived concerning Paul's preferring Justine. But no sooner has disaster been banished to the margins than it returns to overwhelm Lucy in the final paragraphs of the novel. The frame around one picture becomes the picture space at the center of the next frame. This switching is so pervasive and repeated a pattern that we may even come to doubt which is picture space and which is frame.

Lucy's cryptic words about presentiment have multiple relevance. "There is a kind of presentiment which never *is* mistaken; it was I who had for a moment miscalculated; not seeing the true bearing of the oracle, I had thought she muttered of vision when, in truth, her prediction touched reality" (chap. 39). In context, these words mean that Lucy may have been mistaken in her fear of being visited by a ghost risen from the grave. But though that precise fear may have been groundless, fear in general proves all too justified. By the end of the fête reason and imagination have reversed roles. The painstaking use of logical inference would have deferred Lucy's painful, somewhat rash conclusion that Paul and his youthful ward are in love. But in a resolve to know the worst, Lucy's darkest imaginings leap to an acknowledgment of what she prematurely calls a "reality," a given. Truth is now imaginatively intuited, not logically inferred. And what she calls true is both true and not true. She is wrong in her immediate inference about Paul and Justine, but her larger presentiment of loss and disaster is now reason itself "in her most exalted mood." Far from being a graceful frame around a picture sketched by a stoic and withholding reason, imagination is now the artist who paints the picture. And the picture is darker than anything reason had formerly conceived.

As in *Wuthering Heights*, the language of imagination tries to collapse all words back into an undifferentiated language of equivalences. Distinctions that reason would establish among the dead nun beloved of Mr. Paul, the ghost of the nun who materializes in the Rue de la Fossette, and the nun's namesake who appears like a ghost from the grave at the fête, are overridden by imagination, which prefers to annihilate the differences in one fearful synonym. The name Justine Marie is like the montage or ideogram of cinema. The single equivalence of three merged identities, which come to stand for a common burial of love, makes an impression on Lucy that a more logically discriminating use of language could never hope to equal.

Though the propped-up effigy of the nun's ghost, which Lucy finds in her bed after returning from the carnival, reveals that earlier apparitions of the ghost were merely a hoax,[1] this discovery condenses

---

1. A study of Charlotte Brontë's miniature magazines and journals shows how early and deep-seated is her impulse to subvert comically as well as to harness the Gothic formulas. In a dreamlike fragment titled "The Adventures of Monsieur Edouard Clack" (Houghton Library MS. Lowell 3), an oracular voice addresses the young hero, declaiming in verse in the manner of the gap-toothed man in Tennyson's poem "A Vision of Sin." It is hard to translate Brontë's meaning out of these solemn dreamlike fragments, in which characters materialize, then just as suddenly vanish. Paris seems as alien to Edouard when he first arrives there as Villette seems to Lucy. "A lean haggard race of mortals," he concludes, "with sunk eyes, hollow cheeks and sallow tawny complexions." Equally oracular are Brontë's early quatrains to liberty, a Shelleyan effusion reminiscent of Tennyson's rhapsodic ode "The Poet."

But a comic and satiric impulse begins to subvert these conventions in her Gothic parody "In the Poetaster: A Drama in Two Volumes." The drama opens oracularly enough, but soon the poet is racking her brains for rhymes. We are already in the anti-Gothic world of *Villette*, where Madame Beck sneezes out of season and the supernatural drama of the nun's ghost turns out to be a hoax. Brontë alternates between the forced elevation of the majestically dark heavens, "bedecked with many a star," and her parenthetical admission that she cannot proceed until she finds a rhyme for "dark." When she strains the limits of sense to reproduce the sound, we realize that self-mockery has displaced visionary experience as the real subject of this satire. In all the poetic and prose fragments of the miniature magazines, anti-Gothic impulses are always on the brink of subverting some solemn or oracular effect. And yet, as in *Villette*, the meaning of the dream sequences cannot be translated out of the phantasmagory of character and incident in which some passive observer witnesses them. They seem to be expressible in no other medium.

a whole spectrum of scenes in which marriage beds turn out to be occupied by the ghosts of dead or departed lovers. Such terror is at its most intense when Lucy is confronted by a ghost when burying Dr. John's letters in a tree (chap. 26) and when, after nights of insomnia, she is shaken by a dream in which she is forced to swallow a black potion (chap. 15). To escape her oppressive visions, Lucy takes refuge in a church, where she makes an odd confession to the priest, Père Silas. Now the image of drinking a potion is reversed. Instead of being drawn from a bottomless sea, the drink is poured into a vessel, the understanding ear of the priest, "whence it could not be again diffused" (chap. 15). The priest admits that confession is apt to become "formal and trivial with habit." But Lucy reinvents the rite: and like her improvised burial of the letters in a mock funeral service, and like Tess's improvised rite of baptism in Hardy's novel, her performance is felicitous.

In his concluding soliloquy in chapter 36, Mr. Paul ratifies Lucy's Protestant impatience with the burden of signs, just as Père Silas had earlier approved her irregular confession. In a sense, even Lucy's dead ghosts are the ghosts of departed mediations, demanded by her Protestant sensibility. The space filled for a Catholic imagination by mercies and mediations is collapsed for Lucy into direct confrontation, as when, after symbolically burying her love for Dr. John, she has to face a ghost alone. Even Mr. Paul, a kind of Jansenist or French Sir William Hamilton, concedes that God is a signless hub, made more austere by a Miltonic framing of his "center" by four adjectives: a "mighty unseen center incomprehensible, irrealisable" (chap. 36). Beyond time and space, measure and comparison, such a God is a signless mystery, outside consciousness and language altogether. But as the unseen center whose properties are the epithets of negative theology, without any positive content, how is such a sublimely remote God to be distinguished from that dark and bottomless vision that induces Lucy's worst fears during her mental breakdown?

The last chapter in *Villette* dramatizes the void Lucy's language is always trying to veil. In the final paragraphs, where the tidy summaries barely conceal the repressed anguish of her questioning of God's ways, the meaning becomes totally implicit—totally a burden of the subtext. Lucy's imagination of disaster is something readers have already experienced in Miss Marchmont's panic-stricken efforts to bring chaos into clarity in chapter 4. Words are spoken in a double sense, as in an oracle. Frank, the "furious rider," is destroyed by a fate more furious than himself. Even the third-person pronoun is replaced by its most dreadful and impersonal variant, that "strangely dark" and unnameable "thing," that migrates as a fearful unknown through Miss Marchmont's speech. One falsified hope succeeds another. First she confuses the man holding the horse with Frank; then she thinks Frank may be dead. In fact, he is half conscious, and lives to hold her in a dying embrace. In the final chapter everything is resolved once more into mystery, as Lucy contrives to keep the fate of Mr. Paul as ambiguous as possible. On the one hand, the eagerness with which Lucy awaits Paul's return recalls the heightened emotion of Miss Marchmont as she awaits Frank's return. Even the same phrase, separated from the body of a sentence, is used: "the wind takes its autumn moan; but—he is coming" (chap. 42). On the other hand, the sun rises as a bridegroom, "glorious, royal, and purple," as a "monarch in his state." The flaming morning sky seems to presage an epithalamium for Lucy, as her long-delayed lover returns to claim her. Two-way imagery precipitates an intolerable crisis of knowing.

The chronicle ends with studied indirection: "Peace, be still! Oh! a thousand weepers, praying in agony on waiting shores, listened for that voice, but it was not uttered—not uttered till, when the hush came, some could not feel it: till, when the sun returned, his light was night to some!" (chap. 42). Paul was her Apollo. He should have claimed her as the resplendent bridegroom of the Song of Songs. His removal is signaled by figurative transfers. For just as the words, "Peace, be still!" can be either Paul's or Christ's, directed at a different storm (Mark 4:39), so the light can be either the light of Paul's countenance or the literal light of the returning sun. We can feel the ground of that loss, its buried life, in zero values of juncture, elision, and metaphoric displacement. But nothing can translate it. It is like walking on silence.

Paul's death signifies for Lucy what the death of Wordsworth's brother at sea signifies in "Elegiac Stanzas." What has died is her imagination of hope. No more will she paint the light that never was on sea or land—the consecration and the poet's dream. She must resort instead to bare notation, renouncing the seductions of hope and false surmise. The barely repressed anguish and puzzlement that underlie the obituary plainness of the last paragraph also dramatize the fact that Lucy is a survivor. She lives to write the obituaries of the three people whose fate she chronicles. Mme Beck, Père Silas, and Mme Walravens have one fate in common: they appear to prosper and live long. But is such a fate justified? The mind of each reader, thwarted in its search for a common set of qualities that might justify the prosperity of three dissimilar characters, must acknowledge that if providence is in charge, it is a providence that exhausts the freakishness of arbitrary caprice. The happy endings of fiction are not the endings of real life. Because the allotment of happiness and suffering, of prosperity and early death, bears no discernible relation to intrinsic merit, there still lurks a black king on the chessboard, a figure more sinister than any character we have actually met in Brontë's fiction. One looks in vain for any clue to who, or what, or where the black king is. Theodicy and ethics are helpless to deal with this mystery. Lucy's language of oracle and dream can come closer. But though we wonder what energies she might release if she could speak everything she seems to feel at the end, it is as if her reluctance to speak comes from her sense that the blight is so primordial that it must be experienced and explained by each reader in his own way. As the darkness of Lucy's world retreats from the communicative grasp of words, she finds herself withdrawing from speech. Her silence is rooted in the pauses after "great terror, the rapture of rescue from peril, the wondrous reprieve from dread" (chap. 42). It inhabits the empty spaces between the commas and phrases, the places of breakup where we tremble on the brink and vacancy looms as an invisible but potent presence.

CHAPTER 4

"The Signless Inane": Mystery and the Unconscious in Carlyle

Though Nietzsche pronounced Carlyle "an English atheist" who wanted "to be honoured for *not* being one" (Nietzsche 1968, 75), and William James thought he was "an amateur prophet exclusively, having as little real resemblance to Isaiah . . . as Mr. Booth has to King Lear or Shylock" (James, n.d., 15), Carlyle can be read as a Victorian Milton, whose works compose a skeptic's *Paradise Lost*. In Carlyle's cosmology, both paradise and hell precipitate crises in representation, for each has the puzzling attribute of being simultaneously describable and indescribable. On the one hand, paradise is a condition of harmony that seems a product of voluntary design. Hell, by contrast, has all the disadvantage of being involuntary—wild, anarchic, resistant to control, without any of the advantages of being ordered. On the other hand, neither of these highest and lowest regions can ever be defined, since to be outside consciousness, which is a condition of both heaven and hell, is also to be outside language. Only the unfallen world's reflections of paradise and the fallen world's countervailing reflections of hell can be inscribed in words: such inscriptions make the states they inscribe an object of consciousness. But by definition such geographies of the self as heaven and hell are regions of Carlyle's "signless Inane" (1:205): they cannot be described and still remain unconscious.

Carlyle's attempt to regain paradise falls into two phases. First, unfallen nature's reflection of a lost order operates as a positive norm, against which Carlyle can judge the imperfections of the false signs that fill his world. In this first phase, paradise seems to be an order of which Carlyle is not fully conscious, but which is in principle knowable and recoverable. But when Carlyle then tries to produce out of chaos a new set of intrinsic signs, he discovers that his dark oxymorons and prophecies are incapable of being translated. The unconscious is now synonymous with the tropes of veiling and repression. Outside this language of repression there is nothing for the prophet to express. The disappearance of any external referent helps explain William James's alarm. Carlyle is "a harlequin in the guise of a Jeremiah," James protests, "who feeds you with laughter in place of tears, and puts the old prophetic sincerity out of countenance by his broad persistent winks over the footlights" (James, n.d., 16). Though Carlyle's impulse to demolish petrified signs proceeds from an intimation of what paradise might be, his desire to build on the ruins of the signs he has destroyed brings the disturbing realization that there is no paradise outside language for the prophet to recover.

Two contrary impulses operate in Carlyle's early essay "Signs of the Times" (1829): an impulse to erode the signs that have petrified into dogma, and a fear of being destroyed by the madness that overtakes every revolutionist. There is an original innocence of imagination in the inspired but irresponsible dreamer painting glorious triumphs "on the cloud-curtain of the future" (27:56). But when the mind binds itself to such visions and delirium becomes the dream of many waking minds, the ensuing frenzy is terrifying to contemplate unless the enchanter can also be revealed as a prophet wielding his "Aaron's-rod of Truth" (27:57). As the solvent of illusion, irony is used in Carlyle's search for more solid grounds of knowledge. Where the ironist expects to find solid ground, however, he finds mere shifting sand. "The grand encourager of Delphic or other noises is—the Echo. Left to themselves, they will the sooner dissipate, and die away in space" (27:59). The oracular rhetoric sets up an ironic echo within its own coordinate syntax. The phrase "other noises" echoes and appropriately subverts the prophetic pretensions of "Delphic." With no capacity to originate themselves, echoes soon dissipate their energy, and the parallel syntactic units, combined with a bathetic use of the anticipatory dash, establish an echoing pattern of ever expanding diminution and loss.

There are two moments of irony in Carlyle. In its first moment, irony is used as an all-corroding, all-dissolving solvent to erode the mindless proliferation of machines and institutes, whose insectlike swarming is mimed in the alarming multiplication of nouns with like endings: "Hence the Royal and Imperial Societies, the Bibliothèques, Glyphothèques, Technothèques, which front us in all capital cities" (27:62). Carlyle's second moment of irony is more radical. Having subverted idols of the tribe, the ironist must now subvert idols of his own cave, including failed prophets like the fallen Edward Irving.

Increasingly, the distempers of the mad prophets and enthusiasts Carlyle denounces as a humorous ironist begin to afflict Carlyle himself.

In "Signs of the Times" the blur and density of the verbal mazes often lead Carlyle into a centerless labyrinth. Truest to his own sense of dynamism, for example, is his paradoxical pull away from what he is drawn toward. If we are too dynamical, we become fanatics: if we are too mechanical, we harden into robots and machines. Carlyle tries to resolve the mystery by turning it into a problem or puzzle in Newtonian physics: "only in the right coördination of the two, and the vigorous forwarding of *both*, does our true line of action lie" (27:73). But the vectors, too geometrically mapped to ring true, explain away more than they actually explain. In denouncing the "Euphuists of Mechanism," Carlyle is in danger of sounding euphuistic himself. The daylight of truth, which he artfully parodies in the feeble rushlight of closet logic, makes him sound as fastidious and mincing as the "intellectual dapperling[s]" (27:75) he takes to task. Carlyle utters the same vacuous "mouthfuls of articulate wind" (27:79) that he attacks fops like Byron for blowing at him. Because the truths he would name are unnameable, he is finally assailed by opposite phobias. He has nightmares of stifling in a bell jar's "scanty atmosphere" (27:81) but is equally afraid of being annihilated in the heady world outside the jar. As terrified by open spaces as he is by closed ones, Carlyle never seems to know whether the world outside consciousness—plastic, infinite, open—is angelic or demonic. Is it a place of plenitude or a desert of mere emptiness and vacancy?

The moment Carlyle tries to expound the mysteries of the unconscious, he falls into contradiction and paradox. Nowhere are these paradoxes clearer than in his 1831 essay "Characteristics," which opens in a volley of self-subverting propositions, as if in proof of its thesis that all "Inquiry is Disease" (28:2). On the one hand, the "felicity of 'having no system'" (28:2) is a product of the unhappiness of having one. For if there were no systematic inquiry, how would we arrive at the consciousness of any truth, including the truth that "the beginning of Inquiry is Disease"? On the other hand, the division and dismemberment that inquiry introduces are denounced only because they violate the norm they presuppose. We would never know what it is to be partial and broken unless we had some prior conception of what it is to be whole.

"Political Philosophy," writes Carlyle in his notebook, "should be a scientific revelation of the whole secret mechanism whereby men cohere together in society" (1898, 144). But how can "revelation" be "scientific"? And is a "mechanism" ever "secret"? To expound a secret science devoted to the mechanism of the mind's unconscious operations is to tread a linguistic minefield. When language does not explode into oxymoron, its meanings are eroded by negative constructions. The mystery of an unconscious consciousness is best described as a unity "always silent," a "blessedness" not known, a music "unregarded" or a light "unseen" (28:1–2). Such unintelligible mysteries are alone worthy of pursuit: "Manufacture is intelligible, but trivial; Creation is great, and cannot be understood" (28:5).

If, as Virgil argues, happiness is the absence of knowing we are happy, how can we ever be conscious of our happiness? Is it possible to be happy if we never know we are happy? Perhaps the most we can hope is that the loss of happiness may bring knowledge that we were once happy. Just as light, in rendering all things visible, itself remains invisible, so the unconscious, though just out of sight, is the happy condition of our seeing everything else clearly. Even in being granted vision, we are given the gift of blindness. For if we could see the abyss for what it is, the sensation of swimming "fearfully and wonderfully" on an ocean that is truly "bottomless" (28:3) would be as disquieting, though exhilarating, as a free-fall through space.

Since all discourse aspires to abolish itself by achieving silence, which is the condition of unconsciousness, signs are best able to inscribe the "signless Inane" (1:205) when they "sign" their meaning as a deaf-mute might, condemned in advance to be speechless. When Carlyle praises the ancients for making Silence a god, he is thinking of the Athenians' *agnostos theos*: Socrates worships a deity who is in principle unknowable. Unlike the silent, self-withholding Socrates, the Sophists descant at length about virtue, "proving it, denying it, mechanically 'accounting' for it; —as dissectors and demonstrators cannot operate till once the body be dead" (28:10). The alarming multiplication of like endings makes the remorseless dissection sound more like an autopsy than a dispassionate inquiry. Truly moral people like Socrates make no parade of their moral nature. They love goodness but do not make love to it. Though Carlyle is no precursor of George Grote, who proclaims Socrates the greatest of the Sophists, he does anticipate one influential teaching of Grote: the importance of Socrates' negative irony. Every metaphysical system or theory of the universe that fails to incorporate Socrates' capacity for self-criticism and irony is bound to become dogmatic and uncritical.

How can Carlyle distinguish the silence of the infinite and inexpressible from the silence of the nil, the void, the nonexistent? Is silence "not anything," or is it something called nothing because, though unperceived like light, it is still the source of all our experiencing? There are two corresponding sides to Carlyle's oceanic awe before the boundlessness of existence. A boundless ocean inspires wonder, but it also induces vertigo by seeming to be bottomless. Because "Doubt is the indispensable inexhaustible material whereon Action works," there is no true terminal point. Any achieved goal immediately begets a new idolatry, which has to be "torn in pieces," Carlyle insists, so that a less idolatrous certainty may again "be sought for in the endless realms of denial" (28:26). Since the negating power of metaphysics "begins in No or Nothingness, so it must needs end in Nothingness." It "circulates and must circulate in endless vortices; creating, swallowing—itself." Carlyle is overpowered by a nightmare vision of the sinking of all literature, as one colossal *Dunciad*, into a "boundless self-devouring Review." Such commentary on commentary, like Carlyle's own periodical essays, seems pledged to batten parasitically on all the other reviews in an endless regress of words about words (28:25, 27).

Sartor Resartus (1831) half revels in and half despairs of a similar crisis. On the one hand, the book indulges an impulse to dissolve cellular, vascular, and muscular tissues, and even tissues of wool or other cloth, into a whole network of more complex tissues. On the other hand, as everything threatens to become text and intertext, Carlyle is forced to concede that the only essential truth is the absence of any such truth. All properties of man and his world are merely contingent, like the hat or suit he wears. Any exhilarating venture to identify the "grand Tissue of all Tissues" (1:2) ends in the paralyzing discovery that there is only a vast network or tissue of text and intertext, with no privileged god term at the center.

Teufelsdröckh's etymological link between clothes and culture, an "Esprit de Costumes" and an "Esprit de Coutumes" (1:27), is easier to justify in French than in English. But the word play reinforces his axiom that clothes are merely one example of the double potential— creative and destructive—of all sign systems. Symbols may confer individuality, distinction, social polity, even the gift of language itself. Alternatively, they may turn us into mere dehumanized "clothes-screens." A sign system may generate something wholly unforeseen, an entire symbolic network as fertile and self-generating as banyan groves or as poisonous as a forest full of hemlocks.

To walk barefoot or naked into reality, we have to tear away all our signs and masks. But without masks and clothes, would there be anything left to see? All the excitement of unveiling depends on arts of striptease and delay. Though a naked House of Lords is a comic spectacle, it is also disquieting, because it shows how fragile yet pervasive our symbols really are. Is nakedness something we should seek or avoid? To be stripped naked like the descendentalists is to lose one's identity. But it may also be a way of soaking or immersing oneself in the identity of everyone else. Clothes are a precondition of civility, but they both create and conceal our humanity. The same could be said of language. Without it, there would be no humanity to express. But with it, we can deceive ourselves endlessly. We can trap ourselves inside a labyrinth of signs from which there is no easy exit. Though Carlyle is a precursor of contemporary poststructuralists, he is critical of their dogmas. He suspects that the inability to get outside our signs may also be a denial of our true origins and ends. Each choice seems to entail some irreparable loss. If we try to deny that we are Swift's "forked straddling animal," for example, we also conceal our spirituality, the fact we are also an "unutterable Mystery of Mysteries" (1:45) capable of recovering our "royal nature" in our "other body," in our "individual and physical one," as one commentator says of King Lear (Frye 1986, 115–16).

Teufelsdröckh's paragraph on metaphor proves the professor's point that there is no such thing as an unmetaphorical style (1:58). Even the word "attention" is a metaphorical "stretching-to." The more Teufelsdröckh "attends to" and "stretches" the meaning of "clothes," until the word expands to include "the essence of all sciences," the more "these dim infinitely-expanded regions" begin to impinge "on the impalpable Inane," which by definition is signless. In a universe of privileged signs, the privileged referent disappears, and the god term at the center turns out to be just another metaphor or sign. It is as if Carlyle is running away from what he keeps racing toward: the discovery that there is no end term or origin, only an endlessly receding chain of signs linked to other signs.

The impossibility of ever recovering a first cause or origin is dramatized in the story of the stranger who leaves the infant Teufelsdröckh as an "invaluable Loan" (1:66). The noble-looking stranger is a figure of mystery: he is called the "unknown Father" and recalls the "Unknown God" of Socrates. A strict Platonist would argue that character is shaped in a prenatal world and that genius is hereditary. But if the hereditary argument is pushed to an extreme, salvation by election would make all history redundant. Conversely, the editor's argument from experience, if consistently applied, would soon deprive the self of any independent identity.

The truth seems to lie somewhere in the middle. According to Fichte's *Wissenschaftslehre*, which Teufelsdröckh calls "Applied Christianity" (1:156), the general condition of consciousness prior to all knowledge is represented by the tautology A = A. But no individual consciousness could exist unless this generalized subjectivity encountered a nonego within itself. To account for the fall from undifferentiated consciousness into consciousness as we experience it, Fitchte has to posit a limiting activity on the part of the ego. The fall into consciousness is indeed a fall: it requires a limiting of the pure or absolute ego by the nonego. But it is also a gain, because it alone makes intelligible the consciousness as we understand and know it. Teufelsdröckh's truest Fichtean insights occur in incidents like the sudden intrusion of a brutal Russian smuggler into the solitude of the North Pole. The self is never independent of the outside world: isolation and indifference are impossible to maintain. John Holloway has shown how Carlyle appropriates religious language to make authoritative his own practical displacement of theological doctrine (Holloway 1965, 24–26). In Fichte's appropriation of theological words like "Faith" and "Doubt" in *Die Bestimmung des Menschen*, Carlyle would have found just such a precedent for his own rhetorical procedure. Only in practical religion has the highest come home to the bosom of the most limited. The poorest pietists and Methodists are superior to Plato because, instead of worshiping mere copies or simulacra, they actively partake of the divine nature.

Whereas Arthur Hugh Clough opposes a religion of silence to a religion of work, Carlyle equates the two. To create a new religion through work is to proceed silently, he insists. Because speech is grounded in previous truth, it often impedes new discovery. Clough reaches a different conclusion because he defines "silence" differently. Silence, for Clough, is a refusal to profane some mystery. It is a synonym for a contemplation of the unspeakable, and as such it is an alternative to doing. But silence for Carlyle is the silence of the inexpressible, or the silence of what cannot be expressed until some new intrinsic symbol has been made. The life of Christ was once authentically symbolic, and intrinsically so, just as the original Last Supper was a symbolic performance of the utmost daring and genius. If we try too hard or self-consciously to invent a rite or to make our life an allegory, it will become instead a mere piece of theater. Like Strauss's notion that myth is *unconscious* invention, lives that become allegories are unconsciously symbolic. If we try to invent a symbol, like the festivals in honor of a supreme being in *The French Revolution*, we shall soon discover that an authentic symbol can never be legislated. It has to be believed into being in silence, by faith and civic love. True creators like William the Silent do not talk about their projects. Secrecy is to virtue what silence is to doing. Reserved people say nothing till they see. In Robert Frost's phrase, "the love belief ... has that same shyness. It knows it cannot tell; only the outcome can tell" (Frost 1968, 46).

As Augustine discovered when he tried to define time, the harder

Teufelsdröckh tries to define symbols, the less intelligible they become. Symbols require other symbols to explain them. And how, for example, can the invisible be symbolized in man and remain invisible? Either the bodying forth of the symbol is not a true bodying, or the meaning of "invisible" is changing. Most symbolic predications of a living subject try to explain away its mystery. Like Kant's antinomies, which often totter "on the verge of the inane" (1:175), the professor's high-soaring definitions of man keep trembling on the brink of no meaning at all. Logically, it is just as impossible for man to be at one and the same time Bacon's enchanted glass, a dead iron balance, and a digestive machine as it is for Sir William Hamilton's God to be simultaneously infinite and absolute. From owl, man subsides into donkey or ass. If everything is a symbol of man, is anything truly a symbol? Unless some common quality binds together the chain's links, the referent seems to escape through the hole at the center of each link.

Only intrinsic symbols exhaust their subject, and they cannot be analyzed. Only extrinsic symbols can be analyzed, and like the ritual naming by the herald at the coronation of George IV, they tend to trivialize their subject. The new king is not really offering battle to the universe, nor is he in strict veracity the champion of all England. Since he cannot even mount his horse properly, the archaic rite is now no more felicitous than the baptism of a monkey. To the degree that symbols are intrinsic, they become identical with the thing itself and so cease to be symbols. In allowing us to see the referent face to face, such transparent signifiers are indistinguishable from a death sentence: "And Manoah said to his wife, 'We shall surely die, for we have seen God'" (Judges 13:22). To the degree that symbols remain symbols, however, they cease to be intrinsic: the fearful rift between the unnameable God and his attributes begins to reappear. Christ's life seems to be an intrinsic symbol, a continual allegory, because he *makes* it so. But the allegory of his life is not permanently achieved. Each new believer must become what David Friedrich Strauss calls a "Messias of Nature" (1:175). No little symbol or dogma can serve as the unalterable measure of the universe. Religion will perish unless new Messiahs, new exemplars of the divine ground, elicit in each new age an intuitive response that pierces beyond dogma and symbolic definition.

The explosion of aphoristic fragments in the chapter "Natural Supernaturalism" suggests that Teufelsdröckh has reached the limits of language. The foundations of the universe are very deep and cannot be reduced to an engineer's machine, a lawyer's statute book, or an architect's ground plan. But if miracles, properly conceived, are violations of the laws of nature, then the true mystery is merely pushed back a notch. The mystery term requiring definition now is "laws of nature." Are there higher unwritten laws as well as scientific laws? Is resurrection a violation of the latter law but a confirmation of the former? To define anything we must define everything; but this being manifestly impossible, the infinite regress of mysteries quickly induces vertigo.

Teufelsdröckh must find a way that allows the great and the small, the immense and the infinitesimal, to exist together in reciprocal dignity. He comes closest in his use of metalepsis to ascribe a present effect to a remote cause, or a remote effect to a present cause, as in his Ptolemaic image of epicycles. "Who knows... what infinitely larger Cycle (of causes) our little Epicycles revolve on?" (1:205). The parenthesis casually linking cycle with cause turns the synecdoche of the wheel within the wheel into a daring attribution of present effects to remote causes. "Such a minnow is Man; his Creek this planet Earth; his Ocean the immeasurable All; his Monsoons and periodic Currents the mysterious Course of Providence through Aeons of Aeons" (1:205). In linking man, the minnow, to the course of providence, the slowly expanding synecdoche works in perfect alliance with the careful caesural pauses, the use of anaphora, and the expanding syntactic units. The last clause even drops the copula verb, as if to dramatize the final merging of juxtaposed items.

We reach a point when there is nothing further behind or beyond the signs that will help dramatize the mystery or make it more intelligible. The unconscious ceases to be something merely unknown and in principle recoverable. It becomes instead the principle of veiling itself. Unconsciousness, in its more radical form, is synonymous with repression and with the linguistic and other mechanisms responsible for monitoring a perpetual boiling up of the nether deep. "In every the wisest Soul lies a whole world of internal Madness, an authentic Demon-Empire; out of which, indeed, his world of Wisdom has been creatively built together, and now rests there, as on its dark foundations does a habitable flowery Earth-rind" (1:207). The "authentic Demon-Empire" is not a mere mask or covering. Unlike the "Earth-rind," it cannot be used to hide anything. The sentence I have quoted is as much a statement about the irreplaceability of oxymoronic signs and tropes, about the untranslatability of "Wisdom," as it is about psychology, the fragility of culture, or the fashioning of ethical out of cosmic nature.

For Teufelsdröckh, philosophy becomes a battle against the bewitchment of the mind by means of custom—an enterprise that coincides with Hegel's definition of Socratic philosophy. In making "dotards of us all" (1:206), custom proves to be mere bastard morality, what Hegel calls *Sittlichkeit* as opposed to genuine *Moralität*. Lying upon us "with a weight," as Wordsworth says, "heavy as frost and deep almost as life" ("Ode: Intimations of Immortality," ll. 128–29), custom turns the world into a prison rather than the dwelling place of a celestial visitant. It blinds us to the truth that the most miraculous event is what, in our stupefaction, we regard as the most commonplace, the stretching forth of a hand to grasp something. If I can clutch anything, I can clutch everything. To define a single term we find we have to redefine a whole chain of terms, including "God" and "miracle." But the last link in the chain is seldom more explicable than the link we started with. Only tropes like metalepsis and synecdoche can relax the grip of custom by bringing us to the limits of language and possibly beyond them.

The prospect of lifting the veil can be just as terrifying as the prospect of living with illusion. Limits are obstacles, but they are also merciful middle grounds. All we can affirm is that the stormy procession of life is from spirit to spirit, as in Plato's myths; from dream to dream, as in *The Tempest*; and from darkness outside the mead hall back into darkness, as in the great parable of Venerable Bede: "We emerge from the Inane; haste stormfully across the astonished Earth; then plunge again into the Inane" (1:212). Framing all experience is "the Inane," the twice-used metonymy that frames the march of short coordinate clauses. As in section 123 of *In Memoriam*, the full pathos and terror of man's precarious foothold in time comes from a sense that earth itself is unstable. All we can really know is man's stormful hastening across the astonished earth. Spirits are shaped into bodies, then vanish into air.

The climax of *Sartor Resartus* is not an original uttered word, guaranteed by a voice that speaks from the whirlwind or the sky, like the strange voice that talks to Tennyson at the climax of *In Memoriam*:" 'The dawn, the dawn,' and died away" (95.61). In "Natural Supernaturalism" every intimation of unmediated presence has its countervailing intimation of absence or nonbeing. "But whence? —O Heaven, whither? Sense knows not; Faith knows not; only that it is through Mystery to Mystery, from God and to God" (1:212). While Teufelsdröckh is striving for unmediated vision, his readers are left with emptiness and silence. Carlyle repeats Schiller's critique of Western man's infatuation with some absolute proximity of voice and being. From the first paragraphs of *Sartor Resartus*, we sense that Carlyle is a reluctant descendentalist, impelled to strip away the veiling fictions but afraid to face what his stripping will disclose.

Generically, *Sartor Resartus* is a gloss: an editor's marginal commentary on such complex words in Teufelsdröckh's text as "unconsciousness," "silence," "symbol," "clothing," and "God." Like Jacques Derrida, Carlyle interrogates his texts in order to dismantle fictions of presence assumed to exist on the other side of silence. Even the most casual reader knows that *Sartor Resartus* exposes the internal contradictions of utilitarianism. What is less often recognized is that the book also exposes the metaphysical conspiracy in which the post-Kantian idealism of *Die Kleider* is itself implicated. *Sartor Resartus* shows that whenever German idealism becomes less skeptical of its own postulates than the critical philosophy of Kant, it starts to founder on spurious axioms of presence.

At the end of *Sartor Resartus* the habit of seeing all things figuratively is censored as a disease of language. It is a disease for which the editor, infected by the same distemper, must find a cure. But is figurative seeing false seeing? Or is it the only seeing that is ever possible? There is no originating principle, no divine unconsciousness, behind the clothes philosophy and its sign system that the editor can hope to recover or even point toward without the help of tropes. When the masks are finally taken off and the repressed forces from the demon empire are allowed to filter through, Carlyle discovers that the unconscious is not something outside language at all. On the contrary, it is synonymous with repression itself, with oxymoron, catachresis, and all the other tropes of displacement and reserve he has been using.

The paradox of being conscious of the unconscious, like the paradox of knowing that God is unknowable, may seem difficult to reconcile with the general condition of unconsciousness that must prevail if Carlyle's theory of the "signless Inane" is to be valid. And yet the theological implications of these paradoxes would certainly be familiar to Carlyle, since they had just been expounded by Sir William Hamilton in the October 1829 issue of the *Edinburgh Review*, the journal in which Carlyle had published "Signs of the Times" four months earlier. In an influential review essay on the philosophy of the unconditioned, Hamilton conducts a Kantian critique of the philosophy of religion, showing that the concepts of the absolute and the infinite are self-contradictory. Shrouding God in an elusive veil, Hamilton, like Carlyle, is obsessed by self-concealing attributes of the sign, without which language would be forbidden. In replacing philosophies of divine presence with the doctrine of an unknowable power that surpasses all the philosopher or prophet can think or say about it, Hamilton explores, like Carlyle, the difficulty of ever expressing the divine nature, a life without difference, in mere symbolic fictions. Like the dark spot at the center of Hamilton's Kantian critique of religion, the dark spot behind the mask of nature is something that only

Carlyle's endless play of signs can defer and help moderate. But even in delaying exposure, Carlyle finds that the final uncertainty remains. He is left with the mere presence/absence of the trace, with the mere elusive signature of a God who has fled. Nothing in the end can domesticate that mystery or tame the terror of discovering that there is nothing behind the oxymorons and catachresis for Carlyle to unveil.

Like the "signless Inane" in *Sartor Resartus*, the most important truths in *Past and Present* (1843) cannot be understood. The riddle posed by Carlyle's sphinx is "What is justice?", a version of Pilate's "What is truth?", and just as hard to answer. Noisy orators at Westminster are speechless when addressing the great court of the universe: they "have no word to utter" (10:9). Whatever justice is, it is no longer synonymous with the venerable laws of Parliament, but is closer to Antigone's "higher and unwritten eternal laws." But if true justice is higher and unwritten, how can there be any valid emblem of it? Unless heaven's invisible justice can be deciphered, the whole nation, like a Roman criminal, will be pushed over a Tarpeian rock into a pit of destruction. And yet heaven's justice seems to be, in Carlyle's phrase, "a fearful indescribability" (10:14). The whole argument is as circular and self-subverting as a riddle without an answer. For though higher justice is said to be solid as adamant, it is also claimed to be invisible, unembodied, and not yet describable. By adding to the question's sphinxlike quality, the riddling contradictions elevate justice to a sphere high above conceptual understanding, like an Idea of the Pure Reason.

To write as a prophet is to embrace as salvation a condition that, if ever reached, would be the ultimate diaster—arrival at Utopia or the Happy Isles, a destiny synonymous with death itself. Accordingly, every prophet is a living contradiction, like Cassandra, whose fate is always to go unheeded. Because to succeed as a prophet is to stop declaiming, it is also to cease being a writer. Carlyle must aim for goals that, once achieved in *Past and Present*, would be fatal to his own prophetic office. One way of deferring goals is to preserve intact the multiple layering of his chronicle. He is presenting as an editor what another editor, Mr. Rokewood of the Camden Society, has already presented as the work of a third editor, Jocelin, whose ingenuous anecdotes are at once candid and inscrutable.

To preserve the sense of a monastic mystery like Umberto Eco's *The Name of the Rose*, Carlyle attacks as pedantry any attempt to make the history of the abbey more knowable than it is. Saint Edmund's Shrine is "now a mutilated black Ruin" (10:125). If we would capture its past, we must become dramatists ourselves, and decipherers of acrostic fragments, not mere collectors of dry-as-dust parchments and fossil remains. Like the nesting structures of narrative in *Sartor Resartus* and *Past and Present*, shroud within shroud of protective garments conspires to hold more in reserve than is ever revealed. The glorious martyr's body is never seen in the flesh by any of the monks. The culminating moment of Abbot Samson's life is a moment of drawing back and being denied a promised vision. Edmund's coffin is wrapped in garments; the coffin itself is described as a metaphoric garment; and there are even layers upon layers of linen cloth placed inside it. When "Time-Curtains" suddenly "rush down" (10:125) on the abruptly terminated narrative, it is as if Carlyle, like Jocelin, has come too close to penetrating the naked "sacred flesh" (10:122). Some ultimate meaning, or absence of meaning, must be held in reserve.

The judicial version of Saint Edmund's voluminously wrapped body and of Carlyle's many-layered narrative is the vestigial justice lurking somewhere inside the head of the venerable wigged Justice. Carlyle compares it to Dryden's Head in *The Battle of the Books*. If the animating germ, in size no bigger than a hazelnut, could be seen for the small grain it is, we might all despair of the "fraction of God's Justice" (10:132) that is really present. It seems at first that if superannuated symbols of the just could be set aside, something more authentically just might take their place. But there is no such thing as pure justice or a natural language of justice. The words and emblems Carlyle promotes as genuine signs of the just are valued not for their naturalness, but for their imaginative boldness and figurative resource.

Contradiction and crisis face Carlyle at every turn. The surest way of achieving oblivion is to appeal to posterity. And yet the surest way of appealing to posterity is to ignore posterity and appeal instead to eternal God. Words like liberty are equally paradoxical. Is the liberty to die by starvation a divine thing? We try to attach constant emotive meanings to words like "liberty" and "democracy" even after the descriptive meanings have changed. Once "democracy" is redefined as the "despair of finding any Heroes to govern you" (10:215), it can be shown to be to politics what atheism is to religion. Alternatively, by changing a negative emotive meaning while retaining the descriptive meaning, an insulting adjective like "dumb" can be made to operate in the reverse way. "The Speakable" is a mere "superficial film, or outer skin" (10:159). Whereas English, Russian, and Roman people are silent, the French, like monkeys, are forever talking and gesticulating. The "Doable" is perfectly congruent with what cannot be uttered.

Immensities and depths of "Silence unsoundable" (10:200) are the surest sign that anything Carlyle can say about it will be contradictory. The nautical pun on "sounding" dramatizes the truth that faith must be preserved in mysteries beyond the power of human speech to fathom. Only by beginning as a "No-thing," as a pure potentiality conceived in faith, can human creations come to body forth, in Paul's sense, "the forms of Things Unseen" (10:205).

No contradiction runs deeper in Carlyle than the opposition between evolutionary hypotheses of organic growth and prophetic doctrines of cataclysm. On the one hand, all times and places are the single life-tree, Igdrasil. Nothing could be more seamless or total. And yet Carlyle is also the oracle of revolution and cataclysm. Though he yearns for Utopia, he half fears that the dream of an ideal community, where all good things cohere, is conceptually incoherent. He desperately invokes spiritual and political heroes, because he cannot face the loss that each act of choice compels free people to accept.

The curtain is brought down abruptly on Jocelin's narrative. Its rude, cliff-hanging termination in midsentence dramatizes that horror of concluding that, as Dr. Johnson knew, is inseparable from a thinking being whose life is limited and for whom death is dreadful: "The magnanimous Abbot makes preparation for departure; departs, and—And Jocelin's Boswellian Narrative, suddenly shorn-through by the scissors of Destiny, *ends*. There are no words more; but a black line, and leaves of blank paper. Irremediable: the miraculous hand, that held all this theatric-machinery, suddenly quits hold; impenetrable Time-Curtains rush down; in the mind's eye all is dark, void..." (10:25). That the passage ends with two stressed monosyllables hanging in space following a succession of staccato clauses and a lacuna in the middle of the first sentence makes it even more memorable and terrifying as a shadow of the great darkness that will soon blot out the mind. Like readers of Mark's gospel, which ends before the expected resurrection story can be told, Carlyle's readers are left to wrestle in the "real," contemporary world of the chronicle's two editors with the same mysteries of faith that Jocelin presents in the Middle Ages. As in the gospel of Mark, the Johnsonian "conclusion in which nothing is concluded" betrays our expectations. It is as if the fragmented narratives and lacunae were designed in both cases to release the hidden powers of make-belief and faith in each reader.

Carlyle leads us into verbal mazes from which it is often difficult to find an exit. Our bewilderment may not make us his disciples, but at least it acquaints us with the dilemmas and contradictions in which his ideology and intellectual ambition place him. Teufelsdröckh, for example, wants us all to recover our nakedness—to walk barefoot into reality. And he amasses vast amounts of learning in support of his plea. But how truly naked can such a self-conscious and erudite plea for nakedness really be? Without betraying the very unselfconsciousness we seek, how can we be made conscious of the need for becoming unselfconscious?

The elaborate nesting structures and allusive mazes in Carlyle should be treated, I think, not as puzzles to be solved, but as mirrors of ideological plots or systems. As we have seen, works by Fichte as well as treatises by Bentham are "plots" in a double sense—both philosophical structures and conspiracies. And no one but James Joyce, or Northrop Frye or Coleridge perhaps, could hope to be informed or attentive enough to be an ideal reader of *Sartor Resartus*. As a literary representation of the post-Kantian and utilitarian "plots" against us, *Sartor Resartus* is difficult in the way many allusive modern works are difficult. In addition, Carlyle keeps veering away from his previous statements, as if he were afraid of being trapped by some aphorism or learned allusion he has just uttered. An ideal reader would therefore have to be both erudite and ingenuous, capable of being open, fresh, and spontaneous even while being self-consciously adept at taking all the learned detours and at tracking all the allusions without the help of any reliable map or guidebook to the labyrinth.

The substance of Carlyle's ostentatious learning is less important than the fact that he makes such a parade of it. It is the *act* of allusion rather than the *substance* of the allusion that matters. His writing abounds in interpretations of interpretations. Sometimes every second word Carlyle uses seems to be a quotation. How can readers escape from such a web of self-reference? The poet or seer presumably has to originate meaning. But such originating power displays itself in Carlyle mainly as an energetic repudiation of prior interpretations. He uses discrete fragments and broken syntax to sever the chain of commentaries on commentaries. There is an odd combination of dogmatism and diffidence in his writing. The more learned and schematic his performance becomes, the more it seems to conceal something. As Nietzsche recognized, "Carlyle deafens something within him by the *fortissimo* of his reverence for men of strong faith and by his rage against the less single-minded" (1968, 74). What is Carlyle trying to blot out? Is it the roar that lies on the far side of silence? Is it something precariously unbalanced or unstable in his own psyche? It is as if he both deeply desires and deeply fears a divine power, a "signless Inane," that is continually invading and breaking down the comfort of his names and definitions. William James believes that Carlyle is even prepared to degrade the divine power by honoring "it in the flash" and by dishonoring "it in its sublime reserve," in "the awful because *unconscious* wealth of the race" (James, n.d., 79, 81). Like Browning and some modern writers, Carlyle is simultaneously inclusive and fragmented. His desire for silence is exceeded only by a compulsion to talk about silence endlessly. Agitated by a longing for unconsciousness that is acutely self-conscious, Carlyle remains extremely insecure about his capacity to encounter or interpret a divine power that, in continually eluding him as a "signless Inane," as a no-man's-land beyond tropes and signs altogether, is best invoked as "a fearful indescribability" (10:14).

Chapter 5

Incomprehensible Certainties

and Interesting Uncertainties:

Hopkins and Tennyson

When Hopkins tells Robert Bridges that his subject as a religious poet is "an incomprehensible certainty," not "an interesting uncertainty" (Hopkins 1935, 187), he is drawing attention to an important source of mystery in his poetry and to a defining quality of his sublime use of language. But the distinction raises as many questions as it answers. If Tennyson, for example, is a poet of "interesting uncertainties" and Hopkins himself a poet of "incomprehensible certainties," how are we to recognize such differences in the syntax and grammar of their verse? And how can "uncertainty" be converted into "certainty" without losing its incomprehensibility and mystery? Is Hopkins's "certainty" merely the antonym of the skeptic's "uncertainty"? Or is the word "certainty" itself being redefined? Just as incomprehensible as Hopkins's certainty is his audacious oxymoron "incomprehensible certainty": for how can anything of which we are genuinely certain also be incomprehensible?

The uncertainties that Hopkins consigns to the lower realm of mere "interest" appear to attach themselves to propositions that are logically contradictory. But the certainties that Hopkins finds "incomprehensible" are not like that. They are to "interesting uncertainties" what "certitude" is to "certainty" in Newman's *Essay in Aid of a Grammar of Assent*. The latter is a feature of propositions like $2 + 2 = 4$, which are unaffected by the state of mind of the mathematician who affirms or denies them. But certitude is a feature of propositions like "I believe in God" or "I love you," where the affective state of the assenter is an important part of what is affirmed. The certainties that Hopkins finds incomprehensible are rendered certain by reserves of meaning in both God and the believer. Because God is a sublime given, his meanings, though always out of reach, are never in doubt: they are always certain. But because reserves of meaning in the believer—meaning that is subliminal and always partly out of sight—are continually converting mere certainty into certitude, that certitude is also incomprehensible. The sublimity is God's contribution: it confers certainty. But it can do so only because the believer converts the mere certainty of a logical proposition into the incomprehensible certitude of a religious affirmation. In the process the believer adds meanings that are partly subliminal or repressed. His meanings are also the residue of something sublime, however, for which he is not responsible, and which the poet who honestly charts the magnitude of his subject can never quite put into words.

An analysis of the sublime also suggests why sublime poetry should express "incomprehensible certainties." Every sublime subject presents what Keats calls the mere "shadow of a magnitude," a phrase he uses in "On Seeing the Elgin Marbles" (l. 14). The magnitude is conveyed in poetry by appositional devices and by forms of dilation that expand and diffuse a subject. Hopkins uses parentheses, appositional grammar, semantic units of equivalence, elaborate devices of parallelism and antithesis, tmesis, and sundered syntax. But used by themselves such incremental forms might achieve sublime immensity at the price of mystery and incomprehensibility. To keep the magnitude a mere "shadow," the poet must also use such devices of elision as dashes, broken syntax, halting caesuras, and asyndeton. These remind the reader that the poetry is a mere trace of a grandeur that has passed. I want to study, then, two sources of sublimity in Hopkins's and Tennyson's poetry: the use of elision to allow sublime meanings to reach us through fragmentation and caesural breaks, as if these meanings are speaking to us from the other side of silence; and the use of parentheses to intimate sublime meanings less obliquely through devices like appositional naming, sundered syntax, and suspended grammar.

Caesura is a mark of both brokenness and fullness, emptiness and possession. In interrupting the forward rhythmical movement of a poem, the caesura transports the reader, not in the sense of carrying him from the beginning of a line to the end (for it is precisely such a lateral movement that the caesura impedes), but in the sense of elevating him, of carrying him outside himself. Whereas caesuras and dashes may be used to dramatize the truth that what is most worth saying cannot be said, such grammatical and rhetorical devices as parenthesis, syntactical sundering, and tmesis may be used to intimate sublime meanings less obliquely. Sometimes the caesural and parenthetical methods, the uses of ellipsis and dilation, can be combined in a single poem like *In Memoriam* or *The Wreck of the Deutschland*, where silencing may follow a leisurely expansive movement as the poem is suddenly propelled toward an unforeseen stoppage or break.

To make the opening vocatives of *The Wreck of the Deutschland* as expansive as possible, Hopkins uses tmesis to sunder pronouns and adjectives from the nouns they modify. The first example, "Thou mastering me / God" (ll. 1–2), is a mere rehearsal for more dramatic sunderings to follow.

> Thou hast bound bones and veins in me, fastened me flesh,
> And after it almost unmade, what with dread,
>   Thy doing:
>
> (1. 5–7)

The sixth line is broken in three by sharp eighth-and-eleventh syllable caesuras and by a slighter pause at the end of the fourth syllable. Not only does Hopkins sunder the verb "unmade" from its direct object "doing," but he also leaves the pronoun "it" without an obvious antecedent. Does "it" modify "flesh," a depersonalized "Thou," or God's acts of binding and fastening? The undoing of God's creation is also a partial unmaking of English grammar. Grammatical sundering is a two-way device. When its primary function is to break the rhythm, as in lines 6 and 7, it inflicts cuts upon the language, like the caesuras that allow meaning to escape through the breaks in a poetic line. But when sundering functions mainly as a figure of dilation or expansion, as in the tmesis of the opening lines, it has the opposite effect of giving God a spacious dwelling place in language.

> Thou mastering me
> God! giver of breath and bread;
> World's strand, sway of the sea;
> Lord of living and dead;
>
> (1. 1–4)

These lordly vocatives, a feature of the appositional or expansive sublime, collapse in the next stanza into word heaps that are barely grammatical. At the beginning of the poem Hopkins produces numerous verbal equivalents for God, without any ability to relate them except as tautologies. Now he falls prey to the opposite disorder.

> Thou knowest the walls, altar and hour and night:
> The swoon of a heart that the sweep and the hurl of thee trod
>   Hard down with a horror of height:
> And the midriff astrain with leaning of, laced with fire of stress.
>
> (2. 5–8)

As Hopkins elides the narrative of his own fearful depression, his grammar collapses into metonymic fragments. All that the frantic commas and coordinate conjunctions can link is a disarray of "walls, altar and hour and night" (l. 5). The polysyndeton lays Hopkins low with a series of hammer blows. Unless the noun "stress" is meant to function as an object of both prepositions in line 8, God is precisely an absence—precisely what Hopkins omits after the preposition in the unfinished phrase "with leaning of." As the source of violence, God is best evoked as a fearful ellipsis. It is as though the victim of such actions has lost the power to name the awesome agent of his own destruction. As if he were suffering from a form of aphasia, the distemper Roman Jakobson calls "similarity-disorder," Hopkins gives exaggerated importance to sundered prepositions that he heaps up at the head of successive lines:

> The frown of his face
> Before me, the hurtle of hell
> Behind, where, where was a, where was a place?
>
> (3. 1–3)

By stammering over the adverb and copula in line 3, like a stuck record, Hopkins dramatizes the difficulty he has in using name words. He seems to stutter over the triple "where" and the repeated "was" in a desperate effort to summon up the forgotten word for "place." He cannot remember nouns, though in the opening apostrophe, where synonyms for God multiply at an alarming rate, he seemed capable of producing nothing else.

To overcome these verbal disorders, Hopkins must poise himself like a carrier pigeon and hurl himself into the void, in the hope that his fling of the heart will carry him to "the heart of the Host." Like any performative use of words, the hurtling outward is an act of faith, fraught with risk. Hopkins hopes that "wings that spell" will be potent with the charm of the felicitous word, with a power to fan a flame into life where there is no antecedent warmth. If the wings spell truly, they will be answered by a God who is "carrier-witted," like a homing pigeon.

> My heart, but you were dovewinged, I can tell,
>   Carrier-witted, I am bold to boast,
> To flash from the flame to the flame then, tower from the grace to
>   the grace.
>
> (3. 6–8)

Is "My heart" an invocation to "the heart of the Host" (l. 5)? Is it a boast that the celebrant now finds the story of his own heart inscribed

on God's heart? Or is "My heart" in apposition to the human heart
that is said to be flung out in the preceding line? If so, the poet is
boasting of the efficacy of his own dovewinged rite of passing birdlike
from flame to flame. Though it is just as congruous, and less arrogant
perhaps, to ascribe the passion of "carrier-wit" to God, the enfolding
of flame in flame is so complete that the mutual flashing is rightly
celebrated as a mighty towering up, a sublime elation, of both God
and his celebrant.

A moment later, however, we are shocked to find Hopkins reduced
to a mere blank space and dash.

> I am soft sift
> In an hourglass—at the wall
> Fast, but mined with a motion, a drift,
>
> (4. 1–3)

As the "soft sift" of time is said to run down "In an hourglass," so
Hopkins's life is allowed to leak vaguely away through the empty space
created by the dash at the center of the second line. Only in some
counterprinciple, which he tries desperately to name in the last line
of this stanza, can entropy be arrested. If God remains sublime at
such moments, it is because He is a mise-en-abîme, an abyss, who
throws each celebrant into an endless downward spiral or descent.
Instead of saying "credo ut intelligam," Hopkins, like Dante, says that
love of God must wait upon knowledge of God. "I greet him the days
I meet him, and bless when I understand" (5. 8). Unfortunately, such
a benediction may be long deferred. For to understand God is to
"stand under" a being who has just been described as standing "under
the world's splendour and wonder" (5. 6). To understand the very
principle of "standing under" is to grow dizzy with the prospect of
making an infinite descent.

Once released into history, the Word of God spills over the divide
between stanzas 6 and 7, in the poem's first runover between stanzas:

> ...only the heart, being hard at bay,
>
> Is out with it!
>
> (7. 8, 8. 1)

The soul that had been drained and emptied of meaning can be filled
to overflowing in the instant of time it takes to insert the phrase "in a
flash" between the noun "brim" and its detached suffix "full." Hopkins
does not merely mention the idea of fullness: he uses the trope
tmesis— "Brim, in a flash, full!" (8. 6)—to give the idea grammatical

force in his poem. And yet near-antonyms like "winter" and warmth—
"Thou art lightning and love, I found it, a winter and warm" (9.
6)—are so paradoxical as to cancel each other out. In baring a lethal
syllable, "kill," within his "lingering-out swéet skíll" (10.6), God even
reverses the unpacking of the saving injunction "spare" contained
inside the leaden echo's repeated "despair" in "St. Winefred's Well."
Such contradictory invocations ensure that God is still "Beyond saying"
and "past telling of tongue" (9. 5). Even in naming, Hopkins's figures
conspire *not* to name, and so leave God, in his exalted "three-numberèd
form" (9. 2), as sublimely indescribable as ever.

   In the first part of the poem Hopkins says he cannot bless God until
he understands him. But if God is a mere elided Word, if he is the
meaning that transpires (and possibly expires) between the poem's
end-line dashes and caesuras, can Hopkins ever hope to understand
God? In part 2 Hopkins finds that he has still to be tutored by
believers like the nun, whose faith is inclusive enough to embrace
what she can never understand. In learning the right names for her
destroyer, the nun can christen her "wild-worst / Best" (24. 8–9) and
learn to approach what Carlyle would call a "fearful indescribability,"
beyond saying and "past telling of tongue."

   In struggling to apprehend the struggle of the nun to understand a
God who seems also to be her enemy, Hopkins is now writing at two
removes from God. His double removal reaches a climax in stanza 28,
where yawning ellipses break discourse apart, crowding it with unsaid
thoughts, which are censored or amended before they can be uttered.
Language falters, halts, then stops altogether, reduced to fragments
by questions and dashes and by a daring use of aposiopesis, the
rhetorical device of breaking off in the middle of a sentence, as if
from some deep reluctance to proceed.

> But how shall I...make me room there:
> Reach me a...Fancy, come faster—
> Strike you the sight of it? look at it loom there,
> Thing that she...there then! the Master,
> *Ipse*, the only one, Christ, King, Head:
>
> (28. 1–5)

Hopkins, in using the Latin intensive "*Ipse*," strains to speak with
the gift of tongues granted at Pentecost, which both repairs and
confirms Babel's confusion of many languages. But all he can do is
gesture in a desperate reversion to ostensive definition. First he must
verify he is not hallucinating: "look at it loom there, / Thing that she
is." Before he can interpret that awesome indescribability, he must fix

it through acts of repeated naming: "the Master, / *Ipse*, the only one, Christ, King, Head." All names collapse into a single name, as six verbal equivalents press language back into one fearful synonym.

Five lines of poetry concentrate two extremes of discourse. First, the language falls apart into agrammatical fragments, loosely bound by spatial and temporal connectives like "there," "look at it," "then." Such language, a version of "similarity-disorder," is marked by a loss of the all-important nouns and subject words. A moment later the disappearance of deictics like the twice-repeated "there" and the multiplication of nouns that were formerly missing, produce the opposite distemper, a species of Jakobson's "contiguity-disorder." The needle sticks in the groove again, and all Hopkins can do is stammer out six different names for the same thing.

The nun's dying injunction, "O Christ, . . . come quickly" (24. 7), strikes Hopkins as majestic and sublime precisely because it leaves unsaid more than it says: "What did she mean?" (25. 1). What are the unspoken words behind the spoken ones? Hopkins petitions the Holy Spirit, "the arch and original Breath" (25. 2), to attune him to the silent meanings. Sublime truths can be intimated only through words like "lord," which boldly compress opposite tones and meanings: "Do, deal, lord it with living and dead" (28. 7); and through puns that keep the multiple meanings vibrant, as in the nun's rite of "wording" the shipwreck the work of the Word (29. 6). The wreck of the ship, like the disaster of Babel, is also the wreckage or ruin of words, which can no longer express the primal Word behind the bruit of contending words. "Word" means literal word, but also Logos, participatory sign, a creation, and an act of felicitous naming. One source of sublimity is the necessary doubleness of God's "double-naturèd name" (34. 2). He authorizes both unity and diversity. As a unitary presence that expresses itself only in multiple words, God's name both *can* and *cannot* be uttered. Any recovery of primal unity is a reversal of dispersion in an attempt to recover an undifferentiated name, a sublime word, that precedes the disaster of Babel and that contains all language in itself. But how can the poet divide the Word into words without also annihilating the Word? Once a primal language has been lost, how can the process of desynonymizing be reversed?

As master of the tides in stanza 32, God is said to be contradictory things. He is the total plenitude of the sea, but also the point of entry into it, the wharf, and the containing wall itself. He is not only water in motion but also the principle that stays all motion: He is "Ground of being, and granite of it"(32. 6). Metonymies of seawalls and wharves, of curbs and sides that are also said to be the full girth and expanse of what is curbed and contained, remind us that to stand under God is to be God, because God himself is the grounding principle, the means of "standing under." As an elusive surd of mercy, a power we are usually deaf to (*surdus*), God absurdly "outrides" all we seem justified in saying about him. It seems logically absurd to be at once "The all of water" (33. 2), the author of destruction, and the "ark" that safely rides the water. But God is intelligible in no other terms. His absurdities make sense only to the loving "listener," "the lingerer" (33. 3) who attunes his ear to silent meanings. To hear God is to descend to the "underthought," to the subliminal and repressed meanings, too subterranean, too low and deathlike, for speech to fathom. To find Christ we must linger with Hopkins over the dashes and caesuras, the empty spaces in language, listening there for the words that are otherwise inaudible.

Even when typography and word order are briefly allowed to mirror the containment of Christ as a middle term, framed on both sides by the other persons of the Trinity—"Mid-numberèd He in three of the thunder-throne!" (34. 5), nothing can mute the force of Hopkins's realization that God is still "past all / Grasp God" (32. 6–7). In contrast to the mighty storm of a risen giant, who strides prodigiously through history, riding time like a river, Christ's stealthy reentry into the poem, like a thief in the night, may be signaled by nothing more remarkable than "the uttermost mark" of punctuation, the dash at the middle of line 6 of stanza 33. Even in the final line, where six jostling possessives threaten to crowd God out of the poem—"Our hearts' charity's hearth's fire, our thoughts' chivalry's throng's Lord" (35. 8), God reenters only through "the uttermost mark," which is not here, as in stanza 33, a gaping dash, but literally the last word of the poem.

In the end, such a self-concealing God must be petitioned through a mediator, the drowned nun, who is invoked as a "genius of the shore," like the drowned Lycidas. But no mediator allows Hopkins to forget that all names for God are names we take in vain. They are false names, inscribed in poetry only as solecisms, oxymorons, paradoxes, or antinomies. Only in moments of extremity, of emptiness past prayer or communion, in the silence of a prison, or when penitents are drawing their last breath, can God make his long-delayed entry.

> A vein for the visiting of the past-prayer, pent in prison,
> The-last-breath penitent spirits—the uttermost mark
> Our passion-plungèd giant risen, . . .
>
> (33. 5–7)

"The uttermost mark" is literally the dash that precedes the phrase— the mark of ellipsis and caesura. It is the place of fracture, where life breaks apart after being all but exhaled through the hyphens that break apart the monosyllables in the compound phrase, "The-last-breath penitent spirits." God lives in that break; he comes to life in it, even as he came to life from a tomb. Only in extremis, at the brink or edge, in the very site of fracture or breakup, can God's presence be found.

Though the overthought of Hopkins's poems is the flow of all particular words back to a primal Word or Logos, its underthought is often a countermovement of fragmentation and collapse. The moment of reversal, where appositional naming gives way to an anarchy of elision and of sundered things in throngs, is captured most awesomely in "Spelt from Sibyl's Leaves." At first it seems that nothing could be more expansively appositional than the sonnet's opening lines. Assonance and alliteration bind together the semantically equivalent adjectives, making them all "equal," as Hopkins says, all predictably "attuneable" to the delayed subject, "Evening."

> Earnest, earthless, equal, attuneable, | vaulty, voluminous, . . .
> stupendous
> Evening
>
> (ll. 1–2)

But two oddities alert us to subtle differences between this use of sublime naming and the spacious apostrophes to Christ at the opening of *The Wreck of the Deutschland.* There is an ominous double pause after "attuneable," which is marked by an extra-stress sign, and after the adjective "voluminous," which is followed by triple dots. In the absence of a noun to which the adjectives can attach themselves, the first line also threatens to collapse into "word-heaps." In straining to be expansively appositional, the godlike namer has forgotten for a moment how to name. Even in filling the first line with no fewer than seven adjectives, two of them polysyllabic, Hopkins seems to be subsiding involuntarily into an abyss of darkness. It is as though a host of unnamed attributes has been drained away through the caesuras and triple dots, like stars that have just disappeared down a black hole.

Instead of using tmesis to load every rift with ore, proclaiming the plenitude and bounty of the power that is named, Hopkins contrives to have the interpolated elements collapse or fall in upon themselves.

> Evening strains to be time's vast, | womb-of-all, home-of-all,
> hearse-of-all night.
>
> (l. 2)

The grammatical sundering of "time's" and "night" evokes an impression of magnitude. But the swift transit from womb to home to hearse enacts the rapid expansion and quick collapse of a whole universe. When the suspended referent is finally supplied in the noun "night," it simply flaunts the power of the hearse to swallow up not only the three parts of the compound in which it appears, but also the whole triad of compounds, including the womb and the home, of which it forms the final, all-devouring element.

Any attempt to write expansively and comprehensibly about the Word beyond the words, about an undifferentiated unit of equivalence that contains everything in itself, is a sublime but futile task, for the beginning of human language is diacritical. But the beginning of theology is the unity of God and the Word, so human words about the divine Word have to use differentiation to speak of its logical opposite, unity. Even in describing God, as J. Hillis Miller has shown (1985, 261–62), Hopkins uses words of division, marking, striking, cutting, to play variations on various kinds of sundering that the Word itself is meant to repair in a reversing flow of all sustaining difference, all pied beauty, back again to God. The literal meaning of such words often becomes an exact antonym of their figurative application. What cannot be compassed by concrete names, however, may be intimated obliquely as Hopkins pursues the opposite tack of trying to contract language to the vanishing point. God becomes identical with whatever disappears between the caesuras and ellipses of Hopkins's prayerful efforts to say what is not strictly sayable.

In Tennyson's most sublime poetry, as in Hopkins's, it is possible to find in each dash or elision a separate excitement. In section 95 of *In Memoriam*, for example, even before meanings seem to be elided, the strongly marked caesuras at the end of lines and clauses prepare for a contraction and silencing of thought.

> For underfoot the herb was dry;
> And genial warmth; and o'er the sky
> The silvery haze of summer drawn;

> (ll. 2–4)

Grammatical units simultaneously attach to and separate from the units that precede. Syntactical sundering makes the "genial warmth" of the middle clauses more mysteriously pervasive than the predictable result of a known cause—dry ground—would have been. The hint of some logic of reserve, some withholding principle behind the spacious unfolding of short grammatical units, is given in the last word of this quatrain, in the past participle "drawn" (l. 4). Is the silver haze of summer "drawn" over the nighttime sky, as a kind of protective canopy or arch? Or is the silver haze momentarily drawn back, as a curtain? Are we being shown something? Or is something being concealed?

The emphatic parataxis at the opening of the second quatrain, "And calm that let the tapers burn / Unwavering" (ll. 5–6), strains to join a clause that otherwise struggles to free itself of any grammatical bonds. The matching syntactical units couple the clause to the phrase, "And genial warmth," in the first quatrain. But as we have just seen, the status of even that phrase is curiously ambiguous. Meanings seem about to escape through the notoriously open "And"s as well as through the strong fourth-syllable caesura after "Unwavering" in line 6 and the emphatic breaks at the end of both that line and the next one.

> ...not a cricket chirred;
> The brook alone far-off was heard,
> And on the board the fluttering urn.
>
> (ll. 6–8)

What is not heard, the silent meanings, seems more potent than anything the mourner does hear. He passes from the silence of the crickets' *not* chirping, across the silence of the emphatic caesura and line break, to the distant sound of the brook, and then to the even less audible motions of the| flickering flame in an urn. The synesthesia and near-catachresis of hearing moving fire, which is usually seen or felt but seldom heard, evokes a presence like the fire that stirs about the woman in Yeats's poem "The Folly of Being Comforted." Remote sounds, nonsounds, and eerie sounds of mere moving flame intimate the elusiveness of what Tennyson strains hardest to hear. Though line 8—"And on the board the fluttering urn"—makes most sense if an ellipsis of the passive verb "was heard" is assumed after "urn," it is also intelligible as a discrete unit of meaning setting in place one more stage property before the drama begins. This double possibility heightens the strangeness and leaves the meanings poised and hovering, on the quiver, as Hopkins would say. Some neglected potency of language seems always on the point of escaping us, slipping away through one of the emphatic caesuras or loosely coupling "And"s.

There is a recurrent oddity in the language. We never seem to be hearing quite what we expect to hear. The conjunction of bats and fragrant skies is strange enough in itself, but it is not nearly so strange as the slight jarring effects created by minor switches in word order.

> And bats went round in fragrant skies,
> And wheeled or lit the filmy shapes
> That haunt the dusk, with ermine capes
> And woolly breasts and beaded eyes;
>
> (ll. 9–12)

We expect "wheeled" and "lit" to be two further predicates in apposition to "went round." But bats, unlike fireflies, cannot really light up the dusk. We can preserve the sense only by registering the hyperbaton that wrenches words out of their normal order. "The filmy shapes" that act as grammatical subject of the second and third verbs no doubt include bats, but they are more comprehensive. To call them bats is to delimit their potency and mystery. Their grotesque or sublime identity is precisely what slips through the hole at the center of the phrases that are overdetermined at one terminal—"filmy," "woolly-breasted," "beady-eyed"—and notoriously underdetermined at the other terminal: they are mere "shapes" that, though ermine in color, have "capes" instead of more identifiable wing patterns or markings.

The poet reads Hallam's letters in silence and enacts his private commemorations in silence. Even when the silence is broken by words, these words are said to be "silent-speaking" (l. 26). The words in the letters do speak, despite their muteness, perhaps because Tennyson pronounces them subvocally. And they also speak in other ways. Tennyson can imagine the dead Hallam pronouncing the words himself. And the unheard words behind the words—the "dumb cry" of love "defying change" (l. 27)—are audible to a mourner who knows how to interpret them. His victory over silence and death takes place in such subtle and seemingly peripheral ways as the shift from finite verbs to timeless infinitives.

> ...and strangely spoke
> The faith, the vigour, bold to dwell...
>
> (ll. 28–29)

> And keen through wordy snares to track
> Suggestion to her inmost cell.
>
> (ll. 31–32)

The faith and vigor are achievements of the mourner's own imagination, as it utters the dumb or unspeakable words whose only residue can be traced in the spacious runover that spans the divide between the seventh and eighth stanzas, for example, or in repeated modulations from past-tense verbs like "spoke" and "broke" into tenseless infinitives like "to dwell" and "to track."

The two-way flow of the mourner's communing with Hallam is dramatized by chiasmus, the trope of reversing motion.

> And all at once it seemed at last
> The living soul was flashed on mine,
>
> And mine in this was wound,
>
> (ll. 35–37)

But the mourner's phrase, "that which I became" (1. 48), like his tautology, "came on that which is" (1. 39), is a nonnaming locution for the unspeakable or inexpressible. The failure of words to signify such a referent is the explicit admission of stanza 12, where the body of language, "Vague" and "matter-moulded" (ll. 45–46), is no longer a living body but a corpse. At the moment of rupture, when the trance is canceled and the mourner is "stricken through with doubt" (1. 44), Tennyson fears that the flashing of Hallam's soul on his is too intermittent and fitful to be truly luminous.

The repetition of the lines describing the knolls, the repose of the white kine, and the gesture of the trees as they embrace the field (ll. 14–16, 50–52), has the same function as stage directions in a play. It sets the stage for a second act, for an experience of sublime meanings that, in bridging the divide between three successive quatrains, prove far more expansive and appositional than the elliptical meanings first presented. The three climactic quatrains become more and more energetic, in imitation of a storm that slowly builds, gathers force incrementally, comes to a crisis of tempestuous action, surprises us with an astonishing announcement at the climax, then slowly subsides into the silence of "boundless day."

> And sucked from out the distant gloom
>   A breeze began to tremble o'er
>   The large leaves of the sycamore,
> And fluctuate all the still perfume,
>
> And gathering freshlier overhead,
>   Rocked the full-foliaged elms, and swung
>   The heavy-folded rose, and flung
> The lilies to and fro, and said
>
> "The dawn, the dawn," and died away;
>   And East and West, without a breath,
>   Mixt their dim lights, like life and death,
> To broaden into boundless day.
>
>   (ll. 53–64)

The sublime marvel of a talking breeze, which announces theatrically, "The dawn, the dawn," is modeled on God's words in Genesis: "'Let there be light,' and there was light." No sooner has the announcement of dawn been made than the dawn appears. Nature seems as totally responsive to this speaking voice as it is to God's creative fiat in Genesis. The breeze has started rocking the full-foliaged elm trees and has already rocked the rose and flung the lilies before we recognize that this is no ordinary breeze or hurricane. It has even started talking before we register its full marvel and mystery. In the last quatrain Tennyson practices verbal sleight of hand by using the unobtrusive simile "like life and death"(l. 63) to make an argument for the immortality of the soul before we realize that any argument is being made. Until we reread the lines to register precisely what has been said, the most important meanings tend to remain subliminal, at the periphery of consciousness.

The sublimity is partly a matter of concentrated repetition. There are two kinds of trees—large-leaved sycamores and full-foliaged elms. And there are two varieties of flowers, the heavy-folded roses and the slender lilies. The pairing extends to oppositions of East and West, sunset and dawn, life and death, in the last quatrain. The short, monosyllabic verbs are the syntactic staples or rivets, securely joining the animated objects in nature to the supernatural breeze. With each new stroke, the hammering polysyndeton of the paratactic sentence structure drives the rivets home: "And fluctuate," "And gathering," "and swung," "and flung," "and said," "and died away," "And . . . mixt." These concentrated verbs combine with the expansive inventory of paired nouns to create simultaneous impressions of the bounded and the boundless.

A Victorian or modern reader may be downright embarrassed by the archaic belief in whispering spirits or talking breezes. To allay that distrust in section 86 of *In Memoriam*, Tennyson half conceals what he does. Lyric apostrophe has been used for seven lines before the use of optative verbs in lines 8 and 9 requires us to construe the first two quatrains as a rapt invocation to the "air." Like the verbal cunning in section 95, which uses an unobtrusive simile to introduce the notion of immortality, the potent vocatives have already been suspending any embarrassed disbelief for almost two quatrains before we fully register what is happening. The efficacy of invoking ambrosial air is proved by the pervasive motion of the lines. The air's power of animation is brought to life by the spacious runovers, as it rolls inexorably over the ends of lines, over "brake and bloom / And meadow," and even over the divide between stanzas. We are not allowed to pause for breath at the end of the first quatrain, because the participle "breathing" is still awaiting grammatical completion in a direct object, "The round of space," at the head of the next stanza.

The greatest glory, we are told in one of Tennyson's most sublime poems, "The Holy Grail," is a nakedness, a destitution of the majesty God underwent when he "made himself / Naked of glory for His mortal change" (ll. 447–48). Can language and objects be made into participatory signs, like the holy elements into which Galahad actually sees the fiery child fight for entry? Or is all incarnation of God a form of idolatry? If the only godhead that can smite itself into bread is a godhead already divested of its full glory, how can language signify anything more than a shadow of a shadow? And yet is this double divestiture, this twofold nakedness, not what makes the sublime subject sublime, a mere stripped replica of what cannot, after all, be seen in its full radiance and glory?

Until Galahad's crossing is completed, its outcome is in doubt. As if he were uncertain about what he is seeing, Percivale keeps offering double explanations:

> And o'er his head the Holy Vessel hung
> Clothed in white samite or a luminous cloud.
> And with exceeding swiftness ran the boat,
> If boat it were—I saw not whence it came.
>
> ("The Holy Grail," ll. 512–15)

Being robed in "white samite" seems to justify the knight's faith in losing himself to find himself. But the correlative conjunction "or" admits a second possibility. The robe of "white samite" may be nothing but a luminous cloud, itself an oxymoron, since most clouds, like most veils, are not luminous. No sooner has Percivale seen a boat on which Galahad seems to be borne away "with exceeding swiftness" than he concedes the boat may be his own invention: "If boat it were—I saw not whence it came."

The more the heavens seem to open to Percivale, the more they also close. Oxymoron returns in the conjunction of "blazed again" and "Roaring" (ll. 516–17), where it appears as if fire or lightning rather than thunder were the source of sound. Opening even becomes a disguised form of closure when the appearance of Galahad to Percivale—"I saw him" (l. 517)—is likened at once to the appearance of "a silver star." Is it just a star he sees, or the infinitely receding figure of the knight? The language breaks apart with the emphatic end-line dash after "star," the second use of a dash in three lines. So uncertain is Percivale about the content of his vision that he poses two more alternatives, loosely linked by the correlative conjunction "or," and ends the broken sentence not with the expected affirmation, but with a question.

> And had he set the sail, or had the boat
> Become a living creature clad with wings?
>
> (ll. 518–19)

The true referent seems to have slipped through the dash after "star" (l. 517). As dashes begin to punctuate—and puncture—Percivale's vision, the more chance there is for Galahad to exit prematurely, disappearing through one of the holes that perforate the poem.

The "Holy Vessel" is twice asserted to hang above Galahad's head (ll. 512, 520). But how can Percivale be sure, since Galahad is very indistinctly seen at this point? Also, if Galahad is receding from view "with exceeding swiftness," how can Percivale keep him in focus? If the white samite could be just a cloud, and the boat an optical illusion, who is to say whether that other "Vessel," the Holy Grail, is not just the red-rose sparkle of some auroral display? Even at the moment Percivale says "the veil [has] been withdrawn" (l. 522), it may actually be closing. For what strikes both Percivale and the reader is the minuteness of the vision. Though the goal of all the saints, the gateways are no bigger than "a glory like one pearl" (l. 527). Suspended syntax keeps the outcome of vision in doubt. The climactic action of the city's "striking" from the sea is sundered from its antecedent by two and a half lines of expansive apposition, which allows the distant object to swell in imagination, as Galahad tries to confer on the city the kind of aggrandizement that is worthy only of sublime subjects.

> ...and straight beyond the star
> I saw the spiritual city and all her spires
> And gateways in a glory like one pearl—
> No larger, though the goal of all the saints—
> Strike from the sea;
>
> (ll. 525–29)

Offsetting the spacious sundering of the direct object "city" from its infinitive, "Strike," a countermovement of contraction is diminishing the city to one small object, a single pearl. Dashes at the ends of successive lines allow more meaning to escape than is contained, and what is said concentrates rather than diffuses the sense. Expansion and contraction go on simultaneously, as if life were pumped into the vision by some giant bellows, filling a bell jar with air before slowly exhausting it of content.

Though crises of faith and knowing in both poets precipitate crises of representation, the difference between Tennyson's interesting uncertainties and Hopkins's incomprehensible certainties is the difference, it seems, between a skeptic's exclusive use of "either-or" and a believer's inclusive use of "both-and." Certitude converts the "either-or" of mere logical understanding into an incomprehensible "both-and," which is no less certain for being (and remaining) a mystery.

Because Percivale cannot stand the strain of double vision, his discourse falls apart into logical contradiction and uncertainty. The spiritual city may be just a mirage, or a ruin, like the decayed Timbuctoo of Tennyson's Cambridge Prize poem. For Tennyson there is no escape from antinomy and paralogism, because there is no confident and sustained transformation of certainty into certitude. But at his most exuberant and self-assured, Hopkins can sustain such a change, because like his nun's faith in *The Wreck of the Deutschland*, his certitude is capacious enough to include apparent contradictions that he cannot, in a less believing mood, hope to understand.

Hopkins's deep reserves of skepticism and doubt have sometimes been ascribed to the influence of J. H. Newman. Harold L. Weatherby argues that both Hopkins and Newman sacrifice knowledge to intuition and unite "the popular scepticism and subjectivism of the age with a rigorous adherence to Catholic dogma." By "popular scepticism" Weatherby means epistemological skepticism—an apprehension of "the existing individual as the senses apprehend him" rather than an apprehension of "the notion of the individual which the intellect abstracts" (1975, 74–75). By detaching the dogma from the skeptical epistemology, however, such an emphasis can easily be reversed. When we compare Hopkins's "incomprehensible certainties" with Tennyson's interesting uncertainties, for example, we can better appreciate the efforts of both Hopkins and Newman (and even of a less dogmatic thinker like Browning) to make faith intelligible—an "incomprehensible certainty," as Hopkins calls it, rather than a mere uncertainty.

The mourner in *In Memoriam* stretches "lame hands of faith" (55. 17): he gropes for knowledge he can clutch and grasp with his senses. Any truth that he cannot grasp empirically is imperfect knowledge, an "interesting uncertainty." At times Browning seems to speak of faith as objectively uncertain knowledge: "You must mix some uncertainty / With faith," his speaker says in "Easter-Day," "if you would have faith be" (ll. 71–72). But when these lines are examined in context, we see that by "uncertainty" Browning does not mean the mere absence of knowing resulting from an incomplete induction or defective demonstration. A truth that is not accessible to the empirical understanding may be entertained instead as a highly probable explanation rather than as a proof that is necessary or certain. The difficult word here is "probable," which has a different meaning in moral and theological reasoning than it has in statistics.

An important but neglected source of Browning's own belief in faith as a faculty not inferior to reason, but merely different, is the cogent analysis of moral, as opposed to mathematical, reasoning found in a book extensively annotated by the poet's father: the 1816 edition of Levi Hedge's *Elements of Logick*. Offering a new definition of "probable" that helps digest the logic of the "incomprehensible certainties" defended by religious apologists like Hopkins, Hedge insists that "the epithet *probable*, as applied by logicians to the evidence of moral reasoning, has a technical meaning, altogether different from its usual signification. In common discourse, it is applied to evidence which does not command full assent; but in logical discussions, it has a more comprehensive meaning, not only including every *subordinate* degree of moral evidence, but also the *highest*. In this latter sense, it is not to be considered as implying any *deficiency* of proof, but as contradistinguishing one species of proof from another;—not as opposed to what is certain, but to what may be demonstrated after the manner of mathematicians; —not as denoting *degree* of evidence, but the *nature* of it" (Hedge 1816, 89–90). In other words, "probability" in religious discourse does not mean the essentially "uncertain," as it does in statistics, but denotes something logically distinct, something even "incomprehensibly certain." Such is the special meaning of "probability" developed by Joseph Butler in his *Analogy of Religion*, and to which both Hedge in his *Logick* and Newman in his Oxford sermons and *Essay on the Development of Christian Doctrine* are significantly indebted.

Hopkins's "incomprehensible certainties" in *The Wreck of the Deutschland* are not an inferior form of knowledge, but the rapturous and exacting thought of a religious mind. His reasoning is synthetic, rather than analytic, and is based on induction, analogy, and the testimony of the nun. His faith in "incomprehensible certainties" seems to owe a good deal to Aristotle's analysis of moral reasoning in the *Ethics*. If Hopkins did not encounter the idea directly in Aristotle, he would certainly have been familiar with a theological version of the idea in Newman's writings. We know Hopkins read Newman's *Difficulties of Anglicans* and asked Newman for permission to write a "comment" on the *Grammar of Assent* (Weatherby 1975, 77, 153). There is also evidence that Hopkins read the *Apologia*, in which Newman generously acknowledges the seminal influence upon his thinking of Butler's doctrine of probability. A pervasive defense of probability can be found in Newman's Oxford sermons, where faith is said to operate with probability, not facts, and probability is to fact what the soul is to the body. Though Newman's analysis of the subject is complex, his demonstration that faith is the reasoning of a divinely enlightened rather than a weak mind offers the best explanation I know of Hopkins's difficult oxymoron, an "incomprehensible certainty."

It is fashionable today to portray Hopkins as a deeply troubled poet, tortured at the center of his faith. But even in his darkest sonnets, where God is presented as an enemy or an absence rather than a friend, Hopkins never thinks of God as a mere vacancy or void. It is true that the harder Hopkins tries to explain the "incomprehensible certainties" of his faith, the less comprehensible they often seem. The moment he tries to collapse all words back into a single word or Logos, in a reversal of the process Coleridge calls "desynonymization," the more unnameable the supreme Name becomes. But because Hopkins sometimes speaks as if God is a Word or Logos who has created people and the world as semantic objects to refer to himself, this Word that contains all other words inside itself is never, for Hopkins, an "interesting uncertainty." Hopkins himself cannot speak the undifferentiated Word, but he knows it exists. He speaks by means of this Word, and if he could speak the Word itself he would speak nothing else.

PART TWO

Mystery and Identity:
Is Self-Creation Possible?

One would think that if the self knew anything, it would know itself. But in nineteenth-century thought self-identity presents a twofold mystery. How is it possible to preserve a recognizable identity through time? And how, given the deep discontinuities, can we ever hope to be architects of our own humanity and values? The dominant axiom of nineteenth-century thought, the evolutionary model of *continuous* change, provides a model for abiding identity. Darwinian evolution, however, substitutes for doctrines of progressive change the idea of random or nonprogressive change. Randomness fragments and disrupts the continuum: a change that is truly random produces an item that does not seem continuous with any item in the series that precedes it. When flux in the world becomes flux in the self, then self-identity dissolves, as it does for Pater in his conclusion to *Studies in the History of the Renaissance*. Pater's model of discontinuous change in the individual is also Hume's model of a theater in which several perceptions successively make their appearance, pass, repass, then glide away like phantoms on a stage. The logical culmination of this growing sense of instability is F. H. Bradley's *Appearance and Reality*, a metaphysical nightmare that turns Hume's theater of phantoms into a theater of the absurd.

To explain how an object can retain a recognizable identity, Locke posits the existence of a substance and its qualities. But the plot of British empiricism has an unforeseen outcome: when Berkeley and Hume make all qualities secondary qualities, substance itself is shown to be a fiction. Without a substance in which changing properties can inhere, how is identity over time to be maintained? When does change occur in the same person, and when is a person's identity so eroded that we have to substitute a second identity for the first, or the notion of a split personality? Sometimes the changes in characters in prose fiction seem so discontinuous that we are tempted to invoke some psychological equivalent of the theory of cataclysm or special creation in geology. In other words, we are encouraged to remake rather than reinterpret a character. Is the demented exorcist who throttles Miles to death at the end of *The Turn of the Screw*, for example, the same governess admired by Douglas in the introductory frame? At other times a less radical procedure seems called for: Mr. Arabin in *Barchester Towers* has merely to be reinterpreted by Eleanor as she unmasks the integrity concealed by his reserve. Even when a principle rather than a character seems to diverge from an earlier version of itself, like nineteenth-century Catholic doctrine, J. H. Newman can argue in his *Essay on Development* that the church's doctrines are still the closest continuer of patristic teachings.

Nineteenth-century literature suggests that genuinely to possess an identity is to have the capacity for reflexive self-reference. When Browning's Caliban initiates his discourse as a stammer from the mud, his inability to use the first-person pronoun dramatizes his inability to refer reflexively. People who lack positive moral identity, like Becky Sharp in *Vanity Fair*, may speak of the self in the same way, as a mere empty signifier. Like Sophocles' Oedipus, Franklin Blake in *The Moonstone* is the canonical self-referrer whose reference is nonreflexive. Rachel Verinder assumes that when Franklin Blake insists on seeking the aid of the police to bring the thief to justice he is referring to his own arrest. In fact, Blake is using the word "thief" to refer to himself, but not as a form of reflexive self-reference that would justify his use of the pronoun "I." No "I statement" can be derived from a self-referring statement that is nonreflexive.

A self-reference is reflexive if it refers to itself from inside. And self-reference is always a performative utterance, never constative: it refers to something as having a feature that is bestowed in the very act of referring. Browning's poetry of self-making is full of such self-references. In "Dîs Aliter Visum" the speaker's references to herself from inside a past sequence break apart her discourse, producing the mise-en-abîme of a reference within a reference. The "I" does not fully exist until it is referred to from the inside of an inside, from within a discourse that is framed by another discourse. The more interior the reference, the more the reference may contain a whole Chinese box of containing quotations, each nested within the others.

Three forms of self-reference are possible. If the self-reference is nonreflexive, the speaker may possess a merely primordial intelligence like Browning's Caliban, who can refer to himself in the first person only intermittently. Alternatively, the self-reference of a character may be reflexive but externally generated. Thackeray's inveterate actress Becky Sharp has only a theatrical conception of the self. Any character she possesses is conferred on her by her offstage acting. Authentic self-reference is, by contrast, internally generated. This occurs most memorably in Mrs. Bulstrode's donning a plain black gown to embrace humiliation and redefine her situation ritually before joining her husband in grieving but unreproaching fellowship in *Middlemarch*.

The true egotist is the external self-referrer who can generate no reflexive understanding from inside. Rosamond Vincy is such an egotist, because she is incapable of introspection. But introspection by itself is no guarantee of genuine self-reference. Claude's self-reflexive acts in *Amours de Voyage* are no more internally generated than Lavengro's. Whereas Borrow's Lavengro is always living his life as if he were acting it upon a stage, Claude looks at himself with the detachment of a novelist writing an epistolary fiction. He exists not because he acts, but because he writes about himself as a possible hero in a novel: "Scribo, ergo sum." If Rosamond Vincy has too little introspection to be capable of internal, or reflexive, self-reference, Clough's Claude has too much. Rosamond has no consciousness to expend: Claude has an excess of consciousness, which he expends on the invention of imaginary scenarios rather than on the adventure of living itself.

The self may exist independent of all acts of self-making, or (alternatively) it may be wholly self-made. Each view of the self retains its own residue of mystery. If a free-floating self exists totally apart from any self-enactment, how can we expect to know this fact? Such a self would seem to be as wispy as the prior's notion of the soul in "Fra Lippo Lippi": "Man's soul, and it's a fire, smoke ... no, it's not... / It's ... well, what matters talking, it's the soul" (ll. 184–87). If our identities are wholly self-made, however, does such self-making not annihilate our past, creating deep discontinuity in place of continuous change? The dual claims about the self—that it exists independent of any self-enactment and that it is made or constituted by such an act—are massively and inconclusively debated in the nineteenth century by right- and left-wing Hegelians. The need for affirming simultaneously both of these incompatible views suggests that we have reached the limits of understanding: as in any crisis of representation, bifocal vision reminds us that being a self is a mystery. No one can presume to say precisely *what* it is.

Sometimes Browning's characters treat the self as a salable commodity. The Duke of Ferrara exchanges his name for a dowry, and the Comparini barter Pompilia on the marriage market. Perhaps selfhood is not so much a product of self-making as the property of a body. In *A Soul's Tragedy*, however, Browning dramatizes the reductio ad absurdum of trying to treat the self as a negotiable property, like any other quality of an object. Chiappino insists that his rival Luitolfo is the closest continuer of his own past. The two men not only have exchanged clothes, they have also switched identities and selves, for Chiappino claims that Luitolfo's assassination of the tyrant is the act C himself was born to commit. If C can become L and L can become C not just by switching clothes but by exchanging memories and character traits as well, would C be C or L, and would L be L or C? The puzzle is a result of treating selfhood as a detachable property to be transferred at will, like one's money or one's clothes. In the end, only Luitolfo retains a stable identity: he dies for his radical views, while Chiappino, the temporizer, recovers his memories and character, all those more intrinsic, incommunicable qualities that were properties of C rather than L.

Confessional poetry, lyric, and soliloquy seem designed to promote the worship of a private self. Even a poet who writes dramatic monologues by migrating from one impersonated object to another seems too discontinuous from one moment to the next to bear the weight of positive identity. Such a transmigrating Vishnu, as W. J. Fox calls the young Tennyson (Fox 1831, 77), is a pure, featureless mental receptacle. To assume that an abiding self exists behind the negative identity of the role-player is to turn the self into a spiritual substance. But we cannot preserve the idea of an abiding personal identity by inventing a soul substance for the self. As Locke argues, as soon as we postulate a soul as the principle that gives identity to the self, there is nothing to prevent a skeptic from discarding the soul as irrelevant to the self's actual operation. Moreover, as Locke says, "it must be allowed that if the same consciousness...can be transferred from one thinking substance to another, it will be possible that two thinking substances may make but one person" (1924, 191). Being a self is a mystery, and so is the survival of personal identity over time.

The spectator of geological change in *In Memoriam* apprehends the world from outside rather than from a standpoint within it. He apprehends the world as centerless. But as someone inside the picture Tennyson is also an insignificant speck, someone who might easily never have existed. The self begins to dissolve or experience vertigo the moment it has to entertain these two perspectives simultaneously. How can the "I" apprehend the world as centerless while still being used as a kind of window on that world? How can a particular person at a particular time and in a highly localized place also be a spectator of all existence? Hopkins often expresses a similar sense of puzzlement that he can be this particular person rather than another. "Each mortal thing... / Selves—goes itself; *myself* it speaks and spells, / Crying *Whát I dó is me: for that I came*" ("As kingfishers catch fire," ll. 5, 7–8). How can Hopkins be anything so irreplaceable and different? Irreducibly first-person perspectives must exist, for Hopkins's experience of the world would be incomplete without them. But such perspectives also *cannot* exist, for a God-centered world in which "Christ plays" simultaneously "in ten thousand places" ("As kingfishers catch fire," l. 12), including all subjects on a roughly equal footing, seems to exclude the uniqueness of any first-person standpoint. Merging with others to form a higher unity is all very well, but how can this happen to an individual who is "counter, original, spare, strange" ("Pied Beauty," l. 7) and who has the special property of "selving?" It is as if Hopkins's conviction of being uniquely a self both *must* and *cannot* be sustained.

George Eliot's parable of the pier glass in *Middlemarch* explains why even a world that is conceded to be full of people with unique perspectives on the world is still a centerless world. It is centerless because it contains too many local centers, too many "flattering illusion[s] of... concentric arrangement" (chap. 27). A multitude of centers replicates at a second-order level the proliferation of randomness that is found at a first-order level in the scratches on the pier glass. The world contains us all, but none of us occupies a metaphysically privileged position. Reflecting on this centerless world of many ce1 - ters, each observer is impelled to ask how a self that is unique and irreplaceable can also entertain a view of the world that refuses to give the self's viewpoint any privileged status.

In *Amours de Voyage* only the detachment of Claude's reflective observations holds out the hope of genuine freedom. But at the same time it snatches freedom away. At the very moment Claude's detachment allows him to take life into his own hands, it also makes self-creation impossible. For to be really free, he realizes, he would have to act like God from a standpoint completely outside himself, creating his identity from nothing. But no person, including the adventurous swimmer who forsakes the safety of the shore dwellers, can create himself ex nihilo. To do anything, Claude must already be something: therefore creation out of nothing is impossible. Claude's self-making is doubly limited. He is autonomous neither as a shore dweller nor as a risk taker. The more his self is swallowed up in circumstance, the less autonomy he has to act with. He aspires to the kind of freedom to originate that is enjoyed only by God. But as a pursuer of knowledge, he discovers he is part of a world of political and social intrigue he himself would never have created. Any detachment that seems to offer Claude more control of his life also reveals the ultimate givenness of the world.

The more inclusively characters see life, the more they see it as a determining whole, but the less completely they can then view their own participation in it as an exercise of freedom. Sometimes it seems that the harder Lydgate and Dorothea try to act as free agents in *Middlemarch*, the more the small, hampering, threadlike pressures of circumstance constrict them. Such disclosures of constraint are most acute in *Vanity Fair*. Thackeray's characters can act only from inside the world of their puppet stage, and so they never recognize fully their puppetlike status. Though Becky's internal view sponsors the illusion of her freedom as an actress, it is a theatrical illusion that produces mere hopelessness and despair in the end. *Vanity Fair* combines the allegorical strategies of Bunyan with the moral vision of Samuel Beckett in *Waiting for Godot*. Thackeray's novel presents the forms and semblances of an objective moral order without the expected content. Just as Hardy neutralizes moral judgments by expanding the point of view to cover ways in which the tragedy of Tess can be seen as part of the course of nature, part of the evolutionary scheme, so Thackeray inhibits moral response by taking a comparatively detached perspective, further out than usual. It might be argued that the search for values is itself a value, and almost as good as the values themselves. But moral responses are also blocked because the projection into the point of view of the agents is seriously impeded. In *Vanity Fair* the characters do not really have points of view, because they have no interior life beyond the theatrical offstage performances they give. Our morally reactive attitude to Becky Sharp is as effectively defused by her offstage acting as is our moral judgment of Franklin Blake when we discover he removed the moonstone when under the influence of opium.

After problems and puzzles associated with mysteries of identity are introduced in chapter 6, chapter 7 examines Trollope's and James's methods of estranging the familiar. Though the most enigmatic character in *Barchester Towers* is Trollope's self-effacing narrator, even the mysteries of his identity produce a mere silence of reserve: such mysteries do not proceed from the kind of empty space or void that is found at the center of a role-player like Borrow's Lavengro or Thackeray's Becky Sharp. Confidence in a rationally ordered world is still the narrator's ultimate postulate of faith. A trust that virtue is the highest proof of understanding expresses itself as a judicious, morally enlightened use of double irony, which allows Trollope's narrator or James's Winterbourne in "Daisy Miller" to see all around a complex issue. Only when certain links in the detective fiction's model of the concealed but flawlessly connected causal chain seem willfully removed does Trollope's judicious use of double irony turn into a confused or confusing use of the same technique in James's novella *The Turn of the Screw*. Whereas Trollope sacrifices suspense to irony in order to achieve a single effect, James seems unable to decide whether *The Turn of the Screw* is a ghost story or a study in abnormal psychology.

Chapter 8 explores how mysteries of identity in an inveterate offstage actress like Thackeray's Becky Sharp may darken into the mysteries of a void or empty space at the center of her character. Thackeray's growing skepticism about the power of words to inscribe any stable meanings manifests itself in his corrosive use of double irony. When deployed on a massive scale, the habit of endorsing simultaneously two contradictory codes leads us to doubt whether Thackeray's narrator knows the answers to his own questions. The evasiveness may be part of his defensive strategy, designed to protect him from a paralyzing knowledge of the nothingness of human matters.

Chapter 9 examines a dark principle at the center of existential characters like Borrow's Lavengro and Clough's Claude, who perfect in their repeated experiments with role-playing a version of Keats's dramatic art of negative capability. The generalized asyndeton and dismantling of connectives dramatize the discontinuities that appear between one improvised version of the self and another. Characters who refuse to be artists of their own lives are likely to have inauthentic identities. But a constant rotation of dramatic parts may lead the role-player to conclude that his personality is synonymous with his personae: to be is to playact, and when he stops acting he ceases to exist.

The last two chapters of part 2 show how George Eliot and Robert Browning substitute for a categorical understanding of the self a more existential understanding that discards stereotypes and substitutes performative for rehearsed speech. As Dinah Morris discovers in *Adam Bede*, a prepared sermon may communicate far less effectively than a halting colloquy like the half-conversation, half-prayer she holds with Hetty in prison. Punctuated by silences, the prison conversations are improvised rituals of confession and conversion, examples of spontaneous performative speech as opposed to prescripted uses of speech. A similar rite of baptism, too intimate to be profaned by a disclosure of what has actually been said, takes place in Browning's lyric "By the Fireside," where the secret name pronounced by Leonor is said to give the speaker a new identity: "I am named and known by that moment's feat" (l. 251).

In both Eliot and Browning the transition from constative to performative speech is marked by silence and irony. When some new belief is in the making, the silence that attends it testifies to the birth of secret knowledge. As Robert Frost explains, you do not "want to tell other people about [such secret knowledge] because you cannot prove that you know. You are saying nothing about it till you see; . . . only the outcome can tell" (Frost 1968, 46). Because words like "Look up, Nicholas" (*Middlemarch*, chap. 74) can never hope to describe that ironic double movement of the spirit that allows Eliot's Mrs. Bulstrode to accept shame and simultaneously join her husband in "unreproaching fellowship," she must use her words ironically, as a way of speaking but saying nothing. Browning's silences go just as deep. The endings of "Porphyria's Lover," for example—"And yet God has not said a word!" (l. 60)—and of "The Statue and the Bust"—"*De te, fabula*" (l. 250)—are deeply puzzling because they withhold more meaning than they promise to disclose as concluding words in each poem. Browning the ironist is constantly playing practical jokes and tricks, inviting the reader to become a "Maker-see" by discerning what is there but not seen. The silences function as a whiplash, suggesting that a revelation has taken place in a flash, even when the reader cannot say exactly what it is. Anyone who has read Browning knows what it is for silence to speak. The overpowering sensation in many of Browning's monologues is the feeling of being alone. Andrea's solitude is enforced by the presence of his actively silent wife. If his own repressed meanings are one part speech to three parts silence, Mrs. Bulstrode's most important communications are presented wordlessly: they can be shown but not talked about. A simple ironist like Borrow's Lavengro or Clough's Claude says what he means by *not* meaning what he says. More radical ironists like Browning's Andrea or Eliot's Mrs. Bulstrode find that language has lost all vestige of its innocence: they must learn to speak without actually saying anything.

CHAPTER 6

Making up People: Are Moral Values Invented or Described?

In *Paradise Lost* Satan, the Byronic overreacher, is an antihero in a Christian epic. But when Blake and Byron glorify the antihero by detaching him from his original context, they make him the hero of a different genre. In poems like "The Two Voices" and stories like *Dr. Jekyll and Mr. Hyde*, conflicts between the hero and society become internalized as splits within the individual consciousness itself—hence the origin of the split personality or double. Were there Byronic heroes before Byron invented them? Or split personalities before Dickens, Arnold, and Eliot invented the myth of public and private selves? Is the very idea that people are "made up" one corollary of Keats's doctrine of negative capability, his idea that poetic identity is not a gift but a creation, a work of art each poet fashions for himself?

Inductive science would argue that notions of the self, like concepts in science, are empirical collations. It fosters the view that our ideas of character are wholly a posteriori, wholly dependent on experience. By contrast, a stereotyped conception of character is totally a priori. We know what the overbearing Mrs. Proudie and the self-promoting Mr. Slope are like almost as soon as we meet them. Midway between these two extremes are psychological concepts, like the medieval theory of humors, that shape the mind's received impressions of people by fitting them into familiar categories. There is no uninterpreted or unclassified fact. To qualify as a fact is already to have been shaped by a theory of how the received impression of a person fits into a class. Unlike Kant's forms of space and time, however, such classifications change from one culture or historical period to another. At work within Victorian culture is an impulse to historicize and to integrate the data, making static categories of character more dynamic and atomic theories more holistic.

The problem of assessing character in fiction and poetry is often the problem of determining what self-identity consists in. There are at least three possibilities. A character like Trollope's Mr. Arabin or Austen's Mr. Darcy may have a stable identity that is misinterpreted or only partially understood. The mystery is solved by "rereading" the character. Alternatively, the character may have a wholly negative identity, like Becky Sharp and Lavengro, or else a positive but changing identity, like Dinah Morris and Dorothea Brooke. Becky's theatrical conception of the self confuses acting a dramatic part with being a person. To be is to play a role, and to be offstage is to cease to exist. If a character has a stable but changing identity as Dorothea Brooke does, then an interpreter may have to remake rather than merely "reread" her character. Such is the conception of self favored by Feuerbach and Strauss, two authors George Eliot translated, and by the Personal Idealists Pringle-Pattison and F. C. S. Schiller later in the century. Is Dorothea Brooke the same person in the Finale of *Middlemarch* that she was in the Prelude? The answer is that she both *is* and *is not* the same. An identity is given to her, but something new is also made. Her Wordsworthian harvesting of memories might seem to fall rather low on the modern Saint Theresa's earlier scale of value. And yet something with less corporate unity, like a private capacity to see life steadily, may make us wonder whether the more public unity to be achieved by seeing life whole is the best standard available. Dorothea comes to value steadiness more highly than wholeness and moral invention more highly than the imitation of heroic models.

All moral theory is a mere black-and-white photograph of the richly colored picture that a novel like *Vanity Fair* or *Middlemarch* provides. Becky Sharp treats people as adversaries in a war game. Her strategy of pursue and kill never treats them as value seekers. To reduce people like Miss Pinkerton to the status of physical objects, at which dictionaries may be hurled, is to withdraw from them the moral characteristic ethical behavior is based on. Becky is involved in games and offensives against potential husbands in which adversaries are responded to and manipulated as mere maximizers of utility. A military or a social campaign treats the adversary not as a value-seeking "I," but merely as a robot or machine that knows the rules and tries to maximize its own gains.

George Eliot precipitates a crisis of knowing within utilitarian moral theory by suggesting that the best act may not be the one with the best consequences for the most people. Mrs. Bulstrode's compassionate treatment of her disgraced husband is valuable in its own right and it has beneficial consequences. But sometimes doing the act with the highest compassion score is not the same as maximizing the compassion score of the world. Are Maggie Tulliver's deeds in *The Mill on the Floss*, for example, expected to maximize the goodness accruing to St. Oggs? Or are they only to maximize the goodness of the deeds themselves? Instead of maximizing the goodness for St. Oggs by marrying Stephen, as Dr. Kenn advises, Maggie chooses to maximize the goodness of her action itself.

Most value seekers assume there is some preexisting value in the world to realize. But *Vanity Fair* presents a world in which the only value that exists is being a valuer of value. In the absence of any other values, is the value seeking of Thackeray's narrator, a kind of Victorian Bunyan or Dr. Johnson, not itself a valuable characteristic? If we are committed to a descriptive theory of value, then we might deny the value of this characteristic on the grounds that it is now useless, since it is a mere capacity without a target, like a sign without a referent. Generally, we value some characteristic other than the valuing of value: in a different novel we might value Dobbin's altruism or Amelia's capacity for self-sacrifice. But because these characters are seriously flawed, we are tempted to substitute for their virtues manqué a response to value as such. If anything is valuable, then so is the ability of people like Lady Jane Sheepshanks or Thackeray's narrator to value it.

What is wrong, then, with "making up" or inventing characters and values? Why should imaginations and empathies not range over all possible realities and worlds? George Eliot deplores the practice in *Adam Bede* because a responsive connection to the actual world is felt to be more valuable than mere exaggeration. "Falsehood is so easy, truth so difficult... it is a very hard thing to say the exact truth, even about your own immediate feelings—much harder than to say something fine about them which is *not* the exact truth" (*Adam Bede*, chap. 17). Eliot and so-called realists cannot imagine a range of characters more diverse, surprising, and intricately unified than the unidealized people we find in *Adam Bede*. To "make up" imaginary values and characters, requiring no focusing on actuality, will forsake a valuable organic linkage with the given world. Such a maker would be like the Deists' God, who retired from his creation after setting it in motion. "To make up" values that are wholly imaginary, with no tight linkage to actuality, may also consign the maker to solipsism. The world is too rich to be wholly a product of the novelist's consciousness—too complicated, diverse, and puzzling for George Eliot to have thought it all up. Moreover, if Eliot had merely "invented" or "made up" her characters, she would surely have made them better. These arguments, of course, are in tension. Perhaps flawed and ordinary characters like Reverend Irwine are more complex and interesting than their creator realizes. And perhaps George Eliot has unconsciously made them better than they are. Reality is what we experience as most coherent. Dreams, like monstrous "griffins" we "make up"—"the longer the claws, and the larger the wings, the better" (chap. 17)—are less so.

Borrow's *Lavengro*, which its preface describes as "a dream, partly of study, partly of adventure," raises the possibility that of two intermixed series of events, one coherent and unified, the other fragmentary and unconnected, the first might be called the social actuality and the second the dream. But a dream life can be imagined that is as coherent as reality itself. If the reality of a system of experience consists in its coherence, then it might be possible to present two equally coherent systems of experience, as James seems to do in *The Turn of the Screw*, only one of which could be real. A reader then has no way of knowing which series faithfully describes what is given and which is "invented" or "made up."

George Eliot shows that moral people are better off for having more valuable lives. But is she wrong to limit self-making to moral inventiveness? Doris Lessing complains that "there is a great deal [Eliot] does not understand because she is moral" (1973, 11). This criticism suggests there is no guarantee that Eliot's characters are best off behaving morally. An immoral action by Lydgate, for example, may still exercise his value-seeking capacities. By voting for Bulstrode's candidate against his own better judgment, Lydgate may realize and protect the nonmoral values of his medical research. There are intellectual, aesthetic, and even sexual values as well as moral values, and Eliot may too often assume that a value seeker should focus solely on the latter.

In Kantian ethics the moral law is somehow "made up" by the rational agent. It makes a claim upon him because it stems from his rational nature. At a second level, the moral claim concerns other persons and might be described as a claim the others make. But it does not stem from others at the ground floor. If the moral law stems only from my rational nature, however, do I really want to devote my life to observing a law I myself have invented? If, as Hardy suggests in *Tess of the d'Urbervilles*, "the world is only a psychological phenomenon" (chap. 13), and in accepting nature as a moral norm we are accepting an aspect of ourselves, is it really in our own moral interest to know this? There seems little room for maneuver between the autonomy conferred by a theory of "making up" and the authority conferred by what is objectively grounded or given. To be free is to seek an ungrounded value: to pursue a value that is grounded, or already given in our nature like a program fed into a computer, undercuts our dignity and freedom.

Browning's monologues dramatize this dilemma most consistently. Is the suffering of the damned good because God approves of it in the manner of Johannes's predestinating God or the divine despot worshiped by Caliban? Or does God approve of something because it is good, the way Abt Vogler's God approves creative effort in the musician or St. John's God approves love without a limit? Apparently immoral acts are accepted by Johannes Agricola and Caliban on the ground that justice does not exist as a standard independent of God, but rather is defined and created by God's decrees. Though Browning finds morally offensive the notion that good could have been different had God chosen or approved differently, who is to say that morality, as the censors of adultery in "The Statue and the Bust" conceive it, is the highest value in the universe?

The questions raised about God by Browning's Johannes and Caliban are an apparent bombshell. To assume that God must meet the moral standards he himself has legislated seems to limit his autonomy. But to assume God need not meet them, as Johannes postulates, implies either that the moral standard is independent of God or else that the law he has legislated is somehow imperfect. What theology seeks is not a God who approves of value after the fact. Such a view leaves God devoid of values. Browning prefers a scenario in which God has founded the law but, having done so, is not free to abrogate it. In "Saul," for example, David's God chooses that "love" should be his "ultimate gift" to man (l. 266). Once he has made this choice, there then exists an independent hierarchy of value, with love outranking power and knowledge, that is not subject to God's further choice or control. What is true of Browning's God also seems to be true of each of Browning's moral agents. They can decree the existence of a value, but the character of the value is not "made up," since it is not subject to individual control.

Do we realize values that already exist, or do we "make" new values "up"? Victorian literature provides four different answers to this question. At one extreme, religious poets like Christina Rossetti and G. M. Hopkins never doubt that God's values *do* exist: but like the psalmist they often find these values totally independent of the worshiper's own understanding and attitudes. At the opposite extreme are writers like Borrow and Clough, who make both the *character* and the *existence* of values depend on Lavengro's choice of roles or on Claude's experiments in self-making. A third, less radical possibility is represented by Tennyson in *Idylls of the King*. Values exist independent of King Arthur, but inchoately. A moral hero like Tennyson's Arthur merely sculpts or delineates values. George Eliot and Robert Browning present a fourth alternative: a world in which the *existence* of value depends on agents like Maggie Tulliver or David in "Saul," but whose *character* is independent of them. Maggie decrees self-sacrifice after reading *The Imitation of Christ*; but the true nature of self-sacrifice, discovered only in renouncing life with Stephen, is not a value she is ever free to invent.

Though the universe of Thackeray's *Vanity Fair* may contain no antecedent value, why can its inhabitants not cut their losses, like Dobbin and Lady Jane, and choose to live as if their universe did contain value? Becky herself behaves in such a way when she discloses damaging truths about George's past behavior to Amelia. Even in *Middlemarch*, when value seems to have gone out of the world after Dorothea fears Ladislaw is secretly in love with Rosamond, to act as if values *did* exist is also to *make* them exist. If noble fictions about value can make us cherish, seek, and even create value, then to act in a value-depleted world as if value existed is to be no worse off, perhaps, than to live in a world where a sovereign code or a plenitude of values already reigns.

Browning keeps insisting in "Christmas-Eve" and "Saul" that an argument designed to force assent is less valuable than an explanation that concedes the mystery that really exists and merely tries to show how values are possible. A coercive or knockdown argument in ethics or theology is always at odds with the desire for free assent. Choosing that God and values should exist, as David does in "Saul," establishes tighter linkages between the person and the values he affirms than some nonautonomous relation between an arithmetician, for example, and the proposition $2 + 2 = 4$, which is unaffected by anyone's believing or disbelieving it. Tightness of linkage in theological or moral argument is also a mark of organic unity, which in life, as in literature, is itself a value.

For rational moralists like George Eliot and J. S. Mill, to be free is to be morally good, and to be bad is to be enslaved. Rosamond Vincy is more like an amoral cat stalking her prey than like a free agent. Trapped by instinct and ignorance, she seems stuck with her feline qualities. Lydgate is frightened by her, for he feels he has married a cunning pet instead of a wife. Should we not, however, object to such a rational morality for the same reason that Sidgwick in *The Methods of Ethics* criticizes Kant? If badness is a result of not being free, how can bad people like Rosamond be held responsible for their badness, since freedom is surely a condition of moral responsibility?

If we proceed far enough along the path that leads from personal self-making and invention of value to objective description of how people actually behave, we may fall into detachment, indifference, and eventually even nihilism. Clough's Claude, for example, has an uncanny capacity to withdraw from his personal projects and aims. But such withdrawal also begins to undermine those aims by allowing him to see himself as a small, contingent being, what Hardy or Tennyson would call a mere cosmic accident. Detachment starts to erode Claude's commitment to Mary Trevellyn without actually destroying it—leaving him a divided or a split personality. When Claude has to join in with the rest of life and play a part from which he is oddly disengaged, he becomes somewhat schizoid, because he is in significant measure detached from what he is doing. How can Claude be an energetic lover when only half his heart is in it?

The recognition that one's position in the universe is not central has a Stoic (and at times even religious) dimension to it. But if religion cannot supply Clough or Arnold with cosmic meaning, then their detached perspective, in the absence of a religious solution, may generate only skepticism and despair. The trick of morality, like the trick of writing dramatic monologues, as the morally astute Browning seems to have realized, is to occupy "a position far enough outside your own life," as one commentator suggests, "to reduce the importance of the difference between yourself and other people, yet not so far outside that all human values vanish in a nihilistic blackout" (Nagel 1986, 222). Browning sees more clearly than most Victorians that adjustment of internal and external viewpoints, which critics have always recognized as the central issue in the writing of monologues, is also the central issue in ethics.

Few Victorians, however, are as adroit as Browning at walking a moral tightrope. Most of them feel impelled to choose between a potentially trivial and absurd life of moral invention, immersed in mere particulars, and the derangement or sense of lostness that results from looking at existence from so far out that one begins to wonder how anything particular can really matter. Such a view is likely to make us feel giddy, as when Tennyson is confronted by the long perspective of geological time in *In Memoriam*, or when Thackeray's narrator in *Vanity Fair* is momentarily lost in a universe of endlessly receding drawing rooms. The extreme contingency and unimportance of our projects and our values makes us feel a constant undertow of absurdity in the ambitions and goals that drive our lives forward. A detached enough view, like that produced by death, will generate jarring displacements of perspective that leave the eye of a spectator cold and glazed, dispossessed and indifferent.

CHAPTER 7

Estranging the Familiar: Veils
of Reserve in Trollope and James

Mysteries of identity in fiction are not limited to characters like Thackeray's Becky Sharp or Borrow's Lavengro, whose sense of self is unstable and dissolving. Nor are such mysteries limited to persons like Dorothea Brooke, whose identity is slowly being remade. Even characters like Trollope's Eleanor Bold and James's Daisy Miller, whose identities are relatively stable, can be made to seem mysterious by people who misunderstand them—by Dr. Grantly and Winterbourne, for example. Any misinterpretation of a character invites not a *remaking*, but a *rereading* of it. By holding meaning in reserve, such seemingly antithetical methods as Trollope's use of an intrusive narrator and James's much more dramatic use of an unreliable narrator can be made to serve a common end. Each method estranges the familiar by showing that even a representational theory of fiction is problematic and enormously complex. By eroding the boundaries between fiction and life, Trollope's narrator in *Barchester Towers* never allows us to forget that every social novel, like every so-called chronicle or history, is a reconstruction of the past, and so a fiction. These fictions are as strange as each interpreter, for they are constructed over silences, missing information, and events that are still only imperfectly repossessed.

Trollope proves that social and domestic novelists can still estrange us. If nothing were alien to Trollope's narrator in *Barchester Towers*, nothing would be familiar to him either. Unless the strange mechanisms of self-deception, deftly rendered by the ironic grammar of the opening paragraphs, were partly familiar to the narrator, they could not be an object of his sympathetic amusement. But unless they were also strange and a mystery, he could not take pleasure in showing that ecclesiastical preferment is a lottery, exhausting the freakishness of arbitrary caprice. Dr. Grantly's misreading of Eleanor's character, like Winterbourne's misreading of Daisy's character in James, places imaginative obstacles in the way of a leveling and curious mind. By assuring the reader near the beginning of the novel that "it is not destined that Eleanor shall marry Mr. Slope or Bertie Stanhope" (chap. 15), Trollope's narrator seems at first to violate reserve by telling secrets. But often his disclosures are really forms of reserve in disguise. The narrator in *Barchester Towers* is an authorial Mr. Harding, one of the fiction's most reserved and private characters. Like a dramatic interpreter in James, he prevents our possessing too quickly other persons and minds. Both James's use of unreliable narrators and Trollope's use of an oddly self-withholding omniscient narrator distance what is close at hand, estranging the familiar.

A continual source of surprise in *Barchester Towers* is the narrator's power of sympathetic trespass. There are moments of illegitimate sympathy, when the narrator tries to make us feel closer to Slope than we want to feel, reminding us that Slope is "not in all things a bad man" (chap. 15). Through the use of identical quotations, the most important intrusions of Trollope's narrator align him with a character, Signora Neroni, with whom he seems at first to have nothing in common. Such surprising alignments force sudden adjustments of perspective. Contrary to expectations, the narrator's intimacy with the reader never dispels the strangeness and mystery that attach to even the most familiar events and people. Far from resolving mystery, the apparent artlessness of the narrator's disclosures has the opposite effect. Their function is one of the fiction's most interesting and abiding mysteries.

To trust in Trollope's narrator, the reader must behave as if the narrator will never deceive him by planting false clues about the outcome of his story. So Trollope takes pains to cultivate this trust by promising to renounce the cheap suspense of a Gothic novel or detective story. But in encouraging the reader to trust appearances, the narrator is also encouraging him to be less suspicious than he has to be. To believe in the narrator is to behave like the uncritical gossips in the story who are continually deceived by appearances. It is to behave like the Grantlys when they spread false stories about Eleanor's marrying Slope or like the gossips who make wrong guesses about who will be appointed bishop or dean. Conversely, to disbelieve in the narrator is also to behave precisely *like* the narrator, who is constantly exposing the discrepancies between facts and appearances, truths and fictions. Nothing is quite so artless as it seems, and the greatest pitfall is to assume that Trollope is as unreserved and open with his readers as he pretends to be.

No important character in *Barchester Towers* is ever remade. But because patient interpreters are continually having to reassess a character, this most rhetorical of novels also has its shock effects and sudden reversals. A veil falls from Mrs. Grantly's eyes when she realizes what lies people have told about her sister's marriage to Mr. Slope. But the only lies told about Eleanor are ones Mrs. Grantly and her husband have spread. And so the shock for Mrs. Grantly is followed by an aftershock for the narrator and his readers: "But people in this matter had told no lies at all" (chap. 48). Trollope is a master of such understated irony. At the beginning of chapter 47, for example, Slope's stock keeps rising and falling on the capricious market of public opinion. After the rhetorical seesaw of the opening paragraph, Trollope concludes that "when it was ascertained that [Mr. Slope] had taken a first-class ticket for London, there was no longer any room for doubt on the matter." Each surmise of each successive day bounces ironically off this wry conclusion. The more we believe anything the narrator says, the more gullible and stupidly certain we become, like one more victim of his irony. And the more we disbelieve Trollope, the more we behave precisely like him in doubting the conclusion that "there is no longer any room for doubt" (chap. 47). Always undulatingly alive to the nuances that dwell on the shadow side of speech, Trollope is appalled by the brutal assaults inflicted on language by self-promoters like Slope, who lives in a perpetual wind tunnel of gossip and noise. It seems to follow, therefore, that if we behave like Trollope we disbelieve him, and if we believe him we behave unlike him and so misread him. Is there any escape from this dilemma?

Because of Trollope's constant, resourceful restoration of his readers' ignorance, the reserve of his narrator often approaches that of a professional satirist. It is easy, for example, to find in Pope's and Austen's satirical portraits the counterparts of Trollope's innocent queries and sudden erosions of false certitude when reporting the gossip surrounding the appointment of a new bishop in the opening paragraph of the novel. The passive verbs and detached reporting— "It was pretty well understood," "rumour had confidently assigned" —convey the aloof reserve of the ironist. An event seems to conclude with the clauses, "Bishop Grantly died as he had lived, peaceably" (chap. 1). But the multiplication of adverbs and phrases—"peaceably, slowly, without pain and excitement"—makes readers increasingly aware of the narrator's amused hovering, as if in imitation of the refusal of the bishop to end his life until he has ended his son's hope of "possessing the glories of a bishopric."

More baffling is Trollope's occasional use of double irony. In his supposed defense of the architectural purity of Mr. Thorne's manor house, Ullathorne Court, for example, is the narrator censuring the decadent critics of the house's architectural style? Or, while seeming to defend the glories of England's great country houses, is he secretly aligning himself with the critics? The censor can be identified by his holding the more official or solemn view of "the beauties of English architecture" (chap. 22). He is amused by the pilgrim who will undergo every variety of torture to pitch his tent under Mount Sinai yet refuse to venture into the English counties to see the glories of rural architecture. And yet the comparison with Mount Sinai will not sustain the load of cultural significance the narrator is trying to pile upon Ullathorne, which resembles the biblical landmark only in austerity and ruggedness. Ullathrone Court turns out to be more notable for what it lacks than for what it possesses. It has no driveway for horse-drawn vehicles; it has nothing so decadent as a hall or a grand front portal. The ironist never says so, but the interior of the house sounds more like a barn than a manorial hall: it even lacks a dining parlor. Both admirers of Ullathorne and detractors can claim with some justice that the reserved narrator is secretly on their side and only pretends to sympathize with their adversaries. A utilitarian friend who insists that the giving of light "is the desired object of a window" will not deny that the quadrangular apertures with stone mullions have their own charm, even though they give less light than modern windows. "Luxurious" and "utilitarian" are scarcely complimentary adjectives, and critics of Ullathorne's incommodiousness may begin to have an uncomfortable sense that the narrator's tongue has started to curl and that he is secretly laughing at them behind their backs.

And yet utilitarian critics of Ullathorne Court are still charitably addressed as "friends" and even as "kind." The benevolent reserve of such double irony is peculiar to Trollope, and in him it is felt to be balanced and judicious, kind and unpretentious. It allows him to occupy some undefined but wisely balanced position between critics and defenders of Tudor architecture, both of whom may feel he is secretly on their side without explicitly saying so. It may be, as William Empson suggests, that any "consistent programme about double irony" (1984, 144) will eventually bring the ironist to the point of not knowing the answers to his questions. Sometimes Trollope seems genuinely puzzled. Is Eleanor or Arabin, for example, to blame for their misunderstanding about Slope's supposed designs upon Eleanor? Is Eleanor or Grantly responsible for their misunderstandings about the same topic? Why are innocent people like Miss Thorne often made to look as if they were in the wrong (chap. 37)? No easy answers are forthcoming.

The reticence of the likable people in *Barchester Towers* is a psychological equivalent of their theology of reserve. Mr. Harding's music and chanted liturgies discreetly veil in mystery meanings that strident evangelicals like Mr. Slope and Mrs. Proudie might otherwise profane. So reserved is Arabin that when Eleanor first meets him she thinks he may be merely proud or self-absorbed: he "did not apparently take much notice of her" (chap. 21). When he observes that the cult of St. Ewold's priestess of yore is "anything but orthodox," Arabin may seem to be merely solemn and overbearing. Taking her cue from her sister, who in championing the cause of women priests is pert enough to voice her entire disagreement with Arabin, Eleanor observes that Barchester has its own sacred lady in the person of the bishop's wife. Instead of directing this remark to Arabin, however, she directs it to her father, as if approaching the oracle through a third person, treating him with as much mock deference as the sacred lady.

Though Eleanor has made it easy for Arabin to joke at Mrs. Proudie's expense, she does not yet know if he is too aloof to joke. Only when she feels bold enough to address her second observation to Arabin himself does she hear his voice crackle with epigram and wit. "No priestly pride," he declares, "has ever exceeded that of sacerdotal females." He might essay to rule a lowly curate, but a "curatess" would be sure to get the better of him. The invention of a new word and the oracular turn he gives his humorous response mark Arabin as an ironist of quick parts and a fantastic humor. But Eleanor cannot quite tell whether his joking is partly directed at her. In making fun of sacerdotal females and curatesses, is Arabin possibly a male chauvinist, using his frolic humors to mock all women? Eleanor's politically minded sister wants Arabin to be less evasive. How does he feel about the priestess currently enthroned behind the bishop's chair? But Arabin's reserve forbids a direct answer.

Arabin's talent for wittingly improvising on a word or an idea furnished by his auditors immediately displays itself in his conversation with Eleanor. His window affords a "beautiful" observation post from which to view a scene that is anything but "beautiful" in Eleanor's sense of the word. As Wordsworthian pastoral is superseded by medieval warfare in which Arabin, from his command post in the study, can fire away at his enemies in the hospital and the palace, both within easy shooting range, the high irony of his altered picture makes Eleanor suddenly critical. Why should clergymen always fight each other? Arabin conducts a half-serious, half-jocular, defense: contention is a condition of truth, he tells Eleanor. If clergymen are part of the church militant, is it not their duty to take literally the injunction to wage war? Arabin's reserve and quiet earnestness appeal to Eleanor. He takes her questions seriously, and though he is as skeptically critical of his own ideas as he is of Eleanor's, his doubt merely makes him more vigilant. Reserve demands caution and is consistent with the energetic pursuit of truth.

Arabin's wit and irony sound like Pope without the couplets, and he even quotes Pope: "to damn with faint praise, or crush with open calumny." The balanced rhetoric corrects the intemperance of those he criticizes. A discreet adherence to an ill-defined middle ground of "truth" may make a speaker less intelligible. But since this is where truth lies, it is as wrongheaded to censure everything without reserve as it is to praise everything. Arabin is reserved because of the consequences of *not* being reserved. "You condemn what I do; but put yourself in my position and do the reverse, and then see if I cannot condemn you." The chiasmus dramatizes the balance and temperance of Arabin's own mind. If Eleanor were to be more open in her own censure and praise, like her late husband the journalist, would she not be in danger of once again wounding a man like her father? Arabin is redefining reserve as a synonym for discernment and intelligence. It should not be mistaken for complacency, inertia, or moral cowardice.

To be unreserved is to be stupidly censorious in the manner of a sensation-seeking journalist. It is to be intelligible but wrong, and responsible to nobody. Sensationalists are blind to the law that contentiousness and apathy, for example, exist in inverse proportion: the less of the first, the more of the second, and vice versa. To be reserved, conversely, does not imply unbelief in any truth whatever. It entails instead a complex blend of skepticism and faith—a faith that truth exists, but a skepticism that it is as readily attainable as most people think.

Eleanor's initial impression of Arabin as arrogant and aloof is quickly corrected. His character can easily be reread, for as soon as Grantly leaves the room, a play of wit lights up Arabin's whole conversation. The grave proprieties, as he denounces heterodox opinion, give way to more flexible and tolerant attitudes. He uses a phrase like "elegant quotation" to imply the reverse of what he says, and he deploys his "railery" to serious ends. His willingness to discuss complex attitudes with Eleanor may even suggest that he is being polite in more than the proper public sense. He is interested in her good opinion of him and in her own ideas and seems to be taking "much more notice" of her than she realizes. Because Eleanor cannot really adjust to all Arabin's rapid changes in tone, we are told she can only half follow what he says. The double presentation of ideas, with arguments on both sides, is perfectly suited to the combination of skepticism and faith that Arabin's reserve is made to express. Instead of trying to be dogmatic and censorious, he will be content with better understanding. Such irony is not cynicism, but a statement of what sensible people can reasonably expect.

As soon as Arabin hears that Slope is in love with Eleanor, however, he quickly reassesses his own feelings. For a brief moment Trollope, the narrator, draws back his customary veil of reserve to reflect ironically on the imitative nature of desire: "As soon as [Arabin] heard that she loved some one else, he began to be very fond of her himself" (chap. 30). In blaming Eleanor for "not making an enemy of his enemy," Arabin seems now to be betraying his own declared principle of trying to see every facet of a complex truth. Though inclined at first to dislike Slope, Eleanor finds that his intervention on her father's behalf has left her in a quandary shared by none of her friends except Mary Bold. When Mary urges Eleanor to give Slope "the benefit of the doubt," Eleanor passes from the kind of indecision that often characterizes Arabin and Trollope's narrator to an approval of Slope that is just as uncritical as the censure leveled at him by his enemies. To reassess our first impressions of a character may lead us into error, as it does Eleanor in her willingness to think better of Slope. And in trying to think better of someone than she should, Eleanor is encouraged to think less well of Arabin, a character who fully deserves her high opinion.

When Arabin tries to make conversation, paying her oblique compliments about the pleasant month he has spent near her, Eleanor is barely civil (chap. 30). His observation, "Charity should begin at home," though a platitude, is striking in its personal application. "You should show me a little love," he seems to imply. His comments about charity have a teasing variety of meanings. And in refusing to mention his rival Slope by name, Arabin shows the courtesy appropriate to a gentleman. But his request for knowledge of his "special deficiency" angers Eleanor, for it inadvertently suggests that the grounds of her displeasure with him are too irrational for anyone to infer. Or she may construe Arabin's request as a mere hypocritical pretense. He knows how he has offended but is too dishonest rather than too polite to say so.

Arabin and Eleanor are so self-protectively reserved that the narrator has to abandon his own reserve to tell us what would have happened had they behaved more openly. Without reserve, we learn, there would have been no deferral of understanding. And without such deferral, "where would have been my novel?" (chap. 30). Reserve is Trollope's equivalent of Dickens's tmesis: it is a principle of espacement that postpones intimacy and prevents the strangeness or hidden inwardness of a character from being violated.

The imperious gravity of Arabin's pronouncement—"What the

bishop is to Dr. Grantly, Dr. Grantly is to you" (chap. 30)—is forbidding and disagreeable. But his exacting gradations measure more than pride of rank. He speaks as a man of the world and as a friend who is interested in Eleanor's welfare. If he is punctilious and discriminating, it may be because he is in full rational command of a power that is sadly impaired in Eleanor. Arabin may exaggerate the need for precise discrimination, but Eleanor, in trying to see the complex truth about Slope, makes it more complicated than it is. She would have done better to save her charitable interpretations for a complex character like Arabin, who is worthy of such consideration. For Eleanor, every truth about a character like Slope becomes so true that any truth must be false. Such relativism is the perversion of that tolerance and wise withholding of judgment that Trollope embodies in his reserved but judicious narrator.

When Arabin speaks to her later in the archdeacon's garden (chap. 30), Eleanor tries to break down his wall of reserve. She plays upon different meanings of the word "rule" in an unsuccessful attempt to maneuver him onto the subject of marriage. So unable is Arabin to say what he feels that he half wishes for the rule of clerical celibacy. Eleanor reminds him that the Church of England has its own rule, the rule of marriage, but he mistakes her meaning and invokes the rule of the Lord's Prayer. Eleanor's puns on "rule" are in more than a trivial sense jeux d'esprit. Their humorous reserve has a serious point: or rather, it *is* the point. Her ironic meanings are the jokes of an adult mind. Though Eleanor would have responded openly to a direct declaration of Arabin's love, his more devious course of cross-examining Eleanor above her love for Slope makes her equally devious.

One reason Arabin is afraid to speak is that even seemingly safe terrain may prove full of land mines. A polite inquiry so apparently innocuous as the question "Are you returning to Plumstead, Mrs. Bold?" (chap. 41) may be thought to encroach on "dangerous ground." It may be misinterpreted as a devious effort to discover information about Eleanor's marriage plans, since Grantly has made it plain that he will never admit Eleanor to Plumstead as Mr. Slope's wife. Eleanor, for her part, is no more self-possessed than Arabin. She tries to fill an awkward silence not by making conversation, but by rearranging her rings. It is as if any verbal profession of love is incompatible with the condition of being in love. Those who glibly avow their love, like Slope, do not love, and those who truly love do not speak.

Signora Neroni warns Eleanor that to be as evasive with Arabin as she has been with Slope would be disastrously coy and would produce a very different result. Though Arabin is aware of complexities of thought and character, his use of words is unequivocal. "With him, yea will stand for yea; and nay for nay" (chap. 45). Arabin is the opposite of Slope, who is categorical in his judgments of people and their ideas but equivocal about principles. Signora Neroni mocks this impulse to equivocate when she taunts him with the question, "Tell us with what words she accepted you. Was it with a simple 'yes,' or with two 'no no's,' which make an affirmative? or did silence give consent?" (chap. 46). Arabin and Slope use different grammars: a grammar of tact and reserve is not to be confused with a grammar of dishonest equivocation. Only in the grammar of an evasive equivocator like Slope do two "no no's" make a yes.

It is characteristic of Arabin's reserve and gentility that he does not know he is going to propose marriage to Eleanor until he starts to do so. Only schemers like Slope and Stanhope *plan* to propose, but they scarcely qualify as gentlemen. At first Arabin's subtle and incessant intellectual activity unfits him for action. He sounds like Claude in *Amours de Voyage*. Will he use his intellectual perplexities to escape from a commitment to marriage? Will he turn Eleanor into another Mary Trevellyan? Some of his sententious observations seem to be true on more levels than he realizes: "We see so very very little," he reflects. Arabin's proposal never comes in so many words. Reserve produces only a vocative, followed by a dash, and then a modest progression in intimacy as Arabin manages to clear the hurdle separating the formal surname, Mrs. Bold, from the more familiar given name. But that is as far as words go. Gestures and looks do the rest. Even the narrator is at a loss to declare who made the first move. Did Arabin first draw Eleanor to his breast, or was it the other way round? The answers are discreetly veiled by the narrator's own reserve. We are reminded that Eleanor was called on for neither a "yea" nor a "nay nay." Words after speech reach into silence, and the heart of true union lies in that silence.

When Mrs. Grantly discovers that her sister is engaged to marry Arabin rather than Slope, there is no need for either Grantly or his wife to "remake" Eleanor's character. They have only to "reread" it with care. As soon as readers do the same, they see that Eleanor defends Slope as a way of opposing Grantly's overbearing manner. "'My dear Eleanor,' he said, 'I hope you believe me when I assure you that you have no sincerer friend than I am'" (chap. 29). Style and content send opposite messages. There is a verbal tug-of-war between Grantly's profession of sincerity and his wheedling, circumlocutory syntax. Grantly addresses his sister-in-law as if she were a legal client rather than a friend: "But as it is I cannot but think that it must be a comfort to you to know that...." Opaquely roundabout constructions sound like preambles in legal contracts. After such sallies, any advice

Grantly gives must be strenuously resisted. When Grantly seizes Slope's love letter and pronounces it improper, he seems not to recognize that he himself has been talking in the same exaggerated tones as the letter writer. His obtuseness and hyperbole are contagious and encourage Eleanor to call the improper tones of Slope's letter the opposite of what they are: "Quite... proper." Grantly uses a high-sounding moral rhetoric—"it is my duty to tell you"—to give exclamatory force and sanction to what Eleanor takes to be a mere arbitrary crossing of her will: his announcement that he chooses "wholly" to "differ from" her.

Just as Austen's Emma Woodhouse, verbally seduced by Mr. Elton, repays mannered inversion with mannered inversion—"Skilful has been the hand" with "great has been the pleasure" (*Emma*, chap. 6), so Eleanor repays antithesis with antithesis. She is even prepared to lie about her own low opinion of Slope in order to complete the rhetorical pattern established by her sparring partner: "You think Mr. Slope is a messenger direct from Satan. I think he is an industrious, well meaning clergyman" (chap. 29). As the conversation becomes a contest in hyperbole and antithesis, truth is allowed to escape through the middle. Though Eleanor finds she has to lie to tell her truths, we are never in any confusion about her real opinion of Slope. Nor are we ever in any confusion about what the alternatives between Slope and Grantly really are.

Signora Neroni is another character whose veils of reserve keep estranging the familiar and misleading careless interpreters. The growing alignment of Trollope's narrator and Signora Neroni is evident from a metaphor of situation that unites them. After gulling Slope, the Signora taunts him with a refrain from a popular song: "It's gude to be off with the old love—Mr. Slope, / Before you are on with the new" (chap. 46). When Slope much earlier in the novel writes his love letter to Eleanor, the narrator quotes a snatch of the same song to reprove Slope for turning his attention to Signora Neroni before concluding his love affair with Eleanor (chap. 27). Because the narrator and Signora Neroni use the same words, they seem to speak in unison, with the moral authority of "choral" characters. Only by using reserve to maneuver Slope into embarrassing situations can the Signora then throw aside all reserve to disclose the full measure of Slope's own duplicity. The reserve of the moral censor is opposed to the reserve of the hypocrite. And there can be no question, despite the rich ambiguity of the ironic dialogues, where the narrator's sympathies lie. We may have to "reread" Signora Neroni's character, but we are never required to "remake" it. Like Trollope, the Signora's most pestilent jeering is redeemed by large measures of rational feeling. She is as precise in defining her sentiments as she is strict in exacting her moral judgments. Everything she does in her final exposure of Slope is perfectly appropriate to habits of mind both she and the narrator have been developing throughout the novel.

Trollope's reserve saves the familiar social world from overfamiliarity by placing imaginative obstacles before an inquisitive interpreter. To achieve similar restraint Henry James finds he has to view every mind through some other mind. Any desire to know less obliquely "betrays the mystery," as one commentator says, "rapes the past, and lets us possess too quickly another person or mind" (Hartman 1970, 70). Like the complex characters in *Barchester Towers*, most mysterious characters in James's fiction have to be "reread" rather than "remade." Daisy Miller, and even the governess in *The Turn of the Screw*, do not really change: only our interpretations change. And yet to interpret properly, as Winterbourne discovers, we may have to change our own identity.

James's best fictions combine genuine mystery in the central portrait with genuine mystification on the part of an interpreter. A fine sense of the complexity of the character delineated in the central portrait is balanced by a steady—and justified—belief in the interpreter's capacity to arrive at sounder judgments. In "Daisy Miller" and *The Ambassadors*, the interpreters Winterbourne and Strether begin in skepticism and suspicion but end in trust and faith. In *The American* and *The Turn of the Screw* the process is reversed. Newman's initial faith in Claire and the Bellegardes is displaced by skepticism. And in *The Turn of the Screw* skepticism invades the governess, the main interpreter herself.

At the end of the short story "Daisy Miller," Winterbourne concedes that Daisy's manners are "mystifying." Like a reflective critic, he needs leisure to be wise. It takes moral labor to reach the innocence of things. Even Daisy's message that "she would have appreciated [his] esteem" (part 2) is appropriately ambiguous, capable of double interpretations. Indeed, Mrs. Costello's interpretation is precisely the opposite of Winterbourne's. She thinks Daisy means that she wanted to flirt with Winterbourne or possibly seduce him. In fact, her meaning is the exact reverse of this. Like Mme de Vionnet in *The Ambassadors*, she wanted her friend's good opinion, his esteem, his enhancing imagination of her—not his body. The double interpretations include not merely Daisy's innocent remark, but also Winterbourne's admission that he "was booked to make a mistake." He is mistaken, not as Mrs. Costello supposes in his belief in Daisy's essential innocence and charm, but in his suspicion of Daisy's flirtatiousness and immorality.

The double meanings of the ironist persist, but there is now no doubt about which interpreter is right. Winterbourne's sentiments are defined as exactly as his moral judgments. He is as discriminating in his esteem for Daisy as he is in his conviction of her innocence.

Even in his first detailed description of her, Winterbourne holds a fine balance between intimations of Daisy's insolence and appreciation of her candor. Sometimes key words like the adverbs "very forgivingly" are capable of looking two ways at once. Is the narrator forgiving Winterbourne for accusing Daisy's face of being unfinished, or is Winterbourne forgiving Daisy's single physical deficiency? Despite our most scrupulous efforts to do so, it is not always easy to dissociate the narrator's irony from Winterbourne's. The latter is by turns amused, perplexed, and decidedly charmed by Daisy. He is amused by her self-deprecation and absence of pretense, charmed by her unpredictability and candor, but perplexed by her teasing variety of tones.

Mrs. Costello's patronizing assumption of superior integrity is quite foreign to Daisy, who parodies the idea of being "exclusive" by wittily redefining the adjective four times in as many sentences. "I know I should like her. She would be very exclusive. I like a lady to be exclusive; I'm dying to be exclusive myself. Well, we *are* exclusive, mother and I" (part 1). Being his relative, Mrs. Costello is a special person: any aunt of Winterbourne's is bound to be "exclusive." The second time the adjective is used it becomes synonymous with aloofness, the quality that sets a "lady" apart from someone common. When Daisy says she is "dying to be exclusive," she appears to be joking about what hurts her. Despite the banter, Daisy in the end will literally die "to be exclusive." Even now the persiflage cannot disguise an inward seriousness of tone. Daisy's final use of "exclusive" is largely self-parodying. Guessing that Mrs. Costello has refused to see her, and that "exclusiveness" consists in gratuitous insult, Daisy uses the mirroring trope, chiasmus, to reverse the proposition it parodies: "Well, we *are* exclusive, mother and I. We don't speak to everyone—or they don't speak to us." The painful silence of not being spoken to and of therefore being unable to speak is not, Daisy knows, to be equated with the self-imposed silence of the socially important aunt, who is too proud to speak to anyone.

There is a sense in which Daisy speaks the truth when she says she is "dying to be exclusive." Her imagination of romance, of being open to adventure, does exclude the kinds of amorous attachment and seduction that Mrs. Costello and her nephew invariably associate with romance. Daisy is more "exclusive" of complicating personal entanglements than anyone seems to realize. Her exclusiveness in this larger, nonsocial sense accounts for her amazing fluctuations of mood. In her sudden desire for fresh adventure, she asks Winterbourne impulsively to take her out in a boat. All the fun resides in the caprice and promise of the moment. But when Mrs. Miller gives her approval and Winterbourne even makes a formal proposal to take her, the sanctioning of the enterprise seems to rob it of all its allure. Daisy is never merely flirting with a man called Winterbourne. She is flirting with an idea, with a conception of romance, with her own imagination of what human possibility should be like. It is as if, like Kierkegaard's hedonist in "The Dairy of a Seducer," she tires of imagined pleasures before they are enjoyed. In hoping that Winterbourne will not be "disappointed, or disgusted, or something"—a reaction she cannot quite define, Daisy is trying to find words for her own sense of disappointment. Sometimes Daisy seems to be challenging people to put into words ideas that might better be left unsaid. She jokes, for example, about the way Winterbourne, in speaking about his formal offer to take her in the boat, manages to say nothing. "I was bound I would make you say something," she chides. She half realizes that often the most important meanings are conveyed by words that literally say nothing.

The "extraordinary mixture of innocence and crudity" that Winterbourne finds in Daisy is defined for the reader by finely balanced tones. Her crudity is displayed by the disarming directness of her questions. Who, she asks, is the mysterious charmer Winterbourne is hurrying back to see? This supposed rival seems hardly to exist. But Daisy endows her with such vivid life that she is even imagined racing to the boat landing in a preposterous rescue of the seduced Winterbourne. These frontal attacks leave Winterbourne no shred of euphemism or polite fiction to hide behind. The substance of her conversation may be crude, but its teasing tones are various and complex. Though important adjectives like "charming," "nice," and "dangerous" acquire a range of sharply differentiated meanings, each word, when applied to Daisy, also retains an irreducible minimum of mystery.

In the second half of the story a new opposition emerges between cleverness and earnestness. Daisy is on the side of wit and cleverness, Mrs. Walker on the side of moral seriousness. At the party Mrs. Walker's earnestness scores a victory over Daisy's cleverness. And yet the moral victory lies with Daisy in the end. After her late arrival, Daisy talks in a charming but vacuous way. There is an edge of condescension in her voice, as she asks, "Is there anyone I know?" A multiplicity of tonal layers can be discerned in such a question. Is Daisy being cheerfully aggressive to mask her vulnerability? Is her tone exclusive, or only the tone of one who feels excluded? Is her query merely unreflective? Whatever the precise inflection she gives the words, there can be no mistaking the pungent force of Mrs. Walker's riposte. "I think everyone knows you." Daisy is notoriously undiscriminating, she insinuates, and so familiar to everyone.

The rigidity of Daisy's censors is now denounced as moral stiffness. Its opposite is flexibility and cleverness, including a witty ability to score against one's critics. Mrs. Walker's rooms are pronounced pitiably small; and only stiff, earnest people like Winterbourne, who are too grave and censorious to dance, equate clever, entertaining behavior with flirting. Daisy plays verbal tennis with Winterbourne, putting a spin on his language and tossing back his words with altered meaning. To flirt with Giovanelli at the piano, her critic argues, is to engage in behavior that her censors "don't understand." Daisy denies the truth of the observation and insists that they "understand nothing else." "Understand" in the sense of condone is turned into its antonymn, censorious gossip. She is a witty debater, ready to take punning advantage of an opponent by redefining his terms.

When Mrs. Walker inflicts social pain on Daisy by turning her back on her as she formally takes her leave, moral censorship is unmasked as something "very cruel," to use Winterbourne's phrase. The pain is compounded by the unmanageable good temper of Daisy's mother, on whom the insult fails to register. No longer a moral censor like Mrs. Walker, Winterbourne now becomes Daisy's most feeling advocate. "Daisy turned away, looking with a pale, grave face at the circle near the door; Winterbourne saw that, for the first moment, she was too much shocked and puzzled even for indignation. He on his side was greatly touched" (part 2). Though we are told Mrs. Walker resorts to insult to repair "the weakness" of being civil when her guest arrived, it taxes a reader's ingenuity to discover how anyone can call her earlier insinuation that Daisy is promiscuous—"I think every one knows you"—a form of civility. Winterbourne is shocked when this rude and uncivil hostess redefines as "weakness" an observance of minimal politeness and decorum. Mrs. Walker's wit is vicious and destructive. It is unanswerable. Daisy's wit, by contrast, is playful and good-natured, allowing her opponents ample opportunity to answer and defend themselves.

When Daisy hails Winterbourne at the Coliseum, calling him one of the grim old lions that devoured Christian martyrs, the comment is at once jocular and prophetic. Giovanelli hollows out the tone of the oracle by making it merely amusing: the solemn Winterbourne will be censorious, eating Giovanelli first and saving Daisy for dessert. For a

moment an illumination has been flashed upon the ambiguity of
Daisy's behavior: she is merely "a clever little reprobate," no more
interesting than Mrs. Walker has said. Winterbourne is momentarily
exhilarated by this false clarification of the mystery and by his sudden
revulsion from cautious criticism. But Daisy is exhilarated by something better. There is a note of unsettling finality in her meditation.
She is fated to see the Colosseum by moonlight. Like Winterbourne,
she picks up the tone of finality heard earlier in Mrs. Costello's
warning that her nephew, in his naïveté, "will be sure to make some
great mistake."

A subtle and generous interpreter will expend a great deal of
imaginative energy and talent on a subject: his ultimate postulate of
faith is that such energy and intellect will be rewarded. When
Winterbourne sees Daisy at the Colosseum in the company of Giovanelli,
his opinion of her suddenly plummets. We are told "he felt angry with
himself that he had bothered so much about the right way of regarding Miss Daisy Miller." The formality of the last phrase opens a
distance between the interpreter and his subject. People like Daisy
ought really to live up to such a complex and subtle imagination of
them as Winterbourne is willing to sustain. Like Strether in his
enhancing visions of Chad, Winterbourne feels momentarily betrayed
by his materials. In James's view, however, Daisy is both emancipated
and moral. And if she is not moral in Mrs. Walker's sense, then the
word "moral" will have to be redefined. Readers who cannot reconcile
earnestness and cleverness will have to content themselves with a
mystery and try through a careful reassessment to arrive at a better
understanding. Winterbourne's mistake is his failure to see that to be
engaged to Giovanelli or any suitor would betray Daisy's newness and
freedom. Being beyond sex, scandal, and society, such a heroine is
already beyond this world and goes the only way she can—*out* of it.
Married to an Emersonian vision of nature, Daisy is a typically
Jamesian heroine who would rather commune with moonlight in the
Colosseum than with any lover. Such a colloquy is one-sided, like a
prayer, and Winterbourne finds that the only appropriate response is
silence.

The mysteries of identity are most perplexing in a short novel like
The Turn of the Screw. As veils of reserve are stripped off Miles and
Flora, their characters have to be reassessed. And so does the character of their chief interpreter, the governess, who may be possessed by
the very demons she tries to exorcise in Miles. Before the governess
can assess the depravity that lurks beneath Miles's gentle demeanor,
she must penetrate the mystery of the unmentionable crime he has

committed at school. When it becomes clear that Miles was dismissed not for stealing, but for something he said, the governess tries to discover the precise words. "I said things," he concedes, and reflects cryptically, "it was too bad" (part 24). It is not clear what the enigmatic "it" refers to. Were the unnamed "things" he uttered too "bad"—in the sense of evil—for the schoolmaster to repeat? Or does the "badness" consist simply in the pity of the master's writing home to Mrs. Grose about mere trivia? The exasperation of the governess is likely to be shared by every reader who finally loses patience with James for piling up layer upon layer of gratuitous reserve. If the veils cover something, why not tell us what it is? Is the fact to be veiled the mere absence of any fact that would justify the master's letter? If so, Miles does not deserve the governess's suspicion, and the whole edifice of supposition she has built upon it falls to the ground. Some critics have believed Miles and argue that the real subject of the tale is not the veiling of any specific secret but the principle of veiling itself.

But it is as hard for the governess to renounce a favored fiction as it is for critics to renounce a favorite interpretation of *The Turn of the Screw*, which may possess them like an obsession. At the end of the story the governess thinks that Miles is about to confess that Peter Quint is in some horrible way implicated in the child's abjection. But just as the confession is about to begin, the governess has an apparition of Quint. Wrongly surmising that the governess sees Miss Jessel, Miles substitutes the feminine pronoun for the expected "he." By introducing the wrong performer, he threatens to ruin the performance the governess is trying to stage. Instead of identifying Quint by name, however, she invokes the more impersonal and pervasive presence of what she calls "the coward horror" (part 24). The definite article makes it palpable for her, but still generalized enough to impose on Miles the responsibility for naming his accomplice. Miles keeps interrogating, as a learner should. But the governess is a true Socratic mentor, and she answers his questions—"It's *he*?", "*Where?*" —by asking new and better questions: "Whom do you mean by 'he'?" When Miles responds, "Peter Quint—you devil!" the crisis in knowing is signaled by a crisis in language that allows two-way syntax to darken his meaning. What, for example, is the grammatical function of his phrase, "you devil"? Is it a vocative or an appositive? Is the governess the devil, or Peter Quint? A fearful ambiguity is also rendered grammatically by the long delay of direct objects: "he was at me in a white rage, bewildered, glaring vainly over the place and missing wholly, though it now, to my sense, filled the room like the taste of poison, the wide, overwhelming presence" (part 24). Named only in the three concluding words as a "wide, overwhelming presence," the unidentified "it" that Miles misses "wholly" is separated from the sentence's principal verb by a concessive clause whose own subject and verb—"it" and "filled"—are themselves separated by a phrase inserted between another pair of commas. Such elaborate sundering is the grammatical equivalent of veiling and mystery, and it has the same function in *The Turn of the Screw* as Dickens's use of generalized tmesis in *Great Expectations*.

There is an oracular punning quality to the governess's boast that the demonic Quint has "lost" Miles "forever." If death is the cost of exorcism, then Quint has "lost" Miles not because the governess has saved the youth, but because she has killed him. He is "lost" in the lesser sense only because he is "lost" in a greater one. He is saved, and hence "lost" to Quint, only because his life itself is "lost."

The veil of reserve that shrouds the secret conspiracy of Miles, Miss Jessel, and Quint is made more impenetrable by the deaths of all three characters. In this story of a death inside a death inside a death, events replicate themselves like a repeating decimal. Once generated, they are powerless to stop. In the prologue a man who has since died tells the story of how a dead governess presided over the death of the pupil she was hired to teach. It is as if Miles's mysterious death were doubly framed by the deaths of a narrator and a governess. The friend to whom the governess has entrusted her story duplicates the secret love this governess has felt for her employer. But undeclared love does not stop here. It transfers itself unconsciously to her employer's nephew, the young Miles, whom she seizes at the moment of his death "with...a passion" more appropriate to a lover than a pupil. These duplications resonate more strangely when we recognize unsuspected similarities between Miles and Douglas. Both are ten years younger than the governess, and sometimes the same words can be spoken with equal appropriateness by either speaker. When Douglas, for example, says that "she was my sister's governess" (prologue), he means that the governess was hired to teach his nephews or nieces. But Miles might have used the identical words to indicate that he and his sister Flora were taught by the same person. The replications become vertiginous and create in the reader the same dizzying effect that Miles feels when he utters "the cry of a creature hurled over an abyss" (part 24) or that the governess is said to experience when she falls into a bottomless black hole of skepticism that includes disbelief in herself.

Veils of reserve are thrown over all the dark passions and secret loves in the story. And parts of the governess's story may be impenetrably veiled by her own acts of censorship. Her story, we remember, has been recorded by the governess herself and is being read by a subsequent admirer. Just as Henry Esmond's memoir may be subject to censorship by Rachel, the woman he later marries, so the governess's record may bury or place a veil of reserve over truths that are self-damaging. If she has not personally censored the record, perhaps Douglas has. We shall never know to what extent the manuscript has been tampered with.

Until the end of her story, the suspicious governess has been insufficiently suspicious of herself. To be a consistent skeptic, who keeps discerning discrepancies between the masks people wear and the dark secrets behind these masks, she must doubt the correctness of her own interpretations. But that is to adopt the view of Mrs. Grose. Dissolution of stable identity places the reader in a quandary. On the one hand, if we as readers believe the governess is a reliable interpreter who is correct to conclude that Miles and Flora are possessed by the evil spirits of Quint and Miss Jessel, then we shall interpret events not as the skeptical governess herself interprets them, but as the saver of appearances, Mrs. Grose, tries to do. If, on the other hand, readers suspect that the ghosts exist only in the governess's disordered imagination, they will interpret events as skeptically as the governess. And so to be trusting like Mrs. Grose is to *believe* the governess, and to be skeptical like the governess is *not* to trust her. The dilemma faced by each character becomes the reader's dilemma. In reexamining *The Turn of the Screw* to discover what we may have missed in a careless or too hurried reading, we are doing precisely what the governess does when it flashes through her mind that she may have made a horrible mistake about Miles: "it was for the instant confounding and bottomless, for if he *were* innocent, what then on earth was I?" (part 24).

The governess distrusts natural explanations for the same reasons Mrs. Grose trusts them: to save appearances. Miles and Flora look so preternaturally innocent that, to preserve this impression and explain the apparitions she sees, the governess has to conceive of a plot to corrupt the children, even though the plot involves the agency of ghosts. Mrs. Grose offers a more plausible theory of how appearances can be saved. She refuses to believe in the sanity of a witness who strikes as much terror into Mrs. Grose as the ghosts strike into the witness. But in *not* believing the governess, Mrs. Grose behaves exactly *like* the governess, who is an inveterate skeptic. When Occam's razor suggests that appearances can best be saved by reserving one's skepticism not just for the facts that are interpreted, but for the interpreter herself, then even the governess begins to fear that her own *imagination* of horror, rather than any unspeakable abjection in Quint or Miles, may be the true abomination. If so, the most important veil the governess has to remove is the veil that hides her own repressed or darker nature from view. The most important character she must encounter and come to know is herself.

CHAPTER 8

The Dark Principle: Erosions
of Identity in *Vanity Fair*

In Thackeray's puppetlike characters in *Vanity Fair*, the normal priority of face to mask, of life to art, is oddly reversed. Cuticles masquerade as hearts. Passions exist for the sake of the fictions and playacting; things for the sake of images or impressions; and feelings for the sake of words. Whole areas that are usually taken to be the province of spontaneous response seem regulated by experiment. How do Becky Sharp's gestures and movements animate her heart and brain? A dislocation spreads over the whole creature: like the charades she acts out at Gaunt House, her life seems less a coherent action than a puzzle made up of pieces of behavior. Limbs move on cue; facial and bodily expressions become a mere animation of mechanical joints, like the motions of a puppet. It may be dramatically expedient and politically discreet, she realizes, to show affection for her son. But maternal emotion ceases to exist when it is no longer in Becky's interest to express it. Far from being artful supplements to life, the playacting and charades become controlling centers. Life begins to exist for the sake of the art, the face for the mask, the echo or verbal simulation of feeling for the feeling itself.

We discover at Gaunt House that one way of producing a charade for Clytemnestra is to mime an eye and then a nest, and to combine the words that are contained within the proper name to be guessed. Such is Thackeray's own way of miming life in *Vanity Fair*. Like a charade that makes exaggerated *gestures* of meaning, the novel glories not in the plenitude of the meanings it mimes, but in the piecemeal artifice of its own sign system. Reading *Vanity Fair* is like watching the players' play in *Hamlet*. It is to be present at a charade or a puppet show that concentrates on gestures and signs to the exclusion of the content we expect to find. The artifice of the gestures is in inverse proportion to the life and meaning expressed. A consistent allegory like Bunyan's or Spenser's is not improvised: its symbolism is consummated in preexisting concepts like despair or holiness. The meanings are conventionally assigned and could be expressed by different signs. By contrast, the meanings in *Vanity Fair* are inseparable from the charades, puppetry, and playacting that dramatize them. This inseparability is not, of course, the result of any truly iconic symbolism. It occurs only because the conspicuous consumption of symbols exists in direct correlation to the conspicuous absence of any stable meanings behind the symbols. When empty carriages are sent to funeral processions in *Vanity Fair* and long compound names are assumed by the nouveau riche, the more ostentatious the symbols become the emptier of content they prove to be.

Characters like Dobbin and Amelia who seem at first to have stable identities, beyond any role they may happen to play, are in fact simply trapped in stereotyped dramatic parts. They are less versatile actors than Becky. The contrast is not between categorical and existential options but between different forms of role-playing. For Clough's Claude in *Amours de Voyage*, to be is to write. But for Thackeray, to be is to playact, or to change the masks one wears. In *Pilgrim's Progress* Bunyan tells us that the only way to get to the Celestial City without passing through Vanity Fair is to "go out of the world." To stop playacting is either to die or to be sent to Coventry Island like Rawdon.

Though Becky is the most accomplished actress in the novel, in each of her important dramatic roles she gives a flawed performance. She is too aggressive in her first campaign against Jos, too restrained when trying to capture Sir Pitt, and insufficiently sure of Rawdon during the famous discovery scene in chapter 53. That chapter opens with an exchange of letters in which husband and wife seem to be playing familiar roles. In his three-paragraph letter to Becky from the sponging house, Rawdon masks anxiety for himself with a cultivated mixture of contempt for his "captors" and solicitude for Becky: "I *hope you slept well. Don't be frightened* if I don't bring you in your *coffy.*" The whole movement of his letter is from reserve to urgency. He lacks the composure to write complete sentences, and increasingly the edgy, nervous asyndeton creates an erratic syntax, full of dashes and fragmented phrases. In her own letter, Becky reverses Rawdon's plea for sympathy by dwelling on the misery of her insomnia, fever, and headache and by even pretending to write from her sickbed. "Odious monstre" is Becky's affectionate sobriquet for Rawdon. But the tone of good-natured banter begins to effervesce the moment she indiscriminately applies the same word "odious" to Nathan, the hateful moneylender, and to the kind but bullied Lady Steyne, who is wickedly described as a "sheep-faced monster." Even the affectionate use of "pauvre" takes on a disturbing meaning as it is used to describe Rawdon's "poor," ill-spelled letter. Pity is the highest style of intercourse Becky allows herself. It is as if the temple of her affections were a sponging house or a hospital, and all the inmates either paupers or lepers.

When Rawdon, freed from the debtor's prison by Lady Jane, breaks in upon Becky and her lover, Steyne finds himself torn between two possible realities. Is this an accident, or is it planned? Are Becky and Rawdon trying to blackmail him, or is Becky as surprised as he is? If the latter illusion is sponsored, then Steyne should follow Becky's lead and protest his innocence. If the other reality is to be believed, then to confirm her innocence is to admit that he has paid for favors he has not received. When acting as a one-member team in composing her letter to Rawdon, Becky can confidently decide what line to take. She has no team mate to inform of her decision. But in playacting with Steyne, Becky should have told her partner that Rawdon's approval of their affair does not include the granting of sexual favors. And she should not have told Rawdon she was ill when she was actually reveling at home with his rival. As an actress herself, Becky instinctively admires Rawdon's "strong, brave, and victorious" performance, even though it is a heroic role to end all future roles. Unlike Rawdon, Steyne is just as embarrassed by confusion about the kind of dramatic performance he is expected to give as he is by Becky's imagined insult to his intelligence. He does not know what dramatic part to play until cues can be given and received.

Because Becky's performance before Rawdon dramatizes a very fragile reality, it is imperative that she overcommunicate the fact of her technical innocence of adultery and undercommunicate the fact that Steyne has been giving her money and jewels. If Becky's playacting before Rawdon is to succeed, she must control destructive information. Some of her team's secrets, however, are divulged by Steyne when he charges, quite inaccurately, that Rawdon has been receiving thousands of pounds from Becky. The remaining secrets are discovered when Rawdon finds the hiding place in the desk where Becky keeps the banknotes.

At the end of the discovery scene, Thackeray's narrator picks up a question innocently posed by Becky's French maid. " '*Mon Dieu*, madame, what has happened?' she asked. What *had* happened? Was she guilty or not?" (chap. 53). We are never sure which team this narrator is on. Ostensibly, the narrator is addressing the wider moral audience. But he is also a go-between, defending Becky from conventional moral censorship. He never simply condemns Becky, as Steyne, Rawdon, and Lady Jane do. He doubts Becky's technical innocence but concedes that the corrupt heart may in this instance have been pure. To confront the void behind all her role-playing may even take courage. Becky's retreat to her bed, which earlier in the chapter she had merely feigned, is now in earnest. Is the narrator defending her or censoring her? "What were her thoughts?" "Would he kill himself?" "Should she take laudanum, and end it, too?" The battery of questions reminds us that despite the simple dramatic force of the discovery scene, the nature of what has been discovered is still shrouded in mystery.

The stability of the narrator's lists—hopes, plans, debts, and triumphs, "all her lies and her schemes, all her selfishness and her wiles, all her wit and genius" (which are set forth in three rhetorical pairs and made more authoritative by anaphora)—is a desperate stay against confusion. Even the triad of desolating adjectives—"how miserable, lonely and profitless"—tries to erect some bulwark against the nothingness, the zero result, of Becky's "long past life." Confusion is mimed by the heaping together of nouns. How can we reconcile the alliterating "wit" and "wiles"? How does "genius" consort with lies, schemes, and selfishness? We would not ordinarily expect a selfish genius to be bankrupt. The alliterative disorder of the nouns imitates the disorder of the tumbled vanities lying in ruin around her. But the real disorder may be in the vacillation of the narrator as go-between. Moral phrases like "tumbled vanities" and "miserable ruins" are sententious and judgmental. But as a kind of moral spy, commissioned by an actress of genius like Becky to unmask the hypocrisy of her censors, the narrator has also to expose the double standards of most readers. Their harshest judgment of her seems to be that her past is "profitless." Lack of financial profit becomes a shockingly literal judgment, exposing the material basis of her censors' vaunted morality. Becky's boast that she could have been a good woman on five thousand pounds per annum plays upon the same confusion. If we attack Becky for moral casuistry, then we must also attack her critics for the same failing. As a go-between, Thackeray's narrator exposes the darkest secrets of each side.

What is most subversive about *Vanity Fair* is the unexpected collapse of the adversarial teams into a common front of cynicism and indifference. In the end there is nothing to differentiate the moral censors from the dramatic performers. A censor like the narrator uses moral words such as "bankruptcy" and "vanity" without the expected moral meanings. And yet, having evoked a moral meaning only to renounce it, such words continue to hover between the literal and the metaphorical, and in their hovering each meaning feeds off the other. The dramatic performers, for their part, use one-dimensional masks, with the reductive simplifications of a puppet show or charade. Even the most moral character in the discovery scene, the censorious Rawdon, by complaining that Becky could not spare him even a hundred pounds, uses an economic vocabulary like the narrator rather than a moral vocabulary appropriate to a censor.

The passage in the second chapter of the novel in which Thackeray alternates between an amusing account of Becky's theatrical talents and the autocracy of Miss Pinkerton is a superb and typical example of the narrator's double irony. In describing the child's theatrical resource, which qualifies as precocity bred of poverty, he appears to applaud her genius in making fools of censorious creditors and of authority figures like the majestic Miss Pinkerton. But the amusement of father and daughter at the expense of the censor, who becomes the subject of backstage pantomime, turns into something grimmer when the genial Miss Jemima, the benevolent sister who gives Becky jelly and cake, herself becomes a target of mimicry. The doll given by the censor is used to mimic the censor. And then mimicry becomes reckless, as ridicule becomes far stronger than gratitude and Miss Jemmy is derided "quite as pitilessly as her sister" (chap. 2). By the end of the paragraph the negative capability of the heartless mime has got out of hand. The theatrical genius has become an unfeeling renegade, whose backstage pantomimes threaten to move onstage at any moment. For an instant allegiances shift, and the narrator invites us to transfer our loyalties to the abused Miss Jemmy, whose gift of the dictionary has been treated with equal irreverence.

In posing the query, "Oh, why did Miss Pinkerton let such a dangerous bird into her cage?" (chap. 2), the narrator's arch tone and manner prove quite unsettling. Becky may be a raven masquerading as a canary. But because her school-cage retains the restrictive formality of a prison, we may pity the prisoner. The birdkeeper might assume that the narrator only pretends to sympathize with the untamed and dangerous bird. Yet Becky could with equal justice argue that the narrator, while pretending to sympathize with the generous and honest Miss Jemima, is secretly on the side of cleverness and wit. Thackeray seems at first to be holding a wise, balanced position between moral censorship and a subversion of censors. But he implies at times that both attitudes are defective. The hypocrisy of even the censorious Miss Pinkerton is intimated by the presentation to Becky of a doll confiscated from a girl, Miss Swindle, whose name suggest that the confiscated property has itself been paid for with embezzled funds. The narrator uses a whole regress of confiscations and evasions to hint at the subversive truth that moral censors and their critics are equally amoral.

When practiced on a large scale, Thackeray's double irony rapidly erodes any boundaries or moral norms we are tempted to impose. The norms that would sustain a stable form of irony retain only the shimmering mystery of a mirage in *Vanity Fair*. They recede from our vision and our grasp just as we seem on the point of reaching out to touch them. If there are no norms or stable referents, then moral language, like the moral masks of the performers, is empty of content. This discovery may be a source of despair, but also of minimal hope, since it suggests that all inhabitants of Vanity Fair are responsible, in Dr. Johnson's phrase, for "[making] the happiness [they do] not find" ("The Vanity of Human Wishes," l. 368). The clearest statement of this discovery, at once bracing and defeatist, is the narrator's wry reflection: "The world is a looking-glass, and gives back to every man the reflection of his own face" (chap. 2). If the objects of the censor's censure give back only an image of the vanity or emptiness in himself, it is no wonder Thackeray's irony dissolves in skepticism.

As Becky improves as a strategist and an actress, she begins to acquire more of the dramaturgical loyalty and circumspection that are Vanity Fair's substitutes for moral discipline. In performing for her father and Miss Jemima, Becky has no loyalty to anyone but herself. She learns discipline when trying to seduce Jos, but she cannot always cope with emergencies when they arise. The farce at Vauxhall proves that there are dangers in a performance that is too carefully scripted as well as in one that is totally unrehearsed, like the disastrous discovery scene. Jos's incapacity to see why Becky is dangerous to the Sedley-Osborne team is proof that a team may be a secret society even to its own members. Once Becky moves into the world of the Crawleys, she cultivates the goodwill of the rich Miss Crawley and becomes a member of a team that includes old Sir Pitt and Rawdon. But if her seduction of Jos is too unsubtle, she is too discreet in her courtship of Sir Pitt. With practice and experience, Becky has to acquire the proper blend of loyalty and self-serving, discretion and boldness.

As soon as Becky recovers her self-possession after being denounced by Steyne, she devises a plan of retrieval involving the young Sir Pitt. Though Pitt blushes when Becky mentions Steyne's partiality for her, he tactfully protects the fiction of her innocence and the probable fiction of her trying to secure him a peerage. Though Lady Jane sanctions none of these protective practices, Becky is now sufficiently detached from the kind of altruistic suppliant she wants to impersonate to be in full command of her performance. Even her pretense of faltering for the right word, for the noun "esteem," which is generalized enough to convey partiality without conceding intimacy, is studiously contrived (chap. 55).

Becky artfully corrects the trauma of the discovery scene (chap. 53) by staging a performance in which even the intrusion of Lady Jane can be used to dramatic advantage. Becky's stage cue to Sir Pitt—"Tell her that I am innocent" (chap. 55)—exactly repeats what she had said earlier to Steyne. Unlike Steyne, however, Pitt rallies weakly to her defense. And the incivility of her sister-in-law secretly pleases Becky, because it brings Sir Pitt and her together as victims of their sharp-tongued censor. Lady Jane's rhetoric is stiffened by self-righteous anaphora, and she proves in the end to be more unreasonable than Becky. If Becky is not ostracized from their circle, Lady Jane will divorce her husband. The narrator seems to be expressing imaginative sympathy for two opposite codes simultaneously. Becky dramatizes a radical discontinuity between her offstage self (if such a self exists) and the identity she assumes as an actress. By contrast, her moral critics, Lady Jane and Rawdon, dramatize the continuity between what people are and what they appear to be. Ironically, however, the two apostles of continuity precipitate junctures and breaks. If Rawdon and Lady Jane prevail, the old alliances will be broken: no reconciliation will be possible. Conversely, the practitioner of duplicity, the theatrical Becky, wants on this occasion to save appearances. If she and Sir Pitt prevail, some accommodation with Rawdon may still take place, and so to behave as Becky would is to interpret events like her moral adversaries, the advocates of order and continuity. And to behave like her censors is to interpret actions like Becky, the agent of rupture. No escape from this double bind seems possible.

When Becky stages a performance for Jos in her dirty little refuge in the Elephant Hotel, she first puts on an entertainment for the amusement of Max and Fritz, her young German friends (chap. 65). In calling Jos her grandpa, as she had earlier called Steyne her uncle, she is half invoking a polite euphemism for anticipated intimacy and half joking at Jos's expense. Backstage derogation of Jos shows that Becky is as theatrical offstage as she is on it. The reappearance of the brandy bottle and munched sausage after Jos leaves ritually profanes the stage on which the imposter, Becky, has just performed. When she later tricks her backstage friends by selling them tickets for a fictitious concert, her conspiratorial furtiveness seems to know no limits. It might be thought that the same space that functions as a front region when Jos is present immediately reverts to a back region when he leaves. But in a real sense, Becky has no backstage region. Becky is always onstage, always playing a part. When Jos leaves, she relaxes not by ceasing to play a role, but by assuming a more informal, irreverent role. Becky's compulsion to mimic people, and even to dupe her backstage audience, may become so powerful that the mimicry and deception become new forms of acting. To be is to playact: the moment she stops performing, she ceases to exist.

Becky's preposterous fiction that she can never bear to part with the portrait of Jos on his elephant conquers Jos, but it never deceives anyone else. Amelia, by contrast, carries around two portraits of George: his actual picture and the metaphoric portrait of him that exists only in her falsely idealizing memory. Becky correctly identifies this portrait of George as the icon of a fool: it consecrates the idolatry of "a silly, heartless, ungrateful little creature" (chap. 57). The mounting and removal of Jos's picture and the many migrations of George's portrait, which is part of Amelia's portable household shrine, recall the fate of the dead man's picture, which his heirs soon can bear to look at and eventually remove from its place of honor (chap. 61). Though less harsh than the swift disappearance of the picture in Dr. Johnson's poem—"The form distorted justifies the fall, / And Detestation rides the indignant wall" ("The Vanity of Human Wishes," ll. 89–90), the displacements in Thackeray are just as remorseless in enacting the same Fall of man in miniature. The fate of Everyman is nothing more distinctive than that obliteration of outline "in the dark land" to which Mrs. Sedley precedes her husband (chap. 61). Death is another name for the dark principle: it is the empty space behind Becky's flattery of Jos or Amelia's idolatry of George. It may also be the vacancy behind every mask an offstage actress wears.

Erosions of identity bring Becky face to face with the dark principle. She is said to be "without faith—or love—or character" (chap. 64). Much earlier in the novel, many inhabitants of Vanity Fair are described, less shockingly, as "Faithless, Hopeless, Charityless" (chap. 8). The slight but devastating change in the third attribute alerts us to the most potent absence of all. She lacks not merely hope, the second of the three Christian virtues, but something so radically human as character.

Becky's negative capability, as an artist of roles, is reproduced in society at large as a dark principle or void, whose most inclusive name is vanity. Ostensibly, the narrator wants his readers to avert their gaze from this void. But like many censors, his zeal for veiling increases the reader's desire to peep behind the mask. In an amplified paraleipsis, for example, Thackeray invites his readers to provide deleted information. What is omitted by way of tactful elision can be provided by each imaginative censor. "There are things we do and know perfectly well in Vanity Fair, though we never speak them: as the Ahrimanians worship the devil, but don't mention him. . . . In describing this siren, singing and smiling, coaxing and cajoling, the author, with modest pride, asks his readers all round, has he once forgotten the laws of politeness, and showed the monster's hideous tail above water?" (chap. 64). The fiendish cannibals, exuberantly devouring their victims, compose too hyperbolic and entertaining an arabesque of submarine rarities to hold real terror. The true terror is not a gothic horror show, discreetly veiled from view, but a sense of unnameable depths. What one cannot name is indefinite and measureless, beyond the refuge of any picture or definition.

Like a devil worshiper who refuses to name the devil, the censorious narrator seems to be more entranced by unnameable horrors than are the immoral performers he censures. Vices are to be tolerated, he says, if we place decent masks over them. But how does this argument of the moral censor differ from the unprincipled practice of an actress like Becky? In pretending to submit "deferentially... to the fashion at present prevailing" (chap. 64), is Thackeray's narrator not also subverting that "fashion" by collapsing any sustaining difference between the censor and the target of his censorship? In being made perfectly "genteel and inoffensive," is Becky herself not being presented as hypocritically by the censor as she is habitually being "presented" by herself? The collapse of the moral censor and the melodramatic actress into a common posture of hypocrisy, which veils an absence of true identity, is potently intimated by the siren's seductive invitation to the censor to hold up the looking glass to his face. Like the fool in the frontispiece illustration, the moral censor is also studying in the mirror an image of himself. The fool and the censor, like the censor and Becky, are only superficially different.

Vanity Fair's most unforgettable episodes vividly expose the same void or emptiness behind the masks. Becky's fleeting glimpse of Lord Steyne, for example, riding by in his coach with livid face and ghastly eyes, fitfully illuminates a specterlike emblem of depleted sensuality. The pretentious list of names and honors in his obituary notice, like the splendor of his priceless horses and blazing carriage, can do nothing to conceal the puniness and venom of the shriveled hedonist who hides inside the panoply of masks. Though Steyne stares at Becky as if he were Macbeth confronting Banquo's ghost, the true specter is Steyne, whirled "darkling down the torrent of his fate," like an allegorical Everyman out of "The Vanity of Human Wishes" (ll. 346).

The first sentence of "Before the Curtain" presents Thackeray as a kind of censorious god, who surveys mankind from China to Peru, as Dr. Johnson does. But a touch of Swiftian frenzy animates the catalog of jostling activities that crowd the fair and threaten to proliferate

randomly. As the asyndeton combines with like-sounding suffixes—
"smoking, cheating, fighting," the narrator becomes as intemperate in
his censure as the fools he censures. Even the phrase "before the
curtain" looks two ways at once. If the preposition "before" is temporal, it can refer to the time preceding the rise of the curtain that Tom
Fool shares with his wife and little Jack Puddings. If the preposition is
given a spatial meaning, then "before" can refer to the onstage region
where Tom Fool turns cartwheels and cries to the audience, "How are
you?" Because the same phrase can refer to either the backstage or
the onstage region, it raises the question: What is the status of
theatrical performance? Does backstage differ from onstage? And
what distinguishes a washed face from a painted one? Is there
anything worth recording behind the curtain as opposed to what takes
place in front? Or is onstage performance the only reality that exists
or the only reality we can talk about? As Thackeray's version of
Browning's poem "House and Shop," the first paragraph of "Before
the Curtain" suggests that if anything important happens backstage,
the narrator prefers to keep it private. Browning's reticence is sometimes only a temperamental reserve. But Thackeray's silence seems to
veil some deeper absence of meaning.

From the very beginning Thackeray takes refuge in the debilitating
strength of double irony. To save himself from Swiftian imbalance, the
intemperate censor who lashes out at every variety of indulgence must
make room for the laxer attitudes of lazy and sarcastic, even benevolent, observers. The only rule for connecting such discordant adjectives is that there is no rule. Thackeray wants to mask his impatience
and create at least the illusion of balanced judgment. But equally
disquieting is the narrator's boast that his performance is simultaneously
controlled and uncontrolled. He is in control of the puppetlike
responses of his readers, who if they behave like previous readers will
be entertained by his puppets. But he is in control of no moral key or
norm that might make his fiction coherent: "I have no other moral
than this [the response of people to the show] to tag to the present
story of 'Vanity Fair.'" The bewildering array of contradictory impressions exceeds the abundant variety of an ordinary fair as a riddle
exceeds its solution. The double irony of the narrator, who sympathizes with the fools who are censured as well as with the moral
tyrants who censure, also preserves a sense of elusiveness and mystery,
allowing Thackeray to rise to a grand survey of the strangeness of the
carnival.

In pointing to the incongruity between the heroic scale of his survey
and the modesty of his discovery, if it can be called a discovery,
Thackeray is touching, I think, on the central mystery. His only moral

is that his survey justifies no moral. Some censors find fairs and art immoral, others find them entertaining. But that is hardly a moral. His secret message lurks behind these evasions. It has something to do with a disquieting sense that actresses like Becky and artists like Thackeray are hollow people—impersonators who can identify with no single role. To be lucid about who we are is to betray the mystery of who we *feel* we are. And to be true to the mystery of who we feel we are is to be unclear about which role we want to play. Indeed, unwillingness to play a single role, to be limited to the part of a moral censor or a censured fool, is the secret spring of Thackeray's double irony. And a comparable unwillingness is the secret of Becky's skill as a performer. She feels totally herself only when performing onstage: backstage, she is like the wearer of motley who, when he leaves the fairground, goes home to "be perfectly miserable in private" (chap. 19).

In the characterless Lady Rose Crawley we find a parody of what the actress or performer becomes when she is not acting. Rose is a mere machine in her husband's house, of no more use than a grand piano. Beyond her small flower garden, she has no likes or dislikes. A mere echo or emptiness, she has not even enough character to take to drink. Her credentials compose an appalling list of negatives: "she had no sort of character; nor talents, nor opinions, nor occupations, nor amusements, nor that vigor of soul and ferocity of temper which often falls to the lot of entirely foolish women" (chap. 9). As a creature without qualities, she finds that even her hold on Sir Pitt's affections is not very great. In the end, Becky's life proves equally hollow. Her triumphant performance on being introduced to "the best society" excite, elate, and then bore her. Because she is as empty inside as the characterless Rose Crawley, the epitome of placid inertia, Becky is destined never to be happy. The hunger of her imagination is forever simplifying the endless desires of the human heart, as Dr. Johnson says, then finding them wanting. Becky would rather be a dancer, a parson's wife teaching Sunday school, or a sergeant's lady than the wife of Captain Rawdon. Like Borrow's Lavengro, Becky lives in dread of being trapped in a single role. She is the perfect embodiment of Kierkegaard's sensualist, rotating the round of her pleasures in a desperate effort to stave off the inevitable boredom. Like the author of a seducer's diary, she is impelled to experiment with new incognitos. She even playacts at being bored. Unable to be bored in earnest, she escapes from boredom by telling Steyne lively stories about her boredom. Is she honest and good-natured, or a little minx? "Some people . . . said that she was the criminal; whilst others vowed that she was as innocent as a lamb" (chap. 64). It depends on the role she chooses to perform. Playacting is her opium. She needs an audience and can no "more exist without [society] than an opium-eater without his dram" (chap. 64).

Just as Trollope's narrator in *Barchester Towers* is more like Harding or Arabin than anyone else in the fiction, so Thackeray's narrator most resembles Becky. He pretends, for example, to mock the censure of Amelia by female correspondents who write to him in letters that have pink seals attached. Their "kind" remarks consist of complaints that Amelia is "*fade* and insipid" (chap. 12). Is Thackeray mocking the censors, or is he secretly siding with them? The ironist seems simultaneously to be attacking the jealousy of the censors and the foolishness of their victim. For a woman to be despised by another woman is a great compliment to her beauty and charm. But in seeming to mock the envy of Amelia's censors, Thackeray is also behaving precisely like Becky when, after uttering an ironic comment in so wry and detached a manner that her auditors wonder whether she intends any irony at all, she then coolly apologizes for her insult (chap. 51). Thackeray may seem to present Amelia without any benefit of irony. But the ironic remarks that an imaginary female correspondent is said to make about Amelia are clearly Thackeray's way of warning readers that any ironies they may think they detect are part of his design. To assume otherwise is to set too low a threshold of irony. The hollowness or instability that both abets the double irony and takes refuge in it is as characteristic of Thackeray's narrator as it is of Becky.

Thackeray's superb moral essay on the qualities of a gentleman—one "whose aims are generous, whose truth is constant, and not only constant in its kind, but elevated in its degree" (chap. 62)—provides one of the novel's few articulated norms. But who can measure up to such a benchmark? Though Dobbin is the kind of person Thackeray describes, he is immediately subjected to caricature: we are reminded that his hands and feet are too large and that he speaks with a slight lisp. At Vauxhall Dobbin, the unattached bachelor, is treated little better than a servant who is made to carry the shawls; only after years of waiting does he move to center stage to claim Amelia. When norms are embodied in people and institutions, they go unrecognized in Vanity Fair. The true values do not possess the appearance of being true: and what appears to be of value is not really so. There are no transparent signifiers. Signs that seem to be transparent are not really signs but are empty or distoring masks. And the signs that truly signify are too self-concealing and opaque to be recognized.

When Jane Osborne, dragged momentarily from the periphery of the novel to its center, is said to lead "an awful existence" (chap. 42), the adjective "awful" looks two ways at once. It describes, colloquially, the drabness of Jane's drudgery in the patriarchal household. But her existence is "awful" in an oddly solemn, awe-inspiring way, for it evokes the boredom and the horror by which countless other marginal lives are swallowed up and consumed. Branching relative clauses, which amplify the sentences by engulfing nouns in modifiers and protracted present participles—"listening," "sitting," "expecting," "working"—achieve grammatically what is achieved optically by the infinite regress of images reflected off the two facing mirrors. In turning the drawing room into the center of a whole system of drawing rooms, Thackeray preserves the semblance without the substance of an ordered world, just as Becky's offstage acting proliferates endlessly with no circumference or limits in the process, and with no real center to fall back on.

Like the facing mirrors in Jane Osborne's drawing room or the echoes of the piano that awaken echoes of another kind—memories of the banished George—architectural details of the Sedley household allow Thackeray in chapter 61 to enlarge his meanings indefinitely. Invoked as a friend in motley, the reader is drawn into the alarmingly abbreviated pageant produced by Thackeray's sudden three-word contraction—"Life, Death, . . . Vanity"—of a leisurely twenty-line apostrophe to the arch in a London house. The narrator begins with the arch, then moves to the stair. The basic trope is synecdoche: the use of a part to expand into a whole. Looking up and down the stairwell, Thackeray can be as all-seeing as an epic poet. A future event, the death of each reader, is also commemorated in a harrowing inversion of déjà vu. By renovating what is dead in our own complacent platitudes about dying, Thackeray manages to bring into shocking prominence the hour of our own death. We are invited not only to be present at our funeral, but also to witness the desecration of our memory by our heirs, who will remove our picture and soon forget what we look like. The "black ark" in which "the cold tenant" slumbers is like every other mask or veil in *Vanity Fair*. There is nothing behind it that is not already in front of it, already "before the curtain," so to speak. Even though impressions of mortality are always fading from the mind, they are also inscribed on everything around us, waiting to be revived as a motive to virtue by moralists like Bunyan, Dr. Johnson, and perhaps at moments even Thackeray himself, when they invigorate a dead metaphor or jaded impression.

At first we may think that Thackeray is just trying to see all around an issue, like Browning in *The Ring and the Book*. There is more than one code of behavior in the world, and a central purpose of reading is to experience some of this diversity and range. But unlike Browning,

Thackeray is not merely trying to understand many codes so that his endorsement of specific codes will carry weight. In a world without heroes there is no code of behavior that Thackeray can single-mindedly endorse. As William Empson says, the "time must...come, if a man carries through a consistent programme about double irony, when he himself does not know the answer" (1984, 144). I think Thackeray's bewilderment comes very early in the novel. Even in the prologue, a mystery of weird pathos surrounds the manager who presides over a performance whose values he scorns. The teasing quality of Becky, the accomplished actress who accepts Jos's teasing with grace (chap. 3), personifies the teasing quality of the narrator himself and of his novel at large. We are teased into expecting the disclosure of some secret message. But the message is withheld until we begin to suspect that the sphinx is without a secret after all.

There are flickers of gratuitous judgment in Thackeray's observation that Becky's sense of ridicule is far stronger than her gratitude (chap. 2). But the dominance of dramatic over moral sense is not part of a well-made dramatic entertainment for the reader. Though Becky's mimicry may provide improvised local entertainment for her father and his friends, for the reader it cheerfully works the other way round, often producing incongruity of effect. Because the styles and varied performances of the characters jostle each other, instead of settling down comfortably together, the novel enacts on a large scale the jostling of such adjectives as "lazy, dissolute, clever, jovial," applied to Becky's father (chap. 2), and the even more pivotal and oxymoronic conjoinings of lies and schemes, of selfishness and wiles, of wit and genius, at the climax of the novel (chap. 53). The narrator's tone has something almost good-naturedly lax about it, expansive and familiar. But the laxity is combined with a Swiftian impatience and imbalance that are rarely found in conjunction with leisurely amplitude. The tone is dual, in keeping with the subtle and incessant double irony. And the language is often simultaneously terse and expansive. Huge sentences like the one describing the arch in the stairwell (chap. 61) tie themselves into syntactic knots that suddenly come loose. Strands slacken and unravel. Even the chief performer relaxes the strain and drops, as we have seen, into backstage mimicry and farce.

The current of the novel is tidal, bearing everyone at its disposal forward and backward in an incessant ebb and flow that keeps undoing what has been done. The tumbling together and confusion of sensations as Becky sits alone in the discovery scene, her empire of conquest collapsed around her, dramatizes a general helplessness. Even the halting syntax drops connectives, and pronouns often have a double referent: "She knew he would never come back. He was gone for ever" (chap. 53). Is she referring to Rawdon or Steyne? The vagaries of her mind and syntax set her afloat on a frail raft, and sometimes the narrator seems to be as much adrift as Becky. "What *had* happened?" he asks. "Was she guilty or not?" (chap. 53). He seems to lose himself in mental wandering, caught in the toils of incongruous detail. Though the same fatality and sense of inconsequence broods over all performers in the carnival, to cease playing parts is even more disastrous. It is to have all individuality leached out of one's personality, like the *fade* and insipid Amelia or the blond, characterless Lady Rose.

Playacting is as much an art of forgetting as of remembering. An actress has to remember lines but forget everything that exists off-stage. Even Thackeray's narrator seems to forget as much as he remembers. At one moment he tells us he is a lonely and childless bachelor: Vauxhall is no place to go if one is unattended and single. At other times he forgets he is a bachelor and speaks of his wife Julia and his children. Forgetting is equally characteristic of Becky. She forgets about Rawdon Junior until it is in her financial interest to remember him. As an artist of forgetting and undoing like the narrator of *Vanity Fair* and like Beatrix in *Henry Esmond*, who undoes her web by night in imitation of Penelope, Becky is just the person to instruct Amelia in the art of forgetting George.

Earlier allegorists of Vanity Fair, including Bunyan and Dr. Johnson, were never in any doubt about the theological or moral center of their vision. But the only center for Thackeray seems to be the emptiness of Jane Osborne's drawing room. The mystical image of a universe whose center is everywhere and whose circumference is nowhere has been replaced by a system of drawing rooms that, because it has no beginning, no ground outside itself, exists only as a self-generated web. As in any image reflected in a mirror set opposite a second mirror, the recess of vistas is self-replicating and endless. Without a stable center, how can an allegory about Vanity Fair be written? It is the suspicion of the absence of a sovereign power or center that haunts the narrator like the absence of God. Without a power installed behind the social system or within it, which would justify the system, Thackeray's self-replicating vistas of drawing rooms within drawing rooms seem more like a centerless maze than the vision of an allegorist. *Vanity Fair* produces the illusion of a grounded sign system, but its promise of disclosing the ground is never fulfilled. A dark truth that is not strictly speakable, but that seems to lurk as an emptiness or an echo behind every mask and every word, is Thackeray's closest equivalent to celestial vision. To acquire a positive identity that survives the rotation of dramatic masks is to be exiled like Rawdon, dead like George, or else outside language altogether.

Vanity Fair strives for wholeness of vision, but not for stability. To see life whole is to see it is unstable, to see it possesses the shimmering mystery of a mirage, of an unsubstantial pageant like Prospero's that leaves not a rack behind (chap. 67). The titanic plot is necessary for such wholeness of vision. Yet despite its magnitude, the plot's substance is no more solid or stable than a sea during a storm. There is more falling and rising with the waves than any discernible motion forward. And to show that wavering and instability are universal, Thackeray must keep engaging the engine screws of his massive double irony, even when they churn only froth or mountains of ocean foam. The novel has at first the feel of building up like Euclid, but its geometry retains only the *illusion* of incremental design. Though Becky's campaigns move steadily toward a climax, their outcome is bathetic. The form of *Vanity Fair* is majestically synoptic. But it starts with axioms of vanity and playacting that make genuine advance as illusory as one of the ever-receding images glimpsed in the two great glasses that reflect each other in Jane Osborne's drawing room. To put forward a general theory about the vanity of human affairs implies a claim to have wide ethical experience, and such a claimant should be ready to mock his own claims by laughing at himself as well as at his brother wearers of motley. But when Thackeray surveys his world panoramically, as in the scene describing the rise and fall of a wavering Everyman from the vantage point of the arch and stairwell in a Victorian household, his language momentarily towers: it becomes as magisterial and prophetic as Dr. Johnson's august poetry of decline in "The Vanity of Human Wishes." Brooding over the instability and strangeness of human affairs, Thackeray seems simultaneously an omniscient god and a damaged archangel, one of Arnold's ineffectual angels, moving his wings over the darkening void in vain.

CHAPTER 9

The Burden of Role-Playing:

Self-Creation in Borrow and Clough

The word "persona" refers in its primary meaning to a mask: the games and dramatic parts that Borrow's Lavengro and Clough's Claude keep playing are ways of marking out and investigating an identity. But in each case their status as "persons" seems under pressure. In *Amours de Voyage* Claude plays at being a lover, tracking down the girl he wants to marry. And Lavengro keeps amusing himself with being by turns a pugilist, an author, and a gypsy. At first the condition of each person seems wholly one of ceremony and theater, wholly a matter of convincing an audience that each actor is nothing but the pugilist, the gypsy, or the lover he appears to be at the moment. Such role-playing seems to impose no burden or threat to one's personhood as long as the assumed mask represents what Matthew Arnold calls his "buried" or truer self, the self he wants to be. And yet the many precautions we take to lock a person into a single part also suggest that we live "in perpetual fear that he might escape from it, that he might break away and suddenly elude his condition" (Goffman 1959, 76). To be locked into a single role is to atrophy; but to see and create whole vistas of alternative selves soon begins to impose a burden of a different kind. For what happens when a role-player like Lavengro acquires dramatic identities without identity, or a host of vocational beliefs without belief?

The mysteries of identity create a double bind for Lavengro. On the one hand, to seek a ground or "buried life" within the self is to forgo role-playing at the risk of becoming mute and unintelligible: it is to revert to the silence of an autistic child or the muteness of the Moldavian clerk (chap. 51). On the other hand, to be communicative at all, Lavengro must master the secret art of creating a whole series of new identities and surrogate "fathers" by looking into mirrors and seeing facets of himself reflected there. The creator of such masks is in danger of becoming only an actor, only a persona with no authentic self.

The "dark principle" in *Lavengro*, which is capable of both exalting and abasing Borrow's hero, can be interpreted in contrary ways. It can signify the shadow life of self-reflecting images, as of phantoms seen in a hall of mirrors. Or it can refer to the undifferentiated ground, the indescribable "buried" life beneath all the masks Lavengro assumes. Can the impersonator find a grounding self so rich in content that all the personae he creates are thin or attenuated shadows? Or is the self the shadow and the roles he plays the only true substance?

After his attack of unspeakable horror in the dingle, Lavengro concludes that the "dark principle" is inside him: it is his own interior silence, his own heart of darkness. "I could only have got rid of it," he realizes, "by getting rid of myself: it was a part of myself, or rather it was all myself" (chap. 84). Afraid that he has no authentic identity and that all the roles he has assumed are unreal, he prays to "our Father" three times. His second invocation makes the terror more acute, because it formulates his fear of inhabiting an unbegotten, fatherless world. Only the third prayer brings a measure of relief by allowing Lavengro to find comfort in the companionship of a little horse that licks his hand. Though he undergoes what "he cannot describe, and would not attempt if [he] were able," patterns irresistibly impose themselves. Both the triple invocation of the Father and the chiastic rhetoric—"it subsided, came again, again subsided"—provide at least the comfort of a refuge or a limit.

Though Lavengro finds his own history of spiritual depression already recorded in the biblical story of Saul, he is quick to deny any similarity. To acknowledge the replication in himself of a dark principle already written down is to confirm Lavengro's own worst fear of being a plagiarist. Even that fear is only imitative, a mere duplication of the irrational fears of the wealthy author Lavengro has met. If even his despair, like his fear of plagiarism, is derivative, Lavengro is doubly hollow: he not only is empty in himself but is also a mere hollow echo of a hollow man.

When Isopel Berners asks Lavengro if he is afraid of the Flaming Tinman, he says his fear is not so localized. This admission should be compared to the child's observation to his mother that he would be less frightened if he could give his fear a name. But the most precise label he can attach to the terror is "the evil one" (chap. 86). His premonition of evil immediately follows the surge of revulsion he feels when Blazing Bosville asks Lavengro to marry him and make Bosville's wife their drudge. The thought of a homosexual union raises doubts about how far role-playing might go.

When Lavengro tries to find a proper name for the dark principle, his elliptical grammar momentarily settles into an expansive appositional form: "dark one, terrible one, causeless, unbegotten, without a father" (chap. 18). As if in parody of a theological formula: "very God of very God, begotten of his Father before all worlds," the language of theology is used to define a fatherless principle that inverts the very doctrine of the Athanasian creed. The dark principle of being unbegotten, without a first cause or origin, is the terror of echoing hollowly in an empty chamber of near tautologies—ungrounded, fatherless, with neither an identity nor a vocation. Lavengro's fear is the anxiety of a quester, a Victorian existentialist like Clough's Claude in *Amours de Voyage*, who in launching out in search of a new and more authentic identity renounces the categorical living of a shore dweller.

Whereas the rich author is a mirror in which Lavengro sees reflected his own negative capability, Lavengro's brother functions as his antitype. In contrast to the Rubenslike picture of his brother, whose face is always the mirror of his mind, Lavengro's face can never be called handsome. As an autistic being, Lavengro may seem grotesque. But as a prophet in disguise, the oracle of a hidden truth, he may also prove as sublime as Saul. By becoming an array of different people, absorbing the good or bad of a whole nation, Lavengro, like any artist of the self, becomes symbolically what a king is. Lavengro's silence as a child signifies the discrepancy between the manner in which he exists inwardly, as a latter-day Saul, and the external appearance he presents to those who find him mentally retarded and autistic. Just as Socrates is willing to be mistaken for a buffoon, so the young Lavengro, by assuming silence and reserve as his incognito, is prepared to be mistaken for a deaf-mute, even though he has a phobia about dumb people.

Literature and the art of imaginative identification rouse Lavengro from his youthful torpor. He admires Defoe's characters for their willingness to live uprooted lives. To imitate a character like Robinson Crusoe or Moll Flanders might be thought to confer on the imitator a stable identity. But to imitate a resourceful experimenter like Crusoe or Moll is also *not* to imitate. For the genius of such adventurous originators is to reject models. Yet Lavengro fears that his most authentic thoughts are derivative. If there is nothing new under the sun, including the thought that there is nothing new under the sun, then Lavengro is always a belated immigrant to realms of thought occupied before him by more monumental thinkers. The thought that the world is a deception and a cheat was old even when the world was young. Since even the language Lavengro must use to express this discovery is derivative and allusive, a mere echo of Job's lament, "Would I had never been born" (chap. 25), it is no wonder Lavengro staggers and reels under a heavy burden of belatedness.

Far from producing permanent paralysis, however, the dark principle seems to be a source of energy. After his bouts of suicidal depression, Lavengro is strangely renewed. He is not a weary pessimist who is tired of life, but the sworn enemy of every censor and tyrant, every hypocrite and confidence man, who tries to lock him into single roles. Every locked door of repression in the mind masquerades as a form of responsible or reputable vocation, but Lavengro knows they are only prisons in disguise. To escape all locked cells of repression, he resolves to roam the world at large as one of Keats's artists of negative capability.

But in the end the artist may grow tired of his role-playing. The only mental handicap from which there seems to be no escape is world-weariness, the experience of being belated or of merely repeating what has already been said or done. Lavengro's wisdom, like the wisdom of Thackeray's narrator in *Vanity Fair* or of the biblical Koheleth, is devastating. Its essential paradox is that all things are full of emptiness—the root meaning of the biblical word *vanitas*. Even Lavengro's desolation seems merely to repeat the experiences of Saul and Bunyan. The allusiveness of his style is part of the doubter's problem. When Koheleth saw that "not only all was vanity, but that he himself was vanity" (chap. 25), he was struck in part by the vain way he was merely repeating the Buddha's repetition of a similar truth. Part of the vanity is the empty and ungrounded way recognitions of emptiness merely echo each other. The best hope of enduring, Lavengro realizes, is to be self-generating, causeless, fatherless, more original than an originating power like god. As a mere translator, however, Lavengro is overwhelmed with a sense of the hollowness inside himself. Vanity denotes mist, vapor, fog, and by extension the empty spaces of the dreary labyrinth in which Lavengro loses his way when he asks the question, "What is truth?" (chap. 25). And yet the knowledge of his own hollowness spurs Lavengro, as it spurs the rich author, to renewed effort. Since the book *Lavengro* and all the activities of its author are forms of emptiness, Borrow must redouble his own efforts to produce a work that is not totally hollow at the center.

Borrow asserts in his preface that *Lavengro* is neither an autobiography nor a novel but "a dream, partly of study, partly of adventure." As a *waking* dream, the book never completely dissolves the contrast between Borrow, the implied author, whom we seem to overhear most directly in interludes of philosophical reflection like chapter 35, and his dramatic character, Lavengro. And yet as in *any* dream, waking or otherwise, it is not always possible to distinguish between the dreamer himself and the characters who abruptly materialize in his mind and just as suddenly vanish. If readers cannot decide who is being discussed— Is it Borrow or his created character, Lavengro?—the uncertainty is one that Borrow seems to share. Even the stories within stories (Lavengro's stories of the postillion, the rich author, Peter Williams) produce opposite effects. Sometimes they mirror Lavengro's own crises and sharpen our sense of his objective identity. But at other times the dizzying recursions dissolve all the characters in an insubstantial pageant. As Lavengro and Borrow keep melting into each other, only the author himself, as a Prospero-like magician, seems to survive the dreamlike dissolutions and mergings.

Lavengro's search for a single *Ursprache*, behind all languages, which might reverse the catastrophe of Babel, recalls the search for some primal language of identity in *Wuthering Heights*. But when Lavengro thinks he discerns the lineaments of such a universal language in the Romany dialect, distinctions of feeling and of moral value become meaningless and confused. Perhaps "divine and devilish were originally one and the same word," Lavengro suggests to Jasper, since "God" in Romany is "Duvel" and "godly" "duvelskoe" (chap. 17). Gradually, at the edge of his mind, sustaining differences between vice and virtue collapse: "With respect to crime and virtue I was in doubt," Lavengro confides. "I doubted that the one was blameable and the other praiseworthy" (chap. 25). Whereas Cathy's dream of being homesick in heaven expresses a central truth in *Wuthering Heights*, Lavengro's dreams fade in his mind like echoes, disclosing only the dreamer's act of dreaming: "Am I not myself a dream—dreaming about translating a dream?" (chap. 36) Anticipating Jacques Derrida's notion of a "système décentré," Lavengro's world of dissolving identities and words contains no ultimate god term, only an unreal network of differential relations with nothing solid at its center.

Though Lavengro's goal of finding a fulfilling vocation continues to elude him, the moment he runs away from the problem he finds himself running into it again. Goals are achieved circuitously, in ways that resemble the detours and sudden convergences of figures in a dream. Sluggards and drones, for example, are converted into models of energetic activity by the same providential design that reunites the old apple woman and her son after years of separation. The selfishness of the rich author threatens to make him a mere eccentric afflicted by the touch. But because his self-absorption becomes a torment to him, it also impels him to write books. And in case he becomes selfishly fond of what he writes, his vain delusion that each book he writes is vain, a form of empty imitation, makes him doubly energetic. The mental indolence of the scholar who learns Chinese would also have been a vanity had the empty space inside his head not produced a terrible whirring that only study can relieve. The secret of the wisdom he comes to possess is not an Oriental withdrawal from the world but a life of continuous mental energy spent in the acquisition of difficult new knowledge.

Lavengro likes to think that the world is a shadow, and that the substance that creates the shadow will somehow manifest itself when the deceitful phantom of the world is renounced. But the repeated cry "All is a lie—a deceitful phantom" (chap. 25) reverses these assumptions. The invisible world is a concealed revelation. Like air, it is the medium by which the world we live in becomes visible. Lavengro often feels that what cannot be seen is a stifling darkness, a malign disorder that sentences him to wander endlessly in a labyrinth. But he comes to realize, like the Chinese scholar, that the labyrinth exists only in the empty spaces of his mind. Properly used, doubt is not a pretext for paralysis but a spur to continuous mental action.

Not only is Borrow the author of a confession, *Lavengro*, within this confession his narrator Lavengro is the author of a similar genre—a series of Newgate confessions commissioned by the London publisher, Phillips. Many characters are also impelled to make private confessions to Lavengro, as if the events of Lavengro's life were imitating the genre both of Borrow's book and of the books Lavengro has written for Phillips. Often confessional intimacy occurs at moments of psychic strain. During a particularly acute attack of spiritual despair, Peter Williams, the Welsh clergyman, confides to Lavengro his fear of having committed in youth the unpardonable sin. Sacrificing his self-protective distance from Lavengro, Williams induces a backstage solidarity with the stranger. The evangelical cult of public confession is an officially sanctioned genre, an acceptable form of disclosing secrets one would normally conceal. But what Williams cannot say even to his congregation, as part of a public performance, he can say backstage. The support he receives from Lavengro is therapeutic. As a willing auditor and collector of such confessions, Lavengro is continually assembling new sets of skeletons for newly shared closets. Some skeletons, like Bosville's proposal of a homosexual marriage, shock him. But Lavengro is usually willing to elicit confessional orgies of psychological, moral, and even spiritual self-analysis. The confessions seem therapeutic for patient and clinician alike.

In exploring the burdens of role-playing, *Lavengro* also dramatizes the pathos of the incognito, the ironic discrepancy that exists between outward appearance and inward being. In healing Peter Williams,

Lavengro seems to speak with the studied indirection of an ironist and a prophet. But he is an unconscious prophet. Unaware of his power to inscribe holy characters on the ground (chap. 1) or to utter oracular truths, he illuminates the discrepancy between what he really is and what he outwardly *seems* to be. Like Lavengro, many characters in Borrow's fiction lead double lives. The Quaker banker, for example, though an efficient businessman, is also a pious scholar and pacifist. The two sides of his life exist in uneasy tension. Even the novel's subtitle suggests an equally precarious balance in Borrow himself of the priest, the scholar, and the gypsy.

Though Lavengro remorselessly exposes the verbal mystique surrounding respectable vocations and social hierarchies, the sacred compatibility between a man and his job is fostered by the rhetoric of training to which even a practitioner of gypsy lore like Lavengro must patiently submit. Lavengro's mastery of snakes, his command of exotic languages, his skill as a pugilist, all foster the impression of a licensed practitioner. He is subjected to the same rhetoric of training as his brother the painter or as his father the military officer. The mystical range of his wizardry with gypsy dialects and Welsh is just as arcane and disciplined as the Jesuit's priestly craft or as the training of the Methodist preacher Peter Williams.

Whatever sovereign power or standard has given Lavengro's wizardry its authority and mystique is in danger of being subverted, however, by the same "dark principle" that erodes Lavengro's faith in "discrimination" as "the very key-stone" of the social hierarchy. If Lavengro is godforsaken, like William Taylor of Norwich, or if he is fatherless and his life is causeless, then there is nothing behind his masks but an abyss of darkness. No excess of heroism, absurdity, or abomination seems to matter. According to William Taylor of Norwich, the model for the Germanist who dissolves Lavengro's theological and philosophical certainties, any theory about the world and its origins turns out to be a preposterous conceit, a mere arbitrary fiction and nothing more. With some justice, Lavengro's father suspects his son's strange notions have been inculcated by the godless German scholar, who worships Jesus as the hero of Golgotha, as Strauss or Carlyle might have done, but not as the son of God (chap. 23). If Jesus is merely a moral hero, does he not become as fatherless as Lavengro? And if no sovereign power behind the world is watching what we do, how can the German mentor enforce moral decency? Once a truth is recognized as regulative rather than constitutive in Kant's sense, has it not already lost its power to regulate in the moral sphere?

Without a clear origin or end, the German philosopher, like his disciple, seems fatherless and doomed. The baseless, dreamlike progression of characters in *Lavengro* resembles the dark pilgrimage of the German master's life: a pilgrimage without a goal. Like a groundless theology that worships a mere moral genius instead of a Son with a Father, the dreamlike events in *Lavengro* stop rather than conclude. The hero's ceaseless movement toward a light that always remains hidden in the dark, or toward a word that speaks to him from the other side of silence, makes it impossible to write "finis" to his story.

When Borrow interrupts the dramatic action to ask "What is truth?" and to endorse the wisdom of Koheleth (chap. 25), or when in the appendix to *The Romany Rye* he steps forth from behind his other masks to interpret the providential design of his story, he is momentarily suspending the dramatic illusion in a kind of parabasis. But most of *Lavengro* constitutes what Friedrich Schlegel calls a "permanent parabasis." The constant erosion of Lavengro's temporarily assumed identities makes him characterless, neither "fish or flesh," as he says. The kind of irony that postpones indefinitely the goal of Lavengro's quest may finally encompass Lavengro as well as the hollow characters whose positive identity he first postulates and then finds lacking. There may be secure local ironies that erode the pretensions of Francis Ardry, the eternal sensualist and playboy, or of Phillips, the conceited publisher. But these ironies are limited and determinate. Lavengro's inability to identify an underlying father, cause, or origin—a key to the whole phantasm of his "dream-adventure," suspends the possibility of finding any solid ground to stand on. Readers look in vain for any vantage point from which they can confidently assess the whole.

Perhaps like the self-assured commentator in the appendix to *The Romany Rye*, Borrow wants to understand and control his life by becoming a ventriloquist who merely speaks through the voices and masks he assumes. But who, then, is the real Borrow? Who is to say that the bigoted, ale-drinking persona of *The Romany Rye*, who tries to impose closure on his text, is a closer continuer of the real-life Borrow than a role-player like Lavengro? Borrow may hope to master the ironic mode whereby most portraits are discarded before a true portrait can be put in their place. But the skeptic who lives by irony dies by it too. If irony is a permanent parabasis, a suspension of any ground or face behind all the false grounds and faces that are continually being unmasked, then, as J. Hillis Miller says, irony "cannot be used as an instrument of mastery. It always masters the one who tries to master it or to take power with it" (1982, 106).

An artist of constantly changing roles can claim to have no total memory of his life, nor can he see it forming a coherent whole. When such coherence is claimed, as in the appendix to *The Romany Rye*, too many odd and idiosyncratic details of Lavengro's earlier "dream-adventure" have to be elided. The dream presents too many fragments and too little patterned assimilation of them: it provides simultaneously too little design and too much. Any interpretation that tries to be unifying has to omit important configurations in the dream. Indeed, if we are to believe the apologist in *The Romany Rye*, who insists that his purpose in *Lavengro* is to dramatize God's providence, there is duplicity in Borrow from the start: like Kierkegaard, he appears to be a secular and religious writer simultaneously. Pretending to write in one genre, the secular confession, he is really writing in another. But are the apologist's words to be trusted? Is the apologist the face behind the mask, or is he just another mask?

In every character there lurks a secret fear of groundlessness and of exclusion from the truth. Hence Lavengro's obsession with Pilate's question, "What is truth?" and his secret fear that "all [is] a lie—a deceitful phantom" (chap. 25). Lavengro can communicate only with those who share his secret fear. Men of positive identity like his father, who lives categorically, forget the "little Socratic secret" that "truth is spirit." It is better that Lavengro not be understood by his father than that he be misunderstood. Only a profound and hidden inwardness, which refuses to recognize the spirit in any of its accidental embodiments, can preserve the spirit intact and make it live. Anyone who tries like Phillips to profane the secret by indulging in moral bombast about the magnificence of nature and the dignity of man merely proves his own stupidity.

The hypocrisy of Phillips, who makes an ostentatious parade of his spirituality, and the irony of Lavengro, who cannot even recognize the spiritual quality of his experience, are opposite ways of dramatizing the Socratic secret that truth is hidden and inward. Like Phillips's portentous axiom that the world is shaped like a pear rather than an apple, Lavengro's gibe that "German philosophy is all smoke" (chap. 23) revokes in the predicate the profundity it seems to proffer in its subject. The godless German scholar seems to have forgotten that dialectics must keep their passion. He is unhappy because like some contemporary deconstructionists he has turned his search for contradictions into a mindless and arid exercise. Though this cheerless skeptic and mechanical exposer of aporias has forgotten the Socratic secret that "truth is spirit," he has taught Lavengro more than his father has. For he also inspires in his pupil the Socratic fear of error. Arguing that an eternal happiness cannot be based on a historical fact, the German mentor teaches Lavengro to doubt received religious beliefs. He dramatizes Kierkegaard's dictum that "the very maximum of what one human being can do for another in relation to that wherein each man has to do solely with himself, is to inspire him with concern and unrest" (1941, 346).

Lavengro's memory seems at times to be only a depository of chance impressions. Genuine recollections would be investments for eternity, because they would assert faith in continuity. But Lavengro has no recollections; he has only disconnected memories. Most of his sentences seem to be taken from a child's journal, and (to borrow Kierkegaard's distinction) he has the memory of childhood without the recollection of young adulthood or middle age. Since the book contains occasional reflective passages, however, and since Lavengro says explicitly that his true life begins at the moment he learns to see himself in mirrors, perhaps his childlike memories are actually recollections in disguise. The childlike simplicity of Lavengro's narrative may be just another mark of his reserve, another of the Socratic incognitos he chooses to assume.

Lavengro's doubt and unrest seem inseparable from his capacity to reflect. He is overwhelmed by the fear that his identity consists wholly of echoes and reflections. Indeed, doubt itself, according to Keirkegaard, is "a reflection-category," as opposed to wonder, for example, which is plainly an "immediate category" and involves no reflection upon itself (Kierkegaard 1985, 145). The discontinuity of Lavengro's "dream-adventure" is the discontinuity of doubt, which always wages war against whatever belief or attitude precedes it. The unstable transitions in *Lavengro* have the disturbing effect of separating father and son, cause and effect, God and his creation, until the first term in each pair is displaced by the second. By discarding every identity and role almost as soon as he develops it, Lavengro also frees himself from any disciples. Lavengro's own truest teachers—Moll Flanders, Robinson Crusoe, and the German master, cancel the relation of teacher and pupil by encouraging endless experimentation, contradiction, and doubt. The student is acknowledged to be just as practiced as the master. Each identity must be discarded in a different way, and the possibility for new creation seems endless.

Whenever he is questioned about his secret knowledge or about the dark side of truth, Lavengro answers ironically. For as Kierkegaard explains, "it is always irony when I say something and still do not say anything. Isaac questions Abraham in the belief that Abraham knows. Now, if Abraham had replied: I know nothing—he would have spoken an untruth. . . . therefore he answers: God himself will provide the lamb for the burnt offering" (1983, 118–19). If Lavengro had denied he knew the answers to the Jew's questions, he would have spoken an untruth. So he cannot say anything, for what he knows he cannot speak. Instead, he answers the questions by tracing sacred characters on the ground. When Isopel Berners asks Lavengro to describe his suicidal despair, he finds he must speak without saying anything. For to talk about the dark principle is to take its name in vain: it is to profane it. When pressed by his mother, Lavengro says he is afraid of nothing. Does he mean the nothing that is "not anything" or the inscrutable presence behind nature that is called "nothing"? Lavengro is an ironist who "bows before the unknown," and he can answer his mother's question only by saying he does not know how to answer it.

As an artist of dramatic roles like Lavengro, Clough's Claude in *Amours de Voyage* finds that the prospect of living out a single role for a lifetime produces only ennui and despair. He lacks the courage to will a repetition of the part society expects him to play as the suitor and husband. Because Claude lives inwardly like Lavengro, he leaps in his imagination over the whole spectrum of his anticipated life married to Mary, envisaging his own funeral even before he has decided to track down his future wife and woo her. As Kierkegaard says, such an artist of negative capability, who cannot will a repetition of any positive identity he may assume, makes the mistake of standing "at the end instead of the beginning." In Claude's mind the prospect of a train terminus turns into the terminus of life itself. Claude cannot think of signing the marriage contract and of leaving on his wedding trip without imagining the progress of his own funeral train. He lacks an ironic elasticity and seems to think that the moment he commits himself in earnest to anything his life is over. To be negatively capable, he reflects, is to be infinitely capable, to be potentially anything at all. But Claude, like Lavengro, fails to register the countertruth that to be everything in theory is to be nothing in practice. Too godlike in general to achieve anything in particular, Claude cannot see that repetition and recollection are necessary categories, for without them, as Kierkegaard recognizes, "the whole of life is resolved into a void and empty noise" (1964, 53). This empty noise is the inarticulate babble that precedes speech: it is Lavengro's condition as an autistic child, before he learns to recollect what he reads and repeat in himself what he sees reflected from the mirror of other lives.

In an actual reading of *Amours de Voyage* we know less than we may think we know afterward when we summarize the poem and try to provide a plot for it. Claude's references to bonds he may unwittingly have tied raise the possibility of a more serious engagement to Mary than he is willing to acknowledge. Though the moral duty to honor such a commitment seems less compelling if enjoined by a mere possible shadow of deity, Claude's moral and religious skepticism may be less disinterested than it sounds. Are his theology and ethics really casuistry in disguise, a rationalization of his second thoughts about marriage? Even Georgiana may not know the whole truth about Claude. Her view of his inaction may not be totally correct. For there are hints toward the end of the poem that Claude is originally attracted to Mary because she refuses to bind him. Has he rehearsed a scene in which he plans to break off their engagement only to find that Mary pretends no engagement has been proposed? We marry because we see our own funeral train, because no tie or contract lasts forever. Has Claude already proposed marriage to Mary in such unflattering terms? Is his denial that women are capable of thought part of an actual proposal to Mary that she has understandably rejected because it insults her intelligence? We shall never know the answer to such questions. But to take an uncritical, wholly sympathetic view of Claude is to take the view of his most superficial auditor or correspondent. Conversely, to take a critical or judgmental view is to take the view of Claude himself, who is a far more skeptical, probing, three-dimensional character than any of his auditors. And so to behave like Claude is to be suspicious of him, and to absolve him of casuistry is to behave far less suspiciously than Claude himself.

Amours de Voyage dramatizes a lonely, often desperate, quest for personal salvation. Acutely skeptical, Claude is capable of sudden unsettling insights: he is inquisitive about moral meanings he cannot quite formulate, about half-spoken thoughts that are oddly evasive. While the moral imperatives of categorical living are trying to give direction to the poem, a drama of improvised role-playing is leading Claude into uncharted seas, where he finds that truth is less a stagnant attribute of things than something invented or "made up."

As a poem that is helplessly open and oscillating, *Amours de Voyage* requires simultaneous translation of its key images, which have a habit of looking several ways at once. In canto 1, section 12, for example, the salt wave of the sea captures Claude's exhilaration, as he quits Ulysses' ship for Circe's island. Though a more timid swimmer than Browning's "amphibian" in the prologue to *Fifine at the Fair*, Claude exhibits comparable elation. But as he retreats from the sea to the island, borne up on the cliffs by "the great massy strengths of abstraction" (1.12.251), the salt wave of the ocean undergoes a sea change of its own. In section 2 of canto 3 the sea's "billows" buffet and beat its victims till they "sink and are swallowed" (l. 54). The sea now signifies inhuman change, an odious scene of tyranny and destruction. By keeping the images fluid, so that a great many precise meanings are free to dispose themselves in a variety of unforeseen ways, Clough ensures that any moral design that may emerge will establish itself as if by accident, and only provisionally. The reader is challenged, like Claude, to enter into the action of the poem, joining him in uses of language that, instead of producing simple order or disorder, dissolve and absorb the key metaphors.

To maintain an ordered process of discovery, an exploratory activity that is at least as important as any outcome, Clough relies as much on syntax, caesuras, and line breaks as on the resources of his imagery. Because the typographic space after periods, semicolons, and colons produces a space in Claude's world, or at least a gap in his mental processes, Clough can integrate the syntactic breaks into a psychological and moral drama of needle-fine distinctness and refinement.

> I am in love, you declare. I think not so; yet I grant you
> It is a pleasure indeed to converse with this girl. Oh, rare gift,
> Rare felicity, this!
>
> (2.10.254–56)

The denial, "I think not so," reinforced by the midline break between clauses, seems at first to be decisive. But the concessive conjunction, "yet" (l. 254), coming after another emphatic break, forces the reader to absorb and restructure successive clauses instead of taking any one impulse as final. Though the phrase "I am in love" migrates through this section, the imperative to love is most powerful when its demands are most fastidiously qualified or resisted. Like some formal minuet, the finely managed meter leads Claude through steps of decorous wavering; a pace forward in the opening declaration; a hanging back in the next two clauses; a slackening of resistance as he tacitly qualifies his qualification; then, in a rare violation of Clough's metrical practice— in a terminal foot of triple stresses ("Oh, ráre gíft")—a drawing nearer, with a fullness of emotion, and a momentary attainment of all the heart can wish. With his talent for social inflection, Clough's return to a metrical norm of unstressed final syllables brings a modest dropping of the eyes, a disclaimer. But it also brings a hint of Prufrock's precious, mincing manner and a straining for precision in matters essentially ambivalent: "I am in love, you say: I do not think so, exactly" (l. 265).

In these tactical advances and retreats of social exchange, the rich shadings of desire and hesitation make Clough a kind of novelist of manners, the Jane Austen or Trollope of Victorian poets. To capture the flux and reflux of an improvised performance, Clough makes skillful use of crossovers, which allow Claude to pass back and forth over little fractures in the verse. Over line breaks and discontinuities in syntax Clough keeps constructing frail bridges of repeating words and run-ons, which urge the mind to shift direction.

I, who refused to enfasten the roots of my floating existence
In the rich earth, cling now to the hard, naked rock that is left me.

(5.5. 66–67)

Comfort it was at least; and I must take without question
Comfort, however it come, in the dreary streets of the city.

(5.5. 93–94)

Breaks at the end of lines—between "floating existence" and "rich earth," or between "question" and "Comfort"—represent mental gaps, rifts in Claude's mind, that dramatize a pull between contrary motions: between an impulse to live like a primitive organism in the aqueous age of the world and a desire for stable identity, for secure anchorage and mooring. The crossing of such breaks helps sustain the mind's eddying flow. Fearful divides between floating and anchorage, between existential and categorical living, become less intimidating when runovers allow the poet to shuttle back and forth, negotiating a whole series of skillful crossings.

The critic does justice to Clough not by assuming that predetermined design is necessarily a mark of literary virtue, but by acknowledging the strange fluidity and openness of his poem. We being to intuit that his real meanings are conveyed between the letters. They reach us from the other side of silence, in the gaps between sections and cantos.

To dramatize Claude's mental gaps, Clough uses not only syntactic breaks and runovers but also juxtaposition and repetitions. Meaning, Claude muses, is an accident of context. Like his interest in Mary, it is a mere quirk of placement: "it is only juxtaposition,— / Juxtaposition, in short; and what is juxtaposition?" (1.11.225–26). Among other things, juxtaposition neatly imitates the decline of lofty abstraction into casuistry, special pleading, or evasion. Aspiring "evermore to the Absolute only" (5.4.59), Claude is prevented from bringing his love affair to any satisfactory conclusion. Clough uses juxtaposition to write eloquently about the heartbreaking waste of Claude's imaginative gifts. The decline of Hope, the second of Paul's three Christian virtues, into hope: "As for Hope,—to-morrow I hope to be starting for Naples" (5.10.203), dramatizes the decline of the man without "Hope," mastered by mere velleities and whims.

At such moments *Amours de Voyage* creates an effect of resourceful hovering. There is a crossing back and forth of Hope and hope, as if the meaning of the word is escaping us in several directions simultaneously. On the rare occasions, all moments of special uncertainty, when Clough ends a hexameter on a stressed syllable, the effect that such a stress might have of overdetermining Claude's wavering impulse is happily contradicted by other devices. In the poem's first example of a terminal stress—"But a mán was kílled, I am tóld, in a pláce where I sáw / Sómething; a mán was kílled, I am tóld, and I sáw sómething" (2.7.167–68)—the emphasis on the verb "saw" makes the reader hesitate. The repeated object of the verb, the amorphous "Something," is thrown into prominence at the head of a line and given extra force because the reader has to hover over two successive accents. Instead of reinforcing the sudden access of energy, Clough draws attention to the hint of hearsay in Claude's repeated qualification, "I am told," "I am told." Repetition, which normally has the effect of cutting a deeper channel for the flow of feeling, now has an opposite effect. It gives an impression of trying to create certainty where only uncertainty exists.

Claude's long rolling hexameters help defer decisions. Like his talk about endlessly protracted actions, which he expresses in expansive gerunds, the meter encourages interminable buffetings of emotion. Claude rolls and lurches on the surge of his feelings, like a swimmer tossed by the waves but never carried far in one direction or another. Every call to moral action is immediately followed by a rationalization of inaction. If the real victories are all victories of imagination, why leave the private theater of the mind for a public arena that is more likely to resemble a gladitorial contest than a carefully rehearsed play?

Dipsychus dramatizes the folly of making such an exchange. All action is likely to be a decline, a premature entry into the dance while the musicians are still tuning up the instruments. Dipsychus's tragedy is essentially a tragedy of consciousness, like Hamlet's. To do or not to do, that is the question. But whenever Dipsychus tries to act by passing from love to Love, in a reversal of Claude's passage from Hope to hope, he finds that the accomplished miracle of such crossings is easier to achieve in poetry than in life. Love, the Miltonic "large repose / Restorative" (10.30–31), should straddle the boundary between the known and the unknown, as the phrase straddles successive lines. Dipsychus discovers that to yield to the expert urgings of the Spirit, however, is not to pass from love to Love, but to set up an idol, a usurper, on the throne of the true queen.

Grappling, like Lavengro, with a loss of origins, with the dreaded reality of a fatherless world, Dipsychus dreams that instead of facing God the friend or God the enemy he confronts only God the void. In trying to spy the unknown God through a glass, the observer trains his eye on too lofty an object, bringing into focus a mere emptiness or blank. Oscillating between moral theology and agnosticism, between a religion of work and a religion of silence, Clough "bares the device," as Russian formalists would say, allowing the Spirit to mock the antinomies that proliferate in the poem, preventing Dipsychus from bringing anything, including his own life, to a satisfactory termination.

> Yet as for you,
> You'll hardly have the courage to die outright;
> You'll somehow halve even it.

(12.183–85)

Though the Spirit in *Dipsychus* has no use for the antinomies of Kantian theology, insisting that religious language should be unequivocal, Clough himself seems to accept the Spirit's mocking challenge to become a "Critic of Pure Practic" (12.159). By replacing historical religion with a new theology of moral action, Clough tries to solve the dilemma that defeats Dipsychus. He hopes to bypass the contradictory *x*s and *y*s that logic by itself is helpless to reconcile (12.157–63).

The epilogue makes clear that *Dipsychus* is not simply a poem about what to do, but a poem about how to live with the consequences of doing it. As the Spirit invades the mind and becomes increasingly a region of it, Dipsychus finds that only by escaping from consciousness into some sort of saving action can the monstrous things in the mind, too hideous to confront, be appeased. All minds possess a Dipsychus and a Spirit, and the two impulses—the impulse to know and to act—are locked together in a life-and-death embrace.

Readers feel more intimate with Claude than with Dipsychus, because the forces of deception are always inside Claude, never outside him in an adversary called the Spirit. The directness and simplicity of consciousness that we first find engaging in Claude, a noble and spirited observer, are increasingly blocked and thwarted. For example, if Claude decides to marry, he accepts a role to end all roles—a role that makes any further role-playing impossible. On the other hand, if he refuses to marry, then he continues to change roles incessantly, with no fixed identity to anchor him. And so if he changes, he will never change again. And if he refuses to change, he is condemned to endless change, to the rootlessness of a god who must create himself ex nihilo from one unstable moment to the next.

A comparable dilemma destabilizes the reader's attempts to evaluate Claude. To believe that Claude is a responsible narrator, a reader must behave like the omniscient author of the poem's italicized narrative frames. Taking the objective view, such an interpreter concludes that Claude *is* what he *does*: he is an enlightened and generous observer who undergoes no discernible crisis of consciousness. Conversely, to believe that Claude is incapacitated for action and incapable of expressing outwardly the manner in which he inwardly exists is to take Claude's own point of view. Because he lives in the infinite possibility, racing forward in time but incapable, like Kierkegaard's reluctant bridegroom, of repeating anything, Claude is the first to recognize that, though there may be continuity between what he *is* and what he *writes* ("scribo ergo sum"), there is no continuity between what he *is* and how he *acts*. And so it follows, paradoxically, that if a reader interprets events like Claude he is critical of him, and if he interprets events like the omniscient narrator he is sympathetic and approving.

Claude's consciousness grows by concealment. He seems to discover and refine his love for Mary in the act of concealing it from Eustace. The obscurity and mystery in *Amours de Voyage* are not the obscurities of concealed marriage proposals or love affairs. They are the obscurities of not knowing one's own heart and of trying to know oneself. What is concealed in the poem is not some secret alliance or erotic intrigue, but something quite normal and innocent. It is the kind of innocence that extends to Claude's spontaneous enthusiasms and childlike ability to convert ordinary things into wonders.

Clough, like Claude, is reluctant to prearrange the way things should go. Afraid of falsifying complexity, he refuses to see life steadily if the price to be paid is an inability to see life whole. To see it whole, however, seems incompatible with the view from here. It condemns Claude to the detachment of an Olympian view. A man of action like George Vernon feels that one single act of definition, one final discovery of his identity or essence, will bring the search for meaning to an end. But instead of aiming for an apparent single success, Claude believes his mission is to reveal the infinite complications and demands of a flexibly intelligent life. He is too involved with all of life to be wedded to any single part of it. He fails to see, however, that to be united with everything is to opt for nothing, and that the acceptance of rottenness and contagion may be the beginning of regeneration. Mary may be a limited, ordinary girl, but her charms and virtues could help reconcile Claude to the world. Unfortunately, Claude's agonizing obsession with Mary, his desire to know and be in control of their affair, allows his consciousness to spread like a disease, giving him not the positive capacities of a successful lover but the negative capability that Keats associates with the dramatic art of Shakespeare.

Claude's decisions to act are no more effective in banishing consciousness than are Hamlet's attempts to use conspiracy to secure a conspirator's ends. In determining to be a lover and a man of the world, Claude, like Hamlet, discovers how unsuited by consciousness and temperament he is for this goal. Claude has all the wit and charm of a successful lover, but he is compromised by scruples and doubt. His digressions about art, theology, politics, and religion, are the digressions of someone who has forgotten entirely what the poem *Amours de Voyage* is ostensibly about. The disturbing presence of his unfulfilled love for Mary intrudes as a kind of illness about the heart, which cannot be assuaged. And yet Claude is so at one with the medium in which he writes and works that we feel his protests about loving Mary and wanting to track her down are also part of his epistolary role. The more Claude seems to be playing an expected literary part, the more *Amours de Voyage* seems to be just a poem, like the gracefully molded elegiacs that introduce successive cantos. Claude's consciousness is continually being turned aside from its avowed goals into the multifarious life of speculation and reflection. Even his eloquence moves the love poem toward the defeat of its own story.

Works of literature that deal with the risks of role-playing should not be made more stable or conventional than they really are. To offer a plot summary of a verse novel like *Amours de Voyage* or of a fiction about improvising roles like *Vanity Fair* or *Lavengro* is to risk doing violence to what is strangest and most exciting about them. The experience of reading these narratives is meant to be unsettling. Boundaries between what is definitely known and what remains indefinite or unconscious are continually shifting. The satisfactions of Clough's poetry and Borrow's prose are ultimately the satisfactions of consciousness itself. Unconscious pretense and conscious lies give way to the fascinations of what can and cannot be known. The force of all that is unconscious, indefinite, unspoken, continually makes itself felt in both writers. But full consciousness makes words retreat: it is illimitable. To lift the veil may enlarge our vision, but as George Eliot and Robert Browning know, it may also destroy us. To die of the roar that lies on the other side of silence is to suffer annihilation, a breakdown of form. As Claude foresees, it is to eat grass with Nebuchadnezzar (*Amours de Voyage*, 3.10.213) or to stare like Lavengro into the empty space behind all the masks he wears.

Poised between fascination and fear, Lavengro and Claude perform a perilous high-wire act of the mind. They long for expanding consciousness but dread indefinition. They fear that breakdown of language and that dissolution of identity that enlargement may bring in its wake. Claude cannot expand the end of a railway journey into the end of time and the intrusion upon him of some eternal tie without experiencing a measure of anxiety and trauma. And just as Lavengro's narrative stops rather than concludes, so readers can imagine several alternative endings for *Amours de Voyage*, one of which Clough himself writes in the American's tale in *Mari Magno*. The holes at the center of Claude's narrative and the elision of such crucial outcomes as the conversion scene in *Dipsychus* combine with a self-concealing rhetoric and an appositional style to dramatize the peculiar anxiety of someone who is in the uncomfortable position of knowing more than he can allow himself to know.

The expansive, circling hexameters of *Amours de Voyage*, often rolling over and over like huge ocean waves without actually advancing, suggest that there is something comically precarious about the balance of Claude's psyche. He imagines outcomes for things that have not yet happened and will probably never happen. And he keeps running away from what he seems to be running toward. First Claude wants to build up the protective fiction that he is not in love; then he tries to evade his knowledge of what the marriage contract means. Finally, by pretending to run toward what he is trying to escape, Claude shows how a half-dreaded, half-desired knowledge keeps thrusting itself upon his conscious mind.

A poem like *Amours de Voyage* or a novel like *Lavengro* derives its sense of mystery and its power to bewilder or even obsess a reader from the conflict between the fictions that role-players like Claude and Lavengro try to construct and the irreducible facts that refuse to be fictionalized. Mysteries of self-creation both guide the characters' actions and intensify their bewilderment. To survive they may have to create their own facts and choose to live out fictions they themselves invent. The truth about Mary, for example, is what Claude tells Eustace is true. And both Claude and Lavengro have overactive imaginations. They sketch the whole course of a future role before another character has time to understand their present roles. Claude, moreover, is always programming himself as a loser, thrown into the elegiac role of an unsuccessful lover who is lamenting his loss of Mary before she is actually lost. Even Claude's enigmatic praise of Mary creates an esoteric vocabulary to which he alone seems to possess the key. To answer questions about the mysteries of a character's identity is always to delimit arbitrarily a whole terra incognita of unknowables. Obsessive curiosity about what lies behind the role-player's masks is always matched by a fear of knowing too much.

CHAPTER 10

We Make Our Truths but Cannot Speak Them: George Eliot and the Uses of Silence

"If we had a keen vision and feeling of all ordinary human life," says George Eliot's narrator in *Middlemarch*, "it would be like hearing the grass grow and the squirrel's heart beat, and we should die of that roar which lies on the other side of silence" (chap. 20). The heart of Eliot's fiction lies in that silence, and words are to be trusted only when they direct readers to the silent meaning. When Eliot and her characters are silent or profess ignorance, they are not admitting a principle of darkness or unintelligibility, like Thackeray or Borrow. They are often implying instead that meaning can be expressed more economically and perhaps more accurately in other ways. Eliot's heroes and heroines often begin with the verbal stridency and make-believe of highly theatrical behavior, like one of the many offstage actors in *Vanity Fair*. But by coming to believe in the parts they play, they also sponsor deeper understanding and may literally make belief. Mrs. Bulstrode gives a resourcefully melodramatic performance when confronting her disgraced husband in *Middlemarch* (chap. 74). And yet the source of her meaning is not to be found in anything she says. It lies in the question she refuses to ask and in the silences that we are invited to ponder, feel, and remember. Unlike the verbally shrill Ladislaw, who is not really listening to Bulstrode in the exposure scene (chap. 61), Mrs. Bulstrode uses silence to create meanings that did not exist before. The goal of Eliot's fiction is often a new and deeper silence, a silence of reserve and humility, where the narrator can be as strict with her own illusions as she is with the vanities of her characters.

In *Adam Bede* the difference between Dinah's overly rhetorical address to Hetty in the bedchamber (chap. 15) and her address in the prison (chap. 45) is the difference between a rehearsed sermon, like the one delivered to the Hayslope congregation in chapter 2, and an impromptu speech punctuated by silences and halting dashes that are also a source of authentic understanding, deeper scruples, and new belief. There is far too much make-believe in the bedchamber sermon, too much fantastical prophecy about dangers to come, to induce any real belief in Hetty. Make-believe is also the dominant quality of Adam's love for Hetty. He and Hetty are continually talking past each other. Real communication occurs only in the prison interview, which is one part speech to five parts silence. Instead of mounting her pulpit, Dinah is finally tuned to the silent meanings. She allows words to be superseded by a new Feuerbachian love of her neighbor.

Dinah Morris may be more religious than an amiable pluralist like Reverend Irwine, but what is most worthy of imitation in her sermon is the unspoken intimacy between herself and God. What happens at death? Nobody knows, she admits. Only God speaks to us from the other side of silence, and we are without hope if God, the power which "lasts when everything else is gone," is not also "our friend." Dinah seems to be recalling Dante's Paolo and Francesca, who ask the subversive question, "What if the lord of the universe is not our friend?" But there is nervousness and anxiety at trying to contain the boundless God within the limits of so finite a category as "our friend." How can the lord of the universe be addressed intimately, as Dinah addresses him at the beginning of her sermon, as if he were someone quite near her? Dinah must be tutored to extend the intimacy of her colloquy with God to her conversation with other people like Bessy Cranage and Hetty Sorrel. The predicates of otherwordly religion must become the subject of a new religion of man, as they are in Feuerbach's *The Essence of Christianity*, which Eliot translated; and the subject of traditional religion must become a mere godlike predicate.

At first Dinah speaks as a kind of evangelical Renan. The Christ who did good deeds to poor people is as human and unmysterious as a friend who might teach in the village. "Wouldn't you love such a man if you saw him?" (chap. 2). But the rhetorical question dangerously narrows the gap between Christ and his auditors. To restore the difference, Dinah sternly appeals to lost sinners to repent. The divide between God and man is registered by the break of the dash and the fearful pause: "Lost! —Sinners!" The deep meanings are not spoken. They are registered instead in her look of appalled pity, and in the sudden pallor of her face, which restores the forgotten etymology of "appalled." The intimidating exhortation, "See," rivets attention to a fixed point above the heads of the people, where Dinah, like a theological conjurer, a Methodist version of the governess in *The Turn of the Screw*, is determined by half-hysterical fiat to will apparitions into being. Is her hallucinatory vision of a weeping Christ, stretching out his hands, conjured from the sky by her shrill "See," twice repeated, any more believable than her childish fantasy that Mr. Wesley had come down from the sky to preach to her and that he would go back to heaven that night, as in the picture in the Bible? The loving persuasions of a Feuerbachian religion of man make no impression. But the assaults of a stern otherwordly theology, in which God arraigns his people as a kind of divine judge, produce that absolute articulateness of reproach that makes Bessy feel as if the constable has come to "carry her before the justice for some undefined offence" (chap. 2). It seems that a category mistake has been made. Has Dinah not blurred the difference between a doctrinal exhortation and the summoning of an offender before a constable or judge? To what genre does her sermon belong? Is it like one of Wesley's sermons, or is it modeled on a parable like Kafka's *Trial?* The offender's anxiety and sense of guilt are greatly increased by her ignorance of the exact charge against her. The God who strikes terror into Bessy sounds more like the God of Browning's Caliban—a divine despot—than a loving and judicious friend.

Once the rift between a divine subject and its human predicates has been allowed to open, no exercise of intimacy or reserve on Dinah's part seems capable of closing it. In the bedchamber scene, should Dinah go to Hetty's room to comfort her, or should she stay away? She settles the matter by opening the Bible at random and making a literal interpretation of the words she reads. Unfortunately, life may not imitate biblical literature, and Hetty's response falls far short of the Christians' heartfelt reaction to Saint Paul: "And they all wept sore, and fell on Paul's neck and kissed him" (chap. 15). Instead of crying out of love and gratitude, Hetty weeps from sheer fear and vexation. Wanting to play the part of inspired counselor and friend, Dinah finds herself miscast as the prosecutor or judge. Ruskin's doctrine of the innocent eye deserves no more theoretical respect in ethics or psychology than it does in art. Despite what Ruskin says in *The Elements of Drawing*, a blind man suddenly granted the gift of sight would not start painting like Turner or Monet. Nor would he paint one of the Dutch genre pictures that George Eliot recommends as the artistic equivalent of her own method of writing novels. Only by bruising ourselves and incurring gashes in taking things up by the wrong end do we learn how to see. Without arduous apprenticeship in the difficult task of organizing our sensations, we would all be as blind and groping as Dinah.

Self-dramatization, in Eliot's view, makes it "very hard . . . to say the exact truth even about your own immediate feelings—much harder than to say something fine about them which is *not* the exact truth" (chap. 17). Dinah learns to avoid the dangers of self-dramatization and exaggeration in the prison scene, where she finally attunes herself to the silent meanings. Job's comforters would have been justified if they had not spoken. And the main consolation Dinah can offer is her own presence, her just being there. The moment Dinah ventures beyond silence, she frightens Hetty by making cryptic reference to someone who is close to her, beside her cell. Fearing a ghost or perhaps Adam Bede in disguise, Hetty responds in a frightened whisper, "Who?" (chap. 45). Since the invisible God is too impalpable a presence to register on Hetty, as is otherworldly religion in general, it is only as God acts through Dinah that he can make any impression at all.

Dinah's prayer, when it is finally voiced, is a prayer for speech. She prays that Hetty may break through the wall of sullen reserve. When Hetty's words come at last, they are broken and halting. She can barely stammer out her unintelligible thoughts. The unnameable act of child murder is cloaked in a veil of indefinite pronouns: "I did do it, Dinah...I buried it in the wood...and I went back because it cried" (chap. 45). The errant pilgrim is a prodigal, trying even in her desperate words of confession to retrace erratically the steps of her disastrous journey to Windsor and back. The time sequences are all jumbled: first she blurts out the worst deed, burial of the baby in the wood. But then we learn that the baby was still alive when she left it. Hetty had hoped that the covered child would be found. Then she backtracks, confessing that she tried to drown herself in the pool before the infant was born. After the baby's birth, she conceives the idea of drowning it in a pool, as she had tried to drown herself. But all she can find is a hole under a nut tree, like a little grave. She covers the baby with grass and woodchips, but still leaves it air to breathe. Did she kill it or not? Did she want the man in the smock frock to find the infant or not? The exact truth is difficult to tell. All Hetty can say is that the sound of the crying infant in the hollow under the nut tree continues to obsess her. She is tormented by the same power of hallucinatory vision that allows Dinah to see Christ during her sermon. It is almost as if Hetty's idea of leaving the child so that someone will find it is truer than the reality of child murder. The inwardness of the whole scene both concentrates and agitates the mind. Will confession, Hetty asks, ease the pain of her guilt-ridden hallucinations? Dinah cannot answer that question. Their intimacy has nowhere to go but into inaudible sound and invisible air.

The pragmatic human benefits of confession and prayer are richly in evidence in the prison scene. No longer representing empty rituals of an otherworldly theology, the performative language of confession and prayer allows Dinah and Hetty to achieve intimacy for the first time. Neither Hetty nor Dinah has time to reassemble a sense of self or the language that goes with it. Neither is using words for purpose or effect. Dinah's prayerful language is like a kiss or touch. The most moving thing is not their brief togetherness but the apparent incongruity of both Hetty's estrangement from God and her taking Dinah thankfully for granted. There is nothing here of sermon eloquence, but only the odd plain words wrung with effort from the silence.

In *Stages on Life's Way* Kierkegaard says that "the art of the actor consists in seeming to be deeply moved when he is untroubled (if he is really troubled, it is a fault; the art of the reserved man consists in seeming to be untroubled although he is deeply moved. If he is not deeply moved and shaken, his art = o, and he is not reserved" (1940, 329). In *The Mill on the Floss* Maggie's initial ritual of renunciation, when she theatrically embraces humiliation, is too verbal. In her expression of regard for Philip Wakem, as in her ascetic fantasies, Maggie is an actress in Kierkegaard's sense: she is not deeply moved herself (that would flaw her performance) but projects the mere illusion of being moved. The reverse is true in the final sequence, where she becomes a heroine of stoic suffering and reserve, inwardly shaken but outwardly unmoved in the presence of Lucy and Dr. Kenn.

A more scrupulous use of language would condemn people to silence or else minimize the number of consoling lies they tell each other. After Mr. Tulliver is financially ruined, his silences and withheld meanings become more potent than anything his halting language can put into words (chap. 28). The broken eulogy for his wife, whom eighteen years of marriage have "sorely aged," seems part of a funeral oration that includes himself. Carried away by his rhetoric, Tulliver promises to do more for his wife than is really in his power, just as Maggie will promise to do more for Philip. In each case the transports of metaphor, their crossing over from one subject matter to another, abet spurious transports of emotion that falsify feeling and force belief. In dramatizing the pretense of knowing the worst about himself, Maggie's father begins to luxuriate in his own despair. Only Tom, who distrusts metaphor and believes that the meaning of a word lies in its consequence for action, protests against submission. And when the father gives a different performance later, making the ritual of cursing Wakem sound moral, it is to the pragmatic Tom that he appeals (chap. 29). Only in the silences that break apart speech can difficult truths be told. The treachery of language is the treachery of metaphor, which, instead of using transparent signifiers, allows category mistakes to be made about eulogies and valedictions and about antonyms like reconciliation and unsatisfied vindictiveness.

Maggie also makes a mistake about the genre of Kempis's *Imitation of Christ*, which she reads as a medieval romance, another passport to a world elsewhere, like Byron's poems, Scott's novels, or the prose romance *The Pirate*. The quotations from *The Imitation of Christ* enjoin quietness and silence (chap. 32). The divine voice speaks only in whispers, and not everyone has the aptitude to hear. Kempis's injunction to go outside oneself becomes in Maggie a license to have ecstasies. Her best impulses rapidly decline as "the ardour of first discovery," which might have sustained silent endurance, deteriorates into a mere transport of ecstasy, a self-indulgent "panting for happiness." Renunciation is oddly confused with "satisfaction" and with that illimitable craving, that "hunger of imagination," as Dr. Johnson calls it, that, far from being Kempis's object, is the precise temptation he warns against.

Philip does not really have to tempt Maggie with books and romance. Maggie has already set the terms of her own seduction by making the alternatives to asceticism increasingly appealing. By eroding the boundaries between Platonic friendship and love in the fullest sense, Maggie is stretching terms until they produce a blur instead of clarity. "Your mind is a sort of world to me," she tells him (chap. 36). But this implies more than Maggie wants to say. The mistakes of metaphor can be dangerous, because they encourage transports of feeling to match the crossing-over or transgression of categories. In telling Philip she will "never be tired of being with [him]," Maggie allows feeling to rise "high above its average depth, [leaving] floodmarks which are never reached again" (chap. 36).

Having experienced real love, Maggie discovers at the end of her life how painful genuine renunciation is. Transports of joy are reserved for her erotic dreams, for the deep thrilling voice of the man she loves. The oxymoron of his "cruel charm" dramatizes the painful truth that only unsatisfied passion, like her father's unfulfilled vindictiveness, can cross the boundary line between pleasure and pain. But there is nothing confused or oxymoronic about the line she now draws between sacrifice, on the one hand, and seduction, on the other. Formerly, love for Philip was confused with sacrifice. No such crossing of terms is any longer possible. When temptation is genuine, its renunciation brings no transport of ecstasy but a quiet effort of endurance and resolve, too inward to be dramatized and too personal to be talked about.

In the culminating renunciation, when Maggie rejects Stephen's self-pitying seductions for a final time, *The Imitation of Christ* is finally appropriated in the spirit its author intends. The letter from Stephen urging Maggie to stay by him is such a monument of egoism that Maggie can make it seem a real temptation only by refusing to read it a second time: instead, she supplements its deficiencies by imagining it spoken out loud, as an actor might perform the scene in a play, using the letter as his script. Not Stephen's actual words, but the imagined tone of his words, shakes her resolve. Her motion toward the desk to write a one-word letter to Stephen, "Come," is no sooner initiated, however, than it is canceled by a contrary motion. Though the memory of what Thomas à Kempis said restores her power to pray, the true ritual of renouncing is performed in silence, because it is too subdued for words. Her speech is inaudible, lost in the loud driving of the rain against the window and the loud moan of the wind. As Maggie prays a barely articulate prayer to the "Unseen Pity" for strength to endure the new temptations that she knows will come, there is no confident assurance of her own strength, as there was in her original act of embracing humiliation. Some of her words are more like sobs than intelligible utterances. Her words, after speech, reach into silence. And the heart of her meaning is found in that silence.

In *Amos Barton* the banality and terror of death reduce the bereaved clergyman to silence. But the imagination of death, when it is reduced to the more manageable idea of mere departure, allows Amos to perform the proper ritual of mourning that his wife's actual funeral had not allowed. The idea of parting is more terrifying, but also more meaningful, than that of death. The fact of dying is terrible but also stiflingly banal. The real mourning takes place in the mind, never where the staged actuality of a funeral is. It takes place instead when Amos has to leave the community where he and his wife have lived. As he learns of finalities beside the grave, even the raw feelings of pathos and grief have something of the subtle scope and feel of a Henry James novel, because Eliot is trying hard to say the exact truth about grief—always much harder than saying something fine about grieving that is not the exact truth.

The clergyman who has been taught to expect and accept death cannot believe it has come. "She feels no pain now," Mr. Brand says, but Amos disbelieves him: "She isn't dead?" He cannot say anything appropriate, because he does not believe in his sorrow: "it was a bad dream" (chap. 8). Not even the funeral can make him believe his wife is dead. It requires the dismal return to the house after the funeral and the terrible keenness of memory and imagination that bereavement gives to make the loss seem real. Only when the lesser funeral of leaving Shepperton takes place and he visits Milly's grave—for the second-last time in his life—does the real mourning begin. Then he finds the words that failed him at the funeral, where the liturgy had the same dull force as the nanny's platitudes about his wife's being in heaven: fine but inexact. The departure from Shepperton seems to enact publicly the betrayal of Milly's memory that Amos has experienced inwardly but that is too painful a discovery to acknowledge privately, much less put into words. The great loss has to be refracted into some lesser loss, into something outwardly trivial. He weeps for the little things that make him mourn, especially for the insignificance of a gravestone inscription. But the simple words "Amelia, the beloved wife," release a wave of feeling in the mourner, who throws himself on the grave, clasping it with his arms and kissing the turf. That vision and the idea of leaving the simple marker swallow up the story.

"In every parting," in every "chilling entrance on the new and strange," "there is an image of death" (chap. 10). Only once again in his life does Amos visit Milly's grave. His loss is dramatized at no time more pathetically than by the simple communication of the fact that, though he is guilty of no single failure of omission, his feeling of betrayal is still oddly justified. The words of the inscription are terribly banal—"Thy will be done," but in their very poverty and inadequacy they dramatize the oppression of the "blank interval," the hole at the center, which no words or meanings can fill. Leaving the town where one's wife is buried is only a pale imitation of death, but only in that imitation can the meaning of death, otherwise something too stupefying to confront directly, be partly grasped. For to commemorate death rightly is also to magnify the love that makes death terrible.

The interval between death and leave-taking may make grief more manageable. But that interval may also make grief more acute, for it may frighten "love . . . at the intervals of insensibility and callousness that encroach by little and little on the dominion of grief" (chap. 10). The greatest anguish may be an inability "to recall the keenness of the first anguish," as when Emerson grieved because he could not feel more grief when his son died. He could not feel or say anything. When we grieve keenly, is it ever really possible to speak? And when we speak about grief and commemorate it, is that not a sign that grief is already subsiding? In *Amos Barton* we confront Eliot's version of the cryptic Buddhist saying that those who speak do not know and those who know do not speak.

The silences in *Middlemarch* are seldom merely protective. When Mrs. Bulstrode's friends are silent they are not merely trying to shield her from news of her husband's disgrace. For her part, Mrs. Bulstrode strongly objects to their silence, because only by knowing everything can she know what *not* to say to her husband. Ignorance is not synonymous with reserve: reserve is a conscious or voluntary withholding of knowledge, and Mrs. Bulstrode cannot withhold what she does not know. As a form of coyness, Mrs. Hackbutt's silences are cruel and perverse. Torn between meeting and *not* meeting Mrs. Bulstrode, she derives an almost brutal pleasure from withholding any reference to the one topic that is uppermost in each woman's mind. Being more tight-lipped than usual, Mrs. Hackbutt flaunts her silence as a deliberate withholding of secret information. She is a sadist, artfully contriving to make her auditor feel "suddenly rather chill and trembling" (chap. 74). Mrs. Plymdale's silence takes a different form. Her moral bombast can signify either a failure to command the right tone or a displaced referent. The off-key notes send Mrs. Bulstrode in quest of some hidden scandal that would justify "Selina's" offering "edifying answers on the commonest topics" (chap. 74).

The silence of Mrs. Bulstrode's friends renders her panic-stricken with dread. And that dread is contagious. It immediately transfers itself to her brother, Walter, who rashly but understandably concludes that she knows everything. "God help you, Harriet! you know all." Her anxiety is now infinite, because it knows no boundaries. Her brother says the worst, but he also says nothing. His unwitting evasion is the opposite of Abraham's evasive reply to Isaac: "God himself will provide the offering." In saying something, he also says nothing. But instead of leading her auditor to infer the best, like Abraham, Walter forces his sister to fear the worst. In the next few instants, Mrs. Bulstrode has transformed herself into one of Eliot's moral heroines. The plunge from abyss to deeper abyss is almost instantaneous: from the minor shame of monetary ruin, she falls down cliffs to the deeper shame of guilt and public disgrace. But in that chasm she also executes a leap of faith—an infinite motion of the spirit—that joins her "in mournful but unreproaching fellowship with shame and isolation" (chap. 74). The great transitions occur in a "mere flash of time," but they reveal "the bias of a nature, and [are] prophetic of the ultimate act which will end an intermediate struggle." Such agile leaps of the heart cannot be expressed in conversation. There is an absolute disjunction between what she says ("I know nothing") and the dramatized truth of her having already overleaped all knowledge and having learned and accepted everything before her brother speaks.

If Mrs. Bulstrode had done nothing more than embrace public humiliation, she would still have secretly condemned her husband by silently judging him, as Rosamond judges Lydgate. But she does something more. She makes the movement of faith by joining Bulstrode in grieving but unreproaching fellowship. The expression of unreproaching sympathy may be unreproachful in a loyal wife. But how can the decision not to reproach a criminal be unreproachable in any absolute sense? It is unreproachable only by virtue of the absurd, which exalts a single individual above the moral law. Bulstrode enjoys honor and glory as the husband of this heroine of faith. We no longer want him to be sent back to a lower court and shown up as a murderer. Ironically, the substitution of the sympathetic adjective "unreproaching" for the moral word "unreproachable" allows two cognates to chime together and register opposite meanings simultaneously. By a leap of faith Mrs. Bulstrode renders unreproachable what might otherwise be highly reproachable in a unreproaching refusal to condemn criminal behavior.

Irony is the language of such double movements and meanings. Mrs. Bulstrode first accepts the moral judgments that demand sacrifice, then cancels them by being unreproaching herself. To be simultaneously reproachful and unreproaching requires the ironist to say something and still not say anything. Unless one wishes Mrs. Bulstrode to be outside the paradox that allows her to execute a double movement of the spirit, one of simultaneous judgment and acceptance, disgrace and celebration, infinite resignation and infinite fellowship, it is a self-contradiction to demand that she speak. When she talks, she has to say nothing, for what she knows she cannot say. She can merely live out her meaning and try to prove its truth by establishing its beneficial consequence for future living.

When Mrs. Bulstrode locks herself in her room before facing her husband, deeds that were distanced by an interval of twenty years rush together to destroy any vestige of faith in her husband's innocence. The convergence of widely separated events duplicates the sudden conflation of contrary motions in Mrs. Bulstrode's soul in the few instants following Walter's disclosure. But now there is a delay in the double movement, which had at first been so instinctive and spontaneous. The separating out of the two motions of her soul is well dramatized in the rhetoric of the sentence that divides in the middle with a jarring dash: "The man whose prosperity she had shared through nearly half a life, and who had unvaryingly cherished her—now that punishment had befallen him it was not possible to her in any sense to forsake him" (chap. 74). The loving and fond scrutiny of her life with Bulstrode is at such wrenching odds with the harsh truth she must now confront that the sentence breaks apart in the middle, as Mrs. Bulstrode's own life has broken. What starts off as the proud and admirable grammatical subject of the sentence, the "man...who had unvaryingly cherished her," turns into an ignominious object, nothing more distinctive than a twice repeated "him." But though there is a heartbreaking displacement of the proud, intimate tone, censure of such a punished object is made synonymous with "forsaking" someone whose prosperity she has shared through nearly half a life.

Mrs. Bulstrode's setting aside her ornaments and cap and donning the plain bonnet and black gown are a resourceful use of costume. She uses them as a skilled actress would use her wardrobe and stage props. When Mrs. Bulstrode finally confronts Nicholas, there is nothing she can say: she can only support him in silence. To protest his innocence would be to assert what she knows to be untrue, but to say he is guilty is to betray and forsake a partner. The mutual silence of husband and wife is a silence of solicitude and care as well as a silence that proceeds from their sense that the double movement of irony cannot be verbalized. If we have the souls of poets but not their language, then we are condemned to be silent. All she says to her husband is "Look up, Nicholas," and her dress and facial expression speak the rest. In a sense, she speaks without saying anything. But her words reverse the dreadful noncommunication of her brother, when in saying nothing he also says everything: "you know all." Both remarks—"you know all" and "Look up"—are ironical. For it is always irony when someone says something and still does not say anything.

"His confession was silent, and her promise of faithfulness was silent" (chap. 74). The alternative rituals, with their overt questions and admissions, would have been inquisitions rather than sacraments. Instead, Eliot offers non-rites, words that were never spoken: "She could not say, 'How much is only slander and false suspicion?' and he did not say, 'I am innocent.'" It is precisely because the two rituals seem to be empty of content (A confession of what? A promise to be faithful to what?) that they can dramatize the at-oneness of husband and wife. If there is no atonement, there is at least a perfect human at-onement. The confession of guilt that might have seemed appropriate for the husband can become a confession of faith by the wife. And the promise of trust, which might have seemed in character only for the wife, can become a promise by the husband—a silent promise to trust his wife, to be confident she will spare him the misery of perishing slowly in unpitied ignominy. There will be no unloving proximity between the husband and the wife, only the perfect interchange that is dramatized in this crossing-over or exchange of silent rites of confession and covenant, which come in the end to the same thing.

Like Mrs. Bulstrode's "Look up, Nicholas," Dorothea's civil apology, "Excuse me, Mrs. Lydgate" (chap. 77), when she intrudes upon Rosamond and Ladislaw unannounced, is really an evasion, a way of speaking without saying anything. The moment of irony, when words cannot begin to express the meanings registered, the drinking in of a great draft of scorn, characterizes her sudden access of energy, as if she were stimulated and excited. But the illusion of self-possessed energy is only a mask or incognito. Inwardly she is quite shattered, quite un-self-possessed. She is stimulated because shocked, and incapable of taking in the meaning of what she has seen. When Dorothea finally goes home to face alone the terrible collapse of her illusion, the hours of solitude she spends before confronting Rosamond demand more reflection and resolve than Mrs. Bulstrode's brief moments of seclusion before facing Bulstrode. But in both cases a character retreats behind a locked door, and in both cases a wave of feeling sweeps over her. It may take Dorothea slightly longer, but within the compass of a single night she enacts, like Mrs. Bulstrode, a double movement of the spirit: first a burial of dead love, which allows her to vent reproach and scorn; and then, after she wakes in the morning twilight, a kind of self-commissioning to intercede with Rosamond on Lydgate's behalf. Rage and reproach yield to sympathy and the desire to bring merciful relief. The hidden as well as the evident troubles of the Lydgates' young marriage establish a bond of sympathy between Dorothea and her rival far more potent than the mere urge to punish and destroy that had consumed Dorothea earlier.

The discarding of the funeral clothes in favor of a dress that is bright and new reverses Mrs. Bulstrode's ritual of switching from ornamental clothes into a plain black gown. But neither a funeral dress nor more joyful attire can do justice to such double emotion, such simultaneity of elation and despair, as Dorothea knows. Only by using double meanings, as in the altered sense of "morning," can language begin to express the double movement of her spirit, the burial of her private love and the resurrection of a different form of hope. To Tantripp the maid it seems a "strange contrariness" that "just the morning when [Dorothea] had more of a widow's face than ever, she should have asked for her lighter mourning" (chap. 80). All readers are initially in the position of Dorothea's maid. She learns the secrets of her mistress's show by obtaining a backstage view of it, but she remains in the dark about its motives. Tantripp knows more about Dorothea's personal devastation than Rosamond does, since Rosamond is only the audience for whom the performance is designed. But even Tantripp sees only the outward incongruity of a pale-cheeked *mater dolorosa* wearing a bright new bonnet and a fresh dress. Beneath the grotesque visual effect she can register none of the inward spiritual drama, and none of the irony, that justifies it.

The climactic interview between Rosamond and Dorothea in chapter 81 is a series of surprises. Rosamond expects Dorothea to rebuke her for loving Ladislaw, but Dorothea upsets her expectations by talking instead about Lydgate's love for Rosamond. Expecting Rosamond to defend herself against the charge that she was making love to Ladislaw, Dorothea is surprised when Rosamond proceeds to tell her that Ladislaw despises her. Nothing is as it seems. Each fear is ironically averted as the other person does something unexpected. Unanticipated compassion and understanding on Dorothea's side prompt comparable attitudes in Rosamond. Dorothea has to speak about Lydgate's innocence because Lydgate will not speak of it himself and because Rosamond has lacked the tact to accept his silence. Dorothea even says what Lydgate cannot say directly to his wife—that he is sorry he was silent. His silence is like Cordelia's silence. He has a great dislike of saying "I was wrong," but he was wrong not to speak when his wife demanded it.

Dorothea speaks brokenly for two reasons. She does not want to trespass on too private a domain: she has a "dread...of presuming too far" (chap. 81). But she also speaks haltingly because she speaks from the heart about painful experiences of her own. The two women are members of a suffering elite, and such knowledge as they share has something of the dignity of a secret science. Exchanging views on marriage is a more refined and subtle form of passing on recipes that two women might share. The whole movement of their interview is from the iciness of aloofness and suspicion, as Rosamond wraps her soul "in cold reserve," to the intimacy of two drowning women clasping each other after a shipwreck.

Female friendships, according to Simone de Beauvoir, are not like the friendships between men. Lydgate communicates through ideas and projects of personal interest, which his wife cannot share. He is excited by his medical research. But Rosamond and Dorothea are bound together by an exchange of confidences and secrets about marriage: they are in league to create a kind of counteruniverse. A secret working code allows these two women, natural enemies, to share confidences about the difficulties of being married and about a common love for Ladislaw, which under different circumstances might have wrecked two marriages. The unspoken mutual confidence rests on assumptions about the kind of love that murders marriage and makes marriage itself a murder. Dorothea must exercise great discretion and caution. She must be certain that Rosamond does not misunderstand, and that she will not repeat to uninitiated ears what is said. Rosamond has never felt easy about her husband's silences. Will she feel any easier now about Dorothea's silent meanings? There is great complexity about the kind of solidarity Rosamond and Dorothea share. It entails an exchange of confidences concerning the man

Dorothea has loved, and about whom she would normally never speak to a person like Rosamond. But both her silences and her confidences take a great burden from Dorothea, and they serve as a defense as well.

Mystery can sometimes mean mastery, as when Lear says that he and Cordelia can take upon themselves "the mystery of things" (*King Lear*, 5.3.16). The mystery of shared secrets is also a kind of mastery. For this is the one moment in the novel when Rosamond seems to master something. In demanding that Lydgate justify himself by saying he is innocent, Rosamond had insisted he play a part. But his silence is a result of his failure to understand the nature of playing a part at all. Lydgate's nonplaying threatens his wife's whole dramatic conception of herself, which has to be highly verbal. Her husband's refusal to play the part she has written for him makes her overcome this disability by playing the part of the aggrieved wife for all she is worth. But when Dorothea tells Rosamond what her husband has told her but could never say directly to his wife, Rosamond tells Dorothea what Ladislaw has told her about Dorothea but could never say directly to the woman he loves. Her disclosure is the mirror image of Dorothea's own. Dorothea has given her the cue. Inspired by Dorothea's performance, Rosamond gives a stronger performance than she perhaps intended, partly because she feels she is now repelling Will's own reproaches of the day before. Though there is even a species of playacting, then, in Rosamond's responsiveness to Dorothea's tactful gestures, both women are now playing parts that we feel they should try to live up to the rest of their lives.

The scene in which Ladislaw and Dorothea finally agree to marry is dominated by a silence of emptiness and vacancy that nevertheless hovers on the brink of plenitude and full possession. Will's accusations are unanswerable. To renounce marriage is to make light of his love. It is as fatal as murder or any other horror that divides people. Dorothea tries to be encouraging. They might marry sometime. He thinks she is putting him off, that she wants endless postponement. In fact, her silence is meant to be the silence of acceptance. She wants to say she cannot refute his logic. If not to marry is like murder, then the only way to possess wealth and life is to embrace poverty, renounce new clothes, and come to learn what everything costs. Such poverty is the only wealth. But she cannot say this herself. When Will says "Good-bye," it is as if he were the judge pronouncing his own death sentence (chap. 83). And she cannot bear the judgment, because the man she loves has misconstrued her silence. All she can say is that her heart will break and that she hates the wealth that dispossesses her of life. The meanings are unspeakable: like the names for God, they are too inviolable to be uttered. But this does not mean they are inexpressible. They can be intimated through the paradox of loving poverty and hating wealth. Finally, "the flood" of Dorothea's "young passion" bears down all the obstructions that had kept her silent. As the waves of emotion batter down the last walls of reserve, we are reminded of the "great wave" of "new compassion and old tenderness" that sweeps over Mrs. Bulstrode in chapter 74, of the "waves of suffering" that in chapter 80 shake Dorothea "too thoroughly to leave any power of thought," and that later rush over her "with [such] conquering force" that she is left in a state of "speechless agitation, not crying, but feeling as if she were being inwardly grappled" (chap. 81). "She said in a sobbing childlike way, 'We could live quite well on my own fortune—it is too much—seven hundred a-year—I want so little—no new clothes—and I will learn what everything costs'" (chap. 83). The seven dashes in her short concluding sentences are holes in the dike. They allow the dammed-up feelings to come rushing through, like a river in flood or the sea at high tide. In such moments of tacit surrender there are no more words, only the pauses and silences that mark the possession of all words.

In his angry confrontation with Bulstrode in chapter 61, even Ladislaw betrays a simpleminded confidence in the transparency of language and in the capacity of masks to express the reserves of feeling behind them. Because Eliot's narrator does not share this confidence and leads readers to distrust it, we tend to disapprove of characters like Ladislaw or Rosamond when they demand simple and absolute articulateness of judgment. Each actor in the exposure scene seems to be performing in a different theater. Bulstrode wants to treat Will as a father confessor. The theater he envisages is really a confessional. But once Bulstrode hands him his script, Will turns the confessional into a courtroom. He treats Bulstrode not as a penitent, but as a defender in a lawsuit: Will's final speech is shrill and judgmental, the peroration of a public prosecutor. He does not want any answers from Bulstrode, because all his questions are rhetorical. Though Ladislaw is morally justified, we expect the man Dorothea loves to act with more grace and self-command, more purity of heart. Will seems cruel and uncivil, even unfair, since in storming from the room he refuses Bulstrode even the courtesy of a reply.

Like Will in his showdown with Bulstrode, Rosamond demands that her husband play the part of a legal defendant. Lydgate's silence comes from a sense that he is not an actor on trial and that some facts are too private and complex to be turned into public knowledge. Rosamond's own silences cover many motives. At times she is deceitfully silent, as when she secretly writes to Lydgate's uncle for financial help.

But when Lydgate criticizes her for meddling without his knowledge, Rosamond's silence becomes the silence of unspoken recrimination. She affects that "innocent-looking silence whose meek victimised air seems to put [any accuser] in the wrong" (chap. 65). Lydgate's anger switches to alarm when his wife's silences begin to harden into stubborn reserve and unreasoning opposition. Worse than the silence of secret interference is the silent strength of stupidity and indifference. Alarm is to anger what the dread of an abyss is to the resentment of a resourceful but misguided schemer. The schemer can be reasoned with, but the vacancy of a creature neither rational nor fully human can be met only with the silence of despair.

Rosamond is too unsubtle to register facts until they are spelled out with the kind of simple transparency any child might understand. She can infer nothing herself, nor can she accept anything on trust. Before discharging the distasteful task of making his part in the scandal transparent to his wife, Lydgate has to pace up and down the room in a version of Mrs. Bulstrode's ritual of changing her clothes before facing her husband in his hour of trial. But no sooner has Lydgate opened his mouth to begin the painful disclosure than Rosamond raises the quite different issue of her desire to leave Middlemarch for London. The two topics are completely out of focus, and Lydgate feels "miserably jarred" (chap. 75). She ruins the performance he has braced himself to give before he has a chance to start.

The blurred focus in this scene dramatizes with great clarity the slightly blurred focus of Eliot's whole novel. Lydgate wants to be a provincial Vesalius, Bulstrode a pillar of the religious community, Dorothea a modern Saint Theresa. Even Casaubon might be a Victorian Aquinas. But they all have improper stages to perform on, improper talents for the role, or the wrong audience. As a result, none of these characters can quite make sense of what is happening to them. The meanness of opportunity, the absence of the right audience or theater, defeats the acting. The qualities that make Becky Sharp superb when playing charades at Gaunt House are defeated by harsh, resisting circumstance. The most moving moment in the novel is the perfect, largely silent communion that takes place between husband and wife at the time of Bulstrode's disgrace. This is one of the few moments when the meanings and silences of two characters coincide. Mrs. Bulstrode's new compassion and old tenderness surprise her husband. They seem unearned, like grace. And however artful and subtly theatrical Mrs. Bulstrode may be in her switching of clothes, she shrinks from asking questions as she would shrink from touching flakes of fire.

What is comparably affecting in the scene where Casaubon receives news of his terminal illness (chap. 42) is less the brief togetherness of husband and wife than the seeming incongruity of both their earlier misunderstanding and the surprise Casaubon expresses that a husband should be able to take his wife's generosity and concern for him for granted. Because Dorothea cannot find the words that would allow her to say one thing and mean another when Casaubon rebuffs her, or that would allow her to speak but say nothing, she finds herself substituting gestures for words. Though she does not withdraw her arm when Casaubon remains rigid, she cannot speak either, because words would betray her anger. To master scorn and rage with a power to be tender, she must maintain a mask of irony. Casaubon neither knows his wife's love for what it is nor is capable of accepting it. In his smallness of soul, as in his dread of pity, which he mistakes for veiled scorn, Dorothea must confront her own version of death. His hardness of heart is *her* form of emptiness, just as the blur that faces Casaubon when he thinks of his imminent death is the end of strenuous illusion for *him*.

Throughout *Middlemarch* there is a comprehensive sense of human wrongness. The experiences of the characters as we see them do not bear out the kinds of order that gossips like Mrs. Cadwallader, researchers like Lydgate, aspiring scholars like Casaubon, influence peddlers like Bulstrode, and even novelists like Eliot in her parable of the pier glass (chap. 27) all come to rely on in their common pursuit of a variety of web images. As J. Hillis Miller has said, characters in *Middlemarch* are "shown to be mystified by a belief that all the details [they confront] make a whole governed by a single center, origin, or end. In each case the narrator demystifies the illusion and shows it to be based on an error, the fundamental linguistic error of taking a figure of speech literally" (1974, 464). Anything that can be said about webs or heroic prototypes, the kinds of patterns that impose order on the scratches, is likely to seem wrong or off-key. Every reader is to some degree in the indefensible position of Rosamond when she forces Lydgate to put into transparent words meanings that are better left unspoken. Every time characters speak or act, the off-key note of what they have to say seems to come from a primal violation of the need to be silent.

Eliot distinguishes between positive silence, where nonverbal communication can be more precise than speech; nonproductive silence, when words are withheld that should be spoken; and the silence that shrinks from baring pain. Sometimes a character mistakes the second kind of silence, nonproductive silence or the mask of mere opaque speech, for the first kind. Dorothea's misplaced faith in Casaubon, for example, supplies whatever seems to be omitted from his actual conversation. His frigid rhetoric about plucking flowers to place in Dorothea's bosom should have held no more appeal than the bark of a dog or the caw of an amorous rook (chap. 5). It was sincere, but without grace or wit except in the ear that was predisposed to endow it with these attributes. Casaubon is a ghoul rather than a lover. And in conceding that he has been little disposed to gather flowers that would wither in his hand, his proposal says as much. Casaubon does not deceive Dorothea; Dorothea deceives herself by filling in all the ellipses and choosing to ignore the shocking omissions. Equally disturbing is a third kind of silence, which shrinks from exposing private pain. When the erotically exciting Will turns up in Rome, the unspoken sexual frustration of the new wife, treated as a spy in her husband's study, proves too intense and disquieting to speak about. The reader, like Dorothea, is held in the grip of separate obsessions. The strain on these obsessions, which refuse to be assimilated to one another, comes from the fact that Dorothea's initial respect and admiration for her husband must somehow be kept apart from ardor, love, or even "the continuity of married companionship." Secret fears and disappointments shrink from expression, because any public language seems to vulgarize them. The very fact that these experiences are not unusual makes them more banal, part of "the coarse emotion of mankind" (chap. 20).

Middlemarch is really a novel in search of its own genre. Its end is the beginning of the "home epic" Eliot wants to write. But that "home epic," being unrecorded and unhistorical, cannot be the subject of a social novel. Whereas the heroine of a historical epic, like Saint Theresa, needs a sacred poet to tell her story, the heroine of an unhistorical idyll, such as Dorothea becomes in the narrative that takes place beyond the boundary of this fiction, needs no poet to chronicle her tale. In the Finale Dorothea is a "river [which spends] itself in channels." In the Prelude, by contrast, she is a cygnet that lives "in the brown pond, and never finds the living stream." Spending oneself is not to be confused with mere squandering or dispersal. Instead of being dispersed among hindrances, her energy is "spent . . . in channels"; her life does effectively flow, like the unimpeded though constricted motion of a brook. Though Dorothea Brooke is the foundress of nothing that a historical epic can commemorate, the controlled and channeled expenditure of her life in silent acts of unremembered goodness is a fitting theme for the writer of a home epic to celebrate. As the heroine of a historical epic, the genre Eliot evokes in the Prelude, Dorothea is a failure. But judged by the criteria of a different genre, the Wordsworthian pastoral or domestic idyll invoked in the Finale, the wasteful "dispersion" of energy becomes a beneficent "diffusion." We are assured that "the effect of her being on those around her [is] incalculably diffusive." As a thwarted epic heroine, this "late-born" Theresa "sank unwept into oblivion" (Prelude). But as the obscure heroine of a different genre, one whose words reach into silence and whose most important deeds are not commemorated in any history, Dorothea knows in the Finale the rest of an unvisited tomb. The nothingness of oblivion is replaced by the peace of an obscure grave, which at least exists as a place to which a silent admirer like the reader might make a pilgrimage.

The surest way to vulgarize and cheapen *Middlemarch* is to interpret nonactors like Dorothea and Lydgate as characters who are trying to fit a situation or play a dramatic part. The areas of experience that Dorothea and Lydgate find defy speech, that can be lived or acted out only in silence, jeopardize large areas of institutional life. And they also jeopardize the art of fiction. But their threat to society cannot be publicly dramatized like Antigone's. Neither Dorothea nor Lydgate is theatrical enough to "spend...heroic piety in daring all for the sake of a brother's burial." Even if they were more histrionic, "the medium in which" an Antigone's "ardent deeds took shape is for ever gone" (Finale). Not only are characters like Dorothea and Lydgate not made for playing even conventional roles, they are not made for art or language either. Like Mrs. Bulstrode, Dorothea must live her truths, not speak them, because the arts she is a master of are a secret science. Her acquired knowledge possesses the dignity of a lived craft, founded on experience. Though her wisdom is a theology of the marketplace, not of the cell, it is as secretive and committed to silence as any theology of reserve enunciated by John Keble or practiced by such masters of reserve as Trollope's Mr. Harding or Reverend Arabin.

There is something off-key and jarring, by contrast, about all Rosamond's self-centered demands to make people speak. By profaning family silences, she produces in Lydgate the kind of alarm that cannot be reacted to or spoken about. In his fearful foresight of "her irrevocable loss of love for him" (chap. 65), Lydgate feels a terror that defies expression. It constitutes a "dread alternative." A naked exclamation of such dread could not bear acting, for the same reason that some fears cannot be voiced even to oneself.

As a novel about marriage, *Middlemarch* is unremittingly domestic. And yet no husband or wife is quite equal to the part to be played. Rosamond is more repulsive than a monster, and also more trivial. Casaubon is too small souled to be the heroic scholar Dorothea wants to marry. There is little honest passion in either Casaubon or Rosamond, only a sense of being inadequate and exhausted, which Eliot dramatizes with pedestrian accuracy. And for the heroine and hero of even a social novel, too much of Lydgate's and Dorothea's lives is full of home's dull cruelties and venomous whims. The novel accepts the exhaustion and depletion and even exalts the unhistoric quality of their lives. This lack of history is also a lack of what will act or perform well, and an absence of transparent ways of speaking. The Wordsworthian truths about the poet's largely inarticulate feelings and about the process of aging—"the gradual conquest or irremediable loss of that complete union which makes the advancing years a climax" (Finale)—cannot by their pedestrian nature be given a high epic treatment. Because they resist being spoken about, they defeat heroic acting. Silence is justified by the truth that a thought expressed is usually a lie. Since any flattering illusion of concentric arrangement that allows us to make an ordered drama of our lives will betray the complexity of what we see and feel, any role we play and any speeches we make will seem slightly out of focus. Rosamond's failure to shrink from the speech that violates family silence destroys her marriage. She violates the axiom that what a family feels it does not express, and what it expresses it does not fully feel. Wise people like Dorothea and Mrs. Bulstrode learn to feel and live their truths without speaking them.

CHAPTER 11

Browning's Unheard Words:
The Poetry of Silence

It may seem perverse to speak of unheard words and silences in so talkative a poet as Browning. In poem after poem the sense of an interminable voice seems to repress some deep fear of concluding, as if the world would cease to exist the moment he stopped for breath. "Loquor ergo sum." And yet Browning is also a poet of deep reserves and silences, in whose monologues the feeling of being alone is intensified by the presence of silent auditors. Checking the impulse to talk interminably, the sudden stoppages, elisions, and dashes in his poetry express a need for silence and a dread of betraying some hidden inwardness or god. "Contentious and self-justifying," as Geoffrey Hartman says, "Browning's people direct their will at a hidden God. The poet is their advocate, caught in the same condition, and he refuses to give the game away" (1970, 245–46).

Words may be unheard in Browning's poems for a variety of reasons. Most simply, the auditor in a poem may "tune out" or be incapable of "tuning in." As one commentator notes, "the art of the dramatic monologue begins in an acute sense of the circumstances in which strong speech meets strong silence" (Ricks 1987, 154). As the inventor of the modern monologue, Browning is alive to the unheard words, to what Christopher Ricks calls the "essential pressures" of the genre, its "silent interlocutor" (1987, 155). Porphyria, one intended auditor, is dead, and so incapable of hearing anything. Fortù, the auditor of "The Englishman in Italy," is bored by her English admirer and falls asleep during his monologue. Lucrezia keeps tuning in and out of Andrea's odd mixture of sententious sermonizing and harangue. But more important than an *auditor*'s failure to hear or than the sense of being alone that comes from the dying bishop's being surrounded by his actively silent nephews and by the dead Gandolf leering at him "from his onion-stone" ("The Bishop Orders His Tomb," l. 124) is a failure to hear on a *speaker's* part. This is most acute at the end of "Childe Roland," where the knight fails to hear even when the bell keeps tolling in his ear. Most pervasive, however, and the real focus of my interest, are the words never uttered that are nevertheless meant to be heard or overheard by an attentive reader.

There seem to be three reasons for Browning's failure to speak the words a reader most wants to hear. Silence may proceed from a depth of reserve. A speaker may be afraid of telling secrets that betray or profane a hidden god. More disturbingly, the unheard words may be Browning's way of hinting there is no secret to tell. Behind his plenitude of masks, the role-player may find only the silence of a void. A third possibility is that the poet of silence may fashion meanings that are unspeakable not because they are too empty to be uttered, but because they are too full. The silence of reserve and the silence of emptiness may then yield to a third form of silence—a silence that marks the amazed possession of all words.

Pure examples of the silence of reserve can be found in the love poems "By the Fire-Side" and "One Word More," which present the hidden depths of a husband's love for his wife. Only as the husband in "By the Fire-Side" recalls in a silence of long memory and deep gratitude the decisive event years ago when his wife conferred on him a new identity can he celebrate a victory over the tragedy of love— what Yeats calls "the perpetual virginity of the soul." As a foray into the future that loops back into the past to catch up with the present, time becomes, as the husband says, "one and infinite" (l. 181). And yet the opaqueness of the speaker's most important communications, their untranslatability, is also their most profound and cruel truth. We are surprised to learn in the last stanza that a felicitous celebration of the critical past event must still await better inspiration at some future time. The poem is a rehearsal for a poem Browning never wrote. It is full of deferrals and sudden fracturings, in which the most important meanings are either postponed or allowed to slip away between dashes and ellipses. Most curious is the way the interior of one picture becomes the outside frame of a second picture. The branching Greek letters of the speaker's book are the outside frame through which his grandchildren escape his gaze to cut down hazel boughs by the creek. The arch of hazel trees then becomes the outside frame of an infinite regress of other archways, narrowing down within the inmost frame to the accomplished miracle of the autumnal scene in Italy, where he and Leonor were "mixed... / In spite of the mortal screen" (ll. 234–35). It seems the husband wants to defer the commemoration of some hidden meaning he is not sure he can make intelligible without telling secrets or profaning a private mystery.

Only the wife's supportive presence can allay his fear of remembering. But it is not just a backward-looking dread. It is also the dread faced by the woman in Frost's "The Home-Stretch," the dread of closure, of having to pursue "The path grey heads abhor" ("By the Fire-Side," l. 105). The fear of oblivion is dramatized unforgettably by the fall off the "crag's sheer edge" (l. 106) and by the dash at the end of the next line: "Youth, flowery all the way, there stops—" (l. 107). In a poem that celebrates the "moment, one and infinite" (l. 181), such fears of being annihilated seem torn out of context. They are displaced, I think, from their true setting, which is the betrayal of language. Because poetry is composed under the shadow of a *not*, Browning's lyrics of silence are what Paul de Man has called a "persistent naming" of a "void with ever-renewed understanding" (1983, 18). Things may be symbols, as Hegel says, but names are only signs. And signs for sublime and ineffable things are doubly removed from what they signify. The repeated dashes in "By the Fire-Side" evoke as frighteningly as the "cliffs of fall" in Hopkins's sonnet "No worst, there is none," the terror of chasms sundering words from the plenitude of every "infinite moment" they try to name.

"By the Fire-Side" is all beginning, and hence a poem that never really starts. The speaker's heart is like the growing silence of the recollected Italian landscape, which is alive with repressed meanings. The silence grows with the burden of a hidden life, until "it must get rid of what it knows" (l. 159). But that past condition of pregnant silence, of meanings more surcharged for not being spoken, is also a feature of the speaker's present speech. He knows that as a name for what is fashioned out of three sounds or two people, the "One star, its chrysolite" (l. 185) is only a catachresis, like Abt Vogler's star, for the mystery that makes any organic whole the unanalyzable unity it is. The sign is arbitrary: a comet or fireworks might have served as well. Signs of the ineffable cannot without idolatry participate literally in what they name. The trouble that grows and stirs in intimation of aloneness and separation is also a disorder that afflicts all poetic speech. What the speaker calls "the mortal screen" (l. 235) is the partition, the membrane—however thin—that perpetuates the separation of people. It is also the screen dividing words and referents. Friends are not lovers: even the most symbolic words seem consigned to the status of slightly separated friends. No words, only things, can be full participants or lovers. The speaker would welcome the slight gust of wind that blows the last remaining leaf into his face. But having gained a friend, having shaken all but one leaf from the branch, he is too cautious to try for something more.

As in other poetry of silence, the unheard or censored words are the words that readers most want to hear. The forest, as a kind of officiating priest, has mingled the man and woman, but the true ritual is performed by Leonor when she utters the single word that fills the speaker's heart to overflowing. J. L. Austin has taught modern critics the decisive function of performative speech. The name pronounced by Leonor is what Austin would call a "felicitous" performative. Far from merely describing an antecedent love, the act of naming creates love: it makes something unforeseen happen. The act is both a rite of union and a ritual of baptism, giving the man a new identity: "I am named and known by that moment's feat" (l. 251). Perhaps all Leonor has uttered is the speaker's proper name. We shall never know. But it is a potent word, with power to turn friends into lovers and to break down the bar between signs and their referents. If such a word exists, the husband cannot speak it now, nor can Browning hope to fix it in his poem. Even if Browning knew the unheard word, to speak it now would be to tell secrets and betray a mystery. The unrepeated private word, too interior for speech, can be named only in the conversation beyond the poem that the husband plans to speak. But that remains a nonexistent speech, a conversation of the heart's silent speaking, never actually disclosed to us in any poem Browning wrote.

Few poems are more withholding than Browning's "One Word More." It is tempting to assume that the trite but gracious dedication to Elizabeth is the promised "one word more": "take them, Love, the book and me together" (l. 3). But when the formula recurs halfway through the poem, it is only slightly altered: "Take these lines, look lovingly and nearly" (l. 119). If this is the promised "word," why should it take Browning thirteen stanzas to repeat what he has already said in line 3? An alternative explanation is that only the poem as a whole composes Browning's "one word more." But that would make it one of the longest last words in English poetry. The poem is so full of contrary effects of postponing meanings and then silencing them that it is hard not to conclude that Browning's "one word more" has still to be spoken at the end of the poem. Browning implies that we value the single painting by a poet or the single poem by a painter because the unfamiliarity of the art form puts everything at risk. Lovemaking, too, is a risky act. And declaring it in a dedication is just as risky, especially for a dramatic poet like Browning, who prefers to take cover behind dramatic masks, as he does in *Men and Women*, the volume of poems he is dedicating. And yet even Browning's spacious detours through the lost sonnets of Rafael and the lost painting of Dante are more digressive than they need be. Their true bearing on Browning's dedication to Elizabeth must be guessed, because it is intimated rather than openly declared.

Nor is the single privileged reader of Rafael's "century of sonnets" ever directly named. We hear and yet do not hear who she is. What should be a proper naming of her turns instead into a performative rite, a kind of private baptism, in which each reader acts as the celebrant of some hidden inwardness and meaning. "These, the world might view—but one, the volume. / Who that one, you ask?" (ll. 9–10). The compressed grammar requires a reordering of the syntax, so that the pronoun "one" becomes the subject of an elided verb. The question also prepares for Browning's invocation of the heart, which alone has power to instruct the reader in these mysteries.

Like the battery of questions that follows, the rift between the penultimate and last lines of stanza 4 reminds the reader that performative rites are always enacted over absences and voids.

> all Bologna
> Cried, and the world cried too, "ours, the treasure!"
> Suddenly, as rare things will, it vanished.
>
> (ll. 29–31)

As J. Hillis Miller has argued, a grounded performative is a contradiction in terms (1985, 26). The proprietary zeal of the premature cry, "Ours, the treasure!" is immediately followed by a loss that is absolute, because like Rafael's death it is forever. Guarded as a treasure book by Guido Reni, as his eye's apple, the unheard words of the sonnet sequence are now more valued for being lost. In a seven-line parenthesis, Browning also reminds us that Dante's single painting of an angel is a hiatus, a caesura, breaking into his routinely exalted activity of writing sublime poems (ll. 35–41). A parenthetical act is made doubly parenthetical by being broken off by the arrival of "Certain people of importance" (l. 46), Dante's version of Coleridge's man from Porlock.

The peril of any performative use of words is memorably dramatized by Browning's story of Moses. Even the prophet's power to do things with words is fraught with fear and trembling. As Browning's version of Kierkegaard's Abraham, Moses may prove merely "mortal in the minute" (l. 77). To know in advance the outcome of his decrees is merely to counterfeit a truly prophetic use of words. His "tongue's imperial fiat" (l. 98) is also achieved at personal cost. The words we do hear are less potent than the unspoken words he might have whispered in the ear of some unchronicled daughter of Jethro. The private appeals of Moses the man are the precise appeals that the prophet cannot allow us to hear.

If "One Word More" is Browning's substitute for Rafael's lost sonnets or Moses' unrecorded courtship, then it too must be withholding, and its most important words unspoken. More than any other poem Browning has written, "One Word More" is said to be a poem straight from the heart: "cor ad cor loquitur." And yet the very line that celebrates the mystery of the singular—"Once, and only once, and for one only" (l. 60)—is one of the few lines in the poem that is not, in fact, used "Once, and only once," but twice (ll. 60, 70). And the claim to be unique is eroded by the use of the pronoun "one" and its cognates "once" and "only" five times within a single line.

"Poor the speech," Browning laments (l. 143). Having acknowledged the radical failure of words to say what is in the full heart, he then utters the most cryptic words in the poem: "be how I speak, for all things" (l. 143). The phrase "be how I speak" can mean, most tritely, "behave the way I say," but it could also be a loving adjuration, a solemn injunction or plea. Only a reader with "love's sense" (l. 118), who looks kindly and nearly at the lines, like Elizabeth, will be able to discern their finer tone. When the moon finally turns round in its orbit, as God did for Moses, allowing the privileged observer to view its backside for the first time, "What were seen? None knows, none ever shall know" (l. 180). To see the unseeable or hear the unhearable is like a ship's encounter with some giant iceberg. What is barred from sight may be a monster "Hungry with huge teeth of splintered crystals" (l. 171). A moment later the hungry iceberg turns into the hunger of God-intoxicated prophets like Moses and Aaron, "When they ate and drank and saw God also!" (l. 179). Only the near zeugma, rendered less blasphemous by the spacing out of the polysyndeton, can assimilate sublime visions of God to ordinary activities like eating and drinking. Hovering between a dread of calamitous encounter and a hope of being exalted, Browning seems afraid to either confront or expose his own darkest fears.

As a frame around the volume of poems it dedicates, "One Word More" promises to provide at last a glimpse of what is concealed behind the masks of "Karshish, Cleon, Norbert and the fifty" other dramatis personae in *Men and Women*. For a moment frame and picture space seem about to switch positions. We are shocked, therefore, to discover that the frame is only what it seems, a marginal supplement, confined to the mere periphery or edge. If we are never allowed to see the face behind the masks, is it because Browning has no heart or face to show? Failure to provide the "one word more" also seems to come from a fear of closure. The poet is reluctant to bring his volume of poems to a definite conclusion. He experiences that horror of concluding that is inseparable, Dr. Johnson says, from thinking beings whose life is limited and for whom death is dreadful.

The words that should commend his brain and heart to Elizabeth's keeping are therefore pushed beyond the margin of the volume *Men and Women* to its dedicatory frame, and then beyond that frame to the margins of that terra incognita or undiscovered land from whose bourn no traveler has returned. Only after voyaging through "darks undreamed of" (l. 196), can Browning "hush and bless [himself] with silence" (l. 197). To have his beloved take his book and him together, and to have both the brain and the heart, as metonymic substitutes for the book and the poet, lie together, side by side forever, is already to imagine his skeletal parts, stripped of their flesh, reposing in a grave: "Take and keep my fifty poems finished; / Where my heart lies, let my brain lie also!" (ll. 141–42). Only if his heart and brain are taken by his wife and treasured by her can their place of repose in *her* heart allay his fear of dying.

Hovering between historical description and a summoning, Browning's concluding evocation—"Oh, their Rafael... / Oh, their Dante" (ll. 198–99)—reasserts the power of his own poetic naming. Because Browning carefully separates the two grammatical subjects from their principal verbs, his last stanza seems at first to open with the same use of apostrophe as the penultimate stanza: "This I say of me, but think of you, Love!" (l. 187). The two concluding "Oh"s, however, are not the "O"s of invocation, because in the last two lines Browning provides "Rafael" and "Dante" with deferred principal verbs: "Wrote" and "Drew" (ll. 200–01). Yet expectations of apostrophe are not raised only to be disappointed. Though "sing" is indicative, the final "see" is imperative, an elliptical address to the reader.

> Oh, their Rafael of the dear Madonnas,
> Oh, their Dante of the dread Inferno,
> Wrote one song—and in my brain I sing it
> Drew one angel—borne, see, on my bosom!
>
> (ll. 198–201)

Though we see no angel etched on Browning's heart and hear no song in his brain, we do not smile ironically at these patent fictions. For in its explicit impossibility, the command to look at Browning's heart reminds us that the performances most worth enacting are not to be presented on any public stage or spoken in any poem. The "one word more" is always the next word to be spoken, and so it is never heard. Because the shift in grammatical moods is subtly managed, the injunction to see ("look here, the angel is on my bosom!") has the same shock effect as enjoining heart and brain to lie beside each other, like parts of a decomposed body in a grave. And yet the heartfelt "Oh," even in seeming to invoke the song and the angel as silent and invisible presences, also enforces them as events. Nothing need be heard or seen, because Browning's conjuring of these presences is irresistible; his boast about "singing" and his prediction about our "seeing" are themselves his poem's most potent happenings.

"One Word More" takes Mrs. Browning to the threshold of her husband's grave. The coda of *La Saisiaz* reverses this process. Now Elizabeth's heart and brain must repose with her husband, since in real life she has died first. Only by dint of the most strenuous reserve, which also expresses the depths of his love for Elizabeth, can Browning prevent the fissure of his loss from opening up. Even though the flamboyant brand that Browning is said to wield over "night's forlorn abyss" (l. 602) is mocked as a mere "bauble" of wit, its portentous brandishing prepares for something less minimal than what we hear: "Why, he at least believed in Soul, was very sure of God" (l. 604). The critical phrase is "at least," which reminds us that the words we do not hear are more important than the ones Browning speaks. The meanings are also unstable. The chain of arguments for the soul's immortality that Browning had forged in his colloquy with Anne Egerton Smith, who has died in the interval, is said to be "flawless till it reached [her] grave" (l. 608). Does he mean that the links of the chain were so securely joined that they could survive even the brutal shock of her death? Or is the emphasis on "till"? Was the forged chain "flawless" only "*till*" it met the assault of death, at which point its links presumably broke and fell apart?

Whatever the meaning, the last hour he spent with his dead friend has been disinterred, like a corpse, only to be reburied. The buried metaphor is one of desecrating a grave. Even in using the language of disinterment and reburial, Browning has veiled its import by replacing the body with a bulb or seed, capable of germinating when replanted. And yet the more normal use of interment has not been disinterred only to be buried. The unspoken thought seems to be that, just as a bulb is taken out of the ground to be replanted at a time more favorable to growth, so the bodies of the dead may be "stocked with germs of torpid life" (l. 615). But the notion of resurrection is wrenched away from its eschatological context and applied instead to the revival of dead memories. The final optatives are really a variation of the funeral benediction: rest in peace. So brutal but imperious is the urge to tear up old wounds that it is said to pose as calamitous a threat to Browning's mental balance as an earthquake: "rest all such, unraised forever" (l. 617). The optative forbids discovery. In the name of *not* disturbing his wife's grave, Browning is resolved to leave more unsaid than he says. His final words acknowledge his reserve: "Least

part this: then what the whole?" (l. 618). Is the sacred ground of
Browning's faith literally below ground? Is it the mere vacancy of a
grave? Or is it too deep to utter? To leave the important words unsaid
is to make the silence of reserve the equivalent of any empty space or
void, like the grave Browning has reached and from which, at least in
his metaphor of disinterment, he has taken away the body. Removing
the body in metaphor only, Browning refuses to do it in life. And yet
an absence has been replaced by an apostrophized presence, and what
has died in history has come to life in art. Elizabeth's grave both *is* and
is not reached.

So far I have studied the silence of reserve in poems that withhold
some communicable meaning. Now I must look briefly at a second
group of poems in which unspoken words hide some darker secret,
perhaps even some ultimate absence of meaning. Monologues like
"Two in the Campagna" begin as poems of mere reserve. But soon the
reticences of a mere playful game disclose silences more sinister. In
"The Flight of the Duchess" it is difficult to decide which kind of
silence is presented. Are words unheard because they are too private
to share? Or do they hide a vacancy or loss too disturbing for the
speaker to name?

The most important words in "Two in the Campagna" are the
unheard ones, intimated or merely guessed at. The tantalizing thought
that continues to elude the speaker proves as tenacious but as fragile
as a spiderweb. It can be formulated only in the silent spaces that
appear whenever words in the poem break apart, especially after the
emphatic end-stopped dash in line 49.

> —I pluck the rose
> And love it more than tongue can speak—
> Then the good minute goes.
>
> (ll. 48–50)

The jolt of this fracture is anticipated by many lesser jolts earlier in
the poem. There is a divide to be crossed between stanzas 7 and 8 that
the absence of any caesura or dash at first conceals.

> How is it under our control
> To love or not to love?
>
> (ll. 34–35)

> Where does the fault lie? What the core
> O' the wound, since wound must be?
>
> (ll. 39–40)

The desolating candor of the last two questions implies a total reversal of everything the confidently rhetorical first question stands for. Despite the apparent similarity of the matching forms, there is a profound disparity of meaning. In the transition from the aspirations of the ninth stanza to the unnerving "No" of the tenth, nothing in the natural break between stanzas quite prepares for the full disruptive force of the poem's climactic dash (l. 49). Nothing anticipates the magnitude of that break. On its far side, the frustrated lover imagines himself blown like his irrecoverable thought "Onward, whenever light winds blow" (l. 54). Some tantalizing thought transpires in the break produced by the dash after "speak," but it seems also to expire there.

Even if the lover's discovery must assume the form of a reductive maxim, which substitutes aphorism for insight, he seems resolved to name the unnameable in some concluding *mot.*

> Only I discern—
> Infinite passion, and the pain
> Of finite hearts that yearn.
>
> (ll. 58–60)

The emphatic pause after "discern," however, merely serves to dramatize an impassable divide. It is hard not to conclude that the thought the lover tries to fix in this last hurried jotting has once again slipped away through the hole created by the end-line dash. The end of the poem is really no end at all, but an invitation to the reader to help the speaker recover his mislaid thought by circling back to the beginning. Why should the lover's aggressive sexual appropriation of the body of nature be all erotic foreplay, without the expected consummation? What keeps sundering his discourse, driving knives of ellipsis deep into the breaks produced by the reiterated dashes? Why, having touched the woman close, must he stand away, like Joyce's Gabriel Conway in "The Dead," as if he were about to touch a ghost?

Browning's reluctant lover seems unable to will into being the kind of repetition in which Kierkegaard's religious hero delights, but which spells boredom for Don Juan. "Infinite passion" (l. 59) is the infinitude of an endless repetition that exalts the speaker who wills it, and it is the opposite of tedious. By contrast, the pain of finite hearts comes from bondage to a routine that merely bores and exhausts. It is the torture of a routine to which Browning's speaker, like the husband manqué in "Dîs Aliter Visum" or in Kierkegaard's book *Repetition: An Essay in Experimental Psychology*, refuses to submit.

Since words seem capable of retaining only the faintest trace of the speaker's vanished thoughts, it may be that the "core / O' the wound" (ll. 39–40) is an injury inflicted on language itself. To experience plenitude in a concentrating sign, whether in the body of someone we love or in a perfectly formulated thought, is clearly impossible, as the very elusiveness of this thought keeps dramatizing. The difficulty is compounded by the tricky balancing act the lover is called on to perform. If the lover takes literally his parable of earth's lying bare to heaven (l. 33), he accepts nature as a moral norm and so remains only *in* nature. Merely to seduce the woman makes nothing important happen. But if the parable is taken parabolically, if the analogy between earth and body and between heaven and soul is taken in a wholly figurative sense, then nothing happens either. "A great Prince in prison lies," as Donne's metaphysical Don Juan protests in "The Ecstasy" (l. 68). By remaining merely within the analogy, the lover loses in parable as he has earlier lost in real life.

Descent to the body, like recourse to defective words, removes the desired referent. And flight to heaven or soul effaces the signs, corporeal and verbal, without which spirit itself becomes faint and attenuated. To win as a metaphysical Don Juan or seducer is to win in lovemaking but to lose in the imaginative game of transforming fact into analogy, life into parable. Such a victory does nothing to repair the lostness of the unfinished man and his pain. Conversely, to win in imagination only, despising other victories as too reminiscent of the repulsive assault of the "one small orange cup" by "Five beetles, —blind and green"(ll. 16–17), is also to lose. For it is to take parables about spiritual communion as parabolic only. A true victory could occur, as J. Hillis Miller observers of Kafka's discourse "On Parables," only "if the crossing over promised in the parable were to occur in reality" (Miller 1985, 25). The poem's unutterable thought seems to be that you lose by winning the seductive argument and you lose by losing it too.

Equally enigmatic are the unheard words in "The Fight of the Duchess," which hover over silences of reserve, silences of amazed possession, and more frightening silences of unconfessed betrayal and guilt. The gypsy queen's use of words that are to be taken not literally but as nonnaming figures that speak of death as a mighty sunbeam, reversing the more logical association of death with night or twilight, fittingly ends in a dash, in an emphatic caesura of syntactic incompletion.

> Death, with the might of his sunbeam,
>   Touches the flesh and the soul awakes,
> Then—'
>   Ay, then indeed something would happen!
>   But what?
>
> (ll. 687–90)

The long-awaited apodosis of her sentence never comes. The bewildered auditor can record only that at this point "There grew more of the music and less of the words" (l. 691). Sublime meanings exist only in the place of fracture. The speaker calls it the moment of "the snap," when the charm vanishes, as if into the empty space of the dash and the sharp break at the end of the poetic line.

> There came, shall I say, a snap—
> And the charm vanished!
>
> (ll. 705–6)

Every recipient of vision, even a prophet or a seer, is also a semantic stutterer, unable to convey in words more than a fragment of the meanings language should inscribe. The speaker thinks that if his wife Jacynth had been able to clap pen to paper she might have been able to retain "every syllable / With [her] clever clerkly fingers" (ll. 693–94). But he forgets that she is being asked to translate as well as transcribe and to translate music rather than foreign speech.

What does the duchess understand by the speaker's offer to help her? Should the retainer have played Caponsacchi to the duchess's Pompilia? Do the two truly communicate, or is there misunderstanding on both sides? We are confronted with blanks and silences at the very place we expect important questions to be answered.

> And then,—and then,—to cut short,—this is idle,
> These are feelings it is not good to foster, —
> I pushed the gate wide,...
>
> (ll. 784–86)

Three dashes in one line is surely a record, even for Browning. The repetitions enact a kind of paralysis; the speaker seems numbed by tautology. What do these most frantic caesuras in the poem conceal? Are they veils thrown over the secret depths of their love? Or do the breaks conceal the opposite of this, an act of betrayal the speaker is now ashamed to admit? Does the duchess expect the speaker to accompany her? Would they have married had the speaker been less uxorious? What, after all, does the speaker feel impelled to confess? And whom has he betrayed, the hideous duke or his pitiful duchess? Even the final parable of "Smooth Jacob" and "homely Esau" (l. 907) looks two ways at once. The ostensible meaning is that the duke, along with all superficial judges who prefer Jacob to Esau, are traitors. But if the speaker is afraid to discover the duchess's fate while alive, and if he silently hopes that priests may have cheated him about a Last Judgment, which he now seems afraid to face, the real betrayal may be his. Whatever the truth may be, "The Flight of the Duchess" is a poem of confession that continually represses the facts to be confessed.

In many poems by Browning there is never any question of using reserve to displace important meanings. In such well-known poems as "My Last Duchess," "The Bishop Orders His Tomb," and "Dîs Aliter Visum," the dashes and caesuras betray not a plenitude of meanings, but a dearth of them. The silences are masks placed over mental voids or lost opportunities in the life of each speaker. Dramatic monologues might be defined as poems in which lyric apostrophes to inanimate objects like the bishop's tomb or the duke of Ferrara's statue of Neptune continually deflect a speaker's ostensible attempt to seduce an auditor verbally. The speaker's undoing comes from a duality of lyric and rhetorical motives. The duke of Ferrara's monologue is simultaneously a rhetorical poem designed to impress the envoy and a lyric of sublime indifference to any auditor who may chance to overhear.

> she liked whate'er
> She looked on, and her looks went everywhere.
>
> (ll. 23–24)

The paratactic syntax, with its lordly echo of lines 3–4: "Frà Pandolf's hands / Worked busily a day, and there she stands," allows the two expansive gestures to call to each other across the intervening twenty lines. Though audible only to attentive readers, these echoes of God's creative fiat in Genesis resound subliminally and alert us to the presence of other "unheard words." In choosing "Never to stoop" (l. 43), for example, the duke unconsciously parodies the condescension of the Christian God, who stoops to rise, "Such ever was love's way" ("A Death in the Desert," l. 134). The generous stooping of the duchess is a mystery that the duke himself is at a loss to talk about. It can be grasped only through his silences, when narrative flow is interrupted, and the duke concedes, in yet another phrase inserted between dashes, that "Somehow—[he] know[s] not how—" (l. 32) the duchess could feign to be as indifferent to his lofty social rank as the duke himself is sublimely indifferent to the envoy. Into the dark regions that his caesuras and dashes are continually opening up, the only light the duke can throw is the shadow of his own incomprehension.

In "The Bishop Orders His Tomb" a name list beginning at line 56: "The bas-relief in bronze ye promised me, / Those Pans and Nymphs ye wot of," is turned without warning into a chain of vocatives by the sharp break of the seventh-syllable caesura in line 62, which leaves the inventory of treasures grammatically suspended.

> And Moses with the tables... but I know
> Ye mark me not!
>
> (ll. 62–63)

As in lines 4–5, the syntactical incompletion dramatizes a growing rift between two poetic modes: one lyrical and apostrophic, the other narrative and rhetorical. With the shift away from the illegitimate sons to the apostrophized bas-relief in bronze, items that should function as mere backdrop are suddenly transformed into all-consuming foreground. And what should be foreground—the lure of the heavenly rather than the earthly city—finds itself metonymically displaced in the tomb-top's "One block, pure green as a pistachio-nut" (l. 71). Like an Egyptian pharaoh lugging his choicest treasure, his pistachio-colored bathtub, into eternity, the bishop is gradually engulfed in a mise-en-abîme. Strange thoughts of prenatal experiences remove the veil imposed at birth, and then the veil that divides that prenatal life from prior lives, and so on ad infinitum (ll. 91–94). In the vertigo induced by such unsettling perspectives, all grounds fall away, and the goal of some New Jerusalem at the end of time fades into an incomprehensibly distant future.

A more sustained use of the mise-en-abîme is dramatized in "Dîs Aliter Visum; or, Le Byron de Nos Jours," one of Browning's most complex maskings of the mind's desert places. The elaborate nesting structure of this monologue reproduces the intricate evasions of the modern Byron, whose failure to declare his love ten years earlier has ruined four lives. Unspoken conversations are embedded within unspoken conversations, in a bizarre proliferation of receding nonevents. The modern Byron has less in common with his romantic namesake than with Kierkegaard, the author of *The Seducer's Diary*, whose reluctance to propose marriage comes from a failure to will repetition. In an oddly inverted kind of déjà vu, the reluctant lover's future is perverted into a repetition of something he has already lived through in the moments that precede his contemplated marriage proposal, which becomes just another nonevent in the whole receding vista of nonevents that fill the poem.

The mise-en-abîme of embedding one nonevent in another becomes most complex when the woman reconstructs the man's unspoken thoughts at that precise moment ten years earlier when he failed to propose marriage because he could not bear the thought of speaking to her continually in the future. The triple framing of events is pictured typographically by the intricate embedding format of the quotation marks within quotation marks in stanzas 15–20. The speaker's reconstruction of the past event is the outward frame. Within that frame she places the silent words of the modern Byron, who races forward to a future conversation spoken by the woman herself, which is framed within his own framed consciousness of that imaginary speech. This complex framing, though amusing enough to a detached observer, is painful when experienced as tremors of emotion in the speaker's mind. We are spared no intimacies of consciousness. The man seems to think that any proposal of marriage he would have to "blurt out" (l. 47) would profane a mystery he can better honor in silence. For her part, the woman's words are broken apart by pauses produced by dashes—"And then, good-bye! Years ten since then: / Ten years!" (ll. 107–8), until her own elided thoughts contract almost to the vanishing point.

Kierkegaard says that "repetition and recollection are the same movement, only in opposite directions" (1964, 33). The backward repetition of the woman's recollection gives way to the man's forward recollection, which, if executed, promises to be a repetition proper, though a repetition he cannot consent to. By contrast, the woman experiences repetition by reliving her first distress a second time in memory, and then a third time in her elaborate invention of a speech the man imagines her making after a marriage that never took place because he never proposed it. Because Browning has already used two sets of quotation marks, he must now use italic script to frame a speech within two outer frames of speech. Even the speaker becomes confused. She believes that the modern Byron is too obtuse to see what she sees. But her irony at his expense depends on her dropping all the frames outside the speech beginning, " 'Thus with us!' / She'll sigh, 'Thus girls give body and soul' " (ll. 72–73). The instant we restore the two outer frames, this soliloquy of the woman is swallowed up in the continuing consciousness of the modern Byron, which collapses the woman's movement *backward* in time within his own contrary movement *forward*. The will to repeat "An hour's perfection" (l. 70), which would have fulfilled both the speakers' lives, yields instead to the despair of recollection, which makes both of them unhappy.

Ironically, the woman the modern Byron seems to despise means everything to him. The idea of marrying her incites his imagination and makes him a poet. " 'My friend makes verse,' " she observes, " 'and gets renown' " (l. 76). But by meaning so much to him, the woman also signs her own death warrant. The gravelike silences and nonconversations are part of her cruel desire to tear up old wounds. Her mental derangement comes from subjecting every emotion of her heart to the cold discipline of a long deferred postmortem. For his part, by remaining silent when he should have spoken, the modern Byron has betrayed a hidden god. Such at least is the bearing of the poem's title: "the gods' thought was or seemed otherwise" (*Aeneid*, 2.428). In refusing repetition, the man has refused "the daily bread which satisfies with benediction" (Kierkegaard 1964, 34). He faces the same moral emptiness that destroys Kierkegaard's young lover in *Repetition*. The source of all joy, the love of repetition, is replaced by despairing recollection, as if the modern lover were at his life's end while he is still only at its beginning. "Before he begins he has taken such a terrible stride that he has leapt over the whole of life" (Kierkegaard 1964, 38). What greater elision could there be? He is old before he is young. Before he can propose marriage he has become an old man with respect to the whole affair.

In another group of poems, which includes "Memorabilia" and "Any Wife to Any Husband," the use of silence to express plenitude collapses back into a silence of emptiness and confusion. Only in poems like the "Prologue" to *Asolando*, "Caliban upon Setebos," and "Childe Roland," does confrontation with a void allow a speaker who attunes his ear to silent meanings to recover in a *plenitude* of emptiness an odd version of the perfect moment.

"Memorabilia" shows how fragile and even whimsical a genuine recollection may be. To the auditor who merely remembers meeting Shelley, Browning's being startled by that memory seems foolish. But Browning is startled by more than a mere memory. His present recollection of the stranger's memory of Shelley shows that what is exalting to a master of privileged recollection is often merely ludicrous to a descriptive chronicler.

> But you were living before that,
> . . . .
> And the memory I started at—
> My starting moves your laughter.
>
> (ll. 5–8)

The emphatic dash, which breaks apart the grammar at the end of line 7, dramatizes the divide that separates the poet's genuine recollection of an event from his auditor's mere remembrance of it. One function of recollection is to consecrate the item commemorated by stripping away accidental details that might detract from its value. The last two quatrains are Browning's version of Wallace Stevens's "Anecdote of the Jar." A work of art has a power to dominate "the slovenly wilderness," as Stevens says, making it "Surround that hill" ("Anecdote of the Jar," ll. 3–4). Like Stevens's jar, which takes "dominion everywhere" (l. 9), Browning's molted eagle feather, picked up on a moor, preserves the place in memory. Though a mere "hand's-breadth" in size, "it shines alone / 'Mid the blank miles round about" (ll. 11–12). These "blank miles" can be recalled now only because an eagle feather Browning found there has been placed inside his shirt and kept alive in the dwelling place of memory. Though the recollected event is not so much experienced as invented, it is always in danger of collapsing back into a mere caprice or whim, like Browning's gesture of picking up the feather in the first place or his wild idea of associating it with Shelley. Moments of amazed possession may suddenly subside into the silence of a void. They may then seem as emptied of meaning to the celebrant as they did to Browning's stranger, who ridicules as affectation the poet's starting back in wonder in apparent idolatry of someone who merely remembers meeting Shelley.

A similar collapse of plenitude into emptiness erodes the confidence of Browning's speaker in "Any Wife to Any Husband." The wife knows that, despite their memories in common, there is a wound at the heart of domesticity that cannot survive death. So appalled is she by the thought of her husband's infidelity after she dies that she cannot bring herself to say what she has to say. Though her real thought transpires in the empty space between the first and second stanzas, that unheard thought is powerfully intimated by the heartfelt vocative of the opening line, by the two-line appositions that delay the appearance of the subordinate clause's principal verb, and by the hypothetical force of the conditional verbs "Shouldst," "couldst," and "Would."

> My love, this is the bitterest, that thou—
> Who art all truth, and who dost love me now
>   As thine eyes say, as thy voice breaks to say—
> Shouldst love so truly, and couldst love me still
> A whole long life through, had but love its will,
> Would death that leads me from thee brook delay.
>
>   (ll. 1–6)

Since loving truly a "whole long life" is no rational cause for bitterness, we must assume that what is omitted although strongly hinted by the concluding conditional verbs—"had . . . love its will," "Would death . . . brook delay"—is at least as important as what is said. The elided thought, half prophecy and half decree, is that you, who are in every other sense and under every other condition true, will betray me when I die. No wonder the woman represses her prophecy, barely intimating her fears in a fragile web of conditional verbs.

Stanzas 2 and 3 are wholly averted from the unheard words. Only the indefinite "It" at the head of stanza 4 tries to catch in its freely floating net some of the wife's repressed fears and silent thoughts.

> It would not be because my eye grew dim
> Thou couldst not find the love there...
>
>   (ll. 19–20)

It is possible to construe "It" as an expletive introducing a noun clause in the following line. But the ellipsis at the head of line 20 could be filled in more logical ways. Instead of supplying the relative pronoun "that," we might supply the conjunction "and because," making the second line of that stanza syntactically parallel to the first. But if so, the indefinite "It" hangs suspended, a reminder that what weighs most heavily on the woman's mind has not yet been said. Syntactical incompletion in stanza 4 is followed by a return of serial conditional verbs in stanza 5. Only in stanza 6, with the second use of the adjective "bitter" (ll. 1, 31), does the poem round back on its opening, finally voicing the fear that it has taken her a quarter of the poem to state openly. "Thou wilt sink," she bleakly predicts (l. 32). This unbearable thought is uttered now half as a negative command and half as a prophecy. Having tried to use language to celebrate the fullness of their love, she has now decreed only dispossession and loss.

The wife turns the final decrees back upon herself. Though she knows her husband will be false, during the short interval when they are on different sides of the grave "thy love shall hold me fast," she boasts (l. 124). "Shall hold" is a verb of decree and prophecy as well as a use of the simple future tense.

> Thy love shall hold me fast
> Until the little minute's sleep is past
> And I wake saved. —And yet it will not be!
>
>   (ll. 124–26)

Make-believe is temporary: it cannot be used to make belief. The first performative utterance—"And I wake saved" (a triumph of make-believe over fact)—is undone by the second: "And yet it will not be!" The apparent similarity of the two utterances, despite their profound disparity, is reinforced by the paratactic syntax: "And I," "And yet." The last line, like the bond between husband and wife, breaks apart with the fourth-syllable caesura and emphatic dash after the midline period. Her decree of salvation undoes itself, even as she pronounces the words, turning a celebration of unbroken faith into an epitaph not on her *grave*, but on their *love*.

Though the collapse of plenitude into emptiness is repeated in the "Epilogue" to *Ferishtah's Fancies*, this movement is reversed by the recovery of a spare kind of fullness in the "Prologue" to *Asolando*. In the "Epilogue," Browning seems to falter and stumble at the very threshold of death.

> Oh, Love—no, Love! All the noise below, Love,
> Groanings all and moanings—none of Life I lose!
>
> (ll. 1–2)

The wrenching of word order in the second sentence, the persistent dashes, the frantic vocatives, all create more hysteria than assurance. In the chilling disenchantment of the final stanza, when a "terror" suddenly "turns the blood to ice" (ll. 25–26), the spoken words are less meaningful than the words Browning cannot bring himself to hear. Perhaps Browning's unspoken fear is that hope of immortality is a mere hallucinatory "halo irised round" his "head" (l. 28). "Irised" is an odd verb. Its optical metaphor implies that if the poet's eyesight is as abnormal as his diction, the irised halo may be a product of mere diseased vision. Alternatively, the irised halo may be less a mirage than a confirmation that love for Elizabeth, a love that is his noblest creation, will endure. These unheard thoughts are unsettling, because they are Browning's attempt to be faithful to both sides of a paradox. If belief is willed into being by the radical faith of each believer, then God is a ground Browning himself has helped create. But an invented ground is a fiction, even though it may be a supreme fiction, and so not a ground at all. Conversely, if God is the unalterably given, the antecedent ground, then the warrior's energetic verbs in response to God's imperious "Come!" (l. 15), tend to undo themselves. The performatives that make religious belief may be unmasked instead as "mere fool's-play, make-believe and mumming" (l. 13).

The "Prologue" to *Asolando* restores in God's irrevocable otherness one neglected side of the same paradox. The aging Browning of the "Prologue" is most like Moses not when he can present each object "Palpably fire-clothed" (l. 25), but when the poverty of a depleted natural world attunes his ear to silent meanings. When involved with the "alien glow" of the soul's "iris-bow" (ll. 4–5), nature's first green is truly gold. But then leaf subsides to leaf, as Frost says: "And now a flower is just a flower" (l. 6). No alien name will do, because metaphor has lost its power to make every leaf a flower and every flower a ruby or an emerald. Metaphor's consecrating fire is rejected in favor of "The naked very thing" (l. 16). Poetry succeeds by its very depletion and deficiencies. A world of lambent flame, infused with an alien flow by the poet's fancy-haze and bold performative naming, is actually a world twice removed from God. If man is an artist and nature his creation, then art is prior to nature. But if art is posterior to nature, then, contrary to romantic axioms, the prophet or seer who calls nature the art of God is calling nature by its proper name. In composing a lyric of blanks and silences, Browning is composing a poetry in which God's words can at last be heard: "'Call my works thy friends!'" (l. 43), he exclaims. "At nature dost though shrink amazed? / God is it who transcends" (ll. 44–45).

Browning's ability to repossess plenitude in the bleak landscape at Asolo is the culminating act of a drama for which Caliban rehearses in his swamp. Only in an evolutionary theology like the Aeschylean or Hegelian can the wagers and decrees of faith be fully performative. A grounded theology is primitive: unless such a primordial theology, grounded in a voluntarist deity like Caliban's Setebos, can be made to evolve into something less barbaric and coercive, there is no way of reconciling the constatives of its divine ground with the performatives of faith. Unfortunately, Caliban's rite of exorcising the ghost of voluntarist theology, which is the prototype of all dead or static theology, fails in the end, because it is tainted with the very defects of cruelty and hatred it tries to exorcise. The brainless singsong of his spiteful incantation—"*What I hate, be consecrate / To celebrate Thee and Thy state*" (ll. 276–77)—is no true rite of exorcism but a mere imprecation and swearing song, like the delinquent blasphemies of Browning's Spanish monk. At the last minute, however, something unexpected happens. Setebos's sudden materialization to Caliban as a cross-surging of eccentric force in the coming storm gives the emptiness of the exorcist's world a new and potent meaning. It is as if the performative language of exorcism is emptied of its meaning in Caliban's brainless swearing song only in order that this same emptiness can then be transferred to the universe at large. In expelling unworthy gods, "Caliban upon Setebos" turns the silence of moral indifference and emptiness into the plenitude of an oppressive, all-embracing presence. Caliban is never *less* like Setebos than when he is using performative verbs of self-making to imitate Prospero and to anticipate a form of divine self-making in which Setebos will evolve into the Quiet. And he is never *more* like Setebos than when he substitutes metaphors of conquest and force for evolutionary dramas of persuasive agency.

The most enigmatic transition from emptiness to plenitude takes place in "Childe Roland." So potent are the silent meanings and unheard words in this poem that we readily forget that many of its most hideous actions are nonevents, happenings that take place only in the pilgrim's dark imagination. A clue that recollection can radically alter experience comes in line 55, where the first use of a present-tense verb, "I think I never saw / Such starved ignoble nature," dramatizes the truth that remembrance is always now. The starved landscape can be recollected in its essential penury only by comparing it with nonhappenings, with the nonappearance, for example, of flowers and cedar groves (l. 57), or with the imaginary ravagings of a primordial brute that roams the plain pashing out the life of every struggling weed (ll. 67–72). There are far more metonymies than metaphors in the poem, and the cautious use of similes fosters the illusion that objects are being remembered in exact detail rather than projected onto voids and empty places by a mind that is recollecting and recreating the past rather than merely remembering it. The real operations of appropriating and possessing a plenitude of emptiness are being repressed or displaced: no wonder readers have misread the poem. It is almost as if the pilgrim wants to "misread" it himself.

There are surprisingly few poems in Browning's canon (and perhaps in any poet's canon) in which silence marks an amazed possession of all words. Most often the experience of plenitude takes place only in sustained parentheses, as it does in the first half of "Abt Vogler," which is followed by a precipitate fall from grace. The exception to that statement is the last part of "Saul," where suspensions of snytax and parentheses carry the speaker to higher and higher plateaus of knowledge. The strongly stressed anapests and hexameters, often hypermetric, swell with barely communicable meaning. The celebrant is too beset by crowding witnesses "famished for news," like the "runner" (l. 317), to be wholly articulate. He is out of breath, so exhilarated and exhausted by his effort that he can stammer out his meaning only in the breathing spaces between metrical feet, caesuras, and heavily end-stopped lines. A living hand, warm and loving, "a Hand like this hand" (l. 311), is being extended toward the speaker, supporting him and suppressing his tumult. But we can see no hand, nor can David. This "Hand" is a simultaneous presence/absence, thrust provocatively at the reader like the hand in Keats's elegiac fragment, "This Living Hand." David knows that the hand he summons forth is a wild surmise, a daring poetic fiction; but he also shows that the power of this fiction, embraced in a purely lyric or apostrophic time, is irresistible. Because God himself is a poet, a creator through words, performative utterance is prior to descriptive utterance, and prophecies are more potent than mere descriptive statements. As David contrives to make the silence of his culminating benediction an amazed appropriation of all creation, the usual priority of nature to art, of description to performance, is reversed.

Browning shows in "Abt Vogler" that what may be most fugitive and elusive, intelligible only as a silence of amazed possession, may also be most substantial and enduring. To this end he has to reinvent the English language, allowing the convergence and diffusion of syntactical units, which "dispart now and now combine" around the pivot of the repeating adverb (l. 11), to impart the life of spontaneous creation.

> Would that the structure brave, the manifold music I build,
>   Bidding my organ obey, calling its keys to their work,
> Claiming each slave of the sound, at a touch, as when Solomon willed
>   Armies of angels that soar, legions of demons that lurk,
> Man, brute, reptile, fly, —alien of end and of aim,
>   Adverse, each from the other heaven-high, hell-deep removed,—
> Should rush into sight at once as he named the ineffable Name,
>   And pile him a palace straight, to pleasure the princess he loved!
> Would it might tarry like his, the beautiful building of mine,
>   This which my keys in a crowd pressed and importuned to raise!
>
> (ll. 1–10)

The delay of the sentence's principal verb, "Would it might tarry," which comes near the end of a ten-line unit, like the completion of a German *Nebensatz* in its final verb, gives the ebb and flow of the alliterating anapests and midline caesuras a dynamic continuum and a history. The Germanic device of having appositional units precede rather than follow the noun is also recalled by the bold hyperbaton of lines 21–24, where three spacious lines of modification, with one appositional unit enfolded in another, heralds the long delayed subject, "the pinnacled glory." Quick plunges into the hellish region of the lower keyboard are followed by sudden heavenward ascents into the upper registers. The notes dispart and then combine like the grammatical subject and verb of the opening sentence. The double grammatical congruity of the participles "Bidding," "calling," "Claiming," (ll. 2–3), which can modify either "structure brave" or "I" (l. 1), helps enfold the musician in his music, until the two become as indistinguishable as "the finger of God" and the "flash of the will that can" (l. 49). The grammar of "Abt Vogler" not only is paratactic, it is complexly hypotactic too, folding modifier within modifier, envelope inside envelope, until the complicated subordination of one thought to another all but obliterates the kernel inside the first envelope, which must be repeated at the beginning of the second stanza: "Would that the structure brave," "Would it might tarry" (ll. 1, 9). By comparison with Abt Vogler's opening petition or prayer, most English sentences seem stillborn.

Behind the three groups of unheard words I have studied in Browning's poetry stand three theories of language and three critical traditions. The silence of reserve assumes that what is outside consciousness is a forgotten, secret, or hidden meaning that is in principle recoverable. Such a meaning is unspeakable rather than inexpressible, because the poet's silence proceeds less from bewilderment in the presence of a subject that is contradictory or incomprehensible than from reluctance to profane a mystery. Geoffrey Hartman's comment on Browning, which I quoted at the beginning, advocates a reserve of silence typical of Hegel in *The Lectures on Aesthetics* and of his more conservative hermeneutical heirs.

The second mode of silence, which I associate with the more radical Hegel of the *Encyklopedie* and with such contemporary deconstructionists as J. Hillis Miller, assumes that what is outside consciousness, far from being in principle recoverable, is precisely what language can never literally name. If unconsciousness is to be identified with the prelinguistic, as Nietzsche advocates, then it cannot be expressed at all. At best it can be intimated in a language that is neither literal nor figurative. Its unheard words are the silence of a code that defies translation, since its use of oxymoron and catachresis is no longer referential. What is being defined has now no literal name and may seem indistinguishable from nothingness.

The third kind of unheard word celebrates a silence of amazed possession. But the meaning that is possessed is not fully real until the poet uses performative language to appropriate it. J. L. Austin has shown that the efficacy of such language depends on its aptness or felicity. As Browning explains in his "Prologue" to *Asolando*, only burning bushes that have been stripped bare of their "lambent flame" can be possessed by the mind, "know[n] and name[d]" (ll. 31, 37). Such experiences take place in the empty spaces, in the dashes and caesuras that break his poetry apart, culminating not in a sacramental marriage of the mind to nature, but in a proclamation of divorce. The exposure of nature as naked, bare, without inherent meaning, prompts Browning to turn back to mind as the essential element.

"A Bible without difficulties," says Henry Melvill, the theologian who most influenced the young Browning, would be "a firmament without stars" (Melvill 1838, 258). When Abt Vogler boasts "That out of three sounds he frame[s], not a fourth sound, but a star" (l. 52), the "star" is only symbolic shorthand for that ineffable quality that makes any organic whole unanalyzably greater than its parts. Abt Vogler's substitution of the star for a fourth sound may be oracularly "difficult." But without such a difficult leap, how could Browning populate his poem with "a tenantry gloriously distinct," as Melvill says (1838, 258–59)? Like the mysteries of Scripture, the mysterious fullness of Abt Vogler's music can be expressed only negatively, by nonnaming tropes like the star. But were it not for the star's rarefied transmitting light, the ineffable names would disperse in silence, darkness, or mere empty space. Does the unspeakable mystery precede the moment of its being made audible through music or visible through starlight? Or does the mystery exist only in the act of naming it? To put this crisis in faith and knowing another way: Is naming "the ineffable Name" ("Abt Vogler," l. 7) a genuinely performative naming, or is it a constative utterance? Does it merely make visible and audible a mystery that antecedently exists? It seems to be both together, and hence neither. So shrouded in mystery is Browning's worship of hidden gods that pivotal switches from descriptive language to vocatives, or from future verbs to auxiliary verbs of prophecy or decree, are veiled by grammatical ambiguities, silencings, and sudden breaks in the poetic lines.

What is felt in the spacious curve of heaven, as it bends down to touch earth in "Abt Vogler," and in the counterarc of earth as it rises "to scale the sky," is less the actual moment of intersection than its infinite possibility.

> And the emulous heaven yearned down, made effort to reach the earth,
>   As the earth had done her best, in my passion, to scale the sky:
>   ("Abt Vogler," ll. 27–28)

Thrusting out with the fling of a great cantilever or arc, the lines offer the most superb chiasmus in all of Browning: "emulous heaven," "earth," "earth...in my passion," "sky." Faith resounds not only semantically—in the words "emulous" and "yearned," but also phonetically in the echoing sounds in "*year*ned" and in the repeated use of "*earth*," which is the pivot or hinge word, the place at which the two spans of this suspension bridge converge. The firmness of the rhymes secures the juncture, making it as sure a point of contact as God's touching of Adam's finger in the Sistine Chapel painting: "but here is the finger of God, a flash of the will that can" (l. 49). "Earth" harks back to "man's birth" two lines earlier, and "sky" binds earth to heaven by rhyming with "I" (l. 26). In each case Browning anchors his chiasmus on pillars of sound that stand firmly outside the falling and rising arcs. Yet in all his poetry Browning seems to tremble at the brink, as if hesitant to launch forth, even as the massive cantilevers of his verse, like the two sloping spans of his chiasmus in "Abt Vogler," slowly descend in sweeping arcs to touch gently at the center. It is as if Browning is reluctant to track the path of faith, the arc joining description to prophecy, constative to performative speech, while tracing its trajectory all the time.

PART THREE

Mystery and Method:
Is a Centerless View a True One?

To avoid the false teleology of a scientific explanation centered on divine or human will, Charles Darwin favors a centerless view of nature. The accidental variations that he places at the center of his evolutionary theory are really a denial of any center at all. So successful is Darwin in the field of biological science that there is always a danger of forgetting that to be objective in the sense of best accounting for or understanding a phenomenon may require an investigator to be less objective in the sense of being neutrally outside or detached from the object of his inquiry. The objectivity appropriate to Newman's understanding of faith, for example, may require a more interior view than the climb outside the mind required for Darwin's study of evolution or for J. S. Mill's understanding of inductive logic. To renounce mystery and bafflement in search of a single standard of objectivity appropriate to every inquiry is to make the study of both culture and science less challenging than it ought to be. An interior approach to faith, art, or culture may be more appropriately "objective" —in the sense of better accounting for these complex phenomena— than a wholly centerless, nonpurposive perspective like Darwin's.

Part 3 tries to show how each fine tuning of involvement and detachment produces new approaches to knowledge. Promising to raise us above old battles by making us attentive to commonplace facts we are in danger of neglecting, Mill argues that the mystique surrounding the concept of justice is merely obfuscating. When a rift appears between our lofty idea of justice and its lowly ground in an animal desire to avoid injury to ourselves or our friends, Mill advises us to scale down our exalted notions until they accord better with the evidence at hand. To conclude with Mill, however, that the question of universals raised by the syllogism is wholly misconceived, or to attack as nonsense Plato's doctrine of Ideas, as Jowett and Pater do, runs the risk of diminishing these subjects by denying the mystery that a more complex and less reductive approach might disclose. Whereas Mill tends to be a deflationary thinker, Huxley turns out to be a skeptic. Having exposed gaps between idealist and materialist dogmas about the physical world, Huxley advises us to live with them. J. H. Newman represents a third possibility. Though he agrees with the skeptics that rifts are unavoidable, he is resolved to leap across them nonetheless. Such a heroic thinker merely turns his back on the rifts, ignoring the epistemological corpses that reductionists like Mill and skeptics like Huxley find strewn beneath them.

Huxley shows that any advance in science requires that secondary qualities be seen as the effect of primary qualities that allow the chemist or physicist to substitute for idealist forms of understanding new materialist hypotheses. Yet Huxley refuses to reduce spirit to matter, because he refuses to recognize either material or psychological descriptions as privileged: both are mere symbolic fictions, like the xs and ys of an algebraic formula, which no informed thinker would mistake for real entities. Evolutionary explanations of the mind and its capacities have become today a powerful reductionist dogma. But as Darwin's bulldog, Huxley never intended his championship of evolutionary thought to apply universally. Though natural selection may explain all adaptive evolution, there may be developments in the species that are not specifically adaptive and that cannot be explained in terms of natural selection. Moreover, evolution's success in biological science and geology does not justify its application to everything we cannot at present understand. No Victorian treatise more powerfully opposes the pervasive and reductive naturalism of Victorian culture than Huxley's own *Evolution and Ethics*. Morality requires not diachronic but timeless explanations. Though our moral capacities are objective and invite a measure of detachment, they seem to require a more interior perspective than biological science or physics. Huxley acknowledges the chasm that divides the prescriptive statements of ethics from the descriptive statements of physical science. He denies that any evolutionary theory can hope to bridge the chasm or resolve the mystery of how a value can be derived from a fact, or an ought from an is.

Mill's theories of induction tend to obscure the truth that even empirical knowledge must rest on an a priori base. The scientific gaps between data and conclusions are of great importance in any theory of knowledge, and something like Descartes's notion of a nondeceiving God is still required to justify Mill's leap from hypotheses we formulate inside our minds to the world outside. It seems logically impossible ever to achieve a complete induction, which must arrive at a picture of the world that includes within it a theory of the mind and how it knows the world. Such a picture must itself be generated by the mind we are trying to know. At least Mill is an *inclusive* empiricist; far more reductive, paradoxically, is an idealist like Pater. Whereas Plato assumes that something is real if it exists independent of our capacity to conceive it, in *Plato and Platonism* Pater assumes on the contrary that our capacity to conceive of something guarantees it is real. In trying to align Plato's ideas with their grounds in the human mind, Pater often explains away their content. His attempt to cut Plato down to size betrays a lack of humility, as if Pater denies a mystery, refusing to acknowledge that the actual structure of Plato's universe may be constitutionally beyond his grasp.

The strain between objective and internal explanations precipitates crises in knowing. How can Victorians live both from the detached perspective of the surveyor of all geological time in *In Memoriam* and from the point of view of the individual mourner? How can they see the natural disaster in *The Wreck of the Deutschland* both from God's point of view and from that of the shipwrecked victims? We can either alternate between different views of the self, as Carlyle does in "Natural Supernaturalism" or else develop binocular vision. Such large-scale but delicate experiments in double vision as *The Ring and the Book* and *The Moonstone*, both published the same year, try to avoid opposite errors. To look at a standpoint from outside, in a detached clinical mood, is to be too dismissive of the subtle feel and motivation of each agent's values. But to go to the other extreme by converting such partisan qualities into a nonlimitation is to embrace a relativism that says there is no truth that is not peculiar to an individual observer. Browning and Collins know that an objective view is often wrongly equated with the authority of facts, with what is found in the documents or the archives. But the facts are not really given: they are always an interpretation. Nor is reality just a centerless perspective. When Jesus says that *he* is the truth (*John* 14:6), he means that the truth is a personality, not a set of propositions. Browning's religious apologists reach a similar conclusion: since the most objective view is God's, some forms of objectivity have to be irreducibly subjective, for God is a person. The crisis in knowing is inescapable. On the one hand, the use of perspectives makes it hard to ascend to a privileged conception. On the other hand, if we postulate such a conception, how can we pass from it to a world that includes many points of view?

Despite the variety of discordant values, it seems possible to distinguish between values that are relative to internal viewpoints and values that are "agent neutral." Does satisfaction of a desire for liberty, for example, have impersonal utility, as Mill claims? Or does Mill's possession of the liberty he desires have value for him only because he wants it? Would liberty still have value for a person who chose to sell himself into slavery? Perhaps faith, culture, art (and, if Arnold is right, even liberty itself) are merely optional ends. They have value only for writers like Newman, Arnold, Mill, and Ruskin who have chosen them as values in their own lives. If such values are optional, then it is not hard to see why they are most effectively presented through such literary genres as autobiography or essay, where the response of each inquirer is an important part of the inquiry.

But how can an individual's desires confer impersonal, agent neutral value—an objective value that lies outside the self—on something as personal as one's cultural satisfactions or religious beliefs? In his poem "The Two Voices" Tennyson's skeptic observes that in the believing Saint Stephen "The elements were kindlier mixed" (l. 228). If belief is a biochemical accident, or at best an idiosyncratic impulse, how can it possess any normative value? Both Arnold and Newman struggle tenaciously with this question. Is culture, Arnold muses, only the idle curiosity or intellectual indulgence of an Oxford professor of poetry? The mere satisfaction of preferences that depend for their value on the internal viewpoint maintained in such testaments as Newman's *Apologia* and sermons or in Arnold's lectures and essays seems to lose much of its cogency and appeal when viewed from outside. Are Frederic Harrison and Huxley not then right to mock the inutility of a cultural satisfaction like reading Greek? How can so personal a value be impersonally justified?

Bentham concludes that every value is equally important or equally unimportant, depending on one's perspective. He refuses to accord any more value to writing a book or reading Plato than to any other pleasurable pastime. When all such values are agent-relative, then "prejudice apart, the game of push-pin is of equal value with . . . poetry" (Bentham, 1838–43.2.253). If one is a poet or an Oxford professor of poetry like Arnold, then standing outside oneself in the way Bentham recommends will generate humility. Perhaps some proper middle distance between objective detachment and internal involvement can be found, as in the best Victorian monologues, where a just sense of worth seems to fall somewhere between the nihilistic indifference of Caliban the godlike despot, stoning every twenty-first crab, and the blind self-absorption of Caliban the hedonist, a mere sense-bound organism sprawling "Flat on his belly in the pit's much mire" ("Caliban upon Setebos," ll. 102, 2).

In one matter that greatly preoccupied the Victorians, however, no reconciliation of internal and external views seems possible. An objective standpoint seems powerless in the end to accommodate at its full subjective value the fact of death. At death the individual's possibilities not only will not be actualized, they will also vanish—blotted out and obliterated. The brutal shock of this assault is an effect Thackeray tries to register in the scene describing the deaths of Sedley and Osborne in *Vanity Fair*. The picture of the deceased will be covered, then taken down from the wall by his heirs, who will soon forget him: it seems the ultimate form of abandonment. But even more is at stake in *In Memoriam*, where the end of Hallam's life seems indistinguishable from the end of time and the only world there is. There seems no way an objective view of death can retain the seriousness of an internal view. As George Eliot says, we would die of the roar that lies on the other side of silence were we more finely tuned to the death of illusion. It is too staggering to imagine the perpetual "cataract of death / That spends to nothingness" (Frost, "West-Running Brook," ll. 56–57), the avalanche of disaster in which the world comes to an end for countless thousands of people every minute. Perhaps only Christ or Keats's Moneta can maintain the same intense interest in universal death as each individual maintains in his own death. For everyone else the emotional overload is too great.

After introducing the topic of mystery and method, part 3 continues with an analysis of Newman's idea that knowledge is sometimes the revelation of a mystery. As a logician writing in the tradition of Aristotle, Newman finds that his most important model of knowledge in his Oxford sermons on faith and reason is the chain of logically connected statements. But since his subject is faith, he discovers that the chain of logical proof must also be supplemented with the admittedly more mysterious but ultimately more useful model of the explanatory web. The silences in Newman's prose are not just the silences of Tractarian reserve: they are also the silences of a thwarted mind as it tries to make intelligible to understanding the mysteries of an "incomprehensible certainty" that will not quite formulate in logical terms. The art of "persuasive definition," to borrow Charles L. Stevenson's term from *Ethics and Language*, allows Newman, the believer, to keep constant the highly charged emotive meaning of his prize word "faith" while experimenting as a logician and theologian with new descriptive meanings.

In Christina Rossetti's poetry, as in Newman's theological prose, chains of continuity between God and man, or between mystery and knowledge, are constantly breaking down. Chapter 14 shows how links of this chain are restored by Rossetti's heroic use of chiasmus, the trope of crossing over, which allows her to reaffirm the triumphant chiasmus of the Cross. The silences in her poetry sometimes mark the places of fracture and breakdown, but more often they signal a moment of breakthrough as Rossetti uses her contextual definitions of mystery words like "love" or "God" to achieve all the heart can wish.

The short concluding section of chapter 14 examines an apparently identical but actually quite different use of contextual definition in Arnold and Ruskin. Culture, like the products of an artistic imagination, comprises man-made artifacts, yielding the kind of a priori truth that Vico said the mind can possess only of its own creations. But because Ruskin and Arnold are trying to transfer to imagination and culture the spiritual authority that Newman and Rossetti both ascribe to God, they are in danger of making these human entities more mystifying than they need be. Like the statue of Pallas Athene in his poem "Palladium," Arnold's definitions of "culture" are too oracular and remote to be of practical use to anyone. And Ruskin is at a loss to explain how imagination really works. It seems at times that if imagination were more intelligible, it would be less worthy of Ruskin's worship.

Like the silence of a confused Sir William Hamilton, abasing himself before the altar of an unknowable God, the silences of J. S. Mill's adversaries are often equated with the stupefaction and stupidity of minds bewitched by their own confused use of words. In chapter 15 I show how Mill, as a kind of Victorian Wittgenstein, does battle against the bewitching of the mind by means of language. He wants to banish the mystification of obscure essentialist definitions of words so that we can better appreciate the marvels of scientific method and inductive logic that authentically exist. To purify the dialect of the tribe, Mill often translates a mystifying abstraction like the Stoic precept to follow a benign nature into tragicomic scenarios of nature's odious tyranny and cruelty, culminating in some zenith of magnificent inconsequence worthy of the most bizarre and frightening theater of the absurd.

Are knowledge and mystery compatible? Is knowledge a revelation of mystery or is it, like modern science and analytic philosophy, pledged to eliminate mystery? The last two chapters of part 3 argue for the compatibility of knowledge and mystery in two mystery fictions, Wilkie Collins's *The Moonstone* and Robert Browning's *The Ring and the Book*, both published in 1868. Each writer explores the limitations of detective fiction's preferred model of knowing: the chain of causally linked statements. Can a skilled detective, like a good historian, solve the mystery of what happened in the past by providing the causal links that are missing in a chain? Both Collins and Browning show that neither the inductive logic of Sherlock Holmes and the lawyer, Mr. Bruff, nor the scientific historiography of an H. T. Buckle, the ancestor of modern cliometricians who aspire to make history a statistical science, can perform the complex operations required of a criminal investigation or an exercise in historical reconstruction. On the other hand, a highly imaginative detective like Collins's Sergeant Cuff or a myth critic like David Friedrich Strauss forfeits the chance of being proved right in avoiding the risk of being proved wrong. By identifying imaginatively with other witnesses and suspects, only Collins's Ezra Jennings and Browning's narrator can provide a fictional equivalent of Barthold Niebuhr's influential doctrine of historical empathy, according to which historians must exercise their negative capability by reliving the experiences of historical agents.

The silences in *The Moonstone* are usually the result of elided words or missing information. Sometimes a narrator like Betteredge cannot hear what a second character, Rachel, is saying to a third character, Blake. Everything that is said is presented in dumb show, because the conversation is witnessed through a window. Even if Betteredge could hear what Rachel says, however, the most important information would still be missing, because Rachel, as we later learn, refuses to tell Blake that she saw him take her diamond. Such silences result from a temporary withholding of connecting links that are supplied later in the story. The silences in *The Ring and the Book* run deeper and are not as easy to replace with words. Because no bridges are in place to span the empty spaces created by dashes and elisions in *The Ring and the Book*, Browning invites each reader to become an alpine mountaineer, leaping with agility across the cracks and fissures that keep opening in his verse. Unlike the mysteries of a simple detective fiction, the mysteries of Pompilia's faith and of Guido's motiveless malignity come not from something merely unknowable in the work, like the identity of the thief who stole the moonstone, but from something unlimited in it.

CHAPTER 12

Must We Explain What We Believe
and Prove What We Explain?

The Victorian authors studied in this last section of the book are most persuasive not when trying to prove some conclusion, but when trying to explain some leading idea like culture, or some object of belief like religion. Provable propositions like the truisms of Browning's advocates in *The Ring and the Book* tend to be trivial, and important propositions like Mill's belief in the utility of liberty or Arnold's belief in the value of culture, are not strictly provable. But not all methods of investigation need use arguments and proofs. Some methods may be designed to explain something, to render more coherent an idea like culture, utilitarianism, or the scientific method. To be intelligible a thing need not be provable. It is enough for J. H. Newman, given an apparent excluder—the Victorians' penchant for skepticism and doubt—to show that faith is still possible. In view of his contemporaries' incapacity for harmonious, inward, and general development, Arnold may also have to show how culture is possible. And one of Huxley's tasks is to explain how science is possible given the relativity of scientific axioms.

In any strong mode of exclusion, the existence of q seems to imply the nonexistence of p. Logical antinomies in Kant, Mansel, and F. H. Bradley precipitate crises in knowing. They strongly suggest that the subject in question is either nonexistent or not strictly knowable. But perhaps a crisis in representation simply means that the subject exceeds the mind's grasp and can be apprehended only as a mystery. To be a Platonist, one might argue, is to believe in Plato's doctrine of Ideas. But according to Jowett and Pater this doctrine is a mere ontological fiction. Is their disbelief in this fiction logically compatible with their advocacy of Platonism? Newman may continue to doubt some religious propositions, and Huxley may concede the fictive status of matter, but in each case the incompatibility of p with an apparent excluder is denied. The reasoning from these conditions to not-p, the impossibility of faith or science, is shown to be defective. Though explanations may seem to accomplish less than proofs, they can be more valuable in practice. For if we already believe in religion or in the scientific method, it is less important to see how they are true than to see how they are possible. Finding harmony in apparent contradiction and incompatibility is the task of explanation, not of proof, and explanation is at once more and less valuable than proof. Though less rigorous, an explanation's demonstrations may be more useful because less trivial than a proof. We are shown how parts of a picture or a puzzle fit together. Proofs, by contrast, usually demonstrate something we already believe, like the Pythagorean theorem or the equation $2 + 2 = 4$.

Unless a proof starts with premises that carry antecedent conviction, no conclusion will follow from the premises. When an inductive logician like Mill, for example, concludes that all men are rational, his conclusion will follow from the premise that at least all people he knows are rational only if he already believes in the rationality of these people. But an explanation, unlike a proof, may introduce hypotheses or premises that are not widely accepted or believed. I used to think that merely probable premises in Newman's *Essay on the Development of Christian Doctrine* would not in combination produce a conclusion that was any more probable than any of its least persuasive premises taken independently. A chain of logical argument, I thought, was only as strong as its weakest link. But a web of explanatory threads is tougher, more resilient, than any individual thread. If Newman can connect enough authentic attributes of development, then the network of attributes he weaves may produce a conviction that never attaches to any single attribute in isolation. It is appropriate to decide, then, whether the more exact analogy is a chain or a web. A logical proof must forge a chain: the first links must be true premises or premises that are at least believed to be true. Otherwise a plausible end link or conclusion will never be reached. By contrast, an explanation consists of threads of argument that often carry little weight when allowed to unravel. Strong probability is produced only when the threads mesh to form a resilient network of connections. Instead of starting like Mill's inductive logician from principles that are certain and necessarily true, Newman's apologist explains how the unchanging character of Christian truth is possible given the existence of an apparent excluder, the constant change and development of doctrine.

How, we might ask, can an investigation with a foregone conclusion, such as Newman's or Huxley's prior conviction that faith or science is of value, have any value in itself as a methodological inquiry? It may have value in the first place as an explanation, not a proof. Newman, for example, is prepared to explain his beliefs, but he would be the first to concede the folly of trying to prove what he explains. Given his apologetic aims, Newman is right to assert a notion that runs contrary to the idea of a proof: namely, his idea that propositions too weak to induce assent by themselves may produce belief when taken together. As explanations of why Catholic doctrine represents a true development of Christian teaching, the collective "proofs" possess a probability not to be found in any individual "proof." Only, as Newman himself seems half to recognize, "proof" is the wrong word. There is, I think, a second way investigations with foregone conclusions can be valuable. Unanticipated discoveries can always be made en route. Newman may want to reach a conclusion about the accessibility of faith, but his investigations in the Oxford sermons may precipitate crises of knowing that lead him to redefine the meaning of the word "reason." Huxley may want to justify scientific method, but further inquiry may make him increasingly skeptical of the materialist dogmas he is predisposed to advocate. Mill may want to embrace utilitarian conclusions, but there is no guarantee he will reach them. Indeed, few inquirers reach their original destinations without changing and deepening their sense of what is worth investigating.

In using adversaries like Frederic Harrison and the Dissenters as his own strongest advocates, Arnold substitutes for the intellectual karate that Newman uses against Kingsley a form of mental judo or aikido. Most interesting, however, are the attacks that become domestic by posing a threat to one's own belief system. In his essay *On Liberty* Mill's opponents dramatize crises of knowledge in the domestic utilitarian branch as well as in the foreign affairs department of Mill's chosen system of thought. Mill realizes there are rational limits to freedom for any utilitarian, and if he did not know this he would never attribute such theoretical importance to imaginary and real opponents of liberty, who are continually voicing their disagreement with him in the essay.

There would be nothing mysterious about knowledge if a causal relation held between beliefs and facts. But as Browning argues at length in *The Ring and the Book*, our belief that a fact holds is never identical with that fact. If a fact had been removed from the far end of an interpretive chain, how, asks the skeptic, could we tell? This unsettling question leads to the deconstructive operations of Huxley and Pater. The material entities that are posited by the symbolic language of science might be removed from the end of the physicist's mathematical chain, and we could never tell the difference. Similarly, being independent of human perception, Plato's Ideas might disappear from the far end of a metaphysical chain without anyone's being the wiser. A truth that has no consequence for action is a useless cog in a machine, a mere idle wheel; and Occam's razor dictates its removal.

Paradoxically, what is desirable for knowledge—some causal linking with fact and evidence—is threatening for faith. If action is determined by antecedent facts, free will may be impaired and opportunity for the free exercise of faith diminished. The linkage of judgment to fact and evidence must be loose enough to allow for free assent and faith, yet strong enough to permit a measure of knowledge. One sometimes feels that if Browning had made *The Ring and the Book* even longer, his conclusions would be different. One reason the poem is so long is that it seems constantly to be in search of some optional stop rule that will tell Browning he has arrived at the place he wants to be.

The Moonstone shows that facts may continue to elude detection for interesting reasons. The skeptical Collins reveals that especially vulnerable to attack is Rachel Verinder's belief that if it were not true that a thief stole her diamond she would not believe it. But this condition of variance is hard to establish. Something might deceive her into believing p is true when it is false. If some fact were at variance with p, how would she know? Because Franklin is sleepwalking when he steals her diamond, Rachel is deceived into affirming p, when something is actually at variance with p. Instead of trying to steal her diamond, Franklin is trying to safeguard it from theft. He is the opposite of a thief, though Rachel has no way of knowing this. Not-p has occurred, but Rachel is deceived into believing that p still pertains. And so she continues to adhere to p when she should be disavowing it.

The same skepticism erodes the possibility of Blake's possessing knowledge. If the proposition that a thief has stolen the diamond is true, then Blake assumes he will believe it. He will even summon the police to ensure that the thief is quickly brought to justice. But p is true in a sense that Blake does not understand. A theft has been committed that is not a theft, because the "thief" has acted in an involuntary manner.

Evidence for a belief often involves the inquirer in an endless regress of deductions. In *The Moonstone* the evidence for the thief's hurry depends on some further evidence for the assumption that hurry or confusion on the thief's part establishes an evidential tie between the smeared paint and the diamond's disappearance. If e is evidence for d, then Sergeant Cuff has to know an E' such that E' is evidence for the fact that e is evidence for d. How might such a regress be blocked? Only, I think, if E' can be shown to repeat e. Like a symbol in art, which according to Nelson Goodman must exemplify a quality that it also refers to, a piece of evidence must do double duty. It has to be evidence for something while also being evidence that it *is* evidence. Any abnormal detail like smeared paint on a door advertises its status as evidence by being in a novel with family resemblances to other detective fictions in which similar details are important just by being abnormal. Moreover, Rachel's unwillingness to cooperate with the police, the disappearance of the garment that must be smeared with paint, the strange behavior of Rosanna Spearman, all bear evidence of being evidence as well as exemplifying the evidential function they advertise. Since knowledge cannot be limited to deductive chains, however, there is always an irreducible minimum of mystery in detective fiction. To the degree that some forms of knowledge are compatible with mystery, the skeptic seems right: If our beliefs were false, how could we ever hope to know they were false? Only by tracking the conditions under which beliefs vary with the facts can investigators like Cuff, Jennings, and Franklin Blake hope to oppose the skeptics on their own chosen ground.

Stage setting and context are crucial to the application of words like "faith" and "culture." If there is a known context that undercuts a particular application of faith, showing it to be mere credulity or gullibility, and that shows culture to be idle curiosity, then how do we know there is not a still wider context, as yet undetected, that will disclose defects in our present understanding? Newman commends a form of notional assent, which is knowing that one knows. But skeptics argue that reflexive knowledge is exceptional and occurs only rarely. We are often shocked, I think, to discover that the deepest suspicions of skeptics like first-half Rome, Archangelis, and Guido cannot be refuted. If we do not know Pompilia and Caposacchi are innocent, what *can* we know? And yet attempts to avoid skepticism by claiming we know everything that happens between the priest and Pompilia are bound to fail. We are still too reticent about our doubts. Like most things in the world, even the elopement of Caponsacchi and Pompilia is unsettling and bewildering, and it is a mistake to explain away our bewilderment. If God's motives are as inscrutable as Browning's pope maintains, why should God not allow demons to deceive even the pope, if only for his own ultimate good? Can deception not create the conditions of a more understanding appreciation and a deeper faith? Even if a good God exists, might not such a God have his own reasons for deceiving us about the virtue of people who believe in him? Less valuable than a knockdown argument that bludgeons opponents into accepting lean theories and hard data are the bewilderment and doubt of heroic, skeptical, and even reductionist thinkers who, in a constant search for new and better questions, refuse to deny their ignorance or the still imponderable puzzles at the center of their world.

CHAPTER 13

Newman on Faith:

A Heroic Theory of Knowledge

"Faith" is one of those complex mystery words, like "culture" in Arnold and "mystery" in Ruskin, that precipitate crises in representation by defying exact definition. By offering a surplus of definitions in his fifteen sermons preached before the University of Oxford between 1826 and 1843, J. H. Newman generates the paradox of a simultaneous overdetermination and underdetermination of meaning. On the one hand, Newman's definitions of faith are individually so precise that he finds it hard to connect them. On the other hand, by giving too many definitions he presents a superabundance of ideas that leaves faith itself underdetermined. Under rubric 12 of his preface to the third edition (1887, xvi), for example, Newman offers four important but different definitions of faith. He offers three definitions of reason in the improper sense of that word and one definition of reason in its most inclusive and proper sense. Newman keeps saying that reason, like faith, becomes intelligible only by being ordered into larger wholes. But this ordering must ultimately be done by each reader.

Faith may be understood in one of two ways. We can interpolate new definitions of faith between the many incomplete definitions Newman offers, or else we can extrapolate from the known to the unknown, moving beyond an end term already familiar to the mind. In either case we confront a mystery, for no matter how many interpolations we make, there always remain more gaps between the partial definitions. And whatever terra incognita we occupy as we invade the unknown, there will always be more unknowns requiring new extrapolations. Moreover, in defining faith and reason in his preface, Newman is doing what he says is impossible. For he warns that faith cannot be defined in advance of his exploring expedition into "unknown country." Either his definitions are discovered on a prior expedition, in which case they should be withheld from readers until they have finished the sermons, or else faith is necessarily something more than Newman says it is. Like Hopkins, Newman knows the "mind has mountains; cliffs of fall / Frightful, sheer, no-man-fathomed" ("No worst, there is none," ll. 9–10). Though he looks into the abyss separating his faith from his understanding of it and is appalled by what he sees, he leaps heroically across the gap, convinced he has jumped successfully and stands securely on the other side.

All literary language gives at once too little and too much meaning and so is inexhaustible to criticism. And in any discourse about faith the discontinuities are more than just gaps between words and sentences. They are also switches between possible literal and figurative meanings and between changing definitions. The Gospels' parabolic language—indirect, reserved, ironic—is well suited to the exercise of faith. Unless its short, discontinuous narratives concealed as much as they revealed, no heroic qualities could be developed in pursuit of what they mean. "Great objects exact a venture," Newman concludes, "and a sacrifice is the condition of honour" (1887, 220).

Newman concedes there are both a bad and a good kind of mystery. The mysteries of angelic warfare, as the heavenly hosts wage battles against the powers of evil, are one thing. But the battles of the night, like the Syracusan disaster recounted by Thucydides, in which friends are mistaken for foes in the dark, are mysteries of confusion, self-deception, and logomachy. "Controversy, at least in this age, does not lie between the hosts of heaven, Michael and his Angels on the one side, and the powers of evil on the other; but it is a sort of night battle, where each fights for himself, and friend and foe stand together" (sermon preached on the Epiphany, 1839, 201). Miltonic battle scenes in heaven repress the dark side of truth—the trauma of pointless conflict, in which each disputant fails to understand what his adversary means. Arnold's battle on the darkling plain in "Dover Beach" revives Newman's sudden surge of terror, as the epic clarities of Dante or Milton are eroded by the pointlessness of a controversy that "is either superfluous or hopeless" (1887, 201). For a moment of panic, reason seems swallowed up in nightmare, obliterating everything of value.

Perhaps only a systematic expositor like Newman can dispel the terror of the night battle by constantly defining and redefining words like "reason" and "faith." The war of words between fideists and rationalists often arises from a confusion of descriptive and emotive

meanings. Newman hopes to end the conflict by insisting at the outset
that faith is neither better nor worse than reason: it is just different.
Faith operates with probabilities, not facts; and probability is to fact
what the soul is to the body. If the presumptions of faith have no
force, mere facts have no warmth. There are advantages and disadvantages on each side. But Newman's definitions are never ideologi-
cally innocent. An implicit preference for faith is evident in his belief
that faith formed by arguments from design is cold or dead faith.
Rational theology is said to be the product of an age when love was
cold. All the emotion and desire are on the side of faith, all the
coldness and death on the side of reason.

Newman subtly loads the dice against reason in two ways: having
used a definition of reason that equates it with empirical understanding and with principles of scientific testing, he then proceeds to
equate faith with radiant romantic definitions of reason and imagination. Both imagination and reason are given eighteenth-century interpretations that align them with Dr. Johnson's strictures against the
vagaries of imagination. Only faith is equated with Wordsworth's and
Coleridge's Kantian concepts of *Vernunft*. Is Newman not inconsistent—
both epistemologically and historically—in finding synonyms for reason and understanding in the somber, more arid, vocabularies of
Locke and Dr. Johnson, while defining faith in the more glowing
lexicon of the English romantic poets?

Since Newman's sermons have a foregone conclusion, we may
wonder whether their attempt to reach a rational understanding of
faith can have any intellectual value. A comparison of Newman's
conflicting definitions of faith and reason shows, however, that his
destination gets modified en route. How can faith be both a form of
reasoning and something different from reasoning? Either because we
are confronted with what Kant would call a paralogism or an antinomy, or else because the descriptive meaning of either faith or reason is
continually changing, while the emotive meaning remains constant.
Newman seems, in fact, to be redefining "reason," which ceases to be
a principle of empirical understanding or testing and becomes instead
"the faculty of gaining knowledge upon grounds given" (1887, 207).
If by reason we mean our grounds for asserting something, then faith
"is the reasoning of a religious mind." Faith, however, is its own
ground. Unlike reason, faith creates its own keen sense of the intrinsic
excellence of what it assents to. But once again, Newman does not come
out where he had planned. Either faith and reason are totally discontinuous, with the result that faith ceases to be an object of rational inquiry,
or else the two faculties are really identical, with the equally undesirable conclusion that faith loses its distinctive properties and value.

Any identification of faith with reason threatens to turn faith into an inference, dependent on a previous process of clear and cautious reason. But Newman wants to show that faith supplies an alternative to reason. To this end he redefines reason as "a faculty of proceeding from things that are perceived to things which are not" (1887, 206). Yet instead of arguing that faith provides its own grounds, Newman now surprises us by contending that faith, no less than reason, "is an instrument of indirect knowledge concerning things external to us" (1887, 207). And in making faith, like reasoning, an act of gaining knowledge upon given grounds, Newman seems to be making faith itself into an inference rather than a simple assent and so restoring its dependence on reasoning. Doesn't a premise Newman logically accepts imply a conclusion he wishes to reject?

Whenever the logician's conclusions come into conflict with the conclusions the theologian hopes to reach, Newman can either accept the undesirable conclusion or reject one of the previously accepted premises. Newman is momentarily at a loss which course to take. Instead, he ponders the dilemma that the paradoxes of his faith generate: either faith is a faulty form of inference, or else the true premises of faith are undeveloped. Faith is either illogical or recondite, weak or unearthly. Scripture says it is unearthly, the world says it is weak. How should we decide? It seems we have to make an inference, so that the decision we reach will be to that degree rational. But what are the grounds of our inferring? Faith and reason, instead of being true grounds at all, may be merely different means of using prior truths to reach new knowledge. Neither is more privileged than the other. But if this is so, how is Newman entitled to say that faith is the reasoning of a divinely enlightened rather than a weak mind? (1887, 208). Only through an exercise of faith can he make such a statement about faith. If so, then his own argument seems to be just as glaring an instance of petitio principii as those arguments from design that, according to Newman, will convince only the converted, since atheism seems to be just as consistent with physical phenomena as Deist arguments in support of a creative governing power.

Newman's reluctance to reach conclusions about the meaninglessness of faith simply dramatizes a forgotten feature of most philosophical inquiry: the incapacity of investigators to be dispassionate about the questions they find important. Arguments are seldom unrelated to how strongly a philosopher wants certain propositions to be true. If faith remains, as Newman asserts, an exercise of reason and a form of inference, perhaps it is an elided or implicit inference of a special kind. Instead of identifying these inferences directly, however, Newman prefers to show how undeveloped inferences operate in politics and literary criticism. He stretches the meaning of the word "inference" to include valid modes of arguing and inferring not to be found in

Aristotle. And he introduces an important distinction between arguing and reasoning. A reasoner's *explicit* inferences may violate the rules of logic, even though his *implicit* inferences are sound. How else can we make sense of Newman's aperçu that men "may argue badly, but...[still] reason well" (1887, 212)? Yet if the real proofs of faith are merely hidden rather than weak, should Newman not be more forthcoming in identifying the secret nature of these inferences?

So far Newman has been arguing that faith, like reason, is a process of progressing from one object of knowledge to another. Now he takes a new tack by arguing that reason, like faith, accepts axioms and first principles that are incapable of proof. What are our grounds for positing the stability of nature or the uniformity of providence? The rationality of the universe is itself a postulate of faith. Though all acts of inference may seem to be rational, positing any axiom or first principle is an act of faith. Why should we trust our memory any more than our senses or our reasoning? They are all faculties we trust on faith, just as we trust faith on faith. Indeed, just as all knowledge is a form of inference, so all proofs first assume something: we "can gain nothing without a venture" (1887, 215).

In saying that all faith is knowledge and that all knowledge is risk taking or a crisis of faith, however, Newman is using faith and knowledge in two different senses. The first use of knowledge means inference, the process of concluding *B* because of *A*. The second use of faith means the assumption of first principles or axioms. Such an assumption is never strictly provable: rather, it is a precondition of proof. To prove every link in a long chain of argument may be less important and practical than to offer a tentative explanation of how faith, for example, is possible. Newman prefers explanations to proofs, which he debasingly pictures as a form of "creep[ing] along the ground" without any capacity to "soar" (1887, 215). The alternative to proof is the chance to be heroic, an adventurer or risk taker. "If we are intended for great ends," Newman warns, "we are called to great hazards" (1887, 215). God, who loves us, has tested our love of the truth by furnishing us with only partial evidence. Nor do the real triumphs of reason wholly conform to rules of logic and inference, which are only feeble attempts to explain victories that are achieved "as though by invisible weapons." Even mathematical demonstrations, like articles of faith, creeds, or metaphysical proofs, may be "so recondite and intricate that the mass of men are obliged to take them on trust" (1887, 217).

In his sermon preached on Whitsunday, May 21, 1839, Newman observes that whereas reason uses inference based upon premises held to be necessarily true, faith uses presumptive inference. Does this mean that faith, like a philosophical explanation as opposed to a philosophic proof, makes use of mere hypotheses or even premises contrary to fact? Like Mill's "intuitive" inferences, a presumptive inference sounds at first like an illogical inference and hence an abuse of the word "inference" itself. Moreover, if "faith is a judgment about facts in matters of conduct, such, as to be formed ... from the reaching forward of the mind itself towards them" (1887, 224), is the term "judgment" really admissible? Can judgment assume the form of an explanatory presumption rather than an apodictic proof? Newman admits the paradox but proceeds to defend it by establishing criteria for differentiating the make-believe of valid presumptions from the make-believe of invalid presumptions or mere superstitions.

If faith is a presumptive judgment about facts in matters of conduct, what makes such a judgment felicitous or infelicitous, if not exactly true or false? The criteria are close to those that J. L. Austin (1975) develops when differentiating performative from constative discourse. There is no antecedent evidence to be enlisted as proof: instead all so-called evidence is brought into being by a will to believe and "a right state of heart" (1887, 234). Skeptics like David Hume might be less prepared to attack the presumptive judgments of men of faith if they realized that their own judgments are also presumptive. The judgment that judgments of faith are presumptive is not itself a presumption. But Hume's judgment that judgments of faith are false and that the judgments of unbelief are true is precisely that: a presumption of the kind Hume himself is pledged to banish from philosophy.

In his sermon preached on Saint Peter's Day, 1840, Newman compares the theologian who reasons upon his reasons to a mountainclimber who can leave behind neither a literal nor a figurative track of the secret science he practices.

> [The mind of the theologian] passes on from point to point, gaining one by some indication; another on a probability; then availing itself of an association; then falling back on some received law; next seizing on testimony; then committing itself to some popular impression, or some inward instinct, or some obscure memory; and thus it makes progress not unlike a clamberer on a steep cliff, who, by quick eye, prompt hand, and firm foot, ascends how he knows not himself, by personal endowments and by practice, rather than by rule, leaving no track behind him, and unable to teach another. It is not too much to say that the stepping by which great geniuses scale the mountains of truth is as unsafe and precarious to men in general, as the ascent of a skilful mountaineer up a literal crag. (1887, 257)

Newman uses a sequence of five protracted present participles— "availing," "falling back," "seizing on," "committing itself," "gaining" —to suspend the climber perilously in midair. Suspense and uncertainty are an effect of the slowly expanding syntactic units and protracted grammar. Each verb has both a literal and a figurative sense, and the mystery is deepened by repeating the indefinite adjective "some" five times. The skill described is too unteachable to qualify as either a science or an art. It is best called "a living spontaneous energy within us." Only the resourceful but unpredictable hovering of Newman's syntax can make the ranging of the mind to and fro, as it "spreads out, and advances forward," concrete and intelligible.

How pitifully impoverished, by contrast, seems even the most comprehensive logic designed to analyze a process of reasoning whose "subtlety and versatility... baffle investigation." In limiting every act of reasoning to the exercise of the mind "upon neither more nor less than three terms" (the two premises and the conclusion of a syllogism), Aristotle's logic makes a travesty of the process. In his sermons Newman seems at first to be writing as the logician and the critic of faith and reason, not as a creative reasoner. But because his own analysis of the mysteries of reason is itself creative, the achievements of his prose style soon begin to blur the distinction he is laboring to make. If the prose works as prose, its logical argument does *not* work. And if the logic and creative reasoning are as distinct as Newman insists, how can his own grammar and syntax convey his most elusive thoughts as accurately as they do in the quoted passage? Newman's answer seems to be that there is a necessary discount in all theological language. In a sense, all theology is negative theology. God is never what we say he is. Much less can any science of God measure the immeasurable or hope to methodize what is endlessly mysterious and complex.

Newman's sermons keep confronting a paradox: If faith is a presumptive judgment and if its propositions are performative, how can faith be grounded in a truth that is antecedent to a believer's affirmation of it? Are not all performative utterances ungrounded? Either religious beliefs are not fully performative, or else they are not firmly anchored in a divine ground. Each believer may mean something different by a dogma that is shared by a whole community of believers. A dogma is true only in a limited sense: it is a common or a shared truth. Dogmas are like portraits of a person taken as a child and then as an old man. Is Newman implying that Christian revelation grows and changes? Or does our apprehension grow and change? The metaphor of the portraits suggests the first interpretation, but another of his favored metaphors, the book, suggests the latter. Dogmas and many theological opinions are like books, Newman also says. Depending on the accident of the moment, a book at one time strikes the mind "as full of weighty remarks and precious thoughts." At another time, we "see nothing in it" (1887, 271).

Newman defines words as "incomplete exponents of ideas" (1887, 275–76). Instead of reducing a reason to a logical mood and a figure (to an Aristotelian parody of itself), readers should treat argumentive prose as the mere outline of a project, a prospectus. In reaching toward the sense of a passage, skilled interpreters should treat words as provisional programs for action. They should behave like men of faith, launched on an enterprise of presumptive judgment, fraught with procedural hesitancy and risk.

In his sermon preached on Whit-Tuesday, 1841, Newman uses an implicit organic criterion to distinguish between the proper use of a system and its abuse. This criterion is clearest when Newman says that wisdom "communicates the image of the whole body to every separate member" (1887, 291). But the very effort to define his terms, to erect the wall of a limit or an end, which is what "definition" means, seems to be at war with his efforts to break down such divisions. Paradoxically, if Newman's attempt to define wisdom is valid, then it seems to follow that it is not valid. For wisdom appears to override the very imposition of barriers that his definition of wisdom requires.

Though Newman is committed to organic models, he is simultaneously a critical philosopher in the skeptical tradition of Kant and Hume, just as he seems wedded to eighteenth-century definitions of reason and romantic definitions of imagination and faith. To avoid night battles, or wars over words, he scrupulously defines his terms. Heresy and error are produced when an act of faith trespasses upon the domain of reason, or when reason tries to invade the alien territory of faith. Just as the postulates of Kant's practical reason degenerate into idolatry when they are allowed to imitate—and so profanely to parody—the categories of conceptual understanding, so Newman's presumptive judgments are converted into presumptions of bigotry when they pretend to be more argumentive than they really are. Idolatry or bigotry is generated when the statements become insufficiently skeptical and profess a degree of intelligibility that belies their essential mystery.

In sermon 15, Newman tries to explain how the development of true doctrine is possible, despite the skeptical objection that dogmas appear to be propositions "expressive of the judgments which the mind forms," rather than "the impressions which it receives...of Revealed Truth" (1887, 320). Newman argues that the skeptic's excluder is apparent, not real, because it is possible for the mind to entertain impressions or images of supernatural facts and actions even when it is not conscious of receiving them. "It is no proof," he contends, "that persons are not possessed, because they are not conscious, of an idea" (1887, 321). Impressions are fleeting, fugitive, unrecallable, until fashioned by imagination into a more stable and recurrent idea of sense. Such is the function of a dogmatic expression of religious impressions. Ironically, Newman's theory of dogma is clearly indebted to the antidogmatic Hume, the skeptic he keeps attacking in his sermons. Newman is indebted—apparently unconsciously—to Hume's influential distinction between a mere fugitive *impression* and an *idea* of sense that is fully formed and recurrent.

The harsh oddity of dogma seems to be a shock effect of meeting an idea in a medium not native to it, as we may not at first recognize our impressions of a country in a map, especially in a Mercator projection that requires us to move from a three-dimensional medium onto a two-dimensional plane. Dogmatic statements transform "what was at first an impression on the Imagination . . . [into] a system or creed in the Reason" (1887, 329). Religious individuals have ideas or visions of God "as one, and individual, and independent of words, as an impression conveyed through the senses" (1887, 331). But such an impression is a mystery, and its full magnitude cannot be reflected upon by the mind "except piecemeal." Although a creation of our own minds could easily be defined, the object of our religious impressions— an object like God—is not such a creation and may be independent of all our possible representations. God may even be inconceivable to our minds. "A Divine fact," as Newman says, "far from being compassed by [the propositions of a dogma,] would not be exhausted, nor fathomed, by a thousand" (1887, 332). Moreover, just as true ideas are clear and distinct, as Locke said, and memory may be left with only the fading impressions of these ideas, so Newman acknowledges that the awful vision of "Christ in us" is "faint and doubtful in some minds, and distinct in others" (1887, 332). Is it because Newman's pictorial models are so stubbornly empirical that they also become distressingly agnostic and equivocal the moment he tries to stabilize them?

Faced by such crises in representation, Newman tries to differenti-ate between religious impressions of God and empirical impressions of material objects. After all, on each of the three occasions when Hume is mentioned in the Oxford sermons, he is presented as an archadversary. It would be odd if Newman were to uncritically accept— or unconsciously enshrine—one of Hume's most cherished theories. In distinguishing between religious and sensible impressions, Newman seems to me, however, to consolidate the similarities and minimize the differences. Though the mind of the believer may be prepared in a different way from the empiricist's, the actual receiving of the divine impressions is as involuntary and mysterious as the receiving of a sensible impression. Theological language appears to have the same function of fixing and transmitting the impressions that Locke and Hume ascribe to ideas of sense. Moreover, Newman begs the whole question of how sensible and religious impressions differ by observing that "no one defines a material object by way of conveying to us what we know so much better by the senses, but we form creeds as a chief mode of perpetuating the impression" (1887, 333). In fact, the process by which sense impressions furnish the mind with objects of knowledge is enormously complex and begs to be examined. But this is precisely the task Newman declines to undertake, as if such an inquiry might expose disturbing similarities between his own epistemology and the agnostic thought of Hume. Is Newman afraid to find out where his inquiry might lead?

Since dogmatic statements are verbal expressions of the mind's impressions of divine subjects, it is important to examine how far words and names can be used to represent things. Newman now admits that the use of words and names for things, a practice promoted by both Locke and Mill, is a mistake. For the more intelligible our words become, the less they seem to partake directly in the divine impression or in the nature of their referent. Viewed from one perspective, the verbal formulas are true intrinsic symbols of the divine subject, because apart from these words and symbols there is no access to the subject. Viewed in another way, however, the words are intrinsic symbols only in the depleted sense that they express nothing but themselves, since any referent external to the words has ceased to exist.

To apply Newman's implicit empirical mode of perception rigorously is to recognize that just as the impression of a material object presupposes a human mind to receive it, so "the idea of a supernatural object must itself be supernatural" (1887, 338). Since we are not divine, we cannot know divine objects. The words we apply to the divine object—person, substance, incarnation—"have either a very abject and human meaning, or none at all" (1887, 338). Newman seems simultaneously to claim too little and too much for language. On the one hand, to speak of God at all is to take his name in vain. On the other hand, "our ideas of Divine things are just co-extensive with the figures by which we express them, neither more nor less, and without them are not" (1887, 338–39). In the *Apologia* the heavenly facts that fill eternity are said to be locked forever within the embrace of the church and its signs. In the sermons, however, that claim takes on a distinctively skeptical cast. There seems to be no truth outside the church, not so much because the church is infallible as because the idea of any independent truth is rejected as a fiction. The skepctical realist who had affirmed that God extends beyond the reach of our minds now argues the counterthesis that the idea of God either is the idea of something fully within the reach of the church or is no idea at all.

Material objects exist independent of our words, but divine objects do not. That can mean contradictory things. Either our words for God are indexes of his presence, or else outside language God has ceased to exist. No sooner have we assumed that Newman draws the former conclusion than we are shocked to find him drawing the latter. How can we say what divine objects are really like if our only knowledge of them comes from words rather than impressions? When theologians seem to mean more than they actually say about God, they are in fact doing the reverse: they are presuming to say more about him than they can possibly mean.

Whether its real subject is the necessary truth of mathematics or the truth of religion, any attempt to represent supernatural or eternal principles in intelligible signs must sacrifice the mystery of its subject. We can pretend that our symbols and fictions are real things by committing what Whitehead calls a "fallacy of misplaced concreteness." But sooner or later such economies will issue in some great crisis of representation, some impossibility or contradiction, some paradox or antinomy.

Newman's protracted hypotheses anticipate the tense, self-censoring interplay of skeptical and heroic impulses in the fifth chapter of his *Apologia*: "If there be a God, since there is a God." But the agnostic semiotician's anxiety in the sermon is, if possible, more acute: "It is right to speak of [God's] Being and Attributes, *if* He be not rather superessential; it is true to say that He is wise or powerful, *if* we may consider Him as other than the most simple Unity. He is truly Three, *if* He is truly One; He is truly One, *if* the idea of Him falls under earthly number" (italics added; sermon preached on the Purification, 1843, 350). As each creedal affirmation is eroded and broken down by a negative hypothesis, each successive clause discloses a deeper mystery. Any gain in understanding requires a further admission of unintelligibility or a deeper concession of the unprovable status of some prior and more inclusive axiom. At such a moment Newman and his congregation experience the economy of theological language for what it is, a concession to the limits of human understanding. We are left at the end with an experience of eroding boundaries and dissolving definitions, as our words are invaded by something "for which we have not a name, of which we have no ideas, except in ... terms of ... economical representations" (1887, 345) increasingly remote from their divine referent.

The same instability in words impels Newman to struggle with feelings of strangeness in *Apologia pro vita Sua*. No other autobiography opens with so forthright a declaration of reserve. If one's secret is one's own, one would hardly be expected to write the story of one's life unless one were resolved either to betray the principle of secrecy or write a disingenuous autobiography. To make the phrase "Secretum meum mihi" (chap. 1) resonate more strangely, Newman qualifies it with a seemingly unintelligible clause: "but as men draw towards their end, they care less for disclosures." The phrase "care less" suggests at first reading that the reticent Newman, as he grows older, is more averse to confessing or disclosing anything. But like a Delphic oracle, the phrase is capable of being interpreted two ways at once. Does Newman "care less" in the sense of "liking less," or in the sense of "having less objection to"? Usage suggests the first meaning, but the concessive force of a clause introduced by "but" suggests the second. If Newman cares less for the consequences of making disclosures, he will then *not* care less in the sense of objecting to them. The mystery surrounding the utterance "Secretum meum mihi" is due in part to a studied ambiguity in the syntax.

The difficult enterprise of dredging the mind and dragging up to consciousness the traumas and conflicts of the living intelligence, its beliefs and values, leads Newman to adopt two forms of reserve at the beginning of chapter 3. On one hand, he instinctively shrinks from reviving a painful experience, whose recollection is like opening a wound. On the other hand, he is reluctant to speak because he realizes that the intricacies of such a process all but defy expression. The subject is at once too painful and too complex to write about. To penetrate only partway is to open up a wound and allow it to fester. But to go all the way in is to desecrate a grave. What is Newman to do? His response is to follow words wherever they may lead him in an effort to release the full resources of his syntax. His first rhetorical question contains only one appositional clause: the only complication to be considered is the number and subtlety of the influences that act upon him. But the second question he asks seems never to end, so prolonged and repetitive are its qualifying units. A refusal to end evokes the interminable complexities of Newman's past and present trials. The mirror of nature is darkened for him by a weight of perplexity and dismay. And something of that weight is duplicated in the sheer weight of the repeating adverbial clauses, made more emphatic by the ponderous dash before the second "when." "And who can recollect, at the distance of twenty-five years, all that he once knew about his thoughts and his deeds, and that, during a portion of his life, when even at the time, his observation, whether of himself or of the external world, was less than before or after, by very reason of the perplexity and dismay which weighed upon him,—when, in spite of the light given to him according to his need amid his darkness, yet a darkness it emphatically was?" (chap. 3). The darkness extends to the momentarily opaque syntax. There is even an awkward grace in the final clause, as Newman finds it increasingly tortuous to extricate himself from the syntactic knot he has just tied: "when,... yet a darkness it... was." The simple adverbial clause "when it was decidedly dark" would have conveyed the same idea. But much of the meaning, much of the torture of the living mind, would be lost.

The long third question really divides into two questions, as the desire to map accurately the opposing impulses in his mind breaks the syntax apart. The anxiety of the present undertaking is set in simple contrast to a full and calm inquiry allowing leisurely contemplation of the past. But such leisure is precisely what Newman, composing to meet a deadline, lacks in both past and present time. The imminent approach of the hour when his lines must be given to the world seems to prevent his revising the sentence to make it more grammatical. The fracturing of the single question into two parts mimes the haste with which Newman writes, without any "full and calm leisure." But even if the calm contemplation were possible, who would want it, when it resembles nothing so much as premeditated murder? The phrase "in cold blood" is actually used in the next sentence, and it suggests that Newman is performing more than just an autopsy. He is murdering himself and his present peace of mind. Yet he feels it is better to rip up old griefs completely, and perform radical surgery in hope of an ultimate cure, than to allow old wounds to fester. In venturing upon the "infandum dolorem" of years in which the stars of the lower heavens were one by one going out, Newman makes it impossible for a reader not to respond as boldly but fearfully as Newman does.

There can be no doubt that arcane theology is a life-and-death issue for Newman, as culture is for Arnold. We are twice reminded that in reading the history of the Monophysites Newman becomes "seriously alarmed" (chap. 3). The metaphoric shadow of historical analogy, which is said to darken the sixteenth century with the shadow of the fifth, is inexorably lengthening to include Newman as well. He proceeds "almost fearfully." Even the adjective "awful" shifts meaning. Newman is awestruck to find the similitude of analogy operating with such unexpected and implacable power. The analogy is a source of wonder but also of dread, moving silently and inexorably like a life force from the past, which seems to catch him off guard. How embalmed and dead is a past whose shadows can rise like a "spirit... from the troubled waters of the old world, with the shape and lineaments of the new"? Is the ghost a mere specter, to be exorcised with more learning and erudition? Is it a mere demon or obsession? Or is the phantom that moves across the face of the waters, like the spirit in Genesis, one of the guises of the Holy Ghost, disturbing Newman like a ghost from the past only to bring him safely to the farther shore after a stormy crossing? Newman's beloved Virgil speaks in the *Aeneid* of the souls that stretch forth their hands through love of the farther shore: "Tendebantque manus ripae ulterioris amore" (*Aeneid*, 6.314). Like Noah, Newman will be a survivor of the storm, coming "into port after a rough sea" with the aid of the same Holy Spirit rising over history that had appeared to Noah as a dove.

And yet the vivid impression upon his imagination of a shade or ghost from the past may be just a passing hallucination. For when he regains his self-possession the impressions seem to fade. For a moment Newman identifies with Shakespeare's Caliban, for whom the heavens had opened and then closed. Had he had a glimpse into heaven or merely been enchanted? Newman wants to pause: he has to wait till his mind can catch up with the mystery. At times he resembles Clough's Claude, trying to rationalize timidity of response. More often he is genuinely uncertain of the ghost's status, like Hamlet, unwilling to take a leap of faith until he sees better where he is likely to land. The hovering between literal and metaphoric meanings, between actual ghosts and the shadows of historical analogy, between the approaching light of a more abiding apparition and the metaphoric use of light as a figure for reason, allows Newman to dramatize his crises of representation and the difficulty of making the mysteries of his faith intelligible.

A verbal talisman has the same status in language as a phantasm or a vivid image has in the world of sense. Both possess the immediacy of an impression: they are prior to intellection, and in their irreplaceable uniqueness they remain as mysterious and involuntary as those apprehensions of sacred objects that Newman analyzes in his Oxford sermons. The snapdragons outside Newman's rooms at Trinity College have this status in the valedictory coda to chapter 4. Even when Newman tries to turn the snapdragons into an emblem of his perpetual residence at Oxford, their mystery resides in their openness to other representative uses. The poignancy of Newman's idiosyncratic mental association, which is as indelible and strong as the color and perfume of the flowers, comes in large part from the realization that even in conjuring up images of abiding residence, the snapdragons force him to perceive he is dead before he is dead. The horror of concluding even brings a glance forward to the eventual leave-taking of all places and people.

In the Oxford sermons Newman had argued that evidences and proofs carry little weight with minds predisposed to disbelieve in God. Now in the climactic fifth chapter of the *Apologia*, Newman gives his own theological explanation of this mystery. Earlier in the *Apologia* Newman had looked into the mirror of historical analogy and been appalled to see reflected the face of a Monophysite (chap. 3). But worse than seeing oneself as a heretic is the experience of looking into a mirror and seeing no face at all. This appalling experience is itself an analogy for looking into the mirror of the world—this "living busy world" (chap. 5)—and seeing reflected there no image of its Creator. Newman never presumes to *prove* that such a Creator exists. A proof, by coercing assent, makes the heroic assent of faith impossible. For this reason so-called proofs from design and history do nothing to warm or enlighten Newman. Nor do they speak to his conscience or his heart. Newman is content to show that, despite apparent excluders, it is still possible to affirm God's existence. Therefore, since any logical proposition about God leaves the mystery of God untouched, why not entertain a helpful absurdity rather than an unhelpful one? Skepticism makes Newman a believer, as it makes H. L. Mansel a fideist. Our very ignorance about matters essentially unintelligible—the nature of matter or the properties of God—enables Newman to opt heroically for a postulate of faith rather than for some more skeptical alternative. Difficulty and doubt are incommensurate for Newman: ten thousand difficulties do not make one doubt, because atheists who confuse logical difficulty with spiritual doubt are trying to use arithmetic when arithmetic is not known to apply. Even the logical difficulties of a doctrine—its crises of representation—in no way impair the power by which the doctrine is borne in upon a believing mind. And there is always a chance of explaining why a doctrine is possible even when there is no chance of proving it is true.

The sentence beginning "To consider the world in its length and breadth" (chap. 5) is a tour de force of appositional indictment. It has the majesty, the weight, and the intimidating authority of an inventory that searches every state and canvasses every prayer, like Dr. Johnson's poem "The Vanity of Human Wishes." We wait endlessly, it seems, for the completion of the multitudinous items that function as the grammatical object of the infinitive "consider." The qualifying adjectives are strikingly placed to induce a vision to dizzy and appall. Though man's aims are far reaching, the duration of man himself is pitiably "short." The thrust toward "final causes" is thwarted by "unreasoning" elements; the greatness of man is offset by his stupefying "littleness." Even the future is veiled: designs are horribly thwarted, with the result that everywhere good is defeated and evil succeeds. The effect is to create not a Swiftian invective of intemperance and imbalance, but a desolatingly balanced picture that seems all the more honest and heartbreaking because of the apparent accuracy of the portrait. Only with the greatest reluctance does Newman seem willing to have these harsh words wrenched out of him. They have the authority of unwilling testimony, drawn forth from the depth of his conscience in spite of the most strenuous reserve, which keeps trying to silence some unspeakable truth.

To move through the long catalog of grammatical objects, then to be brought up short by the emphatic dash, which eventually supplies a principal clause for a sentence that has been spilling over sixteen lines of print, is to experience something of Newman's own confusion and shock. To read is to be tormented. Newman uses the grammar of suspended meaning and abrupt completion like a weapon. Part of the power lies in the oddly appropriate use of the verb "inflicts." A "sense of a profound mystery" is not usually "inflicted" upon the mind, but his sensation is as sharp as pain and as acute as an attack of dizziness or a sudden headache. Newman's way of concluding exemplifies what the sentence itself has said about the "impotent conclusion of long-standing facts." The catalog produces a lengthy list of incontrovertible truths, but the conclusion itself is impotent in that it concludes or solves nothing.

Newman's simultaneous entertainment of two contrary hypotheses grows straight out of his heart-piercing loss. His reason is bewildered and affronted: "Either there is no Creator, or this living society of men is...discarded from His presence." Either God is absent, or he never existed. As if to temper the audacity of this crisis of faith, Newman spontaneously considers the analogy of the refined and handsome youth, without memory or birthplace, disinherited, as it seems, by parents he has shamed. The analogy deftly corrects certain defects in the stark logical dilemma, which too carelessly implied that in discarding his children God had left behind no tokens of his presence. The tokens are there, but they point toward a desolating disjunction, a great divide between "the promise and the condition" of man's being.

The shocking logical dilemma, the instinctive correcting of it by pictorial analogy, the tentative hypothesizing, "*if* there be a God," converted almost at once (as if by an act of censorship that nevertheless leaves the first traces of skepticism intact) to the more confident and assertive "*since* there is a God," catch the mind in the act of reacting energetically and subtly upon each fact and impression it receives. Newman's conclusion that the race is implicated in some terrible aboriginal calamity has all the power of a cataclysm he has lived through and witnessed. If the world is a fact, then so is God, and so is the terrible break or divide that splits them asunder. The dogma of the Fall and the doctrine of original sin have been creeping up on us as theological explanations, almost like Spinoza's deft identification of substance with God in the *Ethics*, before we know what Newman is up to.

To show how crises of faith and knowing precipitate crises of representation, Newman keeps dramatizing the fluctuations of his fallen reason, the pull back and forth within his own mind, including his reluctance to introduce the logical inference from fallen reason to papal infallibility. He begins with a hypothesis, but before he can complete the consequence of that hypothesis—"in such a case," a doubt occurs to him and he veers off into a parenthetical remark—"I am far from saying that there was no other way"—only to return after the second dash to a statement of the deferred consequence. Instead of asserting the consequence as a fact, however, he presents it as another hypothesis, introduced cautiously and half-apologetically after the conjunction "if." The double hypothesizing breaks down the grammar, but it is as wonderfully effective in dramatizing Newman's own tentativeness and doubt as it is in dramatizing his heroic will to believe whenever a sturdy resolution seems called for. At other times Newman can afford to relax his desire for closure. His very assurance of closure makes him open, admitting into his prose anything disquieting that happened in the past or anything surprising that may happen in the always unpredictable act of allowing oracular, half-understood words to rise unbidden in his mind.

CHAPTER 14

Meaning More Than Is Said: Sources of Mystery in Christina Rossetti and Arnold

Like Newman, Christina Rossetti is a heroic knower: to cross the divide that separates knowledge from belief, she must make such mystery words as "God" and "heart" mean more than she can hope to say. Rather than profane a mystery by scaling it down reductively, as Matthew Arnold tries to do when redefining religion, she prefers to be silent like Clough. Only "love," says Rossetti, can understand "the mystery, whereof / We can but spell a surface history" ("Judge nothing before the time," ll. 1–2; 2:295).[1] By "mystery" she means something like a secret science or withheld truth, as Newman defines these difficult ideas in his Oxford sermons. In her sonnet "Cardinal Newman," Rossetti commends Newman's doctrine of reserve, praising him for choosing "love not in the shallows but the deep" (*PW*, 280.6). As God speaks less openly the more he promises (Newman 1887, 215), so Rossetti speaks more obliquely the more she has to say. Less reserve might have exposed her harrowed heart to the sport of scoffing and insult, to which Newman says any high road open to all men would have exposed the mysteries of religious faith.

George Steiner has argued that language "borders on three other modes of statement—light, music, and silence" (1967, 39). Like Vaughan's "great ring of pure and endless light," the fourth act of Shelley's *Prometheus Unbound* has much in common with an overexposed negative; and Swinburne's poetry often sounds like music for which readers are asked to supply a libretto. Rossetti, by contrast, tends to find

---

1. Quotations are from Rebecca Crump's edition, *The Complete Poems of Christina Rossetti* (1979–), whenever poems are available in the volumes already published. Quotations cited as *PW* are from *The Poetical Works of Christina Georgina Rossetti* (1906).

silence at the limits of language, or else some simple but powerful gesture like the offering of her heart. Rather than saying less about God than she means to say, she prefers to say nothing. To intimate more than she is able to say, Rossetti keeps using dashes and elisions. Often she presents mere deleted fragments of a text she has censored. Such a text may survive only in manuscript or in its resourceful reconstruction by an editor-critic. Her inventive use of repetition and metaphors of situation also confers elusive contextual definitions upon the dictionary meaning of so simple but mysterious a word as "heart" or "love." Finding refuge in muteness, Rossetti draws upon tautologies and tropes of reserve. The signature of her skepticism is a use of elisions, dashes, and caesural breaks, which remind us that she means more than she says. The signature of her faith, by contrast, is a heroic use of chiasmus. This trope of crossing over allows Rossetti to say all that she means. It helps her cross the divide between life and death, knowledge and ignorance, in an ironic double movement that is sanctioned ultimately by the perfect chiasmus of the Cross.

Though deeply personal suffering nourishes many of Rossetti's best lyric poems, we can best grasp her uncanny power to mean more than she says when that suffering has been most carefully displaced, as in the lyric "Listening" (*PW*, 313). Originally the poem was part of a longer lyric called "Two Choices," whose canceled sixth and seventh stanzas contained the following desolating lines:

> He chose a love-warm priceless heart,
>   And I a cold bare dignity...
> I chose a tedious dignity
>   As cold as cold as snow;...
> I chose a barren wilderness
>   Whose buds died years ago.
>   (Bodleian Library MS. Don. e, notebook 9, fols. 13–15)

The graceful bough and tendrils of the vine to which the modern Eve is now compared (ll. 7–8) were initially harrowing metaphors, harsh images of barrenness and waste, prompting the thought that the buds in Rossetti's wilderness died years ago. Her loss is more painful when contrasted with the Eden of delights and refreshing waters—the paradise of soul's sleep—from which Rossetti, while alive, has chosen to remove herself. The husband has chosen in his cushat dove the kind of wife Rossetti could never consent to become. From possible wisdom she declines to cold dignity, then to mere tedious dignity, which is cold as snow. Once we restore the deleted stanzas of "Listening," we realize that its vision of a domestic Eden is the vision of an outsider. Only a study of the poem's revisions can reveal how harrowing is its crisis of representation. The half-satirical portrait of the "cushat dove" discloses the "listening" of a soul in hell, or else the dream of someone who is sleeping at last.

Though the poet's self-censorship is strict, her heartbreaking pain cannot be permanently repressed. Indeed, in the next poem Rossetti wrote, the sonnet "Dead before death" (1:59), all the displaced suffering surges forth. Its bitter outburst appalled William Michael Rossetti. "I am unable to say," he admits in a perplexed tone, "what gave rise to this very intense and denunciatory outpouring" (*PW*, 470). William Michael might better have appreciated the cause of his sister's acrimony had he consulted the manuscript notebook in his possession, which reveals how the domestic paradise of "Listening" had originally been disturbed by countervailing impressions of chaos and hell. We expect the sestet of a Petrarchan sonnet such as "Dead before death" to resolve or at least mute the despair of its octave. But the sestet of this sonnet uses the echoing vault of the poet's despair to set up new linkages of desolating sound. Indeed, this sonnet refuses to honor, as it were, its own generic promise. Even after the expression of despair ought formally to conclude, at the end of the octave, the echoes of desolation continue to sound through the last six lines:

> All fallen the blossom that no fruitage bore,
>   All lost the present and the future time,
> All lost, all lost, the lapse that went before:
> So lost till death shut-to the opened door,
>   So lost from chime to everlasting chime,
> So cold and lost for ever evermore.
>   ("Dead before death," ll. 9–14)

The harshness of the anaphoric triads (ll. 9–11) is relieved only by the reverberating wail of open vowels. "Evermore" answers "everlasting" and "for ever," and "So" and "cold" answer a series of other open sounds; "Ah," "All," and "lost" (ll. 1, 9–11, 14). While the triadic "So," "So," "So" (ll. 12–14) remains rigid, the echoing "lost"s huddle close together (l. 11), then become predictably expansive. The contraction of the chiming "ever"s, converging in the final "for ever evermore," reverses this expanding pattern. Because the speaker's despair persists "from chime to everlasting chime," even after we expect it to be resolved at the end of the octave, we find these echoes that refuse to cease are not crowded with meaning but are mere hollow sounds like the echo of Sin's words in *Paradise Lost*, a reverberation of loss, desolation, and death: "I fled, and cry'd out DEATH; / Hell trembl'd at the hideous Name, and sigh'd / From all her Caves, and back resounded DEATH" (*Paradise Lost*, 2.787–89).

To turn the hell of a stony heart into an Eden of renewal or rebirth, Rossetti will sometimes make literal losses figurative. In the revised version of the lyric entitled "May" ("Sweet Life is dead."—"Not so"; *PW*, 320), Rossetti replaces an active first-person use of the verb "build" with a noncommittal passive form of the verb "freeze."

> 'Twixt him and me a wall
> Was frozen of earth-like stone
> With brambles overgrown:
>
> ("May," ll. 17–19)

The lyric was originally titled "A Colloquy." In the extensively revised second stanza we can see most clearly how a love lyric has been turned into a nature poem. Initially, in building a wall of stone between herself and her lover, Rossetti had only her own stony heart to blame for their separation and estrangement:

> But love is dead to me;
> I watched his funeral:
> Cold poplars stood up tall
> While yewtrees crouched to see
> And fair vines bowed the knee
> Twixt him and me a wall
> I built of cold hard stone
> With brambles overgrown;
> Chill darkness wraps him like a pall
> And I am left alone.
>
> (Bodleian Library MS. Don. e. 1, notebook 9, fols. 55–57)

The funeral she watched in the original version was not just the funeral of the "worn-out year" (l. 12) but the funeral of a lover for whose death she seemed personally responsible. By contrast, in the revised version the colloquy between two voices evokes an unlocalized event, which cannot be given just one name, as it could in the first version where a specific lover had died. In the dividing wall of frozen "earth-like stone" (l. 18) there is something now that exceeds the picture of a literal wall as a riddle exceeds its solution.

> "But Life is dead to me:
> The worn-out year was failing,
> West winds took up a wailing
> To watch his funeral:

> Bare poplars shivered tall
> And lank vines stretched to see.
> 'Twixt him and me a wall
> Was frozen of earth-like stone
> With brambles overgrown:
> Chill darkness wrapped him like a pall,
> And I am left alone."
>
>   ("May," ll. 11–21)

If the masculine third-person pronouns in this stanza refer not just to "Life" but to a lover who has died or from whom Rossetti is actually estranged, then the "earth-like stone" is less an image than a phantasm. The pictures in the stanza possess hallucinatory power. Their obsession with wailing winds, shivering trees, stretching vines, and earthlike stone is indeed strange. But as tokens of estranged and suppressed guilt, these dark phantasms dramatize a crisis of knowing: it is no wonder Rossetti can never quite shake them off. By turning a poem about thwarted love and guilt into a triumphal nature lyric, however, she is able to displace self-blame. Restorative power comes not in the form of another lover but as a life force from nowhere, catching the poet off guard.

> I meet him day by day,
> Where bluest fountains flow
> And trees are white as snow
> . . . .
> He makes my branch to bud and bear,
> And blossoms where I tread.
>
>   ("May," ll. 2–4, 30–31)

Stirred into being by pregnant caesural pauses between "branch," "bud," and "bear" (l. 30), and by strong rhymes such as "flow" and "snow" (ll. 3–4), as compared with the weakly trailing feminine rhymes "failing," "wailing" (ll. 12–13), this new power imposes itself stealthily but irresistibly. Bound by obligation and love to the springtime scene as she never could be bound to another heart, Rossetti finds that her throttled affections also start to bud and grow.

Originally, the mother in the ballad "Seeking Rest" (*PW*, 296) was not a literal mother but Mother Earth. In its earlier version, preserved in Bodleian Library MS. Don. e, notebook 6, fols. 22–26, the ballad opened with the following words of the child: "She knocked at the Earth's greening door. / O Mother, let me in." In seeking the greater objectivity of a ballad, Rossetti decides to delete the child's suicidal longing and her powerful echo of the old man's petition in "The

Pardoner's Tale": "And on the ground which is my modres gate / I knokke . . . / and saye, 'Leve moder, leet me in' " (ll. 441–43). But in no sense are the silences of the final version marked by neatness and composure.

> My Mother said: "The child is changed
>   That used to be so still;
> All the day long she sings and sings,
>   And seems to think no ill;
> She laughs as if some inward joy
>   Her heart would overfill."
>
> My Sisters said: "Now prythee tell
>   Thy secret unto us:
> Let us rejoice with thee; for all
>   Is surely prosperous,
> Thou art so merry: tell us, Sweet:
>   We had not used thee thus."
>
> My Mother says: "What ails the child
>   Lately so blythe of cheer?
> Art sick or sorry? Nay, it is
>   The winter of the year;
> Wait till the Springtime comes again,
>   And the sweet flowers appear."
>
> My Sisters say: "Come, sit with us,
>   That we may weep with thee:
> Show us thy grief that we may grieve:
>   Yea haply, if we see
> Thy sorrow, we may ease it; but
>   Shall share it certainly."
>
> How should I share my pain, who kept
>   My pleasure all my own?
> My Spring will never come again;
>   My pretty flowers have blown
> For the last time; I can but sit
>   And think and weep alone.

("Seeking Rest")

"Seeking Rest" is a deeply disturbing ballad, partly because of what it leaves out. The breaks at the end of the poem, "I can but sit / And think and weep alone" (ll. 29–30), are too sharply and strikingly placed to be only rhythmic breaks. Like the breaks between the stanzas, especially between stanzas 2 and 3, where incommunicable joy turns to equally unfathomable grief, the caesuras are designed to juxtapose actions and thus avoid plot and explanation. The child is autistic. In her inexplicable joys she is as totally isolated from her mother and her sisters as she is strictly alone in her immedicable woes. These are "woes that nothing can be done for," as Frost would say, the woes of someone for whom "spring will never come again" (l. 27), "woes flat and final" (Frost 1968, 67). Though grief is merely a blank in this ballad—the absence of a joy that has been—enough of the original loss survives to unnerve the reader and intimate an absence that is expressed in silence, a silence of private mourning and unshakable reserve. Contrary to what the mother and sisters assume, the silences do not result from the absence of something nameable such as spring. The child is silent because she has a mute sense of the larger strangenesses of life. She is also in the presence of a nothingness, a void, that successive stanzas of the ballad forcefully intimate but that no inquiry or surmise of the mother and the sisters can successfully explain.

Like the child in "Seeking Rest," Rossetti finds there are mysteries about which she can either say nothing or say too much. In "Winter, my secret" (1:47) cutting, eliding, and covering up are all means of preserving silence about such mysteries. Volleys of multiple rhymes set off humorous chain reactions in the poem.

> Perhaps some day, who knows?
> But not to-day; it froze, and blows, and snows
> . . . .
> Come bounding and surrounding me,
> Come buffeting, astounding me
>
> (ll. 2–3, 15–16)

By the time we reach the fourth internal rhyme in the second example, however, the joking has ceased to be merely amusing. Prying readers may be less hostile or bitter than the fierce Russian snows, but Rossetti prefers to leave that assumption untested. Winter destroys, she muses, and springtime renewals are precarious at best. Perhaps the only time to reveal secrets like hers is late midsummer. These seasonal images are nonnaming figures for the secrets of Rossetti's inner weather. As charades for the mysteries Rossetti has locked up, these figures betray a Zenlike propensity to tease the reader. Rossetti jokes about what frightens her and coyly hints that her secret may be the absence of any secret after all. The poem means more than it says because it keeps postponing its disclosures. Like all the lyrics examined so far, it appears to present a mere deleted fragment of some less withholding testament Rossetti has chosen to suppress.

In other groups of poems Rossetti contrives to mean more than she says by creating elusive contextual definitions for the dictionary meaning of so apparently simple a word as "heart." Each metaphor of situation that Rossetti uses points enigmatically to a mysterious "overmeaning" for "heart" that she is unable to dramatize fully in any single situation in the poems. One of the most potent of these definitions comes at the end of "A Christmas carol" ("In the bleak mid-winter") (1:216–17). The sudden exaltation of the lowly "maiden" (l. 30) prepares for Rossetti's insistence at the end of the carol on the sufficiency of a single unadorned word—the poet's "heart." The gifts of the Magi and of the heavenly cherubim and the gifts of the poor coexist, both plainly established, now without conflict and in reciprocal dignity.

> What can I give Him,
>   Poor as I am?
> If I were a shepherd
>   I would bring a lamb,
> If I were a wise man
>   I would do my part,—
> Yet what I can I give Him,
>   Give my heart.
>
> ("In the bleak mid-winter," ll. 33–40)

After the dash, the poet catches her breath before offering her heart. She drops the "I" and repeats the verb. The poet is poorer than a shepherd, who at least could bring a lamb. And like Mary, she has no wisdom. But at the end of the carol Rossetti's intimate offerings of her heart and her art are wholly congruent. The confidence sponsored by this congruence can be felt in the lyricism of the last verse, which implicitly rebukes the stiffness of the bleak opening stanzas. Its trochees are at once rigid and lilting, spare and weighted. As one of those rare lyrics in which apparent artlessness seems the greatest achievement of the poet's art, "In the bleak and mid-winter" is really a response to Mary's directive in the sonnet "All Saints" (*PW*, 148). The greatest gift Rossetti can give is poetry of etched austerity and unadorned words, a poetry expressing her love of God—an art of the heart.

Contributing to our sense that by "heart" Rossetti means something more than she can say is her use of a different situation to define the word in the lyric beginning "Lord, when my heart was whole I kept it back" ("'Afterward he repented, and went,'" 2:300). In this lyric, now that her heart is broken, Rossetti wonders whether she can ever achieve at-onement with God. Why should God be expected to accept damaged goods? And yet God operates by love and is not bound by logic, she reflects. The broken heart she offers may be most like God's, since his too was once broken on a cross.

In another lyric, "A heavy heart" (2:305), the heart is at first the ponderous grammatical object of a transitive verb: "I offer Thee this heavy heart of me" (l. 2). In the last stanza the lightened heart is lifted, and it becomes grammatical subject instead of object.

> Lifted to Thee my heart weights not so heavy,
> It leaps and lightens lifted up to Thee.
>
> (ll. 11–12)

In the final line, "Thy Face, me loving, for Thou lovest me," the first-person pronoun is twice framed by the divine "Thou" in an empathic merging of persons. The mirroring effect of the midline caesura and the chiasmus of "me loving, . . . lovest me" are devices of a poet who knows how to use the chiasmus of the Cross and who loves to handle varied grammatical elements, turning them over with fond and exact scrutiny. In finding the proper language of prayerful petition in "Sursum Corda" (2:311–12), Rossetti also finds the means to lift up her heart, an action she is powerless to perform at the beginning of the lyric: "I cannot, Lord, lift up my heart to Thee" (l. 2). The proximity of "Lord" and "lift" and the remoteness of "I" and "lift" suggest who the real agent of the lifting must be. In a powerful chiasmus and an increasingly intimate progression of principal verbs, Rossetti implores God to take what she is powerless either to keep or to give away: "Stoop, Lord, and hearken, hearken, Lord, and do, / And take my will, and take my heart, and take me too" ("Sursum Corda," ll. 8–9).

Of all Rossetti's poems on bruised or broken hearts that seek at-onement with God, the lyric "Twice" (1:124–26) is most affecting. It condenses most powerfully the repressions of both human and divine love and is therefore the riskiest of Rossetti's experiments in this genre. There is always a disquieting possibility that in experiencing the disappointment of her earthly love, Rossetti is simply rehearsing for a disappointment after death. Can religion entirely overcome the exhaustion, despair, and suffering reiterated in her secular lyrics? If God is as cruelly stringent as Rossetti, will her afterlife not be as resolutely chastened and impoverished as her present life? These are fearful questions for Rossetti to ask. She has staked all on God's love for *her*: she does not want to lose a wager twice.

"Twice" establishes a precarious but potent relation between the "You" of the first half of the lyric and the "Thou" of the second. Is God going to be any more generous or loving than the contemptuous "You" who coldly studied then rejected the proffered heart as he might have studied, then discarded, a flawed work of art?

> You took my heart in your hand
>   With a friendly smile,
>   With a critical eye you scanned,
>   Then set it down,
>   And said: It is unripe...
>
> ("Twice," ll. 9–13)

As in "A Fisher-Wife"(2:109), in which the "heart sits leaden" in the fisher-wife's "breast" until brought into her "mouth" (ll. 4, 8), there is in this lyric a powerful interaction between figurative and literal meanings. Part of the human anatomy can be made to achieve metonymically what the whole body can never achieve: "You took my heart in your hand / ...Then set it down, / ...As you set it down it broke" (ll. 9, 12, 17). As the critical friend, who cannot really have loved Rossetti, handles the heart as he might handle a piece of pottery, the metonymy is made to come to life with shocking literalness and force.

The last three stanzas repeat the drama for a second time: two of the agents—Rossetti and her proffered heart—are the same, but God is substituted for the critical lover.

> This contemned of a man,
>   This marred one heedless day,
>   This heart take Thou to scan
> . . . .
> I take my heart in my hand—
>   I shall not die, but live—
> Before Thy face I stand;
>   I, for Thou callest such:
> All that I have I bring,
>   All that I am I give,
> Smile Thou and I shall sing,
>   But shall not question much.
>
> ("Twice," ll. 33–35, 41–48)

In revising the original version of line 33, "this heart, contemned of man," Rossetti seems too ashamed even to name her proffered gift and deletes the word "heart" (1:273). In the final version the heart becomes nothing more distinctive than a displaced object, a mere demonstrative pronoun detached for three lines from its proper referent: "This contemned..., / this marred..., / this heart take Thou to scan" (ll. 33–35). But even while intensifying the shock and pain of her earlier rejections, Rossetti now uses the altered refrain ("You took my heart in your hand" [l. 9], "I take my heart in my hand" [ll. 25, 41]), the new form of scanning and criticizing (which is now refining, not dismissive), the smile of God, which replaces the cold stare of the friend, and the "I"'s singing instead of questioning, to recall and correct other uses—not only in this lyric but also in other poems on bruised or broken hearts. "All that I am I give" (l. 46) harks back to the ending of "A Christmas carol": "I would do my part,— / Yet what I can I give Him, / Give my heart" (ll. 38–40). As Rossetti in her carol falters after the dash, she wonders if she will be able to make her offering and complete her song. Will the whole enterprise totter and come to ruin, as her heart has so often faltered and failed her? Even in the poem "Twice" the dash after "live" (l. 42) puts the outcome in doubt.

But Rossetti is saved by devices that are now familiar. In "A Christmas carol" the remote is made homely, an art of the heart, as biblical commonplaces are renewed and the ordinary becomes miraculous again. And in "Twice" the poet's simple promise to "sing" (l. 47) reverses the bleak ending of the third stanza: "Nor sung with the singing bird" (l. 24). Even the last line recalls and completes the meaning of line 22: "nor questioned since." Though the poet refuses to question in both instances, she does so for opposite reasons. "To question" in the third stanza was to be self-critical, or perhaps to question God's justice. Originally Rossetti had lacked the heart to examine her own heart; she had not enough courage to be critical of others. Now she "shall not question much," not because she is afraid of any injustice she may expose, but because she is confident God's treatment of her will be just.

In refusing to close the divide that separates her faith in God from her understanding of him, Rossetti is simply refusing to reduce deity to the compass of her own imperfect mind and heart. To pretend that the gap does not exist, as a reductionist like Arnold does when he redefines God as the higher self, is simply to annihilate that distinction between nature and grace—that divide between God and man— that any heroic theory of knowledge and faith must struggle to preserve as its precondition and sine qua non. Her skepticism is inseparable, then, from the ironic double movement that reinstates faith at the moment of doubt, when caesural breaks inflict wounds on her poetry and God comes to life in the silence of a dash or a negation—at the very site of fracture or loss.

This skepticism is most apparent in lyrics that use tautologies, depleted diction, and tropes of reserve. In one of her most exacting lyrics of depletion, for example, "'A bruised reed shall he not break'" (1:67–68), Rossetti makes the end lines of successive stanzas decline from the modest to the minimal: "Alas, I cannot will" (l. 8), "I cannot wish, alas!" (l. 16), "I do not deprecate" (l. 24). Each time the soul seems capable of doing less. But at least the final negation is an affirmation in disguise. To deprecate is to negate, but to negate that negation is already to prepare for a reversal of the soul's will-less state. Though no self-activity may be possible, Rossetti can at least anticipate the first faint stirring of affective life.

We think that God will appeal to the soul's memory of the Crucifixion as a way of restoring the poet's love. He will chastise her by asking, How can *you* forget? But this is not what Rossetti's God says. Rather, if God was crucified for this will-less (though not unwilling) soul, the question to be asked is: How can *I* forget?

> For thee I hung upon the cross in pain,
>   How then can I forget?
> If thou as yet dost neither love, nor hate,
>   Nor choose, nor wish, —resign thyself, be still
> Till I infuse love, hatred, longing, will. —
>   I do not deprecate.
>   ("'A bruised reed shall he not break,'" ll. 19–24)

Over the expected platitude Rossetti has inscribed her own censorship of platitude. On behalf of the poet's bruised and damaged soul, God has already suffered too much to forget her now. Nor does he presume to criticize or minimize her anguish, for he has known the same anguish himself.

Everything depends on the power of contraction. The final line is the most contracted of all, for here the utterance of both speakers— God and the soul—is gathered into a single concentrated phrase. Indeed, for the first time in the poem God and the soul are able to speak in unison. The last line, "I do not deprecate," is equally in character for either speaker. Though readers are shocked, I think, to find "hatred" included in the catalog of affective states God chooses to "infuse"—love, hatred, longing, will—it is part of Rossetti's honesty that she should make God the author of her hatred of himself. "All poetry is difficult," as T. S. Eliot reminds us, "almost impossible, to write: and one of the great permanent causes of error in writing poetry is the difficulty of distinguishing between what one really feels and what one would like to feel" (1932, 361). In this lyric about bruised and broken hearts Rossetti is trying to find in life's most minimal offerings something residual that will suffice. In examining the depletions of a skeletal life—the renunciations of a soul that has perhaps renounced too much, Rossetti contracts language to the vanishing point. But even as the refrains decline from the modest to the minimal, Rossetti shows how the last trace of a false refuge or comfort must be broken down and abandoned. Her exacting honesty makes her exhaustion and depleted diction harrowing, but that honesty is part of her greatness as a poet.

In another of her most charged but depleted lyrics, "All heaven is blazing yet" (2:317), Rossetti manages to mean more than she says by using many connecting strategies that are all part of the verbal sleight-of-hand and the contrived economy of means. The tremor of open vowels, including the four exclamatory "O"s, sends a quaver of barely suppressed emotion down these lines. The tones range from hopeful to despairing. Linking patterns of similar length and shape invite the reader to compare "O hope deferred, be still" (l. 12) with "O hope deferred, hope still" (l. 16). Lines 4 and 12 have the same shape, as do lines 5 and 6 and lines 13 and 14. Even the rhyme words in these similar pairs are nearly identical: "choose," "Will" (ll. 13, 14) and "chose," "will" (ll. 5, 6). The huddling together of repeated sounds is the shudder of a soul that laments what it has lost but that also resolves to gather up and concentrate its now diminished powers.

> All heaven is blazing yet
>   With the meridian sun:
> Make haste, unshadowing sun, make haste to set;
>   O lifeless life, have done.
> I choose what once I chose;
>   What once I willed, I will:
> Only the heart its own bereavement knows;
>   O clamorous heart, lie still
>
> That which once I chose, I choose;
>   That which I willed, I will;
> That which I once refused, I still refuse:
>   O hope deferred, be still.
> That which I chose and choose
>   And will is Jesus' Will:
> He hath not lost his life who seems to lose:
>   O hope deferred, hope still.
>   ("All heaven is blazing yet")

Linkages of shape and sound are most arresting when there is some disproportion between the members. Thus there are slight variations in the rhyme words, and the pattern of syntax in "be still" and "hope still" (ll. 12, 16) is only apparently identical. The first "still" is an adjective, meaning "quiet" or "serene," and the second "still" is an adverb, a synonym for "perpetually" or "nevertheless." Lines 5 and 6 are almost tautologies: "I choose what once I chose; / What once I willed, I will." Tautology is the most withholding of tropes, and part of Rossetti's private theology of reserve: it enables her to mean more than she says. But in lines 13 and 14, which bear a deceptive similarity to these analytic statements, the poet switches to a synthetic judgment. Now she adds in the predicate a meaning not given in the subject, an identification of the poet's will with Jesus' will.

The rhyme words "will," "still," "chose," and "choose" recur ten times in a sixteen-line poem. The shadow of depletion is on such chastened diction. It is as if a computer had been given a limited number of rhymes and instructed to produce a minimal narrative. The austere poetic economy extends to individual words such as "only," which pack maximum meaning into Rossetti's unlavish idiom by looking two ways at once. "Only" (l. 7) might mean "were it not for the fact that the heart in its aloneness is clamorous and unruly." Or it might mean that the heart and nothing but the heart "its own bereavement knows." Lines 5 and 6 produce chiastic inversions of each other: "I choose what once I chose; / What once I willed, I will." Lines 9 and 10 repeat the same syntactic pattern as lines 5 and 6 but use different accusative forms. Line 11 has approximately the same semantic shape, but there is some disproportion now in its greater length: "That which I once refused, I still refuse." Coincidence of syntactic units and line lengths concentrates the energy with astonishing economy of means. The final "hope deferred" (l. 16) is the hope of earthly joy, but what it hopes "still" is the hope of Paul. Renunciation and deferral are made more acceptable when they allow Rossetti to cross the divide that separates hope from Hope, the second of Paul's three Christian virtues.

Closely allied to such lyrics of tautology and depleted diction are oracular poems that manage to mean more than they say by hiding thought in multiple or punning uses of a single word. Ordinarily, the comfort provided by a predictable refrain helps protect the mind against invasions of powers it is helpless to control. But when a familiar phrase takes on unpredictable new meanings, as does the phrase "Astonished Heaven" in Rossetti's lyric "Her seed; it shall bruise thy head" (2:295), the comfort of a limit is continually being broken down. By using changing grammatical functions of "astonished" Rossetti can create an *experience* of that very astonishment that is evoked by what is indefinite, unlimited—ultimately beyond the power of any single word to define.

Refrains are a familiar form of domesticating mystery, of trying to bring the strange into the orbit of the commonplace and known. First heaven is astonished at the miracle of man's creation: "Astonished Heaven looked on when man was made" (l. 1). This is merely conventional wonder and is appropriately conveyed by an adjective modifying a noun. But the oracle about the second Adam astonishes heaven in a different sense. To define the typological mystery of the lyric's title, which prefigures the victory of the second Adam over Satan, Rossetti seems to use "astonished" as a transitive verb that turns "heaven" from a grammatical subject into an object:

> Surely that oracle of hope first said,
> Astonished Heaven.
> ("Her seed; it shall bruise thy head," ll. 3–4)

But how can "heaven," as the author of "that oracle," be astonished by its own invention? The absence of any commas in the 1892 version of line 3, the use of two commas in the 1904 version, one before "first" and one after "said," and the use of only one comma in the version preferred by R. W. Crump, which is the version I have quoted (2:455), suggests the grammatical instability of the lines, which waver in emphasis between the effect on heaven of the oracle's pronouncement and the burden of the oracle itself. If we register the latter emphasis, it is as if the stanza's last line circles back on the opening phrase, making the oracle's content nothing less than the first quatrain of Rossetti's poem.

Most astonishing is the third use of "astonished." In confronting the mystery of a final transformation we might expect Rossetti to use a subjunctive verb: "Till one last trump shake earth, and" astonish Heaven. Instead, she writes "and undismayed / Astonished Heaven" (ll. 10–11). Perhaps in the eyes of God the Last Judgment has already occurred. Or is the past tense of "astonished" used to remind the reader of the instability of all time indicators? "Astonished Heaven" may simply be a nominative absolute construction, syntactically severed from the phrases that precede, as the soul that awakes at the end of time is astonished to find a disintegrating world fall away around it. Or is "Heaven," along with "earth," another direct object of the verb "shake"?

> Till one last trump shake earth, and undismayed
> Astonished Heaven.
> ("Her seed; it shall bruise thy head," ll. 10–11)

If so, why is there a comma after "earth"? And if Rossetti is saying that the trump did not dismay "Astonished Heaven," why does she use the past tense to describe a future action? David A. Kent reminds me that the active grammar may restore to life a buried pun in "undismayed." The trump that "unmakes" earth is able to astonish but not undo an "un-dis-made" or undismantled heaven, invulnerable, at the end, to the grand annihilation. The ever-present alternatives to any single interpretation come from Rossetti's conviction that God's vision of the end of time is not her own, and that each renewed insight about change will disclose deeper problems concerning a mystery she can never quite adjust to, a strangeness she continues to ponder with fresh wonder.

In the lyric "Praying Always" (2:304), it is the mystery of "forever," already latent in the commonplace adverb "always," that is first being limited to the measurement of a clock, then imperceptibly transformed into something immeasurable. The repeating phrase "The clock strikes one" (ll. 2, 7) is a time indicator that localizes events "after midnight" and "after mid-day." But the third use of "one" terminates the action like a stopwatch "after noon and night" (l. 11) when, in the final stanza, time stops altogether. Although the preposition "after" appears to be used similarly in all three phrases, there is in fact a profound disparity between the first two "after"s and the final one. The first phrase of stanza 3, "After noon and night," is not another adverbial phrase like "after midnight" (l. 1) or "after mid-day" (l. 6). Because this third phrase is introduced by a nontemporal preposition, by an "after" *after* all befores and afters, its meaning is not to be found in any dictionary.

> After noon and night, one day
>   For ever one
>   Ends not, once begun.
> Whither away,
> O brothers and O sisters? Pause and pray.
>   ("Praying Always," ll. 11–15)

Like Arthur Hallam's summons to Tennyson from "that deep dawn behind the tomb" (*In Memoriam*, 46.6), the summons to all brothers and sisters is a summons that speaks to Rossetti from the other side of silence.

If tautologies, depleted diction, and a punning or oracular multiple use of words are the signatures in Rossetti's verse of her skeptical conviction that meaning is always in excess of anything she can say, her heroic use of chiasmus is the signature of her equally strong conviction that mysterious truths, though beyond the power of words to compass fully, can at least be *intimated*. In poems of heroic crossing

between doubt and faith, death and life, Rossetti combines two attitudes to God that are seldom found together. She speaks as if there
were a divine attribute of justice that must be appeased. But she also
shares the mystic's sense that the only atonement she has need of is an
at-onement or becoming one with the divine nature. Too often in
seeking the comfort of a limit, Rossetti builds a wall between herself
and God. This wall can be broken down only when the poet learns to
tutor her heart and discipline her affections. Though the simultaneous search for limits and for something unlimited or boundless
precipitates a crisis in representation, Rossetti finds that only by
achieving at-onement with God in the mystic's sense can she understand how atonement in the traditional sense is possible.

In "Weary in well-doing" (1:182) Rossetti must learn to make her
life a chiasmus, a crossing-over from despair to hope, from brokenness
and fragmentation to at-onement with God. But this crossing is at first
a mere vexing: God simply crosses her will.

> I would have gone; God bade me stay:
> I would have worked; God bade me rest.
> . . . .
> Now I would stay; God bids me go:
> Now I would rest; God bids me work.
> ("Weary in well-doing," ll. 1–2, 6–7)

The first two lines of the second stanza are the chiastic inversion of
the first two lines of the first stanza. God's will seems an arbitrary
reversal of everything Rossetti seeks. With the predictable midline
caesuras in the first two lines and the strong breaks at the end of line
3 and 4, "He broke my will from day to day, / He read my yearnings
unexpressed / And said them nay..." ("Weary in well-doing," ll. 3–5),
Rossetti's emphatically rhymed tetrameters and dimeters compose a
sequence of pauses filled by words. The caesuras are more than just
breaks. They are cuts, deliberately inflicted to batter down and wound
the heart. As Rossetti's broken will turns into a broken heart "tost to
and fro" like damaged merchandise (l. 8), the mere deciphering of
unexpressed desires becomes the more frightening terror of the
doubting soul, who begins to question her faith in God.

The true chiasmus of a crossing-over from emptiness to plenitude,
from brokenness to true communion, comes only as a different kind
of crossing—as a crossing of the line lengths in the final question:

> I go, Lord, where Thou sendest me;
> Day after day I plod and moil:
> But, Christ my God, when will it be

That I may let alone my toil
And rest with Thee?
                    ("Weary in well-doing," ll. 11–15)

In the first three lines of stanzas 1 and 2, semantic units and line lengths coincide. The one-line units tend at first to isolate the "I" as a mere cipher confined to singular statements. But in the last stanza the line lengths of the semantic units begin to expand. The pattern of lines per semantic unit is 1, 1, 3 instead of 1, 1, 1, 2. The movement into the more spacious three-line unit provides a crossover from the individual to God. Through a slight augmentation of the two-line unit Rossetti shows how a soul that is broken and not at one strives for wholeness and at-onement.

In another lyric of crossing-over, "Love is strong as death" (2:164), the soul's initial neglect of God—it has not sought, found, or thirsted for God—sets the metaphorical terms for its own recovery of at-onement. So appropriate is the changed perspective in the second stanza to both the transformed soul and God that by the end of the lyric the poet and God, locked together by three binding verbs—"look and see / And clasp" (ll. 11–12)—can slip into each other. Lost in a coupling of pronouns, God and the soul are no longer divided as they were at the end of the first stanza: "Thy perishing me." Instead, their union is celebrated by a syntactic convergence, by a fusing of "thee...Me" (l. 12) in an empathic merging of persons.

Poems of quarreling and fractious debate usually set the terms of their own resolution. A lyric of crossed wills may turn into a lyric of genuine crossing, but only if the poet's aimless questioning has a destination as well as a destiny. Even in a lyric such as "Up-Hill" (1:65–66) the reader has a sense that the pilgrim's questions and the stranger's answers could go on forever. The inn is said to contain "beds for all who come" partly because the pilgrim is eager for rest and frames the appropriate question: "Will there be beds for me and all who seek?" (l. 15). Like a skilled Socratic ironist, the stranger withholds information. Instead of consolidating the mental level on which the pilgrim's questions are asked, the stranger's laconic answers are only as satisfactory as the pilgrim's questions. Better and fuller answers must await better questions.

The soul's ability to set the terms of its own recovery is nowhere more evident than in another poem of anguished crossing-over, the sonnet "Have I not striven, my God, and watched and prayed?" (2:205), which rivals in intensity and despair the dark sonnets of Hopkins. The triad of alliterating verbs in the middle of the sonnet, "I grope and grasp not; gaze, but cannot see" (l. 7), recalls the leveling hammer blows of the opening line, with its polysyndeton and harsh triple stresses on the past participles: "Have I not stríven, my God, and wátched and práyed?" But this triad allows Rossetti to launch her final fearful question. When she is herself as God is now, out of sight and reach, will the God who has reduced her to nothingness in every other sense reduce to nothingness her shame ˙as well? If so, the loneliness that has contracted her soul in the one-line questions of the sestet, generating the near insolence of her query "Is Thine Arm shortened that Thou canst not aid?" (l. 4), has still to achieve that curious blend of intimacy and reverence that by the end of the sonnet must once more make her whole.

> Have I not striven, my God, and watched and prayed?
>   Have I not wrestled in mine agony?
>   Wherefore still turn Thy Face of Grace from me?
> Is Thine Arm shortened that Thou canst not aid?
> Thy silence breaks my heart: speak tho' to upbraid,
>   For Thy rebuke yet bids us follow Thee.
>   I grope and grasp not; gaze, but cannot see.
> When out of sight and reach my bed is made,
> And piteous men and women cease to blame
> Whispering and wistful of my gain or loss;
> Thou Who for my sake once didst feel the Cross,
>   Lord, wilt Thou turn and look upon me then,
>   And in Thy Glory bring to nought my shame,
> Confessing me to angels and to men?

One of this sonnet's curious features is the way it breaks at the end of the seventh line. The querulous self at the beginning is given only seven of the octave's normal eight lines, while the drive toward at-onement occupies exactly half the sonnet. The spacious expansion of the final question, which occupies one more line than a conventional sestet, hesitatingly sets forth the search for wholeness. After the broken, halting syntax of the first seven lines, where the one-line anaphoric questions collapse into elliptical half-line confessions of heartbreak and despair, Rossetti is able to cross by the bold bridge of her spacious seven-line question to an imagined state of recovered wholeness and simplicity. This striking dramatic effect is lost in the sonnet's original manuscript version. Initially, the premature crossover at the end of line 5 made Rossetti's indictment of God too studied and rhetorical.

> Or is the load of one more sinner laid
>   On Thee, too heavy a load for even Thee?

(ll. 5–6)

This original version, which appears in the manuscript notebook in the British Library, is recorded by R. W. Crump (2:410). But in the revised version, the anger is more desolating and is allowed to break out into stark bereavement: "Thy silence breaks my heart." It then turns into an oddly abased but still reproachful prayer: "speak tho' to upbraid, / For Thy rebuke yet bids us follow Thee." In the final version all the steps of feeling are embodied in the short clauses, the sharp midline break after "heart" (l. 5), and in the strong end-line pauses. The chiasmus of the sonnet's last two lines, which encloses the phrases "my shame" and "me" between God's "glory" and the approval of his angelic witnesses, is a climactic crossing-over from nothing to all. The crossover ratifies and puts its seal, so to speak, on the syntactic and semantic drive of the brokenhearted petitioner who, though shattered and unwhole, also rediscovers the meaning of again being one with God.

Rossetti's best lyrics of elegiac crossing combine so many forms of mystery that each time we read them they reveal a different facet to the mind. Some readers may feel that, in crossing over from human to divine love, a lyric such as "Twice," which I have examined as an example of conferring contextual definition upon the word "heart," should culminate in an act more impressive and less homely than the poet's taking her heart in her hand. But then, one realizes, this is an exact and powerful gesture. The offering of her heart is the most important gift she can make. The plain honesty of statement, intimating an almost mute depth of feeling, reverberates with the last line of "A Christmas carol" and has the same reassuring ordinariness and truth. More immediate and poignant than the solemnities of her marriage feast in "Revelation" is Rossetti's vision in "Twice" of a divine lover, capable of picking up her broken heart and offering it such solace as he can. When the devotional poet stops looking at her brokenness and looks instead at the wholeness of Christ, she has already set the conditions for her recovery. Instead of remaining self-abased and depleted, Rossetti must learn to merge with God: she must trust that her broken heart will be acceptable to him and that she can find in her at-onement with him all the heart can wish.

In order to mean more than she says, it is important that Rossetti, even in crossing the divide between death and life, doubt and faith, human and divine love, should continue to use withholding tautologies and tropes of reserve. Rossetti worries more than most poets about what cannot be said, about the places in personal life where hope winds down and possibilities of renovation seem to die. Her tentativeness can be more compelling than positiveness, and her most weighted moments are emphasized by lack of insistence. Even when recorded in little operettas or domestic melodramas of the soul, Rossetti's losses are a touching memento of human limits, a reminder of all that can never be fully grasped or loved or said. I suspect this is another way of saying that Rossetti's art of reserve is simply human in the fullest sense.

I do not want to imply, however, that Christina Rossetti and Newman are the only Victorians who contrive to mean more than they say by conferring mysterious contextual meanings upon the dictionary meanings of such apparently simple but actually complex words as "heart" and "faith." A simplicity in complication is also the hallmark of Ruskin and Arnold, who are equally adept at fashioning complex contextual definitions for such seemingly straightforward words as "imagination" and "culture." Ruskin is as baffled by the true greatness of artistic imagination as Arnold is by culture. The more Ruskin honors the mystery of imaginative genius, the less he can explain it. Even his theories of imagination in the second book of *Modern Painters* leave more unexplained than they explain. Ruskin's theory of the Imagination Associative, for example, does not presume to solve the riddle of how the mind of an artist can intuit in advance the precise arrangement in which a series of imperfect parts will mysteriously compose themselves into a perfect whole.

In "The Mystery of Life and Its Arts," Ruskin's third lecture in *Sesame and Lilies*, the very word "mystery" becomes a mystery. The precise relation between the paradox that all things are full of emptiness, the paradox of Koheleth in Ecclesiastes, and the discovery that comes with the wise man's detachment from life—which is not to be confused with withdrawal—is a mystery Ruskin potently intimates, without ever presuming to explain, by his riddling, refrainlike use of the phrase, "is this not a mystery of life?" Ruskin keeps meaning more than he says, but readers must decide for themselves what that elusive fuller meaning might be.

By some perversity of fate, Ruskin muses, the finer Turner's art becomes, the more invisible it seems to ordinary eyes. Genius is like the air, an invisible medium. And yet, as one commentator has observed, "if we could see air we could see nothing else" (Northrop Frye 1982, 124). A genius like Turner may be the means of seeing. But that genius itself may remain as invisible as the enabling medium of light, the real subject of many of his paintings. The greater any work of art, moreover, the less it can be explained. As Yeats said, an artist may live his deepest truths, but he can never speak them. He can embody his secrets but never know them. Ruskin insists that "no true painter ever speaks, or ever has spoken, much of his art" (18:166). His art remains a secret science. When critics like Joshua

Reynolds write about art, they are "utterly silent respecting all" they can do themselves (18:167). Like Carlyle, Ruskin honors silence: "the moment a man can really do his work he becomes speechless about it" (18:167). A true artist would no more presume to offer a course on his own art than he would presume to teach love or friendship.

Whatever Arnold and Ruskin may say about culture or artistic imagination, there is always some deeper truth about these subjects that both writers hold in reserve. The harder Arnold tries to define culture, for example, the less comprehensible he finds it. If he is to invest culture with spiritual authority, then it must mean more than he is able to say. Surprising as it may sound, we can read the whole of *Culture and Anarchy* and never quite discover what Arnold means by culture. Arnold might well have said of culture what Augustine said of time: he knew what it was until asked, then found he could not say.

To behave disinterestedly, as a true apostle of culture, is to forsake rhetoric for logic, dialectic, and pure vision. But Arnold excels in the very practice of partisanship, applied rhetoric, and persuasion that he deplores. To the degree that Arnold succeeds in using rhetoric to abolish rhetoric, he is putting at risk his most signal achievement as a writer. Arnold wants to retain the authoritative emotive appeal of truth, but he also wants to give it a new descriptive meaning. He wants to equate it with self-making, with a capacity of individuals to develop harmoniously all their conflicting aspirations and powers. But how can "reason and the will of God" be identified with the humanization of man in society without losing its authority as a spiritual ground? And what if some of the conflicting aspirations and powers cannot be reconciled? What if the power of reason and the power of good exist in inverse proportion? Is Arnold trying to meet a necessary challenge, or is he trying to achieve the impossible? Is he a heroic adapter, as Ruth apRoberts thinks, or just intellectually confused, as F. H. Bradley and T. S. Eliot charged?[2]

Ironically, what is most real and intelligible for Arnold is the

---

2. Ruth apRoberts's *Arnold and God* (1983) is the most inclusive recent attempt to rehabilitate Arnold as an original religious thinker. The harshest Victorian attack on Arnold's religious thought comes from F. H. Bradley in *Ethical Studies* (1876, 318–19): "Most of us, certainly the public which Mr. Arnold addresses, want something they can worship; and they will not find that in an hypostasized copy-book heading, which is not much more adorable than 'Honesty is the best policy,' or 'handsome is that handsome does,' or various other edifying maxims, which have not yet come to an apotheosis." T. S. Eliot takes a similar line in his essay "Arnold and Pater" in *Selected Essays* (1951, 432): Arnold's religious writings "have served their turn and can be hardly read through. In these books . . . reasoning power matters, and it fails him; furthermore, we have now our modern solvers of the same problem Arnold there set himself, and they, or some of them, are more accomplished and ingenious in this sort of rationalizing than Arnold was."

harmony of the truly cultured and cultivated self—the individual. But such individuality lacks the authority of a true ground, which for Arnold must be communal and social. Accordingly, Arnold keeps constructing around the harmoniously cultivated individual public extensions of that individual. But these extensions, as they find themselves mirrored in the classes of society and the polity at large, are mere fictive concords, what Plato would call "noble lies." Some of these concords, especially the religious ones, have to be exposed as "fictive." But other fictions must be accepted as mythology. As a highly selective deconstructionist, Arnold finds it is not in the interest of culture and poetry to have their myths exposed as lies, even as "noble lies."

In Arnold's view, the "grand language" used by religion must mean far more than it actually says. Its true referent is not the relative moral perfection Puritans denote by it but "an absolute inward peace and satisfaction" (5:101) that religion as such cannot attain. Conversely, Arnold shows, Nonconformists are continually saying more than they can possibly mean, or much more than they have any right to mean. They attack T. H. Huxley for trying to cure vice and hideousness by scientific rather than religious means. But by applying the twist of his *tu quoque* argument, Arnold shows how Huxley's religious critics, despite the pretensions of their language, are no better equipped to cure vice and hideousness than Huxley. Their "sublime and aspiring language," the language of religion, is "an immense pretension." It speaks of themselves as "children of God." But how can such a narrow, unlovely unattractive people use such exalted language to describe their own squalor of both body and mind?

When Arnold speaks of the sacrifice of his enemies, he is in a sense saying more than he means. "Sacrifice" might better translate as deserved destruction. And yet to speak of their sacrifice is at the same time to mean more than he says. They are indeed offered up as sacrificial victims on the very altar of that world spirit that, as revolutionaries, they are ironically pledged to oppose. As the home of lost causes, the university of Oxford has built a bridgehead to the future, and the quotation from Virgil—"Quae regio in terris nostri non plena laboris?" (5:106)—appropriately alludes to Newman's un- forgettable allusions to the same classical author. What subtler way of Arnold's meaning more than he says than by evoking the pervasive influence of Newman and the Oxford Movement in an allusive contemporary use of a classical allusion?

Paradoxically, the authoritative style of *Culture and Anarchy*, with its short syntactic units and intimidating rhetoric, seems to subvert the doctrine that Arnold preaches about culture's hostility to any would-be prophet or rabbi. Culture is restless, forever dissatisfied with any guru or seer. But if this is so, then it must distrust Arnold himself. To write like Arnold is to be authoritative and subvert the doctrine he preaches. Conversely, to preach hostility to any rabbinical formulation of perfection, which can become intelligible only at the inadmissible cost of profaning the mystery, is to try to erode the oracular authority of Arnold's own style. The man of culture is a critic in the Kantian sense, reminding us of the limits of rational inquiry. He is merciful to individuals but harsh in his judgment of pernicious doctrines. By contrast, culture's adversaries try to demean its true function by equating its practical application of critical philosophy with a "turn for small fault-finding" and with that "fierce exasperation which breathes, or rather, I may say, hisses through the whole production" of Mr. Frederic Harrison (5:112). The deft placement of the verb "hisses," made more dextrous by the artful pause for self-correction, transforms Harrison into a modern Satan, exposed to ridicule before his hosts in Pandemonium. Though Harrison's attack is converted into Arnold's strongest defense, there is still something unwittingly ironic about Arnold's use of shrill satire and partisan rhetoric on behalf of a perfectly equable and serene form of mastery, praised by Arnold as "humanized knowledge" (5:113). Like morality in Bradley's *Ethical Studies*, Arnold's rhetorical appeals on behalf of culture aim at the establishing of an ideal condition that, if ever achieved, would do away with books like *Culture and Anarchy*.

In judging liberty by its consequences for action, as he would judge any other idea, Arnold, it seems to me, proves a more consistent utilitarian than J. S. Mill, because he is unswervingly loyal to "antiessentialist" notions of language and truth. For Mill and Bright liberty is one of the ultimate qualities of perfection: it is as much a mystery word as "culture" for Arnold or "heart" for Christina Rossetti. Liberty is useful for Mill because it is accepted a priori as authoritative and true: it is not accepted as true because it has first proved itself useful in practice. Its sacred status is too mysterious and inviolable to be put to any pragmatic test. But as Arnold shows, liberty sounds less divine when translated into practical equivalents like the middle-class maxim: "every man for himself in business, every man for himself in religion" (5:118). The consequence for action of the sacred doctrine of liberty is nothing less than anarchy. "Doing as one likes" is more than just a slogan. The consequence of entertaining it is unforgettably dramatized in the shrill disintegration of Arnold's language wherever the phrase, "he likes," is used (5:119, 122). The activities sanctioned by the doctrine progressively decline, as the verbs descend from the formal arrangement of "marching" to coarse hooting, devious threatening, and finally open rioting and looting (5:119).

Oddly enough, the mystery of a genuinely humanized perfection is not to be found in the mean, the defect, or the excess of any of the classes Arnold analyzes. He has made the state of the nation intelligible only at the cost of allowing the mystery of genuine culture to escape from his analysis. The mystery of true culture depends on an unanalyzable genius or talent. It is heaven bestowed and is found only in men who are aliens to their class. What is intelligible is bathetic, and what might serve as a "sound centre of authority" (5:155), like the statue of Pallas Athene in Arnold's poem "Palladium," is shown to be too remote and mysterious to be of practical use to anyone.

Arnold's theories about culture, literature, and education by poetry, like Ruskin's theories of imaginative genius and Christina Rossetti's understanding of the love of God, always retain something of the shimmering mystery of a mirage. His ideal is real but elusive, always just beyond his grasp, just on the point of passing out of sight. Arnold never quite succeeds in defining culture, because he does not seem to know what a harmony of Hellenism and Hebraism, of the powers of beauty, manners, knowledge, and conduct, would be like. No Victorian writer can combine Arnold's audacity as a satirist with his toleration as a critic, his concern for tradition with his disregard for authority. But if Arnold continues to mean by "culture" more than he can hope to say, is it not partly because he also secretly despairs of making intelligible or even conceptually coherent the notion of a perfect whole in which all good things cohere? The constant oscillation in Arnold's poetry between spontaneity and control, calm and passion, contemplation and action, suggests that the idea of a perfect whole may never be attainable. Arnold seems afraid to face up to the painful truth, more honestly recognized by Clough, that some great goods cannot live together. We are all doomed to choose, and every choice between equality and restraint, for example, or between the goods of the moral and intellectual life, is likely to entail some irreparable loss. Though experiencing such losses is one of the events that make us human, Arnold cannot bear to admit, I think, that values worthy of being pursued as ends in themselves—values such as Hebraism and Hellenism, justice and mercy, liberty and equality—may actually exist in inverse proportion and so be incapable of being reconciled in some greater whole.

CHAPTER 15

The Bewitchment of Words: J. S. Mill on Saying More Than Is Meant

As a subtle and inclusive thinker, J. S. Mill is critical of both mystification and reduction. It is as dangerous to appeal to what *is* as a measure of what *ought* to be as it is to appeal to what *ought* to be when trying accurately to describe what *is*. The first kind of appeal should mean more than it actually says: it is intelligible at the price of being simplistic. It confuses the descriptive ends of physical science with the prescriptive ends of ethics. The second kind of appeal says more than it can properly mean. Its high-sounding names for obfuscation and ignorance constitute Mill's primary target, for as an enemy of mystification Mill, like Wittgenstein, conceives his task to be "a battle against the bewitchment of our intelligence by means of language" (Wittgenstein 1972, 47, proposition 109).

A key question is whether utilitarianism, Mill's chosen school of thought, can furnish the tools he needs to demystify phrases like "duty," "a good and all-powerful God," and "the authority of the state," which are too often used as masks for self-interest or deceit. In theory, utilitarianism should serve Mill well. For in utilitarian thought, what happens is appealed to as a definition of what is: a preconception of what ought to be is not appealed to for an understanding of what actually occurs. Thus conceived, the utilitarian method can embrace even the genius of Darwinism, which, instead of explaining what has happened by appealing to what we would like to have happened, explains what is by the accidental variations that have in fact occurred. In practice, however, Mill's own utilitarianism may prove to be as vulnerable to his weapons of demystification as the deontological and other fictions he is resolved to expose. In his influential *Methods of Ethics*, for example, Henry Sidgwick argues that in positing a convergence of the individual's pursuit of happiness with the greatest happiness of the greatest number, utilitarianism is positing a principle that cannot be established by utilitarian means. It can be established only by appealing like Joseph Butler to some motive of prudence or expedience that, as an intuitional motive, has no place in an ethical theory like Bentham's or James Mill's. Is J. S. Mill's utilitarianism any less vulnerable to Sidgwick's attack? Does Mill's thought not fall by the same weapons it uses against deontology and all essentialist notions of meaning and truth?

Why is good to be equated merely with happiness and pleasure? And if certain kinds of pleasure cannot be measured or quantified, then is it not valid to conclude that certain forms of good cannot be empirically tested? If this is so, then consigning certain actions to the class we call good because productive of happiness cannot properly qualify as a true-or-false classification. It should be viewed instead as a proposal or recommendation to view such actions as good. But then the distinction between rational, or empirically verifiable, morality and an obscurantist intuitional ethic like Kant's cannot logically be maintained. As a metaphorical proposal about values, like deontology, rather than a true-or-false classification of the kind we find in the science of taxonomy, Mill's own thought seems no more capable of empirical testing than the value system he hopes to displace.

In his essays on Bentham and Coleridge Mill sets forth most clearly his method of exposing verbal deceit. Bentham, for Mill, is the great practitioner of such exposure. By showing how the mystifiers say more than they mean, Bentham restores order and clarity to logical inquiry. But Mill is the first to concede that Bentham has his limits. Not all difficult discourse is gratuitously mystifying. Coleridge's language is often obscure because his ideas are genuinely difficult: it is seldom difficult because his thought is obscurely expressed. Bentham, by contrast, is usually comprehensible. But his discourse may be clear because his ideas are simple and reductive. His empiricism is that of a thinker whose own experience is too limited. Bentham chooses to be obtuse about some matters so that he may be clear-sighted about others.

Mill's three essays on religion expose the contradictions that lie buried in mystery phrases like "the ethics of naturalism," the Stoic precept "follow nature," and unexamined religious concepts like the simultaneous goodness and omnipotence of deity. Religious dogmatists who affirm that God is both good and God are saying more than they have any right to mean. Advocates of an ethics of naturalism are guilty of the opposite error: they are guilty of saying less than they ought to mean.

In the essay titled "Nature" Mill hopes to banish wrongheaded emotive meanings that have no true connection with the proper descriptive meaning of "nature." In presenting himself as a critic of verbal bewitchment, Mill argues that if thinkers who use the word "nature" are allowed to say no more than the word really means, then serious ethical fallacies can be avoided. By exposing fallacies of equivocation, Mill aspires to write the dialogue *On Nature* that Plato might have written. In it Socrates would have dissected "large abstractions..., fixing down to a precise meaning" the elusive word "nature" (10:373), as in other dialogues he fixes the meaning of "virtue" or "knowledge."

Whereas Newman, Arnold, and Ruskin delight in the mysteries of indefinition, in the refusal to formulate of mystery words like "faith," "culture," or even the word "mystery" itself, Mill and Huxley follow Socrates in attacking the illogical contradiction of an "indefinite definition." A "definition" (from *finis*, limit or end) that refuses to set limits is etymologically no definition at all. Most inclusively, nature can be defined as "everything that happens." But then the term "nature," precisely because it is a "term" (from *terminus*, boundary or end), denies the essence of the comprehensive phenomenon it tries to name, just as the phenomenon eludes the term. Sensing the difficulty, Mill proposes a narrower definition: "nature" is now said to be whatever "takes place without the agency... of man" (10:375). Following the Socratic practice of defining words precisely, Mill now exposes the Stoics' error of enjoining men to follow nature. If nature means the laws of nature, the injunction is as meaningless as ordering people to do what they have to do. An injunction properly implies some choice, some freedom to follow advice or reject it. But since acting "according to nature" is "what nobody can possibly help doing" (10:379), the injunction is an injunction in form only. Moreover, it makes a rather serious mistake in philosophical grammar, for it uses an imperative where only an indicative is called for.

The Stoic injunction to follow nature may be preserved in a proper grammatical form, but only by assuming that the laws of nature are a proper model for the laws of veracity and justice. In that case, however, the fiendish cruelty of a nature uncontrolled by human agency makes the injunction patently absurd. Either the doctrine is trite but true and the grammar in error, or else the grammar is correct but the doctrine an enormous falsehood. The ingenuity with which Mill lays these traps for his readers encourages us to be equally resourceful in finding escape routes. The only escape from the first horn of his dilemma seems to be a more precise use of language. Thinkers who advise us to follow the laws of nature often mean that we should study them so they can be used to forward a purpose. But then these thinkers should use the verb "study" or "know," not the misleading verb "follow." To escape from the second horn, we have to show why the maxim to follow nature as "that which takes place without human intervention" is not as palpably absurd as it sounds. The maxim has force, perhaps, if we accept religious arguments that condemn as an impious usurpation of God's power any intervention in natural operations, such as contraception. But the argument from natural law strikes Mill as a vestige of outworn superstition, and he has little patience with it. A God worthy of worship is not going to chain Prometheus to a rock for stealing fire from heaven. Nor is he going to banish Adam from Eden for eating from the tree of knowledge or for practicing birth control.

Though we may admire, like Kant, the sublime immensity of nature, we can never truly admire, Mill insists, her amoral economy or her refusal to turn "one step from her path to avoid trampling us into destruction" (10:384). The essay on "Nature" was rewritten at at time when Mill and his wife were dangerously ill, and the prospect of death gives special force to his dark anatomy of nature's horrors. The balance of the prose momentarily breaks down, as short asyndetic units, achieving a crescendo of aimless carnage, allow Mill to flail blindly at an indecently cruel nature, almost as savagely as Swift might have done: "Nature impales men, breaks them as if on the wheel, casts them to be devoured by wild beasts, burns them to death, crushes them with stones like the first christian martyr, starves them with hunger, freezes them with cold, poisons them by the quick or slow venom of her exhalations, and has hundreds of other hideous deaths in reserve, such as the ingenious cruelty of a Nabis or a Domitian never surpassed" (10:385). The leveling asyndeton evokes a panic-stricken sense of nature's mindless brutality. "Nature's holy plan" is a mere mystification, exploded by its own inventor, Wordsworth, in more searching lines like the movingly honest coda to "Elegiac Stanzas." And yet Mill's oblique personifications remind us that nature may be not so much cruel as indifferent. The only fiction more pervasive and falsely consoling than Wordsworth's fiction of nature the moral guardian and nurse is the fiction that nature is malign and cruel rather than merely blank, stupid, and indifferent, the "Vast Imbecility" of Thomas Hardy's description.

Nature's indifference is a terrible bereavement for Mill. "Perhaps," as one commentator says, "the most important discovery was that there was no Garden of Eden; the Eldorado of the spirit turned out to be both desert and jungle" (Bloom, 1987, 163). The only way Mill can reconcile a partially imperfect and evil world with the existence of a benevolent God is to conclude that God is good but not omnipotent. Man must be enlisted as a "not ineffectual auxiliary to a Being of perfect beneficence" (10:389) who is not, alas, all-powerful. Mill's attempt to save God's "goodness at the expense of his power" may subtract from the mystery of the godhead, but at least it makes theology intelligible. Mill deplores as a gratuitous mystification any attempt to attribute involuntary impulses—the mysterious ones—to God, and the voluntary impulses—the more intelligible ones—to man. The consecration of instinct at the expense of reason is a peculiarly romantic predilection. It is dangerous because it asks us to defer to the authority of an unknown, a mystery, simply because it is thought to manifest some inscrutable, higher purpose. We defer to such a mystery only when our rational faculty has not yet "acquired the authority of prescription" (10:393).

In his essay "Utility of Religion" Mill ascribes religion in cultivated minds to the fact that "human existence is girt round with mystery" (10:418). Like poetry, religion penetrates the regions of mystery with the aid of imaginative analogies drawn from human agency and design. But the analogies will be accepted or rejected not because of their truth or falsity, but because of their felicity or infelicity, as J. L. Austin (1975) would say. Religion is useful, Mill concedes, in helping each individual cultivate an idea of perfection. But why cannot such an idea be cultivated inside the boundaries of the world we inhabit? Why should mystifying notions of perfect unseen powers be better able to inculcate an idea of perfection than more intelligible notions about ideal communities on earth? Comte's religion of humanity, like Marx's secular but essentially religious version of the classical religious dream, satisfies the same needs as supernatural religion, but in less alienating, more comprehensible ways. One argument against the transfer of allegiance from heaven to ideal communities on earth is the short duration of such communities and the brevity of life itself. But though individual life is short, Mill believes the life of the species is not. The improvement of human communities is not a petty object, but "large enough...to satisfy any reasonable demand for grandeur of aspiration" (10:420). It has all the mystery of religion without any of its otherworldly obscurity. And it has the intelligibility of a doctrine like Epicurus's without any of Epicurus's indifference to higher values.

Only the living oxymoron of a "sophisticated heart," Mill insists, can worship without embarrassment the deity in nature and the deity in the Gospels as the same God. Of thinkers who try to derive their morality from religion, it is truly said that "the better logicians they are, the worse moralists" (10:425). The only possible advantage of supernatural religion over a religion of humanity is the prospect of life after death that the former sometimes offers. And the only utility of such a prospect is that it fosters in some sensitive natures a hope of reunion with people they love.

But how many of Mill's own proposals about the benefits to be derived from a religion of humanity are actually capable of being verified? We have never had a religion of humanity, nor have we been able to transfer love of family or country to love of humanity at large. So in what way are Mill's proposals about a transfer of religious allegiance from God to ideal communities any less mystifying than the otherworldly religions he criticizes? If the utility of an idea is not capable of being empirically tested, it seems to be only another imaginative proposal, like the proposals of the supernatural religions Mill seeks to replace, rather than a true-or-false proposition designed to win and retain rational assent.

In "Utility of Religion," Mill tries to show that the utility or inutility of theological belief is not a mere matter of opinion: it can be classified as a true or a false statement. But in his better-known essay "On Liberty," he argues the opposite proposition: the utility of any belief is a mere opinion. As a recommendation incapable of either proof of disproof, it cannot be used by religious dogmatists to suppress free discussion of religious ideas. It is one thing to demolish a utilitarian argument when it is abused by defenders of religious mystification, but if utility is a mere matter of opinion, a mere proposal or recommendation, what happens to utilitarianism's truth claim in general? Is it any less mystifying than the system it replaces?

Two competing models or pictorial fictions keep operating in Mill's essay *On Liberty*, and they do not always seem consistent. One is the economic model of the freewheeling entrepreneur operating on the open market. Free individual enterprise allows each entrepreneur to forward his own interests. This economic picture informs Mills' advocacy of individual enterprise in the realm of ideas. But a second quite different rhetorical fiction is employed: the organic metaphor of biological growth as opposed to mere mechanical operation. Individual development entails the unfolding of a leading principle, a version of Aristotle's final cause, and the metaphor is one of a living whole in which the totality is more than the sum of its component parts. Sidgwick points out the logical incompatibility of the two models in his *Methods of Ethics*. How can free enterprise in the selfish pursuit of one's own goals ensure the attainment of organic unity and growth in the state, or even in the lives of those who make up the state? Insufficient attention has been paid to the antinomies in Mill. Man is asked to operate in the realm of intellectual inquiry like an entrepreneur in a free market. At the same time the individual is expected to harmonize his values, to be many sided like Pericles rather than one dimensional like John Knox or Alcibiades. Instead of operating as a computer programmed to maximize his pleasures and intellectual gains, the egoist is also to function as a complex social organism—as a monad rather than an atom—increasingly attuned to other people's welfare.

If a defense of liberty must rest on a mere postulate of faith that man is rational, then perhaps the utility of the postulate can be used to justify it. But Mill denies in *On Liberty* that utility can be divorced from truth, and he argues against the opponents of free inquiry that the assumed "usefulness of an opinion is itself matter of opinion" (18:233). If truth is to live and be fully possessed, we need some contrivance like the negative dialectic of Socrates to keep thought awake and alert. To hold ideas passively is to behave like the data bank of a computer. To develop organically is to affirm, by contrast, a continuity between the truth that is professed and the way it is appropriated and possessed. Surprisingly, Mill's idea of truth resembles Newman's idea of faith. Irrational people are often condemned as too impulsive. But the false opposition between feeling and reason must be broken down, as reason (the more inclusive term) comes to absorb feeling in itself. It is not feeling or impulse that makes men act immorally and irrationally. If anything, there is not enough impulse. Men are too timid and unfeeling to act in sane and ennobling ways. Their ideas have to become inspiring as the architect of their purposes, imaginative and feeling as the poet of their dreams.

Even when Mill's essays seem internally consistent, problems may arise when we start to compare them. In his essay *Utilitarianism*, for example, Mill proceeds to restrict the prize word "rational" to an inductive morality like Bentham's. In doing so, however, is he not committing in ethical theory the same error for which he condemns the advocates of an ethics of naturalism in his essay "Nature"? Free enterprise in the realm of ideas, the postulate of faith in *On Liberty*, also consorts oddly with the subjective "desire to be in unity with our fellow-creatures" (10:231), the natural sentiment that is said to be the ultimate sanction of the utilitarian morality.

Nowhere, however, is Mill a more astute critic of verbal bewitchment than in the fifth chapter of *Utilitarianism*, where he attacks the view that "justice" has been inscribed on things as an essence, as an "inherent quality." Though subjective mental feelings of justice or injustice seem in excess of any emotions we normally attach to issues of mere utility of expedience, Mill wants to demystify the word "justice." In an attempt "to seize the mental link which holds" all meanings of justice together, Mill turns in some desperation to the word's etymology (10:244). *Justum* is a form of *jussum*, that which has been ordered. Unlike Horne Tooke, who confuses present meanings with original meanings, Mill is resolved not to commit a genetic fallacy. But he still asserts that the *idée mère*, "the primitive element, in the formation of the notion of justice, [is] conformity to law" (10:245).

Recognizing, however, that the sentiment of justice has always attached itself not merely to existing laws but also to laws that were perceived as ideal and that ought to exist, Mill wants to cross the ethical chasms dividing "is" from "ought." There is a great danger, Mill admits, that a floating signifier like "sentiment of justice," which has cut loose from its anchor in any specific ground or referent, will attach itself to a mere fictitious essence. Inventors of such an essence imply a meaning beyond anything they can intelligibly say about it. Mill now tries to reverse this process by anchoring the sentiment in its original ground, even if that ground should prove disappointingly homely and commonplace.

To determine whether justice is a special dispensation of nature or an arrangement of general expedience, Mill distinguishes between justice and morality. A right conferred by law imposes an obligation that Mill calls "perfect" or legally binding. Moral obligation, by contrast, is imperfect, since it does not involve a legal right. As Mill says, "no one has a moral right to our generosity or beneficence" (10:247). But "imperfect" moral obligation therefore seems to be more perfect in a human sense than so-called perfect obligations, precisely because the generosity is not required by law. What is more perfect in the legal sense is less perfect in the moral or human sense, and vice versa. This is the crux of Mill's argument, and at first it sounds paradoxical. Moreover, even the gracious deed, the conferring of beneficence and generosity, is made to depend on expediency, when it is just such self-regarding behavior that the deed seems designed to supersede.

In reattaching the "sentiment of justice" to its true referent, an animal desire to avoid hurt to oneself or to those one sympathizes with, Mill argues that sympathy for others, though incapable of being attached to definable rights, does account for the general utility of behaving as one does. Why are laws that protect the individual against a violation of his rights perceived to be just? Not, in Mill's view, because the rights are ordained by God or nature, but because it is useful to have these rights guarded in the name of that security that no human being can afford to do without. Sentiments of justice do not change the object they are attached to: those objects are still grounded in utility and expedience. But the feelings concerned are so powerful that we mistake their referent. The claim to which sentiments of justice attach themselves "assumes that character of absoluteness, that apparent infinity, and incommensurability with all other considerations, which constitute the distinction between the feeling of right and wrong and that of ordinary expediency and inexpediency" (10:251). The "perfect" obligations of justice would not have to be defined as so perfect if the sentiment of justice—the animal desire to avoid being hurt—were not so primitive and imperfect. And the obligations of moral duties as opposed to legal rights can afford to remain "imperfect," as we somewhat illogically say, because the sentiment of sympathy that makes individual justice moral is a more "perfect" or ennobling feeling than the animal desire to retaliate. By demystifying the language that is meant to bewitch us, Mill can show why the persuasive redefinitions are rhetorically powerful, however inconsistent logically.

As a critic of verbiage that is emotionally loaded but deficient in content, Mill might be thought to argue that justice is no more sacred than simple expedience. Is justice anything more than a high-sounding name for expedient policy? Mill denies that his method is quite so reductive. Justice is useful because it guarantees the safety all human beings require. And moral rules that ensure it are "incomparably the most sacred and binding part, of all morality" (10:255). If the true sanctions of justice are animal desires tempered by human sympathy, why should this capacity of enlarged sympathy be denied the emotively laden epithet "sacred"? By dispelling the fog of obfuscation that shrouds the word while retaining the prescriptive force that necessarily attaches to it, Mill shows that justice is a clearly intelligible and even provable concept, easily subject to pragmatic testing.

Paradoxically, however, Mill the advocate of liberty seems to put liberty itself at risk by making his theory of justice depend not on a rational selection of liberty, but on the influence of a wayward sentiment, a mere animal instinct or feeling. Truer to Mill's own advocacy of liberty than Mill himself is a contemporary theorist of justice, John Rawls, who enshrines as his first principle of justice the "equal right" of each person "to the most extensive total system of equal basic liberties compatible with a similar system of liberty for all" (1971, 302).

Mill seems unaware of another paradox. After praising his wife for making him critical of fallacies of limited induction that confuse "limited generalities" with "universal principles" (1:257), he proceeds to assert a causal relation between the merits of *On Liberty* and his wife's coauthorship. But Harriet's "cautiousness of practical judgment" cannot have been as great as Mill thinks, for it has not included the notion of influence, itself a causal concept. Perhaps such binds can be avoided by a theory of types, as Bertrand Russell suggests. According to such a theory, it is impossible to define a class that contains itself: the class of invalid causal relations in Mill's example contains as one instance of itself Mrs. Mill's own influence on Mill.

In his discussion of fallacies in his *System of Logic*, Mill identifies the great peril of assuming that such sentiments as justice are grounded in natural law. As we have seen, this is a view Mill valiantly combats in the last chapter of *Utilitarianism*. The same deference to essentialist notions of truth invalidates defense of the major premises in syllogisms on the grounds that these premises define the essence or nature of the subject to be defined. Thus "all men are mortal" is said to mean it is the nature of men to die. In both examples "the words Nature and Essence are grand instruments of . . . begging the question" (8:822). Arguments from nature and essence, as in Scholastic theology, exhibit "*petitio principii* in one of its most palpable forms" (8:822). As bewitching abstractions, Mill's personified Nature and Essence assume in their very definitions of a subject the conclusion to be proved. It is no more intelligible than Aristotle's dictum that bodies move up and down because it is the nature of bodies to do so.

Instead of rendering his subject more intelligible, a logician may sometimes make it more mystifying and opaque (7:276–79). Sir William Hamilton, for example, uses the principle of contradiction to deny that substance can be simultaneously infinitely divisible and atomic. He then enlists the principle of the excluded middle to add that substance must be either one or the other, since there is no third term between infinite divisibility and the doctrine that division has a limit. In this way Hamilton makes his subject, an unknowable God or thing-in-itself, resonate with mystery. The two logical principles become "chinks through which [one small] ray of light finds its way to us from behind the curtain which veils from us the mysterious world of Things in themselves" (7:277). But it is Hamilton's own illogical logic that creates and sustains the mystifying remoteness of his subject. The sphinx is said to have a secret: it must be either infinitely divisible or else atomic, but we have no way of discovering which it is. The real secret, Mill suggests, is that the sphinx is without a secret after all. For the properties of the absolute that Hamilton presumes to name seem to be neither true nor false but unintelligible. Their mystery is a verbal fiction, a bewitchment of the intelligence by means of excluding a third possibility not covered by the law's unwarranted assumption that truth or falsehood exhausts the field of possibility. What if propositions about the unknowable are examples of the unmeaning, like Abracadabra (7:278)? Moreover, Hamilton is using attributes of divisibility and indivisibility to define a subject to which these attributes are not even known to apply. Does the mystery of his subject not result from an illegitimate transfer of attributes from things he can touch and see to things that are imperceptible?

Mill's exposure of verbal bewitchment coincides with the method of scientific advance, which often consists in replacing fictitious theories with accurate descriptions. When the Greeks posited the existence of revolving material wheels to explain planetary motion, they were saying more than they really meant. And yet their potential explanation, however false, increased understanding. As Robert Nozick says, "seeing what in principle could give rise to a phenomenon illuminates some of its aspects by the way it latches onto these" (1981, 11). The fiction of the Greeks prepared for a less eccentric possibility when, by a great step in philosophy, "the materiality of the wheels was discarded, and the geometrical forms alone retained" (7:295). Mill values the resolve of later astronomers to emancipate the mind from a "fallacy of misplaced concreteness," as A. N. Whitehead would say, by locating the planets in a solar system containing nothing more than can be seen or verified by actual observation.

It has been said that the key to longevity is to have a chronic incurable disease and take good care of it. Mill's long and incurable disease is to be Bentham's advocate, as Huxley's is to be Darwin's bulldog and gladiator general. Their chronic and insoluble problem is how to make Darwinism and Benthamism universally applicable. Neither system of thought seems quite worth the effort, since fields like politics, poetics, and ethics may stubbornly resist the methods of each school. If Mill, for example, were as critical of utilitarian fictions as he is of the bewitchment of Sir William Hamilton's mind by metaphysical language, he might have exposed as a mere chimera, comparable to the materiality of the wheels in Greek astronomy, Hume's idea of a sympathetic observer able to maximize in his own person the total number of social satisfactions. Classical utilitarianism, as John Rawls has said, "is the ethic of perfect altruists" (1971, 189). And were Mill as rigorous in unmasking the fictions of the utilitarians as Bentham was in unmasking everybody else's fictions, he might have realized that "for a problem of justice to arise at least two persons must want to do something other than whatever everyone else wants to do. It is impossible, then, to assume that the parties are simply perfect altruists" (Rawls 1971, 189). Just as Arnold fails to see that the choice of Hellenism may rule out the benefits of Hebraism and that some values cannot live together, so Mill fails to see that, because even a benevolent utilitarian may be torn by a conflict of loves for different people, some goods can simply not be maximized simultaneously.

And yet in the hands of such undogmatic and resourceful thinkers as Mill and Huxley, an attempt to extend the legitimate province of utilitarian and Darwinian thought, pursued in a spirit of restless curiosity and wonder rather than in a mood of militant discipleship, accurately tracks the way new discoveries are made. The key to having insights and making breakthroughs is to have a chronic, insoluble problem—like the application of utilitarian principles to axiology and aesthetics, areas of inquiry where they may prove in the end to be inapplicable and alien—and to keep working on it. Mill's chief problems may be insoluble, but because they generate endless, chancy inquiries, done in puzzlement, they extend the frontiers of knowledge. Because he is always ready to inhibit utilitarian dogma and quicken truth in pursuit of the wider premise, the more inclusive synthesis, we can learn more from Mill when he is wrong than from most philosophers when they are right.

CHAPTER 16

The Critic as Detective:

Mystery and Method in *The Moonstone*

Two mystery fictions, *The Moonstone* and *The Ring and the Book*, both published in 1868, present theories of criminal detection that bear striking resemblances to theories of history proposed by Barthold Niebuhr in his *History of Rome* and by such English disciples of Niebuhr as A. P. Stanley and Thomas Arnold. Like Niebuhr's historian, the reader of *The Moonstone* has to exercise the vigilance demanded by any act of going outside oneself, any act of interpretive scrutiny. But because not even the recent events surrounding the theft of the moonstone are fully recoverable, radical faith is also necessary. Just as Niebuhr and his disciples insist that the historian must become a historical agent by exercising negative capability, so a reader of *The Moonstone* must empathize with each of Collins's narrators as he would with historical witnesses. At the same time interpreters must be critical of the witnesses, registering subtle differences between their own thought and that of witnesses belonging to a different class, like Betteredge, a different religious persuasion, like Miss Clack, or a different profession, like Mr. Bruff or Sergeant Cuff.

Browning's and Collins's true adversary turns out to be not the influential German historiographer Leopold von Ranke, who is too often narrowly opposed to the historians I have named, but the positivist historian H. T. Buckle, who tries to make history into a statistical science.[1] Is history the recovery of data that allow the

1. In his *History of Civilization in England*, originally published in 1857, H. T. Buckle argues, for example, that "it is now known that marriages bear a fixed and definite relation to the price of corn; and in England the experience of a century has proved that, instead of having a connexion with personal feelings, [marriages] are simply regulated by the average earnings of the great mass of the people" (1864, 1:23–24). For a timely caveat against too ready and uncritical an assimilation of Leopold von Ranke's theory of history to the positivist school of Buckle, see Mary Ellis Gibson, *History and the Prism of Art: Browning's Poetic Experiments* (1987, esp. 6, 68–69).

statistician to make accurate predictions? Or is history an open, self-constituting process, as David Friedrich Strauss assumes at the left-wing, Hegelian end of the spectrum? Because history as self-making seems to be in conflict with history as a synonym for the statistically quantified and given, every attempt in *The Moonstone* and *The Ring and the Book* to combine these two contradictory views of history—the Hegelian and the positivist—precipitates a crisis in representation. Despite the like-sounding names of the detective and the lawyer in *The Moonstone*, for example, the contradictory methods of Sergeant Cuff and Mr. Bruff have to be carefully distinguished. Truth that evolves historically in Strauss's sense is not at first accessible, because it does not authentically exist until an investigator like Collins's Ezra Jennings devises an experiment to discover it. Jennings is a heroic thinker, prepared like Sergeant Cuff to take a leap of faith over the chasm separating his beliefs from their grounds, even though he tries hard, like Mr. Bruff, to verify each of his hypotheses.

Mr. Bruff is the H. T. Buckle of *The Moonstone*, and Sergeant Cuff the David Friedrich Strauss. The one is a mere inductive logician, too passively deferential to so-called facts, the other a poet manqué, eager to weave mythic constructions. Cuff tends to make the truth more complicated and ingenious, more like a detective novel, than it really is. The true detective, by contrast, has the qualities of a good historian. Like Ezra Jennings, he has the imaginative sympathy necessary to become the person whose life he is trying to reconstruct. Such a detective-historian must possess the negative capability Keats associates with the poetic temperament. Instead of being imperious and dictatorial, imposing his own ideas on others, he is as humble before their experience as Bacon's scientist is before the facts of nature. By comparing Ezra Jennings's self-effacing character and his methods of detection with those of Bruff and Sergeant Cuff, we can better understand why Collins writes the fiction he does. To read the novel as Collins has written it every reader must become a kind of Ezra Jennings, supplying the missing elements by practicing a version of Jennings's own arts of impersonation and empathy.

The French, English, and German sides of Blake's character are versions of the three methods of historical reconstruction and criminal detection Collins explores. Misty German metaphysics inclines to imaginative constructions more ingenious than the truth. And English empirical methods tend to be too naively inductive. Only the French method seems capable of perfecting a genuine experiment in the arts of detection. Having lost himself in a maze of useless speculation, Blake receives Betteredge's letter mentioning Ezra Jennings, and immediately afterward Blake devises a more rational procedure, a product of his clear-headed French side, that anticipates Jennings's own methods of inquiry.

If Candy were not actually deprived of his memory, the scene in which he summons Blake to impart information he cannot quite remember in narrative 3, chapter 8, would be a simple repetition of the practical joke he plays on Blake at the dinner party (first period, chap. 10). The unintended insult about Candy's having to make a memorandum to remind him what he wants to say also recalls Blake's cruel joke at the dinner, when he equates a course of groping in the dark with a course in medicine. Now Blake seems to be implying that as a result of his fever Candy is literally groping in the dark. Instead of being overbearing and insensitive, however, as he was at the party, Blake is a model of discretion. He has to raise a delicate subject—what the mentally enfeebled Candy actually remembers—without seeming to insult him. Intricate maneuvering and indirection are at war with the desire to learn something. Blake even allows Candy his innocent deception. The trite comment about the pleasant party allows Candy to save face by sustaining the fiction that he has a clear memory of an event Blake himself has admittedly forgotten. There is an oddly subliminal feel to the whole scene. It is just similar enough to the events of the dinner party to give the reader a sense that he has experienced a version of this exchange before.

In the earlier scene, the comedy of the disastrous birthday dinner dramatizes each character's inability to command quite the right tone of persiflage or banter. The party could be out of *Barchester Towers* or *Emma*. But as at Ullathorne or the Box Hill picnic, the comedy is inseparable from the moral seriousness. Indelicacy toward the feelings of other people, to invoke Mr. Knightley's criterion of ungentlemanly behavior, offends against moral as well as social proprieties. All we can hear in this comedy of misapprehension and unintended insults is a cacophony of voices talking past each other or at cross-purposes. In his exchange with Mrs. Threadgall, as in his joking with Blake a moment later, Candy is a puzzling mixture of solicitude and obtuseness. He is indelicate because of his inattention to Mrs. Threadgall's widowhood. But he is also civil and generous, eager to help the professor by recommending he consult some "remarkably fine skeletons . . . at the College of Surgeons" (first period, chap. 10). No one knows how to gauge the doctor's tone. Is he making a macabre joke about a dead professor, now a skeleton in his grave, about to pay a visit to other skeletons? Is he trying to insult the widow, amuse her, or simply be indecorously civil? "The loud cheerful voice" in which he offers his comment suggests he is really talking past his auditor, addressing the company in general, and so committing an unwitting indiscretion in a desperate effort to keep the conversation going.

But the more times Mrs. Threadgall tells Candy her husband is dead, the less he seems to hear. Candy is not really addressing Mrs. Threadgall at all. Because he is a kind of comic-opera version of the doctor, entertaining the company at large with amusing anecdotes, he fails to register the cues she keeps sending him. Her discreet euphemism, "My beloved husband is no more," twice repeated, yields first to the ironic metaphor identifying the professor's present address as the grave and then to an exasperated overflow of direct speech: "The Professor has been dead these ten years." When Candy blurts out, "Oh, good heavens," realizing now that nothing can redeem his indiscretion, indecorous giggling by the two Ablewhite girls is followed by embarrassed silence, as if everyone present had just seen the professor's ghost.

At the birthday dinner Blake proves just as incapable as Candy of commanding the right tone. He seems to be performing on a revolving stage, and he gives the wrong performance to each of his changing audiences. He talks as an Hegelian Idealist to a pragmatic English authority on cattle breeding and as a racy French wit to a staid Victorian spinster. The proper way to breed bulls, he tells the cattle breeder, is to look deep into your own mind, evolve out of it the idea of a perfect bull, and produce him. In poking fun at the Oxford of Jowett and the Cairds, and at the incessant Platonizing of Hegel, Collins is gently ridiculing the overly ingenious deductions of a historian-detective like Cuff, the fictional counterpart of a German Higher Critic like Strauss. Betteredge is also critical of Blake's disdain for facts, for what Yeats calls "this pragmatical, preposterous pig of a world" ("Blood and the Moon," l. 26). The conservative defender of England's vested interests is inappropriately answered in Blake's Italian, aesthetic manner. If our ancient safeguards are lost, we still have three things left: love, music, salad. But even when the German manner is discarded in favor of the Italian, Hegelian triads survive as a formal feature of the rhetoric. A moment later, Blake drops foreign smoothness and becomes openly insulting, exposing in his banter with Candy his brusquer English side.

The one character who remains a mystery, even at the end, is Jennings. The sympathetic imagination that allows him to identify with Candy, Blake, and most of the other characters seems to prevent his having any history of his own. He wants to obliterate his past, to be as silent and untroublesome as possible. Not only are Jennings's diary, in many locked volumes, and his unfinished book buried in his coffin, but he also insists that his grave be unmarked. Such a grave is a fitting memorial of the detective-historian of true negative capability, who is as self-effacing as the alloy that mixes with the gold in *The Ring and the Book*.

Candy's drugging of the drink requires a reader to compare three texts: Betteredge's summary of the heated exchange between Candy and Blake during the birthday dinner; Jennings's transcript of Candy's "wanderings" during his fever; and Jennings's interpretation of that transcript, including its red-ink supplements. Comparing the three texts reveals that at no time are the facts to be found in an uninterpreted or undistorted form. Betteredge's account would more nearly approximate a reliable firsthand transcript had he reported the actual conversation instead of a mere summary of it in indirect discourse. In some details, Jennings's black-ink transcript of Candy's mental wanderings is more accurate than Betteredge's account of the dinner, because in addition to reporting the spirited banter recorded by Betteredge, it provides Candy's own thoughts about Blake, whom Candy finds generally agreeable. In Betteredge's narrative Candy's temporary disappearance from the room, and his mysterious return, are all but buried in a heap of trivia. Only in Jennings's transcript does the purpose of Candy's disappearance—to obtain laudanum—begin to be clarified.

The equivalences that Candy finds hard to reproduce in his delirium are supplied with resource and ingenuity by Jennings. Roman Jakobson (1956) would say that Candy's highly elliptical discourse exhibits traits of similarity-disorder. Prepositions and connectives survive intact, but nouns and synonyms tend to disappear. The name "Blake" is produced with some difficulty, and the synonyms he wants to apply—"agreeable," "clever" (narrative 3, chap. 10)—can be supplied only in part. The repeating elements tend to be spatial prepositions like "down," twice repeated, and unattached adjectives like "excellent," also twice repeated. Toward the end of the transcript, the preposition "out" and its variants start to multiply at an alarming rate. The needle seems to stick in one of the patient's mental grooves, and advance becomes difficult. Because Candy's power to name and find synonyms is impaired, he seems constantly in danger of saying everything about nothing. Sergeant Cuff, in his eccentric search for novel solutions, sometimes faces the opposite problem of saying nothing provable or factual about anything. Jennings, as usual, finds a middle ground by recovering some of the metaphors that Candy's metonymies have elided or suppressed.

Jennings's humanitarian concern for his employer, Candy, qualifies him as an ideal detective and solver of mysteries. By contrast, Bruff errs on the side of legalistic pendantry, like Browning's advocates in *The Ring and the Book*, and Sergeant Cuff errs on the side of deductive ingenuity and of a rationalism that has lost direction. Whereas Bruff is deficient in imagination and has to be tutored by the more resourceful Mr. Murthwaite, Cuff is always in danger of being carried away by his own ingenuity, making the truth more complex than it is.

In dramatizing the defect of the unimaginative Bruff, Collins shows that this empirical solicitor admits only evidence that would persuade a court of law. In playing the public prosecutor, for example, Bruff begins assailing Miss Clack as he would a defense attorney for Godfrey Ablewhite. Three pieces of evidence implicate her client: he was in the house the night the diamond was stolen; he was the first person to leave for London afterward; and he was mauled by rogues who seem involved in the diamond's theft. By introducing the kind of circumstantial evidence that would carry weight in a court of law, Bruff finds arguments that would also be useful to a historian-detective trying to reconstruct events in the recent past. But Bruff is lost when he can no longer recreate the world in the image of a courtroom.

He relishes the logical and rhetorical maneuvers of a court case, admiring the skill with which Miss Clack has momentarily caught him off guard, opening "the full fire" of her "batteries" on him when he "least expected it" (narrative 1, chap. 3). By insinuating that Rachel, in Cuff's view, is an unreliable witness and possibly has stolen her own diamond, Miss Clack has tricked Bruff into admitting that Rachel is absolutely to be relied on. Once Bruff has rallied to Rachel's defense, Miss Clack can spring the trap of her cleverly constructed dilemma. If Rachel is to be trusted with her own diamond, then she is also to be trusted in her strenuous defense of Ablewhite. It is logically inconsistent to accept her testimony about one matter and discredit it about another. This is the legal equivalent of peripeteia on the stage. And Bruff admits temporary defeat as Miss Clack gloats at her "unholy" triumph. But when she tries to press home a second forensic victory, arguing that the same circumstance that implicates Ablewhite in the theft also implicates Blake, Bruff withdraws his praise. The touch of hypocritical self-deprecation in her use of the word "unholy" has already diluted her triumph for the reader. And even the most ardent feminist critic half approves when Mr. Bruff, having just conceded defeat, blunts his compliment by saying that Miss Clack would have done great things as a lawyer if only she had been a man. As a woman, presumably, she is inferior and still excluded from his circle.

In a codalike summation, as if he were delivering a peroration to a jury, Bruff reduces the arguments against Blake to a threefold absurdity. Yet Bruff's own bewilderment—"it baffles me, it baffles you, it baffles everybody"—discloses a chink in his armor. He unwittingly gives the clue that should alert readers to his own deficiencies. "What is the use of my experience," he asks, "what is the use of any person's experience, in such a case as that?" (narrative 1, chap. 3). Like Jeremy Bentham, Bruff is an empiricist whose own experience is too limited. Moreover, were he a consistent empiricist, he should be more critical of the evidence supplied by Miss Clack and Rachel in support of Godfrey's innocence. Too deferential to the evidence of his senses, Bruff is quick to take offense at the vulgar Mr. Luker but is illogically charmed by the more dangerous Indian visitor, who is grave, gracious, and polite and speaks excellent English (narrative 2, chap. 2). Bruff is just the kind of empiricist to be deceived by the gracious Indian, in whom doing and being seem curiously at odds. Camouflage is part of the Indian's stock-in-trade. He is not trying to secure a loan but wants to gain a piece of information extraneous to the nominal purpose of his visit. Bruff, who believes in transparent continuities, is out of his depth when confronted with this puzzling personification of duplicity, an expert in deception. It is no wonder that Bruff needs the subtler, more Socratic Murthwaite to instruct him.

In contrast to Bruff, Sergeant Cuff is a student of double meaning and duplicity. An empiricist like Bruff, accepting the evidence of his senses, suspects Ablewhite stole the diamond, because he is the kind of hypocrite and scoundrel who would stoop to theft. But a suspicious interpreter like Cuff tends to suspect innocent-looking people like Rachel. What Rachel's probity *means* is undone by the *way* it means. The withholding of what she has seen Blake do destroys each interpreter's position, Cuff's as well as Bruff's. To preserve Rachel's innocence, the empirical Bruff must treat her refusal to tell Frank what she sees as unmotivated and out of character. To affirm continuity, in other words, he must deny it. Conversely, in construing Rachel's behavior as perfectly in character for a deceptive person, the suspicious Cuff is affirming the very principle of continuity he is pledged to deny. In order to deny continuity, both interpreters must affirm it. Readers who try to adjudicate the dispute find themselves back in Jennings's camp. To judge between the naïveté of the empiricist and the suspicions of the ironist, for whom realities are never what they seem to be, an interpreter like Jennings must be attuned to both conscious and unconscious meanings. The differences between the detective's and the lawyer's ways of interpreting (Cuff inviting comparison with Bruff) are shown to be based on a repression of differences within a more comprehensive act of reconstructing a recent past event. Jennings proves that powerful but subtle effects of both suspicion and trust, irony and innocence, are already at work within the illusion of a binary opposition between induction and deduction, between deference to facts and a distrust of facts, each of which is superseded by his own more inclusive methods of inquiry.

The division between Sergeant Cuff's private and public lives, the key to his character, is continuous with his suspicion that other characters are not what they seem. Indeed Cuff, a detective by vocation, chooses roses as his avocation in order to create as wide a rift as possible between the two. "Show me any two things more opposite one from the other than a rose and a thief; and I'll correct my tastes accordingly" (first period, chap. 12). He cultivates oddity in order to exercise his keen distrust of any congruity between form and meaning. Cuff is even prepared to sacrifice to the shock effect of a witticism or a neatly turned antithesis the real complexities of the case. Like Browning's Gigadibs, he is in quest of such journalistic paradoxes as the tender murderer or superstitious atheist and is enamored of the perpetual contradictions that seem to characterize Blake.

Truth in criminal investigations is an imagination that succeeds, an intuition that happens to guess the art of deception in its practiced forms. Cuff is a good psychologist and tactful diplomat, but many of his hunches are wrong. His deductions are therefore a tissue of true insight, partial apprehension, and outright error. From the correct assumption that the diamond has been lost, he passes too hastily to the surprising announcement that nobody has stolen the diamond (first period, chap. 12). That statement is untrue in the sense Cuff intends it but true in a sense that Cuff himself does not yet understand. Committed to the belief that signs are ambiguous and face several ways at once, Cuff may discern duplicity where it does not exist, in a character like Rachel. And he may miss the duplicity that is really there, in the split between conscious and unconscious experience in Franklin Blake.

What Betteredge says of Rachel's interpretation of Cuff might apply with equal propriety to Cuff's own methods of investigation: he interprets everything "in a glass darkly" (first period, chap. 13). Usually Cuff would prefer to be a Socratic midwife rather than a direct purveyor of information: thus when Betteredge asks for a name, Cuff encourages him to provide it himself. Like Sherlock Holmes, Cuff is also a master of mental broad jumps, able to connect a murder with "a spot of ink on a tablecloth" (first period, chap. 12). There is always a danger, however, that "detective-fever," as Betteredge calls it, may be a disease of Cuff's imagination, a merely fanciful use of the investigator's faculties. One symptom of "detective-fever" is a tendency to make everyone as subtle and suspicious as the detective. If the footsteps on the sand are confused, it is because their suspect wanted them to be confused. "I don't want to hurt your feelings," Cuff tells Betteredge, "but I'm afraid Rosanna is sly" (first period, chap. 15). Everyone is "sly" to Cuff, because duplicity is the idol of his cave. Cuff is so accustomed to secrecy and cunning in himself and others that he often withholds information when there is nothing to hide.

Collins's use of multiple narrators resembles Browning's experiment in *The Ring and the Book*, but Browning's poem retells essentially the same events. There is a deepening of meaning, but no advance in the story. For Browning's nonprogressive narrative, Collins substitutes a slowly advancing story that is often impeded by detours, digressions, and unheard words. A generalized asyndeton dismantles continuity. Immediately after the theft, for example, Rachel's conversation with Blake is witnessed through a window, and so her words are not reported. We know Rachel is angry, but we never hear what she says. Even if that conversation was reported, it would have a blank in the middle of it. For Rachel, we later learn, does not tell Blake what she has seen him do. The most important meanings are elided, either because conversations are seen but not heard, or else because conversations are really nonconversations—speeches that omit the most important information the speaker has to impart. Speaking at cross-purposes may induce silence in others. Insisting he will bring the thief to justice, Blake speaks when he should have been silent. As a consequence, Rachel is silent about something she should have said.[2]

Two of Collins's narrators, Betteredge and Blake, narrate more than once. Two of Browning's narrators in *The Ring and the Book*, the implied author of the first and closing books and Guido, also narrate twice. But there is little sense of temporal flow in Browning's poem. If time enters at all, it enters as a kind of spatialized fourth dimension. The time warp of Guido's second monologue is different from the warp of his first monologue. In *The Moonstone*, by contrast, time moves in a self-retarding spiral. It advances even as it coils back on itself in impeding loops.

Insisting in a footnote (first narrative, chap. 1) that it is important

2. Collins is a master of the mystifying use of silence. Like the unheard words that pass between Rachel Verinder and Franklin Blake, as Betteredge observes them through a window in *The Moonstone*, the dumb show in Collins's stage version of *The Woman in White* (Houghton MS. *Ec 85. C6977. 871W [B]) greatly intensifies the mystery. In revising act 1 of the script, Collins adds a silent version of Count Fosco's entreaty to the birds before presenting an audible version. Later Laura Fairlie, with her back to the audience, speaks to Walter in dumb show before exiting. Like the unheard words in *The Moonstone*, these silent conversations are often more memorable than the conversations we hear.

his adversary, Miss Clack, be allowed to indulge her eccentricities and thus expose her true character, Blake is doing as editor what Browning does in the first book of *The Ring and the Book*: he is "baring the device," as the Russian formalists would say, or "tipping his hand." The fancy or prejudice of each witness is exposing or undoing itself as crude alloy in the very act of showing that without the alloy no meaning could ever be recovered. Fancy is the indispensable condition of displaying any fact, of making it malleable. Without the alloy the gold of fact, so prized by empiricists like Betteredge and Mr. Bruff, could never be displayed. History is more than an imaginative invention, but it is never available as a given. Its grounds must always be painstakingly recovered through imaginative identification with historical witnesses and agents. Hence, as in the theories of history championed by Barthold Niebuhr and his disciples, the need to empathize with a colorful gallery of eccentrics and their conflicting testimonies can never be dispensed with. Historical reconstruction, like detective work, is most successful when it clearly acknowledges its reliance on imaginative appropriation and empathy. According to Niebuhr, whom Jowett credits with founding the modern school of biblical criticism a generation before Strauss, the historian will write better about the past, and his "interest...will be the deeper, the greater the events he has witnessed with a bleeding or a rejoicing heart" (Niebuhr 1831–32, 1:xiii). Betteredge's partisanship—his sympathy for the hapless Rosanna and his friendship with Blake—no more disqualifies him as a witness than Jennings's sympathy for Candy during his illness disqualifies him as a transcriber and interpreter of the doctor's mental "wanderings." On the contrary, far from being an impediment, the imaginative interest of a partisan is an asset in any detective or historian. As in any storm front, serious imbalances will rectify themselves. A zealous partisan like the irrepressible Miss Clack is certain to redress any excess of sympathy Betteredge expresses for the editor.

Both Collins and Browning recognize that history is a fiction, a story we make up about the past. And if faith is to be faith in history, as Thomas Arnold had argued, then it must be faith in something that is now irrecoverable. The elusiveness of history has another cause: the limits of language. Like Carlyle in his essay "On History," Browning has an acute awareness that "Narrative is *linear*; Action is *solid*" (Carlyle 1899, 27:89). Even when the poet can approximate a past event, how can he or the historian represent a three-dimensional object in two-dimensional language? It seems to me that the real answer to the important question Carlyle posed in "On History" lies in the historian's use of multiple narrators, such as Collins deploys in *The

Moonstone and Browning in *The Ring and the Book,* or else in the ability of a poet like Browning to perfect a poetry of silence, whose true meanings transpire between caesural pauses and dashes. Effects of simultaneity in Browning depend also on his uncanny power to reinvent the English language. The long grammatically suspended sentences in *The Ring and the Book* or *Sordello,* interrupted by branching modifiers and parentheses, counter the tendency of normal English to break thought down into its smallest, self-contained components. When Browning, like Hopkins or Carlyle, seems to do violence to ordinary English, he is using a form of shock therapy to expose the injuries the language has allowed itself to suffer. These injuries are a result of prescribing clarity at all costs, in the manner of Bentham, whose edicts are rigidly enforced by a grammar that solidifies action into static nouns and that substitutes products for processes, properties for actions and histories.

Collins's and Browning's theory of historical appropriation was defined most clearly six years after *The Moonstone* and *The Ring and the Book* appeared by the philosopher F. H. Bradley in his pamphlet *The Presuppositions of Critical History.* When a historian-detective reconstructs the past, Bradley argued, it is not *in spite of* the presuppositions and biases that oblige him to relive the past from his own point of view, but *because* of them. "To assert within the sphere of history the existence of any causes or effects, except on the conviction that there is now for us something analogous to them, is no better than a self-contradiction," Bradley insisted (1874, 101). The requisite analogies and sympathetic identification are possessed preeminently by Ezra Jennings, and they make him the hero of the novel, just as similar qualities make Dorothea Brooke the heroine of *Middlemarch.* Every historian and detective, in seeking analogies between himself and some event in the past, is using a combination of method and mystery. There are methodical ways of testing analogies, but there is no rule to be learned for inventing them. Every history is self-replicating, because one of the truths it maps is the truth that every history is about the historian, every act of detection about the detective himself. Collins dramatizes this paradox most forcefully in the case of Blake. When Blake opens the box containing the smeared gown Rosanna Spearman buried, he experiences J. H. Newman's shock in the *Apologia* when he looks into the mirror—the mirror of historical analogy—and discovers to his horror that the face that stares back is the face of a heretic, a Monophysite. Blake has been searching outside himself for a truth that is inside him all the time. That is why the most important discovery comes when the buried knowledge of his own crime swims into focus, like repressed materials coming to consciousness in psycho-analysis. The final mystery is oneself, the soul, which in its myriad facets can be seen only as it is reflected from the testimonies of other characters, like an image in a mirror.

CHAPTER 17

Browning and Mystery: *The Ring*

and the Book and Modern Theory

Problems associated with contemporary deconstruction and hermeneutics were familiar to Browning, and he already understood them
in his Roman murder mystery, *The Ring and the Book*. This conclusion
may seem less contentious if we recall that critical theories, though
rich in their accidental varieties, are poor in their essential types.
Deconstruction, for example, was a favorite exercise of Victorians like
Pater, who dismantled metaphysics in *Plato and Platonism*, and of the
agnostic theologian H. L. Mansel, who dissolved the idea of God into
logically contradictory concepts in *The Limits of Religious Thought*. Mansel
takes the idea of the infinite, the idea of the absolute, and the idea of
a first cause and argues that they cannot all be predicated of God at the
same time. As for hermeneutics, though it is sometimes said to be an
invention of Schleiermacher in the nineteenth century, it is surely as
venerable a pursuit as patristic exegesis and as old as biblical commentary itself. Let me proceed at once to a definition of terms. By
deconstruction I mean Browning's subversive use of double binds and
antinomies; and by hermeneutics I mean his study of the simultaneous preservation and transformation of a text's original meaning. In
The Ring and the Book Browning comes to deconstruction via a
hermeneutical dilemma. The more scrupulously he tries to transcribe
his source book's facts—the facts in the Old Yellow Book—the
stranger, more "invented," they appear to be. The passage of events
into history is not itself fictional. But every story an interpreter makes
up about the past, especially if it is the story of a partisan or an
advocate, is precisely that: a historical fiction or a fictional history. As
J. Hillis Miller has said of both *The Ring and the Book* and Melville's
Benito Cereno, "knowledge of the historical sources makes the story

based on them not less but more inscrutable, more difficult to understand" (1982, 37). The more Browning wrestles with this dilemma, the more double binds and contradictions of other kinds he discovers. For example, a doctrine of historical continuity is developed by Browning's pope, who discerns behind the literal events of the Roman murder story the lineaments of a biblical myth of rescue and deliverance. Opposed to his belief in a continuing Bible or testament is the assumption of discontinuity favored by the skeptics, Tertium Quid and Guido. This opposition, which pervades the poem, starts to unravel, however (in a process critics have not so far discussed), when Browning shows how opposite critical methods unexpectedly converge. Thus to accept the premise of Pompilia and Caponsacchi that truth is constant and that surface meanings do not deceive is to interpret events the way Guido, the skeptical exposer of discontinuity, finally does. Guido insists that he is fiercely loyal to a single set of values. *He* is more consistent that his *adversaries*. If the pope decides to play Higher Critic and changes the rules halfway through the game, why should Guido be punished for being more consistent? Conversely, to argue like Guido that action and being are fatally at odds in the adulterous priest who masquerades as a deliverer and in the unfaithful wife who pretends to be undefiled and pure is also to interpret events the way Caponsacchi and Pompilia do. For it is to allow for right-angled conversions and for the discovery of hidden moral and theological meanings in a story that means more than it appears to mean. Caponsacchi, after all, is what Kierkegaard would call "a knight of the hidden inwardness." He wears a mask or incognito: he is *not* the worldly cleric he *seems* to be. The same is true of Pompilia: she lives from a depth of inwardness that cannot be outwardly expressed. And so, as in many deconstructionist readings, to interpret suspiciously or inconsistently like Guido is also to interpret consistently or in a spirit of faith, like Pompilia and Caponsacchi, and vice versa. There seems to be no way out of this double bind.

When Browning's narrator in book 12 asserts that human speech is naught and all testimony false (12.838–39), he is laying claim to knowledge of the ultimate order of things—a knowledge for which his own theory of consistent skepticism makes no provision. Browning seems aware of this contradiction. How can his narrator deplore the general warping of critical insight and still maintain the fiction that his own superior mind is unaffected by the general distemper? His irony is necessarily a two-edged sword. There is no possibility of reserving enlightenment for the narrator and consigning all other interpreters to darkness. Any systematic school of suspicion includes the skeptic in its net. Though the discrepant testaments of *The Ring*

and the Book and the endless progeny of critical commentary that such
testaments breed are all problematic, all equally suspect, the pervasive
skepticism of Browning's own narrator in book 12 obliquely elevates
the subversion of standards into exactly such a standard—one that is
miraculously true of every testimony it examines. The program of
dismantling a center by leading us through a centerless labyrinth
implies recognition of a center after all. Unlike modern deconstructionists, however, Browning finds such dismantling as riddled with
contradiction as any theoretical position he tries to dismantle. The
narrator in book 12 is no more exempt from Browning's irony than
any other commentator. When criticism cannot become a systematic
body of coherent premises, arguments, and conclusions, then it may
degenerate into an effort by each commentator to impose his own
ideas by sheer force of will.

The clash of judgments among *The Ring and the Book*'s speakers
replicates itself in a clash of opinion among the poem's readers.
Carlyle thought that Pompilia was guilty; Judge J. M. Gest insisted
that "Caponsacchi was a frivolous young fellow,... light in thought
and unscrupulous in action" (1925, 624); and Morse Peckham has
concluded that Browning never presumes to resolve the issue (1970,
124–25).[1] Such continuation of a critical quarrel that the poem itself
initiates assimilates events of the narrative to events of reading in the
approved poststructuralist manner. Equally prophetic of some contemporary attitudes is the impatience of Tertium Quid, who despairs
of criticism altogether. To the ironists and the literalists Tertium Quid
says in effect, "a plague on both your houses." He reminds us that
double irony is evasive. The trick of presuming to understand both
sides at once but favoring neither is liable to be unpopular in any
historical period, not just among contemporary adversaries of
deconstruction. As poststructuralist critics like to point out, the deeds
of the characters are also the reverse of what we might expect from
their nature. The pope is sententious and reflective, yet in sentencing
Guido on impulse he commits a violent act. What the sentencing of
Guido means is undone by the *way* it means. The judgment and
deliverance should be justified as instances of continuity between

---

1. J. M. Gest, *The Old Yellow Book* (1925, 624). Morse Peckham, in "Personality and the
Mask of Knowledge" (1970, 124–25), writes: "There is no doubt that [Browning]
believes he has found the truth of the story, the answer to the only real problem in it:
Was Pompilia guilty of adultery with Caponsacchi? His answer is no, yet so well had he
worked that Carlyle, for example, said it was obvious she was guilty. The argument over
whether Browning had found the 'truth' of the matter, which has gone on for a
hundred years, is quite beside the point, as so much of Browning criticism is beside the
point. He does not assert that he has found what the truth really is, or even what it was,
but only that he has found a 'truth' which is satisfactory to *him*."

being and doing. But the way these acts are done affirms a discrepancy between being and doing that calls into question the principle affirmed.

As the deconstructionists of *The Ring and the Book*, Tertium Quid and Guido deserve brief separate treatment. Like some deconstructionists, Tertium Quid constructs aporias and antinomies with a facility that is mechanical and at times almost mindless. Forgetting that the mind's ability to lose facts unpredictably and to get relations wrong distinguishes it from an archival bank or a computer, Tertium Quid tries to feed every fact through a grid of disjunctive propositions. He thwarts the intellect by contriving to trap it inside two alternatives that are made to exhaust the field of possibility. As in any disjunctive proposition, p and q cannot both be true, though there is no way of deciding which of the logically contradictory propositions is true and which is false. Tertium Quid is so wedded to disjunction as an interpretive method that he even splits apart so undivided and spontaneous an act as Caponsacchi's decision to leap forward at once as Pompilia's champion. Tertium Quid must first invent a counterspeech for Caponsacchi, in which the priest counsels Pompilia to bear alone the heavy burden of her marriage, before inventing a speech pledging his service to her, which he then pronounces "best" (4.826).

Tertium Quid realizes that if Caponsacchi makes the right choice, there is no way of knowing he makes it, since to "try" the "truth . . . by instinct" (4.1009) is to dispense by definition with rational proof. Either Guido was jealous of Caponsacchi and tortured Pompilia because he suspected her of committing adultery (4.914–15), or else he was not jealous and wanted Pompilia to leave behind her dowry by eloping with the priest (4.749–55). Since the two alternatives are in logical contradiction, one must be false. But since they exhaust the field of possibility—either Guido was jealous or he was not, either he plotted in cold blood or he acted out of passion—one alternative must be true. Which that alternative is, however, Tertium Quid has no logical way of knowing. Tertium Quid realizes that either people are not what they seem, or else being and action are in contradiction. But Guido, who avows consistency between his action and his being, ironically charges Caponsacchi, the priest whose incognito as an eloper hides his reserves of faith and inwardness, with the greater consistency in vice. And Caponsacchi, sworn to discontinuity between mask and motive, action and being, charges his adversary Guido with the greater inconsistency in pretending to be what he is not. If Caponsacchi "must look to men more skilled / In reading hearts than ever was the world" (4.1111–12), then he must seek an interpreter like Tertium Quid who can accept the principle of discontinuity without being immobilized by the uncertainty that results from any incessant use of disjunction and any incessant exposure of contradiction and deceit.

So much for Tertium Quid. What about Guido? Like some analytic philosophers of language, Guido is a reductive interpreter, a Benthamite, who is resolved to make comprehensible the great mystery words of his adversaries—faith, love, religion, truth—even if he must explain them away in the process. In Guido's two orations everything is subject to reductionist explanations except reductionism itself. Should a thoroughgoing reductionism like Guido's not be courageous enough to reduce and devalue even itself? Should Guido not perceive that he is debunking Pompilia and Caponsacchi out of a resentful envy of their values? In rooting out the concealed poetry in language, Guido even tries to revise downward the mystique attaching to his own social rank. He shows how simple supply and demand curves useful in economics can be made to quantify and give exact, noninflationary meaning to a mystery word like "count," which he can then, like the duke of Ferrara, barter on the market "with all other ware" (5.463).

To convince the court of his honest resolve to strip away all false pretense, Guido concedes that he forced Pompilia to trace over the letters he had written in her confession. But this admission of coercion is a more damaging concession than Guido seems to realize (5.845–47), since how can we reconcile Guido's exposure of deceit in his present oration with the general condition of deceit that must exist throughout the monologue if the exposure is true? If the confession of pervasive deceit is true, it seems to follow it cannot be true. The only escape from this dilemma seems to be the axiom that an offhand admission of deceit like Guido's may have greater validity than direct testimony because, as Levi Hedge observes in his *Elements of Logick*, a book highly esteemed by Browning's father, "there is less reason" to apprehend in any act of casual self-incrimination a "deliberate intention to deceive" (1816, 112).

So far I have been concentrating on the exposure of double binds and contradictions appropriate to skeptics like Tertium Quid and Guido, the principal deconstructionists of the poem. Equally prophetic of modern theory is the hermeneutical criticism of Browning's pope. Distinguishing between the Bible's essential meaning and the accidental significance it acquires for particular readers, the pope asks how a sacred text can have both an original meaning and a new meaning for each successive generation. Faith in Christianity seems to be faith in a historically grounded religion. But the pope recognizes that this claim is paradoxical. For if faith is to be faith in history, as

Thomas Arnold had insisted, then, as the skeptical W. G. Ward argued as early as 1841, in a review of Arnold's *Sermons*,[2] it must be faith in a fiction we make up about the past, or else faith in something that once happened but is now irrecoverable. Moreover, even if the past could be recovered, how could an adventurous knight of faith like Caponsacchi have faith in what is merely given? Such historical faith does not seem to qualify as faith at all, for like any proof that bludgeons its opponents, reducing them to silence, it leaves no room for free assent. Christianity is a historical faith only in an altered nineteenth-century sense of the word "historical," which equates history not with the antecedently given, but with a self-constituting process of development through time. Truth that evolves historically in this second sense is not at first expressible, because it does not authentically exist until knights of faith like Caponsacchi will it into being. Though history as self-making appears to be at odds with history as a synonym for the received and given, only some combination of these two easily confused and incompatible theories of history seems to explain how both the transformation and the preservation of biblical meaning is possible.

The object of the pope's faith is the proclamation that Pompilia was delivered and saved. She has to be offered up to another world before her goodness deteriorates. In a sense Guido is required to play the role of priest, sacrificing his wife so that she can die without blemish. Her great love for Caponsacchi, like Juliet's for Romeo, does not go wrong. It goes in the only way it can go—out of this world, which is also the way Christ's love went. The hermeneutical dilemma facing Browning's pope is that his faith in the resurrected or redeemed Pompilia, which is his equivalent of the Gospel's proclaiming faith in the risen Christ, does not involve any assent to a verifiable proposition. It is not an assent to a scientific classification, nor is it grounded ultimately in the kind of historical or factual evidence admissible in a court of law. Such laws have only a negative function. They can tell us what cannot have happened but can offer no proof of what did happen.

"Unless you introduce the 'resurrection,'" says Henry Melvill, the preacher who most influenced the young Browning, "you will not make intelligible 'the life'" (1838, 111). As a continuing Bible, *The Ring and the Book* proclaims the importance of "resurrection experiences" that break through the barrier dividing life from death. The

2. W. G. Ward asserts that "history by itself, if we knew it ten times better than we do, could prove little or nothing" (1841, 318).

pope distinguishes between the knight of faith and the historical Caponsacchi, between the hidden Word through whom God shows just "sufficient of His light / For us i' the dark to rise by" (7. 1844–45), and Caponsacchi, the public figure, who is half an embarrassment to the court, just as the historical Jesus was clearly an embarrassment to the establishment that had to deal with him. We begin to know God only when we know we know nothing about him. The imminent deaths of Pompilia and the pope invite us to discover the connection between death and the kind of goodness that must pass out of the world because, like Christ's goodness, that is where it already is.

An extraordinary experience, too good for this world, can break down the barriers not just between life and death, but also between life as we live it now and life as it might be lived. We can experience new life when we allow our faith in someone like Pompilia or Caponsacchi to articulate a new understanding of human possibility. One does not first call Caponsacchi an exemplar of Christ and then experience an enlargement of life. It works the other way round. Grasping the significance of what redemption might be like enlarges and liberates the reader. Radical faith depends on an act of God that, though historical, is also curiously transhistorical. The pope's belief seems to be both an object of historical knowledge and *not* such an object. But if faith has no historical content, it seems difficult to distinguish from Guido's formless faith, which is faith in nothing.

I associate "formless faith" with Paul Tillich's idea that faith cannot be identified with conscious assent to any truth. Faith is present whenever ultimate concern is expressed, and this concern—a theological equivalent of I. A. Richards's doctrine of "objectless beliefs"—is independent of any particular symbols or beliefs (Tillich 1951, 1:11–15). Though Browning refuses to embrace such a formless faith, he is equally critical of any kind of historical faith. If history is the basis of saving faith, it also seems to follow that it is not such a basis, for historical facts are never recoverable. Truths of faith are never identical with historical truths anyway, and it is a disastrous distortion of faith to confuse them. The Higher Criticism cannot erode the grounds of saving faith. All it can subvert are the grounds of historical faith, which for Browning's pope is never real faith at all.

Despite what the pope says about correcting the portrait by the living face (10.1873), Browning knows he can never get behind the pictures to encounter the historical Pompilia or the historical Mrs. Browning, any more than he can ever encounter the historical Jesus. And even if he could, it would not be necessary. For what kindles faith is not the original but the portrait, not the historical person but the picture. There must be analogies not between portraits and real-life originals, but between pictures and other pictures, especially between portraits like Caponsacchi's and the portrait of Jesus, which expresses as no other portrait can the cruciform nature of faith. That faith is no more to be eroded by any perceived discrepancy between these pictures and their historical originals than the Gospels' picture of Christ can be invalidated by historical criticism of a figure called Jesus of Nazareth.

It might be argued, however, that though all pictures are selective, some are more imaginatively transformed than others. Pompilia's picture of Caponsacchi as a lesser savior-god, like Saint John's picture of Christ, alters and transforms the tradition of deliverance found in Hebrew and classical sources, just as John's picture transforms the more historical selections of Saint Mark. We can profitably speak of two kinds of interpretation: interpretation as selection, which is more inductive and judicial like the pope's, and interpretation as imaginative transformation, which is more metaphorical like Pompilia's. Interpretation as selection, because it retains more trace of a historical referent, can incidentally provide a canon for criticizing both the selective interpretation itself and the more imaginative interpretation of a Pompilia or Saint John. But this hermeneutical refinement does little to affect the relative unimportance of a real-life original. For more is at stake than some residual historical trace. Browning and Pompilia want to know if the last power can be trusted. Is God gracious? Or is he a mere vacancy and void? Is life significant in some sense that breaks through the barriers of ordinary experience and allows us to go outside the world? Because these are life-and-death issues, questions of faith, which no distinction between selective and imaginative interpretations can hope to settle, some new chasms will always open up to divide the objects of faith from their grounds.

Hermeneutics teaches either that faith can be dissociated from historical narrative or that it cannot be so dissociated. There is no third alternative. In either case biblical criticism illuminates and is not discontinuous with any other mode of criticism. If it teaches that faith is historically grounded, then it abets the strictness of interpretive precision: critical freedom must then operate only within the boundaries prescribed by the author's text. Such is the theory of biblical interpretation advocated by Benjamin Jowett in his essay "On the Interpretation of Scripture" (1860). This essay exercises an important influence on Browning, especially on a poem like *Balaustion's Adventure* (1871), the most hermeneutical Greek poem in Browning's canon. As a classical scholar Jowett wants to interpret the Bible with the same scholarly rigor and critical good sense that he brings to the study of Plato's *Dialogues*. Like Jowett, Browning seems to think we should interpret the Bible as we interpret a work by Homer or Euripides. And if so, the converse is also true: we interpret secular literature as we interpret the Bible. But just as historical criticism can erode faith but cannot supply the grounds of it, so the text an author has supplied can invalidate a critical reading but cannot guarantee that any particular interpretation will begin to appropriate the text's full meaning. Though the presentation of contradictory testimony requires the reader, like any member of a jury, to ask, "Is this what really happened?" readers must always project their own values, applying the warrants of their own beliefs as well as the warrants of history, logic, and the law courts. If Pompilia's deliverance were just another historical event, indistinguishable from other events like the marriage to Guido or the forgery of the love letters, then it could never be a true deliverance capable of shattering the boundaries of ordinary experience. An abnormal historical event would produce only the *illusion* of shattered boundaries. A real breakthrough must be a nonhistorical happening by which all other events in the story are bounded. To be fully meaningful, in other words, an event must be ungrounded, beyond history—and perhaps beyond truth or falsity—altogether.

It is precisely this paradox that keeps encompassing the pope in contradictions. On the one hand, he has to refute the testimonies of Caponsacchi's critics, which are factual and historical, by making historical assertions about what Caponsacchi and Pompilia actually did. On the other hand, having made such assertions, he illogically claims that no historian, detective, or legal witness has a right to assess them. One wonders whether a historical assertion that is incapable of being either refuted or confirmed is genuinely historical. It seems to me that if we want to claim the advantages of historical judgment, we have to assume its risks. And if we want the warrants of faith, we have to assume a whole different set of risks. It is hard to have the faith without the loss of critical autonomy, and hard to enjoy the advantages of history without losing our beliefs.

Saving faith must see in an event a significance that revolutionizes the believer's self-understanding. But because of Browning's deep Protestant distrust of any continuity between faith and works, person and office, a character's motives tend to remain a mystery, even to the character himself. How can the pope hope to read the hearts of Pompilia and Caponsacchi with any confidence when these characters cannot read their own hearts? If a transformation of their self-understanding is to be the proper object of faith and the true meaning of correcting the portrait by the living face, on what a slender thread the whole enterprise is made to hang! The leap involved in passing from historical faith to saving faith is the kind envisaged by E. D. Hirsch in any transition from interpretation proper to the value judgments of "criticism," by which he means the elucidation of significance as opposed to the examination of a given textual meaning. "It is not the meaning of the text which changes," he insists, "but its significance.... *Meaning* is that which is represented by a text.... *Significance*, on the other hand, names a relationship between that meaning and a person" (Hirsch 1967, 8). Browning recognizes, however, that the distinction between criticism and interpretation, significance and meaning, is too simple, because the value judgments of a critic may be just as much an antecedent fact as the events a historical interpreter tries to reconstruct. Like a contemporary commentator, Francis Sparshott, Browning also seems to doubt whether "the pure distinction between meaning and significance can be explicated or maintained in practice, except in cases where the significance is plainly idiosyncratic," as in the eccentric interpretations of the two advocates. "A meaning that is of no significance to anyone [else] is of no interest" (Sparshott 1982, 260). Moreover, is the distinction between significance and meaning a true-or-false proposition or merely an evaluative proposal? As a proposal of a critic rather than a discovery of the interpreter (as a "significant" claim, in Hirsch's sense, rather than a "meaningful" statement), it seems to be an evaluation rather than a true-or-false proposition. And so if the distinction is true, it seems to follow that it cannot be true: it can at best be a proposal, a significant suggestion that is more or less felicitous or apt.

In the last book of his poem Browning caricatures a variety of critical positions, several of which have found favor in our own time. The Venetian visitor to Rome and Don Celestine (the first and fourth interpreters) are both to be commended for seeking self-enlightenment. But too detached from the events they interpret, the Venetian visitor degenerates into a dupe and Celestine into a proud Olympian. Mistaking Guido's execution for a Crucifixion, rather than the capital punishment of a criminal, the visitor assumes that every falsehood is so true that any truth must be false. Don Celestine makes the opposite mistake of taking every sign agnostically, as a mere empty signifier, which allows the true referent to escape through a hole at the center: "God is true / And every man a liar" (12.600–601). Assuming that the truth is so true that any expression of it must be false, Celestine embodies the vice of all ideological critics (from the theological or

Hegelian commentator to the Marxist) for whom the study of art or history is never, like the pursuit of virtue, its own reward, an endotelic enterprise, but is merely a means to some external end.

The second interpreter, Arcangeli, and the third interpreter, Bottinius, both subvert the Socratic premise of self-enlightenment by using knowledge, like the sophists, to gain power over others. Whereas Arcangeli resembles the untenured professor eager to secure his next commission, the bachelor Bottinius is the established critic, attempting to convince himself that his reputation for insight is well deserved and trying desperately to mask his obvious inferiority to rival critics. Arcangeli is the interpreter as uncritical partisan, prepared to argue anything if it seems likely to influence a judge or client. Bottinius, the critic as jealous exhibitionist, who would rather lose an argument than invite the collaboration of some more gifted colleague able to make the case foolproof, glories in the relativist's axiom that every truth is so true that any truth must be false.

The commentator who intrudes at the end of the poem to assert that "human speech is naught" (12.838) is the critic as disillusioned skeptic, who assumes that every interpretation is so false that no interpretation can be true. He is a precursor of some deconstructionists, who despair of reaching any consensus about the meaning of litera-ture except the consensus that no consensus can be reached. The skeptic shares the pessimism of the Augustinian monk Don Celestine, the critic as proud Olympian. But if every man is a liar and only God is true (12.600–601), how can we hope to learn this truth from a witness who, according to his own testimony, is a liar? The condition of falsehood that must prevail if the claim is true, the unreliability of all testimony, is incompatible with the claim that is made. Bottinius, a fame seeker himself, is quick to spot a similar contradiction. The monk's claim that he seeks only obscurity cannot be allowed, for what else is his celebrated sermon on Pompilia's death if not a direct appeal for "just the fame he flouts" (12.649)?

What is most subversive and unsettling about Browning's poem? The constant source of anxiety, I think, is Browning's repeated intimation that even if Guido's suspicion about Pompilia's adulterous liaison with Caponsacchi was justified, even if the myth of deliverance and redemption turned out to be nothing more than stylized adultery, we still would not believe his suspicion was justified, and so we have no way of knowing that what Guido suspects is not true. The skeptic realizes that we could be living in a world conceptually identical to the one we think we are living in, but in which everything we believe is false. Pompilia and Caponsacchi would then be as guilty as Guido says they are, and we would have no way of knowing this. Different worlds can lead to our having the same beliefs, just as different three-dimensional objects can have the same two-dimensional plane projection. Two worlds that produce identical beliefs can be different enough for everything believed in one world to be false in the other. The worlds inhabited by Second Half-Rome, Bottinius, and the pope, for example, produce roughly identical beliefs. But could any worlds be more bizarrely different?

How, in retrospect, are we to identify the critical positions of the main speakers? I have argued that Tertium Quid and Guido are the deconstructionists of *The Ring and the Book.* Tertium Quid sets forth all the wrong ways of interpreting. He parodies the assumption of some of the more doctrinaire poststructuralists that there is a teachable method of deconstructing texts that will enable him to dismantle truth at will. His method is an uncritical, reflex demonstration that every truth is so true that any truth must be false. His indifference is a perversion of the skeptical critic's detachment, and his anxiety about ever reaching truth is a perversion of the hermeneutical critic's concern. He is anxiously indifferent instead of disinterestedly concerned.

Guido, for his part, feels that the absence of standards turns critical judgment into a mystery exclusively controlled by the high priests of the Vatican. One might think that the pope's scrupulous sifting and weighing of the testimony allows his own critical authority to be earned. But as Guido reminds us, the pope discovers that any critical theory, like any scientific theory, is "underdetermined" by the evidence: it is never tested proposition by proposition but stands or falls by grids of other theories it is locked into. Though the pope keeps refining and exercising his interpretive capacities, they are ultimately of little use to him. At the end of his monologue a heroic leap to truth, followed by a self-congratulatory announcement that he has arrived safely on the far side of doubt, comes to the rescue of a theory of knowledge that has proved too unruly to be useful. But if judgments are reached by the use of some favorite code word like "the Unknown God" or "the Genius of the Vatican," as Guido charges, or by some ritual initiation into the mysteries guarded by the high priests of criticism, then no standards of evidence and no intentions seem worth assessing.

One Victorian version of these priestly exercises is the typological criticism of Scripture advocated by John Keble in *Tract 89*—a theory of criticism vigorously attacked by Browning's friend Jowett in his essay "The Interpretation of Scripture" in *Essays and Reviews.* Jowett's critique applies with equal force to the secularized typologizes of many structuralist critics today. In their hands the only setting in which *The Ring and the Book*'s historicism can survive is the verbal labyrinth, a literary haven for every historical phantom or ghostly abstraction that has lost its grounding in a world outside the maze. And yet, with its chain of commentary on commentary stretching as it seems to infinity, *The Ring and the Book* often abets such an enterprise: the poem is curiously unincremental and exitless. Browning has little sympathy with Jowett's straightforward, demystifying view that the meaning of the Bible is its plain, historical sense. How are we to extract such a sense, assuming it exists? And how are we to identify or judge an author's intentions or the meaning these intentions had for his original audience? Indeed, once in the labyrinth of *The Ring*, it is difficult to find either an escape route or a center. And who in the poem is any longer capable of creating or initiating anything? Certainly not the poet. All Browning's narrator can do is play the role of ghostly resuscitator. As a poetic Elisha breathing life into the dead facts, he may, if he is lucky, revive a corpse (1. 760–71), but genuine creation is beyond him.

Unlike the two deconstructionists Tertium Quid and Guido, Caponsacchi and Pompilia are both myth critics. Their aim is not to classify texts or verbal propositions but to make metaphoric proposals. Their recommendation of projected values is the stabilizing principle that enables them to see life steadily, as the reenactment of some biblical or classical myth. And their empathy with other characters is the liberating principle that allows them to see life whole.

The pope, by contrast, is a critical historian or judge, a surrogate for each reader, trying to infer what happened by harmonizing prior inferences. On the one hand, the interpreter must be certain that the witnesses brought the same consciousness to the past event as the interpreter would have had he been there. Only such an assumption allows him to *empathize* with the witness, to *become* the witness, by exercising negative capability. On the other hand, the interpreter must be critical of his witnesses: only by registering the differences between his own thought and that of a different historical time can his interpretation be an invention, a "coming upon" or a "finding," in both the constative and performative senses of that word.

Even when a prior event is unearthed, however, it has a way of turning out to be not the first in a series, but an imitation of earlier events. Browning is an oddly belated, even parasitic, poet whose most authentic creations often seem a product of archival research or historical reconstruction. The most apparently original metaphor in the poem, the metaphor of the ring, proves not to be original with Browning at all. The poet who praised Elizabeth's "rare gold ring of verse" cannot have been Browning himself, because Browning is associated, like his dead wife, with "our England," while the phrase "his Italy" is reserved for the poet from whom Browning has borrowed his metaphor.

> Might mine but lie outside thine, Lyric Love,
> Thy rare gold ring of verse (the poet praised)
> Linking our England to his Italy!
>
> (12.872–74)

What we wrongly took for an original metaphor—the rounding of "the rough ore...to a ring" (12.869)—is only an instance of an instance, an example of a prior example.

What finally emerges, then, from *The Ring and the Book*'s many caricatures of critical positions? Positively, we may say that any single interpretation is provisional. What we say about a text or an event is for the time being. A second conclusion is the futility of trying to abase ourselves before any positivist model of historical research. Except in the mind of H. T. Buckle, such a model does not exist. As the pope reminds us, a scientist's acoustical charts of the sea's wrath are just as fictive a construction as a poet's description of the angry roar of the waves, even though the scientists looks for abiding cause-and-effect relations while the poetic interpreter tries to place himself at the center of energy, inside the waves themselves (10.1400–1402). Competing models of how sound waves work cannot be entirely adjudicated by theory-neutral rules and data. And even though choices are agent relative, the rationality of science itself is never impaired. A final inference to be made is the importance of critical strategy. A resourceful interpreter will be able to capture and possess symbols like Molinism or rallying cries like "Quis pro Domino?" (5.1549, 10.2100), which the pope effectively takes back from Guido, who thinks he has permanently captured it from the church. A critic's ability to demystify his adversaries' rhetoric, however, often prompts him to obfuscate or mystify language for his own ends. The strategies of obfuscation are universal, and they allow Browning to sharpen our sense of irony by discriminating between critical positions like perspectivism, which partially ranks its views, and relativism, which holds all views equally deficient.

If there seems to be no center at the middle of Browning's ring, it is not because Browning knows the center of every ring is necessarily an empty space, like the hole in the middle of a doughnut. Browning works on the contrary assumption that his ring *has* a center. But the interpreters with the greatest claim to centrality are least prepared to press their claims. For they know that to declare any point of view central at the expense of other viewpoints has disastrous results. The

so-called center then becomes a mere still center, like the superannuated symbols of a church that is all machinery without any vivifying
soul. Browning's own position is not relativism, because his points of
view are ranked. And yet no single view is adequate by itself. Though
Browning writes monologues in order to step outside himself, he
discovers that something of himself always remains behind the lens.
Because something in the poet must continue to determine the
resulting picture, Browning will have reason to doubt, whatever
window he looks through, that he is really getting any closer to a
detached view. As one commentator says, "the same ideas that make
the pursuit of objectivity seem necessary for knowledge make both
objectivity and knowledge, on reflection, unattainable" (Nagel 1986,
67).

Browning and his speakers are involved in a contradictory enterprise. On the one hand, they are hard pressed to explain how critics
can arrive at valid interpretations. On the other hand, they refuse to
take refuge in the conclusion of some poststructuralist critics that
skepticism justifies a reluctance to interpret at all. They continue to
criticize and comment even when they half recognize the futility of
doing so. The alternative would be to offer interpretations that are
merely "interesting." But who is to arbitrate disputes about intrinsic
"interest"?

If no one interpreter is infallible, perhaps a whole interpretive
community devoted to accurate knowledge of texts can preserve the
goals and values of historical scholarship. In the most enlightened
speakers in *The Ring and the Book* Browning seeks his own hermeneutical
equivalent of David Friedrich Strauss's community of believers. Instead
of equating truth with Strauss's community of faith, Browning equates
it with a community of experienced and devoted critics—some of
them Higher Critics—committed to accurate knowledge of what is not,
strictly speaking, knowable. Yet Browning's hermeneutical community
is not to be confused with the "interpretive community" of a contemporary critic like Stanley Fish.[3] How can a community of interpreters
confer stable meaning on a text when each individual reading is
unstable?

The individual reader turns out to be the real hero of *The Ring and
the Book*. He is invited to take some middle ground between the errant
structuralism of the two advocates and the lunacies of Guido. Browning
knows that prolonged study may rob the mind of its elasticity, and that
erudition may make critics like the two advocates duller and sillier

3. Stanley Fish, *Is There a Text in This Class? The Authority of Interpretive Communities*
(1980, esp. 303–71).

than they naturally are. Unless readers think for themselves, every truth they discover will adhere to them as a mere excrescence, like a false tooth or an artificial limb. Beguiled by the a priori, like Swift's projectors in the Grand Academy of Lagado, the advocates begin at the roof and work downward to the foundation. Their lack of method helps Browning dramatize a recurrent dilemma. If the biggest archive in the world is in disorder, it will be less useful than a small but well-organized library. The interpreter can organize only what he knows, but how can he know anything until he has organized it? If the facts are in perpetual disorder, the biggest archive in the world will never produce organized thought. Schopenhauer says, "you can think about only what you know...; on the other hand, you can know only what you have thought about" (1970, 89). Until original thinking has already taken place, it is difficult to imagine how it can ever get launched.

Browning shows that immersion in a text and in its history is a reader's best antidote to slavery to fashion, and so his best hope of thinking originally for himself. I am not suggesting that Browning would advocate a return to historical criticism and research. He is saying, I think, that interpretive purity of any kind breeds self-destruction: a variety of critical modes is called for. Critics should recognize the limits of every single method of interpretation, and when one method threatens to become dominant they should endlessly advocate the restoration of disorder. To resist change and even strife in the name of methodological purity is a philosophical mistake. It is even a mistake to banish a new interpretive method because it seems wedded, like some contemporary critical schools, to an uncongenial jargon. A jargon-ridden critic like Bottinius is the first to object to the jargon of the monk, whose discourse he rejects as mere "ampollosity" (12.647). Someone else's critical jargon is the first refuge of ignorance and the eternal refuge of disciples too stupid or fossilized to learn anything new.

Browning's pope realizes that the surest way for the church to commit institutional suicide is to try to stem the rising tide of skepticism. He tries instead to assimilate the tide, empathizing with people gifted for experience of new adventure—people like Caponsacchi, Pompilia, and presumably the much maligned Molinos. Conservative critics denounce Molinos in the name of morality and the authority of existing methods of interpretation. They frustrate reasoned argument and refuse to join in a critical debate that should be seized as an intellectual opportunity instead of denounced as a heresy. Browning's poem suggests that the cry of vested interests against interpreters who ask new, difficult, even embarrassing questions, and then question the answers, has always been wrongheaded, whether it is the attack of theology on science in Victorian Britain or the attack of historical scholars on theorists or of theorists on historical scholars in our own time. Such rearguard attacks never succeed, it seems, in stemming the tide. Like Browning's "old Pope," who "totters" for a moment "on the verge o' the grave" (12.38), all things sway forward on the dangerous flood of history. And the more we try to stay the tide, the more we find ourselves engulfed.

At the end of the poem Browning's narrator proclaims the existence of a latent meaning behind the manifest sense. He has written a book, he boasts, that "shall mean beyond the facts, / Suffice the eye and save the soul beside" (12. 866–67). Phrases like "Beyond mere imagery," "beyond the fact," "Deeper than e'en Beethoven dived" (12. 863–66) continue to intimate a hidden meaning. Inside the outer ring of the poem there is always some secret inner sense, which bears the same relation to the manifest meaning as the rougher ring of Browning's own commentary bears to Elizabeth's rarer inner "ring of verse" (12.872–73). For all the boldness of these proclamations, however, the text is reluctant to disclose its hidden sense. At the end of this inordinately long poem it is as if Browning, like Guido at the end of his second long monologue, has spoken not "one word" "Out of the world of words [he] had to say" (11.2417–18). What is Browning trying to drown out inside him with the fortissimo of his long declamations and fear of closure? We should remember that only with the publication of *Men and Women* in 1855 did Browning become as popular a poet as his wife. Will the publication of *The Ring and the Book*, his first long poem since *Sordello*, consign him to obscurity for another twenty years? Is he afraid to face the verdict of his "British Public, ye who like me not, / (God love you!)" (1.410–11, 1379–80)? Moreover, until it has been concluded that there is something to conclude, how can the poet conclude his poem? Since the data are so hopelessly patient of all interpretations, they are an endless source of pleasure but also a necessary disappointment. Obscure order can be a blessing, but only because more definite order proves delusive.

After line 363 of the first book, the poem should conclude. "This is the bookful": all else is adulterating alloy added to untempered gold. Carlyle thought Browning's story could be told in ten lines and only wanted forgetting. Either the poem must end almost before it begins, or else it can never end at all. It becomes a book that is all beginning, without any end that is not imposed by an arbitrary stop rule. Like the Old Testament, the poem is in search of an ending, of a design that will fulfill it. But the ending is endlessly deferred. We

cannot even satisfy our desire for an ending by regarding the concluding use of the ring metaphor (12.873) as a synecdoche for the
ending that is not there, the way we construe *"De te, fabula"* in "The
Statue and the Bust" (l. 250). The ring parable simply returns us to
the use of the same parable in book 1, and it intensifies our bafflement
rather than eases it.

It is always hardest to think accurately about parables we have taken
most completely for granted. At the beginning of the poem Browning's
fact-loving narrator is more adept at fashioning excessively precise
descriptions of the ring than at explaining what they signify: "A
thing's sign: now for the thing signified" (1.32). The narrator poses as
a puzzled semiotician. Prejudging the referent by assuming it will be
as material and thinglike as the ring, he gives the impression of
stalling for time, trying to work out the exact meaning of his sign. His
injunctions to the errant reader—"beseech you, hold that figure fast!"
(1.142)—seem to be reminders to himself as well. Concluding that the
gold in the ring is "Fanciless fact" (1.144), he is at a loss to say what the
alloy is. If it is mere fancy, what use is it? Because the critic as positivist
simply omits all reference to that part of his parable that resists
analysis according to scientific methods, it remains for a second
interpreter, the poet-critic, to assert that "Fancy with fact is just one
fact the more" (1.464). Is that statement made as a fanciful interpretation of fact? Or is it offered as what his positivist adversary would call
a "fanciless" fact? If it is a fanciful interpretation, then it is an
interpretation of an interpretation, and the interpreted fact seems to
recede further and further from view. Conversely, if the claim is
offered as a fact, it seems to follow it cannot be a fact. For the
condition that must prevail if the claim is true—the union of "Fancy
with fact"—is incompatible with the claim's being a "fanciless" fact.
Moreover, the additive quality of the model—fancy superimposed on
preexisting fact—precipitates a crisis in representation that puts at
risk the more appropriate metaphor of the alloy's informing and
transpiercing the gold until the two are no longer distinguishable.

The parable can support two contradictory interpretations, depending
on the point in the process when the alloy is examined. Early in the
operation, the alloy is thoroughly mixed with the gold to make it
malleable. Imaginative interpreters are drawn into the parable itself,
as the alloy of the poet's own interpretation is drawn into the gold.
And yet the second half of the parable reminds us of an unsettling
truth: interpretation, though necessary, is bound to seem intrusive.
Like the alloy that flies free after the acid is applied (1.24–25),
interpreters may find themselves expelled from the parable by their

very desire for access. They are free only in the sense that, like the alloy set free by the acid, they are released from the secret sense of the parable. Readers are dispossessed and excluded by the very parable that seemed at first to admit them. Because interpretation is always as obtrusive an act as the alloy's penetration of the slivers of gold, the illusion of being an insider is only a more elaborate way of being kept outside. It is as if Browning had written a parable about parables. For the more we seem to penetrate a parable, the more we are also kept on its periphery: no great parable has ever been exhausted by our meditations.

Any theory of *The Ring and the Book*'s latent order is put in question by the narrator's manifest playfulness. The "one lesson" to be learned, he says ironically at the end of the poem, is "that our human speech is naught, / Our human testimony false, our fame / And human estimation words and wind" (12.836, 838–40). If the text has a secret meaning, it is certainly not this "one lesson" half facetiously, half defensively extracted by the poet-narrator. Like some mysterious Ur-text, Browning's hidden meanings are as obscure as a sunken object whose qualities we must laboriously reconstruct from the splash it makes as it falls in the pool. The waves generated in the water then become "vibrations in the general mind," quite unable to fathom the "depth of deed already out of reach" (1.844–45). The phrase "depth of deed" focuses both on the inscrutability of human motives and on the very rapid removal of events from the closest, most knowledgeable observers.

It is as if Browning were writing an ongoing testament or Bible and does not yet know which germs in his mass of narrative detail exist merely in their own right, like some original covenant that is meaningful in itself without later typological "fulfillments" of its meaning, and which are going to be fulfilled in some new testament, some new *Life of Jesus*, still to be revealed by a future David Friedrich Strauss. In *The Ring and the Book* we are puzzled because we cannot always tell which details resemble Candy's mysterious disappearance and return during the birthday dinner party (a detail that will grow immensely in importance later in *The Moonstone*) and which are merely gratuitous touches, a means of making the surface of the narrative more like the crowded surface of everyday life.

There are intermittent fulfillments in *The Ring and the Book*, but nothing sustained. The mystery poem is less like a book than like an archive of newspapers, a cupboard of scrolls, which is the form Browning uses in the manuscript roll that both records and comments upon Saint John's testament in "A Death in the Desert." Codexes promote figural designs; rolls discourage them. As Frank Kermode observes, "the Jews, upon whom the end of time had not come, whose prophecies of a Messiah were unfulfilled, kept the roll, but the Christians, having the desire to establish consonance between the end of the book and the beginning, needed the codex" (1979, 88). *The Ring and the Book* has the logic of a newspaper, and because nothing seems organized sequentially, quotations that stick in one's memory are often hard to find again in the text. Contributing to the enigmatic, scroll-like quality of the text is the fact that narrative in the source book generates the character of agents in the poem and the character of commentators like Half-Rome, Other Half-Rome, and Tertium Quid, who keep interpreting the story recorded in the source. These characters generate new narratives, which often take their form from the narrative of the source book, the way parts of Matthew's gospel are thought to be modeled on the narrative of Mark. And yet the total effect is less that of a Gospel codex than of an Old Testament roll, because Browning's canon, unlike the New Testament's, is never closed. Though the story in the Old Yellow Book is to the hidden or latent sense that Browning is continually trying to extract from it what the old covenant is to the new covenant in figural readings of Scripture, the poem's typologies still require completion in the life and mind of each interpreter.

It is both important and unimportant that the source book be historical, for the same reason that it is both important and unimportant that the Old Testament be historical. It is unimportant because, in one sense, the whole historicity of the Jewish Bible is to be sacrificed to a validation of the historicity of the Gospels. But historicity is also important, because the whole authority of a historical Jewish Bible is needed to establish the historicity of a figural reading of it. The more fictitious and typological Browning's narrative becomes, the more historical it must also claim to be, because typological readings always assume the historicity of the types they try to fulfill.

In interrogating the Old Yellow Book, Browning seems to be writing and reading simultaneously, like a Victorian Derrida. Even in Browning's source book, which recalls the midrash of accumulating commentary in "A Death in the Desert," presumably only three-fifths of the book is a true source, for the rest is said to be "written supplement" (1.119). *The Ring and the Book* repeats this process by offering glosses on a work that, like Jennings's transcript of Candy's delirious testament in *The Moonstone*, already consists in part of marginal glosses. In Goethe's aphorism, "Alles factische ist schon Theorie." A fact is not even a fact without its interpretive supplement. The combination of F_1S_1 becomes a second fact, F_2, only by adding a second supplement, S_2. And F_2S_2 generates F_3 only by adding S_3, and so on. Even the source book's interfilleting of cramped Latin with Italian streaks replicates this seemingly endless regress of transcribed testaments and "written supplements." The only way to block an infinite regress of facts and supplements is to assume that one of the facts to be blocked is the fact that every fact requires an interpretive supplement. The "stooping" of the testament to "mother-tongue" (1:139) recalls the use of "stooping" in "A Death in the Desert" as a metaphor for incarnation (l. 134). The "mother-tongue" is like the alloy of the ring: it gives the precepts and axioms body. But it also suggests, in approved poststructuralist fashion, that figures of body and supplement, text and gloss, are easily reversed. The full-blooded Italian commentary may be more meaningful than the cramped and bloodless Latin axioms that seem at first to enjoy privileged status, just as the alloy may prove more important than the gold, which is the most prized but least useful of metals.

Browning's Roman murder mystery looks for mysteries and finds only Mystery. By "Mystery" I mean an ultimate principle that does not have an explanation. In this sense God's treatment of Pompilia, like the laws of quantum mechanics, is a mystery. To write "R. B.—a poem" (where "R. B." stands for both Robert Browning and *The Ring and the Book*), Browning must also rediscover the mysteries of identity. To achieve a positive identity by speaking at last in propria persona, he must first experiment with a host of negative identities. Or as Jorge Luis Borges says, Browning must "live by forgetting himself." He must "be the face [he] half-see[s] and forget[s]" and also Guido, "who accepts the blessed destiny of being a traitor." He must even "be the friend who hates" him, the "British Public, ye who like me not, / (God love you!)" (1.410–11, 1379–80).

> Agonies, masks and resurrections
> will weave and unweave [his] fate
> and at some point [he] will be Robert Browning.
> (Translation of Borges's poem, "Browning Resolves to Be a Poet")

Equally mysterious is the way the world becomes intelligible in *The Ring and the Book* only as a nesting structure of sacred books, of commentaries on commentaries. Browning knows that there is no single sense or truth in the world and that dreams of transparent meaning are at best consoling fictions. But he also knows that he must keep trying to entertain such fictions, because only by worshiping at the shrine of transparent sense, in a quest for some sacred Ur-book or Bible that "shall mean beyond the facts" (12.866), can he discover the intermittent radiances, the moments of luminous seeing, that make both the book and the book of the world an endless source of meaning.

Conclusion:

Crises in Representation

Moving through three phases of Victorian thought and culture, this book has explored fourteen sources of mystery—classed as mysteries of unconsciousness, mysteries of identity, and mysteries of philosophical and historical method—in a representative cross section of Victorian literature. From the vantage of retrospect, what features of the landscape are worthiest of comment? Most striking, surely, is the Victorian discovery that, contrary to what modern science usually assumes, knowledge reveals mystery: it does not dispel it. Such is the conclusion of ancient Greek and biblical authors and of Victorians as dissimilar as T. H. Huxley and J. H. Newman. Except for Jeremy Bentham and H. T. Buckle, the Victorians value literature, like childhood, as a dwelling place of mystery. As Wordsworth knows and as Mill lives to discover, a culture that skips over childhood will never grow up.

Also striking are the unsuspected similarities our vantage point reveals. Such dissimilar authors as Carlyle and Mill, for example, or Browning and Eliot, all conduct existential experiments in living. By aligning each type of mystery with a form of silence, a theory of knowledge, a use of language, and a crisis of representation, we can also discover in Browning and Rossetti, in Hopkins and Newman, similar problems of combining a performative theory of faith with a descriptive theory of a divinely grounded truth, even though a grounded performative seems to be a mystery or an anomaly, even a contradiction in terms. Sometimes we make discoveries of an opposite kind. Because a literary device like double irony can be used to create widely divergent mysteries of identity, its deployment discloses unexpected differences between novelists like Trollope and Thackeray, for example, whose moral comedies we might expect to be more alike.

As if by some Newtonian law that posits for every action an equal and opposite reaction, the early Victorians rebel against romantic individualism. When their efforts to restore traditional centers of moral and spiritual authority lead to a skeptical backlash, however, we can also see how the vacuum that skepticism leaves in its wake is slowly filled by new pragmatic and existential theories, by doctrines of self-making, moral vocation, and salvation through work, which diffuse throughout Victorian culture at large.

Such critics of romanticism as Irving Babbitt attack the movement as a parody of grace, an appeal to the heart in protest against the dogma of original sin. The romantics' moral intuitionism, their justification of feeling as of moral value, is denounced not merely because it sentimentally ignores Gradgrind's law that the Good Samaritan is a bad economist, but also because it debases earlier classical notions of ethics, according to which good and bad deeds are unaffected by the motives of the agents. Romantics, like Marxists, have been succinctly defined as latter-day Pelagians, optimists who do not believe in the Fall of man. In trying to bring heaven down to earth, these Utopians collapse the distinction between nature and grace, challenging so central a doctrine as theology's belief in a fixed and abiding human nature, created in the image of an unchanging God.

Under the influence of evangelical theology, Victorianism, at least in its initial stage, can be seen as a reaction against such romantic tendencies. As early as *Paracelsus* (1835), Browning exposes the Faustian quester's restless move away from history as a form of immaturity and impatience. Reflecting the impact of his mother's evangelical piety and Henry Melvill's sermons, Browning quickly replaces romantic doctrines of endless questing with biblical notions of human limits and ends, including a radical dependence on God. Chasing holy grails and rainbows may be all very well for saints like Galahad or visionary geniuses like Shelley, but salvation for most Victorians will depend upon work in their allotted field and service to humanity. During the 1830s and early 1840s Tractarians like Keble encourage a revival of typological interpretations of the Bible, based on the fixity of God's word and its types. A figural reading of Scripture confers "as it were the signature of God on his work," guaranteeing, as one commentator says, "the authenticity of [the book]" and the unalterable design of its author (Daniélou 1960, 30).

This earliest authoritarian phase of Victorian culture, like the agnostic and existential phases that later dominate it, precipitates in each of its literary manifestations a crisis of representation. The most stereotyped notion of human identity is to be found in Dickens's flat and fixed characters. The basis of his Jonsonian theory of comedy, this stereotyping allows him to dispense with human nature, as Henry James complained, by creating a community of eccentrics. Oliver Twist, for example, is a mere Platonic essence of virtue. His type of purity is so totally uninfluenced by the fallen world of criminals that his salvation seems predetermined, as it were, by a doctrine of election. Equally fated is the chain of collapsing metaphors of situation in *Great Expectations*, which converge upon Pip in chapter 39 like a tragedy upon its recognition scene. By spacing out events that belong together, the generalized tmesis creates in both Pip and the reader a repressed or subliminal knowledge of knowing more than they know they know. Nothing can postpone, however, the fated moment of discovery and reversal that swims implacably into focus, like repressed materials coming to consciousness under relentless psychoanalysis. The determinism in Dickens's world precipitates a crisis of representation. For when Pip and Estella discover they are not the free agents they seem to be but are mere puppets in the hands of the older generation, the expanding context that seems to confer mysterious new meaning on their lives suddenly deprives them of value. The more value the less meaning, and the more meaning the less value. There seems no way of avoiding this dilemma unless we conclude ironically that the fatality of a world of predetermining laws is merely another of Pip's consoling fictions. It is always possible that Pip is all too aware of the irony of fate but unware of the profounder irony of his own vanity and self-deception.

Just as a spectral trace of the doctrine of election casts its shadow over Dickens's world, so Hardy cannot quite dispel from the fatalistic tragedy of Tess the ghost of a predestinating deity. His "President of the Immortals" is a vast imbecility whose blind and groping attributes sort oddly with the omnipotence of a departing and all but vanished godhead. As soon as the unknowable thing-in-itself becomes the subject of predicates like volition, we might have expected Hardy to see that it is no longer possible, in F. H. Bradley's words, "for any one who cares for consistency to go on calling it the Unknowable" (1876, 323). But Hardy apparently cannot forgo this last infirmity of the noble God of voluntarist theology, the God of Augustine and Calvin. Under Schopenhauer's influence, he continues to project a blind and groping human will, an attribute of the phenomenal world, upon the ghostly noumenal world, where it becomes the most barbarous attribute of a curiously mindless Mind.

A saner, less fanatical version of voluntarist theology can be studied in the comic moral dramas of Trollope and Henry James, where moral centers operate as a secular residue of a stable, God-focused world. By using their characters' speech as a tuning fork, Trollope and James can register even the slightest deviations from a moral and linguistic norm. Whether Trollope's narrator in *Barchester Towers* is deploying double irony to endorse simultaneously two contrary codes, or whether his antithetical rhetoric is eroding the authority of what he says, his classical irony is inconsistent with relativism, for it presupposes that reader and author share the same moral norms. Only in *The Turn of the Screw*, where James seems unable to decide whether the ghosts are real or his governess is mad, does the judicious and balanced use of double irony turn into purely negative irony.

Like Trollope's classical irony, the religious orthodoxy of Newman and Rossetti posits a center of spiritual authority. Yet Newman tries to combine two contradictory models of knowledge. Like Plato and the church fathers, Newman identifies knowledge with the revelation of a mystery. The knower must learn to glimpse intermittently the heavenly facts that fill eternity. At the same time he must verify what he sees by using an empirical model of knowledge, according to which a true object of knowledge will be more vividly apprehended than a false or faint object. Rossetti confronts a different kind of crisis. She combines the orthodox theological distinction between nature and grace with a romantic, almost Pelagian doctrine of her intimacy with Christ. The first doctrine dramatizes the worshiper's removal from God, but the second celebrates her mystical at-onement with him. The more at-onement in the mystical sense, the less atonement in the biblical sense, and vice versa. And the more rigorously Newman tries to forge the links of a logical chain of argument, the more incessantly he spins the thread of an explanatory web. But the more explanation, the less logical proof; and the more argumentive the proof, in the manner of Aristotle or the English empiricists, the less explanation Newman can offer of the mysteries that really matter. How, for example, can the truths of theology be eternal and unchanging yet still be consistent with a constant development of Christian doctrine? And how can the author of the *Oxford Sermons on Faith and Reason* continue to be a rigorous empiricist while still leaving room for the free assent of faith? It seems that the more empirical rigor, the less opportunity for free assent, and the more free assent, the less rigor.

I argue that at the heart of the Victorians' attempt to revive traditional centers of moral and spiritual authority lies a negative, agnostic moment of self-questioning and doubt. One might say that the rise of agnostic theology even precedes the revival of evangelical theology. For the agnosticism that Huxley traces to Sir William Hamilton's influential 1829 *Edinburgh Review* essay antedates by several years the influence of evangelical theology on Browning's 1835 poem *Paracelsus*. Instead of being at home in a God-centered world, the Victorian agnostic is a metaphysically displaced person, uprooted and alone. Some official custodians of Victorian culture try to conceal such knowledge. Their defensive strategy can be found in its most complicated form in a "closet agnostic" like Carlyle, whom Nietzsche accuses of being "an English atheist who wants to be honored for *not* being one" (1968, 75). The most subversive Victorian texts, "an agnostic's *Christian Year*" like *In Memoriam* or a revolutionist's handbook like *Sartor Resartus*, are conscripted into the service of some official Victorian gospel of moral duty or salvation through work. There is always a risk of making them tamer than they are, despite the fact that Carlyle goes out of his way to indicate his subversive post-Kantian sources. Too little attention has been paid, moreover, to the influence on Carlyle of the agnostic Sir William Hamilton and to the influence on Clough of his Oxford tutor, the skeptical fideist W. G. Ward.[1]

In a fanatic like Browning's Johannes Agricola, the evangelical doctrine of election generates its own version of agnosticism: Johannes protests that he could not praise God "If such as [he] might understand, / Make out and reckon on his ways" ("Johannes Agricola in Meditation," ll. 57–58). But the main source of the agnostic turn in Victorian thought is the skeptical development in Britain of the critical philosophy of Kant, who argues that God is not an object of knowledge as such, but a mere regulative principle. In his 1829 *Edinburgh Review* essay on Victor Cousin's *Course of Philosophy*, Sir William Hamilton goes one step beyond Kant. Any attempt to understand God, he argues, generates antinomies that are intrinsically unresolvable. H. L. Mansel in his Bampton lectures for 1858, *The Limits of Religious Thought*, maintains that the divine nature can never be logically grasped by the mind's mutually exclusive concepts of a being that is at once absolute, infinite, and a first cause. In part 1 of *First Principles*, "The Unknowable," Herbert Spencer argues that the absolute escapes from conceptual thought but not from consciousness in general. Victorian agnosticism reaches its logical culmination in the first book of F. H. Bradley's *Appearance and Reality* (1893), where the mind-made relations that T. H. Green had defined as the signature of the real are shown to be as incurably contradictory as Kant's paralogisms, hence indeterminate and unreal.

It is only a short step from the inquiring, critical, agnostic side of

---

1. For a fuller treatment of these subjects than I have an opportunity to provide here, see my discussions "Agnostic Semioticians: Carlyle and Sir William Hamilton" and "Clough's Agnostic Imagination: The Use of Uncertainty," in *The Lucid Veil* (1987, 126–29, 136).

Victorian philosophy and religious thought to the skeptical theories of language and knowledge to be found in Carlyle and the Brontës. With the fall from some primal state of unity and unconsciousness, language has suffered the fate of words after the catastrophe of Babel. In *Wuthering Heights* and in the trancelike, hallucinatory sequences of *Villette*, the only way to reverse this catastrophe is to collapse the multiplication of words into one primal synonym or dark tautology. By allowing the name "Justine Marie" to resonate eerily at the Villette carnival, Charlotte Brontë is able to reproduce an equivalent of the montage in cinema. Half-formed thoughts create out of depictable phantasms of ghosts, buried nuns, and apparitions of young wards a representation of a lover's darkest imaginings, which are not graphically depictable. Yet the pathos of the proper name lies precisely in the fact that it is *not* proper: "Justine Marie," like the repeated name "Catherine" in *Wuthering Heights*, is capable of multiple applications. To recover a primal synonym, the chain of intelligible explanations that Cathy tries to piece together in response to Nelly's catechism must suddenly fall asunder: she can express her at-onement with Heathcliff only by reverting to the oxymorons of dream and to the fearful indescribability of her near tautology: "Nelly, I *am* Heathcliff" (chap. 9). To be understood at all, a speaker must repeat the crimes of Milo and Edgar Linton, splitting apart a whole that was never meant to be divided into a sign and its referent. Such a view of language precipitates a crisis of representation: the more intelligible the word becomes, the farther down the slope of ever expanding antonyms it falls. And the more successful a speaker is in reversing this skid down the slope of verbal entropy, the more the collapse of language into one primal synonym induces the frightful paralysis of what, in Heathcliff's phrase, is not strictly speaking utterable.

Carlyle's agnostic theory of the merely extrinsic sign precipitates a similar crisis in his chapter on "Symbols" in *Sartor Resartus*. One would think that if any sign is intrinsic it is the Cross. But Carlyle surprises us by saying that even the Cross, "the highest ensign that men ever met and embraced under, ... had no meaning save an accidental extrinsic one" (1898–1901, 1:178). To be genuinely intrinsic, as Vico argues, a symbol must be made or designed out of literally nothing, as God created the world in Genesis. In other words, the mind can have a priori knowledge only of the signs and symbols it fashions out of nothing. In Vico's famous formula, "the true (*verum*) and the made (*factum*) are convertible" (*verum et factum convertuntur*).[2]

2. According to Isaiah Berlin, "this bold statement was first published in 1710 in the treatise allegedly concerned with the ancient wisdom of the Italians, ... hereafter referred to as *De Antiquissima*. The question of whether the doctrine of the interchangeability of *verum* and *factum* has medieval roots has been much disputed" (1976, 15–16).

By arrogating to man the creative prerogative that the Bible had reserved for God alone, however, Carlyle produces a thoroughly agnostic theory of the word. To the degree that a use of signs is authentically creative and new, it will produce an intrinsic symbolism that is immediately intelligible. But because any such symbolism by definition floats free of any antecedently existing ground, it ceases to be a symbolism that can give us knowledge of God. To the degree that a symbol like the Cross is divinely anchored, it is merely extrinsic: it opens a rift between the unknowable ground and its properties. As a semiotician, Carlyle finds no easy escape from his dilemma: the more intrinsic and intelligible a symbol becomes, the less it continues to function as a symbol: the more it becomes the *Ding an sich* or the sign system itself. Conversely, the more symbolic the sign tries to become, and the more heroically it struggles to say something intelligible about its unknowable ground, the more thoroughly extrinsic and agnostic it is condemned to remain. Like Hamilton, Carlyle must ultimately consign the divine ground to the limbo of Teufelsdröckh's "signless Inane," a no-man's-land beyond tropes and signs altogether.

In *Vanity Fair* this limbo or no-man's-land at the heart of Carlyle becomes the hole at the center of an allegorical fiction conceived by Thackeray on an epic scale. Like the god of the Deists and agnostic theologians, the sovereign power that we expect to find installed behind the elaborate machinery of a traditional allegory like *Pilgrim's Progress* is nowhere to be found in *Vanity Fair*. In the God-deserted world of a novel without heroes, such conventional signs of value as a mother's love for her son become mere empty signifiers. As part of Becky's repertory of dramatic parts, her fitful displays of affection for Rawdon Junior are as devoid of expected content as the ostentatious carriages sent, without passengers, to attend funerals in the novel. The more Thackeray tries to write an allegory in the tradition of Bunyan and Spenser, the more he ends up writing an agnostic testament that is allegorical only in the generalized Coleridgean sense: *Pilgrim's Progress* becomes *Waiting for Godot*. In allegorical discourse, as Coleridge explains, words are used to express "a *different* subject... with a resemblance" (1905, 182). Instead of producing the desired form of tautegorical discourse, in which words and their referents express "the *same* subject... with a difference," Thackeray is left with what Coleridge might call the mere "allegorical" husks of such referents. The more the allegorist's emblems try to gesture tautegorically in the direction of some sovereign power, the more their failure to inscribe this power in words may lead us to doubt that such a power exists.

Though Borrow's Lavengro speaks of a "dark principle," this equivalent of the black hole or void left by the departure of a sovereign power in *Vanity Fair* is an emptiness that Borrow's hero learns to fill by creating for himself a host of proliferating masks. The invention of such masks may be a defensive strategy designed to protect Lavengro from knowledge of the hollowness at his core. Lavengro fears that, as an artist of negative capability, he has no positive identity to express, no residual self that has not been inflected into one of his constantly rotating dramatic parts. The same fear assails an inveterate role-player like Browning, the author of dramatic monologues, and Clough's Claude in *Amours de Voyage*. Claude's heightened consciousness keeps exposing him to every fresh sensation, breaking down, then multiplying resolve. He even imagines outcomes for events that have not yet happened and probably will never happen. In trying to escape from one form of darkness, however, Claude like Lavengro encounters another. For the more such characters try to run away from a core of darkness in a God-deserted world, the more they find themselves running into an equally dark principle at the core of their own role-playing. In each case the absence of a ground leads Claude and Lavengro to fear they are spectral and unreal. Neither the "dark principle" outside the role-player nor the "dark principle" inside is capable of being inscribed in more intelligible words. Perhaps we should not try to decipher or inscribe more of the "dark principle" than humankind can bear.

In *Culture and Anarchy* Arnold assigns the same function to culture that Borrow and Clough assign to role-playing: he tries to make it a surrogate god. Arnold's persuasive redefinition of "culture" retains the venerable emotive meaning of religion but changes its limited descriptive meaning to include three other powers of the human person. Should Arnold not have realized, however, that culture, as a human invention like literature or science, yields the same kind of a priori truth that the mind can possess only of its own artifacts and fictions? His determination to make "culture" a mystery word, like Newman's "faith," is an attempt to substitute a mystification of his own making for the mystery that is really there. The more Arnold invests culture with the mystery that attaches to an unknowable God, the more he divests it of the value it actually has. Like the Brahm of Indian thought, which Arnold studied, the more oracular culture becomes, the less he can say about it.

As doctrines of utility and self-making encourage Victorians to conduct experiments in living that allow them to evolve their idea of the world from their experience of the world rather than the other way round, Victorian culture enters its third and final stage. The origins and influence of utilitarianism are well understood, but a word should be said about the origin of the equally influential doctrine of self-making. Allied to the moral theology of the evangelicals and the Christian Socialism of F. D. Maurice and J. M. Ludlow, the teaching that we forge an identity for ourselves through moral vocation and work is a legacy of the post-Kantian idealism of J. G. Ficthe in *Die Bestimmung des Menschen* and of the left-wing Hegelianism of David Friedrich Strauss, especially in *Das Leben Jesu*. Both treatises are important sources of Carlyle's thought. By salvation through work the Victorians mean primarily good deeds and social reform. But "work" is a complex word and includes all forms of creation, including that incessant discipline of imagination through practice that Ruskin sees as the incommunicable possession of the true artist. Work brings release of energy only when it is pursued "honestly," as Ruskin explains, and "with all [our] might" (18:181). Though work is energy expended with a further end in view, it must be engaged in as if it were play, an expenditure of energy for its own sake, as in the pursuit of art or a liberal education. Better than talking, which too often mistakes logomachy for wisdom and pugnacity for piety, are the silent communal acts of fellowship and work that enable us to see the real form of wisdom as creative and not simply as doctrinal or learned.

Equally influential is Feuerbach's *The Essence of Christianity*, translated from the German by George Eliot, and F. H. Bradley's *Ethical Studies*. Feuerbach's teaching that theology is veiled anthropology, a repressed knowledge that man is divine (or more precisely, that God is man in alienation from himself), celebrates the self-maker's forgotten supremacy over the rest of creation. And in *Ethical Studies* Bradley offers the most rigorous Victorian exposition of the doctrine of self-making. His later metaphysical treatise, *Appearance and Reality*, represents the conservative side of Hegel's legacy. It removes the absolute to a stratosphere so rarefied, so stripped of even the attributes of personality, and so far above the world of ordinary appearances that even the Brahm of Hindu theology would think twice before entering it. But his earlier *Ethical Studies*, the most Hegelian of Bradley's writings, presents a very different picture. For as well as asserting the irrevocable otherness of God, Hegel also insists that God is perpetually in motion, always in the process of shaping his own divine identity. Influenced by this radical side of Hegel, Bradley argues that morality is a drama of self-realization, a pilgrimage that, in constantly refining and correcting itself, cannot logically terminate and still remain moral. When Pringle-Pattison in *Hegelianism and Personality* (1887) and F. C. S. Schiller in *Humanism* (1903) and *Riddles of the Sphinx* (1912) turn Hegel's doctrine of absolute or eternal self-making from a statement about God into a statement about man, their teaching merely carries to its logical conclusion an existential notion that Bradley had dramatized with an exciting tautness of implication in *Ethical Studies*—a *Bildungsroman* of the moral pilgrim's coming to more and more self-knowledge.

The existential doctrine of self-making exercises a threefold influence on Victorian literature. It substitutes performative for descriptive language; it promotes new nonessentialist definitions of words like "justice" and "duty"; and it replaces the empirical-scientific model, according to which knowledge is given in the data, with a humanistic Viconian model, according to which literature and history provide the privileged forms of knowing: *verum/factum*.

Though Tennyson accepts Vico's teaching that nature remains opaque, he also believes that the world man's creative spirit makes is a world in which each of us is sovereign. In section 123 of *In Memoriam* the external pageant of *mens* in nature, which God alone can understand because he is its author, seems about to end in terrifying absurdity. Yet the dissolution of this external world, which must always seem opaque and inscrutable to observers like Tennyson's mourner, because they have not made it, brings the exalting discovery that, since there is also *mens* in human affairs, each individual self, by birth and by nature, is an artist, an architect, a lesser god, capable of fashioning new and better worlds.

Vico's own doctrine of self-making "stems," as one commentator says, "from the Augustinian dogma that God by knowing creates, that for Him knowing and creating are one, a doctrine that goes back to the conception of the Divine Logos; God alone knows all because He creates all" (Berlin 1976, 116). But Vico's revolutionary move is to apply the *verum/factum* formula not just to God's creation by verbal fiat, but to human history in its widest sense. The more faithful Tennyson is to Vico's revolutionary idea, the greater the gulf he creates between *mens* in nature and *mens* in human affairs. The more translucent the mourner's dreams become, irradiated by his own creative spirit, the more opaque must seem the mind of God, that "wild poet" who has designed a hostile nature and who seems to work "Without a conscience or an aim" (*In Memoriam*, 34.7–8). If man is truly a self-maker, as Tennyson argues in his late poem "The Making of Man," then he cannot be fashioned in the image of a mad creator: and if God is truly what Augustine says he is, then such a deity has set fixed limits to the man-made world in which each creative self is a true citizen. Crises in representation arise when Tennyson's doctrine of self-making comes into conflict with the official Victorian teaching that God alone is a creator.

Hopkins and Browning both try to resolve such a crisis by making the believer's performative acts, his wagers of faith, lesser but still authentic versions of the performative language God uses to create the world in Genesis. In *The Wreck of the Deutschland* the nun's extraordinary act of christening "her wild-worst / Best" (24.8–9) is assimilated, through a daring performative use of words, to Job's heroic act of acknowledging that the God who has created has also taken away. Even in destroying, God is still to be blessed. If the nun's "worst" is also "Best," because she *says* it is, then she is using words creatively, as God does in Genesis, to make something happen.

Like Hopkins in *The Wreck of the Deutschland*, Browning in "Saul" wants to discover how far a worshiper can be humanly receptive of God's gifts while still rising through faith above mere receptivity. The speaker, David, must work at the height of his imaginative and intellectual powers, but he must also celebrate the otherness of God by remaining the seer in whom revelation takes place. No matter how hard Hopkins's nun and Browning's David try, however, to make the performative language of faith a lesser version of the *verum/factum* doctrine of Augustine's theology, they find it increasingly difficult to find the right names for God. The crises of representation become the crisis of their faith. If their performative language is ungrounded in the performative decrees of God, then it annihilates the condition of religious faith. As I observed elsewhere, "the dangerous, mysterious power of performative positing, which tends to erode the believer's knowledge of a gift God has already bestowed, appears to be one of the paradoxes of religion. Like Hegel, Browning speaks as if God's gift both *is* and is *not* fully real until a believer like Browning's David works at the height of his powers to bring that gift into focus and receive it" (Shaw 1987, 265).

Attempts by Browning and Hopkins to reconcile the Augustinian notion that God alone has knowledge of the world, because he alone created it, with Vico's doctrine that man too is a creator, equally knowledgeable in his own sphere, present no problem for George Eliot. She resolves the crisis by denying that an opaque and inscrutable otherworldly God exists. Theology, according to Feuerbach, Eliot's favorite philosopher of religion, has traditionally suppressed the truth that when we say God suffers, what is truly divine is the human predicate "suffering," not the subject "God." In Feuerbach's words, "he who suffers for others, who lays down his life for them, acts divinely, is a god to men" (1957, 60). Only as Dinah Morris forsakes the rhetoric of otherworldly theology, which alienates listeners like Bessy Cranage and Hetty Sorrel, can she discover in the prison scene's half-silent fellowship a version of the new Feuerbachian religion George Eliot has been seeking. Doctrines of self-making encourage Eliot to experiment with pragmatic redefinitions, not only of words like "theology" in *Adam Bede*, but also of the very idea of "heroism" in *Middlemarch*. In retaining the favorable emotive meaning of "heroine," Eliot is able to give the word a new descriptive meaning, which identifies the concept with its use. What is the use of being a Victorian Saint Theresa or a modern Vesalius if one has no theater to perform in? Eliot, like the utilitarians, has little sympathy for "geniuses" like Casaubon, too clever in general to achieve anything in particular. She approves instead of dedicated but unglamorous characters like the reformed heroine of the Finale, whose "unhistoric acts" exercise an "incalculably diffusive" influence on "those around her." And yet a new problem arises: If the value of Dorothea's life is conferred by its limits, by the channels that direct the brook's flow, and if the meaning of her life continues to derive from the wider historical theater of a Christian Antigone or a Victorian Saint Theresa, the more valuable Dorothea's life becomes, the less meaning it seems to possess, and vice versa.

New existential definitions of words like "theology" and "heroism," which equate meaning with experiments in living, are most evident in J. S. Mill. Essentialist definitions of "morality," "justice," and "duty" have petrified into blank counters that block intelligent thought. They must be translated either into blueprints for action or else into stories about past events that explain the historical origin of the concept. Justice, for example, has to be redefined to accommodate the humble circumstances of its origin. What has in fact occurred in the past and is likely to occur in the future is made the measure of what ought to be. What ought to be, as in Kant's categorical definition of what is moral, is not appealed to as the sanction of what works. But conflicts naturally arise. Because a proper utilitarian definition of "happiness" is likely to generate as many different conceptions of happiness as there are people to define it, the more liberty people have to conduct their own experiments in living the less consensus there will be about what is useful. Why should Mill's pursuit of his own happiness be expected to maximize the happiness of the greatest number? The more liberty Mill has to cause mental pain to the pious, the less general utility, and vice versa.

The theory of knowledge assumed by most detective stories and mystery fictions is the chain of logically connected events; though some of its links will be missing, they are in theory recoverable. But if F. H. Bradley and Barthold Niebuhr are right, and the mind of the critical historican or detective can possess knowledge only of its own controlling analogies and fictions, then the simple empirical model of the inductive chain will have to be supplemented by a model of inquiry in which the interpreter supplies essential ingredients of his own knowledge. The truly revolutionary move in Bradley's *Presupposi-*

tions of Critical History is the application of the *verum/factum* principle to the study of history. If Barthold Niebuhr's historian can come as close as possible to the attainment by a human being of divine knowledge, it is because the interpreter's empathy with historical agents turns history itself into a human invention.

In a detective fiction like *The Moonstone* competing models of knowledge begin to precipitate crises in representation. The scientific historiography of H. T. Buckle, who assumes that a close study of the data allows history to write itself, minimizes the contribution of the historian. And the mythical theories of Strauss, who allows the fertile imagination of the mythmaker to erode the factual base of history altogether, minimize the contribution of evidence and testimony. As Collins dramatizes a similar clash between the naive empiricism of Mr. Bruff and the fanciful hypotheses of Sergeant Cuff, it seems as if the truth about the moonstone's theft is doomed to escape through a hole at the center. The more imaginative the detective, the less his theories correspond with the facts; and the more inductive the investigator, the less understanding he displays of Bradley's and Vico's *verum/factum* principle. Only the empathetic and long-suffering Ezra Jennings can resolve this crisis by supplying the balance of critical detachment and sympathetic imagination that Bradley and Niebuhr call for.

A similar crisis of knowing arises in *The Ring and the Book*. The positivist's simple chain model of the "A B C of fact" (1.708) clashes ironically with the narrator's more pragmatic model of engendering truth upon the facts: "Fancy with fact is just one fact the more" (1.464). One might think that, after going to great pains to forge a coherent chain of logically connected argument in support of his verdict, the pope would then use the links in that chain to arrive inductively at a conclusion. Instead, quickened by a voice that asks "Quis pro Domino?" (10.2100), he takes a leap in the dark and sentences Guido on impulse. The center of truth in *The Ring and the Book* is the "circle" of meaning in which each enlightened interpreter must come to stand. But as Schleiermacher notes, this "hermeneutical circle" gives rise to a crisis of knowing. For to grasp the whole, we must first understand the parts; but to understand the parts we must also grasp the whole. How can the process of understanding ever get started? Only, presumably, by taking a leap of faith. Such a leap allows Caponsacchi or the pope, in a process that resists analysis, to understand the whole and the parts together. But the more heroic a knight of faith appears, the less induction he can utilize; and the more logic and induction he displays, the more he is paralyzed by indecision.

Part of the intellectual equipment of the historical interpreter is his sense of mystery, his feel for the strangeness of the human world and the queerness of its laws. No amount of analysis or historical empathy can remove this sense of mystery. The more we read *The Ring and the Book*, the more it keeps disclosing new and profounder mysteries. Both the dogmatism of the positivist historian, confident of his "very A B C of fact," and the skepticism of Tertium Quid, who turns deconstruction into a dry and mindless exercise, breed arrogance and encourage these extremists to say more than they mean. Bewilderment, by contrast, breeds humility and teaches the narrator at the end of the poem, in telling "a truth / Obliquely" (12.859–60), to say less than he means.

Sometimes a crisis in representation is meant never to be resolved. If knowledge is the revelation of a mystery, as Newman and Hopkins argue, then the purpose of a crisis may be to bring into sharper focus the mysteries of faith that really exist. I do not want to imply, however, that most crises of representation are incapable of being resolved. Crisis means "choice," and in adjudicating the competing claims of irony and suspense, for example, or utility and individual liberty, such writers as Trollope and J. S. Mill have enough intellectual courage and honesty to make decisions when decisions are called for. In sacrificing suspense to irony in *Barchester Towers*, for example, Trollope is not forgoing mystery. He is merely forgoing one kind of mystery—the mystery of an unknown outcome—in order to explore the more complex and satisfying mysteries of human identity. Arnold, by contrast, refuses to choose among incompatible goods and sometimes seems intellectually confused as a result. He wants culture to combine four different powers of the human person, but he seems to forget that Athens is not Jerusalem. Socrates would be "terribly at ease in Zion," and would Shakespeare really have been welcome on the *Mayflower?* Arnold of all people should have realized that the more strictness of conscience, the less spontaneity of consciousness, and vice versa.

J. S. Mill is as consistent a utilitarian as it is possible for any major philosopher to be. But because he is more intellectually honest and less confused than Arnold, who wants culture to be all things to all people, he is prepared to make difficult choices when contradictions in life or thought demand them. Mill knows that to choose between a God who is beneficent but not omnipotent and a God who is omnipotent but cruel is bound to cause some irreparable loss in our understanding of deity. But he is prepared to sacrifice majesty and mystery to moral intelligibility, even though he invites the wrath of more mystified philosophers than himself. Even when pursuit of liberty comes into conflict with Mill's cherished doctrine of utility, he has no hesitation about which choice to make. Instead of maximizing the happiness score of the world, he will maximize his personal liberty.

A conflict is bound to arise between "utilitarianism proper" and the "preliminary utilitarianism" that requires each individual to conduct his own experiments in living. But only such preliminary inquiries and experiments can make utilitarianism a compelling doctrine. As Richard Wollheim explains, "each person arrives at his conception of utility by projecting on to some tried and tested way of life a certain inner state of mind. Utility is emblematic of bliss." And as he goes on to say, "if the loss in utility [proper] is not too great," the loss that comes from a reluctance to maximize the happiness of the greatest number, then "the claims of preliminary Utilitarianism should be preferred. For better than most things is that persons should develop their conceptions of utility" (Wollheim 1984, 223–24). Having identified a conflict and opted for personal liberty, Mill then goes to great lengths to balance the claims of "preliminary utilitarianism" and "utilitarianism proper," the claims of both value and moral obligation. As Wollheim concludes, "it is failure to recognize what was at work in Mill's reasoning that has led critics to accuse him of inconsistency when in fact he was guilty of nothing worse than subtlety" (1984, 224). The world, I think, ought to live up to Mill's intellectual conception of it, and if there are crises of representation and even conflicts in Mill's thought we may feel that these come from a limitation in life itself, not from a defect in Mill.

The Conclusion to this book has been drawing distinctions between mysteries that are unspeakable and mysteries that are inexpressible; between meanings that are conferred by enlarged contexts and values that attach to particular people and places; and between crises in representation that are incapable in principle of being resolved and crises that involve decision or choice. This third distinction invites us to differentiate between unfathomable mysteries, or mysteries proper, and mysteries that can be solved by turning them into puzzles and problems. To make all three distinctions as clear as possible, I shall end with brief separate treatments of each.

Mysteries, Puzzles, and Problems

When exploration of a subject precipitates a crisis in representation, that crisis can be treated in one of three ways. If the crisis seems incapable of being resolved, then the inquirer may be exhorted to live with it and accept it as an inescapable feature of that subject's mystery. Such is H. L. Mansel's response to his discovery that attributes of deity like the absolute, the infinite, and a first cause are in logical contradiction. In the impotence of his reason, he resolves to take refuge in faith. Like Newman and Hopkins, Mansel affirms that God is an "incomprehensible certainty" that exceeds his comprehension. An alternative response is to treat a crisis in representation as a puzzle that a philosopher of religion is capable of solving. When Mill discovers that God's goodness and omnipotence are in conflict, he treats the contradiction not as one of Mansel's or Sir William Hamilton's religious mysteries, but as a puzzle to be solved. The apparent mystery is dispelled by clarifying what we should already know: that the God of rational theology, like the God of the Gnostics, is benign but not all-powerful.

A third response to a crisis in representation is to treat it neither as a mystery that defies solutions nor as a puzzle for philosophy to solve but as a problem to which science alone can find an answer. According to T. H. Huxley, puzzles about whether the world is material or spiritual can be solved in science by determining which formula or notation—the materialist terminology or the spiritual one—best facilitates comparison and best extends our knowledge of physical nature. But the solution to the puzzle, Which terminology can best control and predict natural phenomena? never presumes to resolve the mystery of what the external world is really like. Indeed, it is fatal to mistake these materialist fictions for metaphysical dogmas. And the reason for originally accepting as true notations these mere "names for . . . imaginary substrata of groups of natural phenomena" (Huxley, 1:160) is the same reason for treating them later as fictions: namely, the desirable or undesirable consequence of doing so. Invested with a misplaced concreteness, materialist explanations, instead of solving problems and puzzles, become new forms of mystery. And they have the disastrous effect of paralyzing the mind's energies and destroying the beauty of its world (Huxley, 1:165).

If a problem is defined as "something which can be solved," as one commentator explains, "and which ceases to be mysterious when it is solved" (Foster 1957, 18), then the mystery of fatality that hangs over someone like Hardy's Tess is fundamentally different from a problem, for it proceeds from a sense that there is a way things are, but only fools assume it is knowable or known. Nor is the crisis that arises in *Wuthering Heights* from Brontë's collapse of all words into a fearful synonym the kind of crisis that can be solved by providing an answer to a crossword puzzle or a coded message. The mystery in *The Moonstone* is largely annihilated when the puzzle of who stole the diamond is solved. But as Newman knows, there are other mysteries that cannot be solved by "paper logic" alone. No matter how fully an object of faith is understood, as an "incomprehensible certainty" it will still retain a residue of mystery.

Genuine mysteries are likely to be found in a poem like *The Ring and the Book*, which pushes beyond its natural length and finally stops abruptly, like Mark's gospel, instead of reaching a logical conclusion. By contrast, the mysteries in a detective fiction like *The Moonstone*, which reaches a natural conclusion once the crime is solved, are likely to be mere puzzles of devising opium experiments or of deciphering transcripts and coded messages. The self-conscious mysteries in *The Ring and the Book* and *Sartor Resartus* are also the mysteries of metafictions in which a commenting narrator and editor parade their awareness that both the narrative world of the source books and the "real" world of the commentators are imaginative fictions. The arbitrary stopping points in such fictions send a reader in search of some vanished Ur-book or lost original, of which the texts we have are mere copies or traces. What has been concluded in such books that there is anything to conclude? Like the last line of *La Saisiaz*: "Least part this: then what the whole?" (l. 618), a mystery text that stops rather than concludes, and that cannot be explained away as a mere problem or puzzle, always remains a mere metonymy for something unsayable, something the writer who honestly charts the truth of his feelings can never quite put into words. When a text breaks off suddenly, like Jocelin's narrative in *Past and Present*, it has the same effect as the abrupt ending in Mark's gospel, which stops before the expected resurrection story can be told. In Heathcliff's phrase, the meanings of a true mystery story are "unutterable." Carlyle's abrupt ending encourages us to break out of the mystery world of his medieval narrative for the "real" world of history, where we are invited to make such sense of the mysteries as we can. Do mysteries of medieval faith fade away in the light of day? Or is the "real" world the shadow that must learn to grow into the substance of Abbot Samson's vision?

A writer who treats mere puzzles and problems as mysteries proper bewitches our mind with mere mystification. The problem with a mere mystification is that it prevents the exploration of a real mystery. According to Huxley, mystification includes all examples of "lunar politics," all inquiries into the existence and attributes of unknown entities like God, as well as fruitless speculations about necessary connection.

The opposite tendency, represented by a reductive thinker like Pater in *Plato and Platonism*, is to turn a metaphysical mystery like Plato's doctrine of Ideas into a mere puzzle or problem to be explained away. Though Heraclitus offers a readily intelligible doctrine of flux, its principle of lapse and waste erodes all grounds. By contrast, Plato's doctrine of immutable ideas, though barely intelligible in itself, becomes the condition of intelligibility in everything else. Though Plato's doctrine of Ideas is the granite beneath the wasting torrent of phenomena, Pater contends that whenever Plato expounds this doctrine he is trying to make language mean more than it can intelligibly say. Quixotic quests in search of a true Substance, a One, or an Absolute are doomed to fail, because they pursue nonexistent ends. If Pure Being is as colorless, formless, and impalpable as Plato says, then as far as Pater is concerned it is as spectral and fictitious as a ghost. Once we demystify such words, we discover they are "after all but zero, a mere algebraic symbol for nothingness" (1910, 40).

Pater is baffled by other crises of knowing in Plato. On the one hand, Plato makes "the largest possible demand for infallible certainty in knowledge" (188). His constant dissatisfaction with what passes for knowledge, which is really ignorance in disguise, comes from an exacting conception of what precise knowledge entails. On the other hand, Plato permits "the utmost possible inexactness, or contingency, in the method by which he proposes to attain" knowledge. His method is informal, unsystematic. The inexactness and hesitancy, the scruples and reserve, are not, however, a result of the illusory status of knowledge itself. It comes instead from Plato's sense that knowledge reveals a mystery and from his fear of obtruding such knowledge on an unworthy receiver. Pater's Plato resembles a late-Victorian Keble, a defender of mystery who anticipates Tractarian doctrines of reserve.

In Pater's view, philosophic fictions are hard to recognize as fictions, for they are always the prisoners of their own grammar. If Plato were to concede that his doctrine of Ideas is true only in an allegorical or a poetic sense, like one of his myths, Pater would not object to it. But metaphysics, like religion, must deceive to tell the truth, and so every friend of truth must oppose it. Yet if Plato were to admit that his doctrine of Ideas is only the poetry of truth, such an admission would rob the doctrine of its efficacy. The paradox is that metaphysics, like religion, has to lie to be true. It is in the nature of metaphysics and religion to proclaim true fictions, what David Friedrich Strauss would call "unconscious fictions," or lies that cannot be perceived as lies. But is a "true lie" not a contradiction in terms? If metaphysics is true to its essence, it also follows that it cannot be true, for to be true it has to lie. Conversely, if metaphysics truthfully exposes its lies as lies, it falsifies its essence, and so also lies about itself, even though it may be telling the truth for the first time. Though Pater honors Plato's feel for the strangeness of nature, he keeps exposing crises of knowing in Plato that tempt Pater to explain away as mere perverse puzzles and conundrums the metaphysical mysteries, the unfathomable ones, that are really there. Pater can never quite grasp, I think, that for Plato, as for the biblical authors, knowledge does not eliminate mystery but reveals it.

The Unspeakable and the Inexpressible

I have been exploring ways that crises in knowledge and faith produce crises in literary representation and different kinds of silence. Some truths, though capable of being spoken about, seem too private or interior to profane with words: they are unspeakable. Other truths can be lived but not known: they are inexpressible, because they must be presented wordlessly. Different uses of irony help clarify the situations in which the silence of what is merely unspeakable begins to deepen into the silence of what is not strictly speaking expressible. At other times it may be hard to distinguish between the two kinds of silence.

In his classic analysis of ironic encounters, W. H. Empson shows how an ironist, A, fools a censor, B, while appealing to the judgment of a reader, C (1984, 132). In Empson's first scenario, where a writer uses silence to hold meaning in reserve, the identities of the ironist, A, and the censor, B, converge. The reserve that Browning uses at the end of La Saisiaz to protect the memory of his dead wife allows the poet to hint at the deepest source of his belief without desecrating her grave. In such a crisis of representation, the truth is unspeakable: that is to say, the roots of Browning's faith are known to him, but they cannot be profaned by words without causing psychic shock or "earthquake" (l. 616). Perhaps the elegist is conscious of a wound at the center of his life and his poem that he is afraid of opening up. In either case the censor who veils the truth is also an ally or friend who protects Browning from profaning a mystery or from facing another crisis of knowledge or faith. But the ironist's censorship is never total. By veiling the truth from scoffers while obliquely communicating its mystery to sympathetic readers, the ironist half-defeats the censor in himself.

In Browning's "Prologue" to Asolando, by contrast, God is said to transcend nature, and an ironic sense of the limits of our knowledge is the only truth to be expressed. As in the first crisis of representation, the ironist, A, and the censor, B, are conflated, but for different reasons. When Browning urges the reader to "Bend knees, / Drop eyes to earthward" and then renounce language altogether in favor of the "Silence . . . awe decrees" (ll. 28–30), there is no longer any prospect of going behind a censor's back to see what the truth really is. The revelation of God is at the same time a veiling of God: for Kierkegaard the Incarnation is the assumption of an incognito that obscures as well as reveals the divine nature, as Browning's Caesar veils his identity in "Imperante Augusto Natus Est." If God's holiness derives from his hiddenness, then his truth is inexpressible, and all formulations of godhead deserve to be censored. In scenario one, when silence is used as a form of reserve or as a means of veiling some emptiness or blank, a limited form of censorship is used by the ironist as a means of protection. But if large tracts of truth are always inconceivable to our minds, then censorship may be said to constitute a principle of ironic veiling or venerable concealment with far wider application. Such veiling is a precondition of any teaching that the world exists independent of our capacity to know it.

In a third scenario, where the ironist, A, and the censor, B, begin to part company for the first time, the writer may persuade both an ironist who believes the truth is inexpressible, as in scenario two, and a censor who feels the truth is unspeakable, as in scenario one, that he is in partial agreement with each of them. As in any form of double irony, however, it seems illogical to entertain these two interpretations of secrecy or silence simultaneously. As in *Amours de Voyage*, where Clough can sometimes be felt behind the seeing eye of the spectator who watches life from the sidelines and sometimes behind the risk taker who rejects knowledge in favor of action, the double ironist refuses to affirm, unequivocally, which of the two dramatized minds is right. Is the truth merely unspeakable, as the censor of Claude's timidity implies? Or is it actually inexpressible, as the ironist seems to discover when he tries to put into words his subversive thoughts about marriage and life?

Similar questions arise about the "silent-speaking words" of Hallam's letters in *In Memoriam* (95.26). Is the silence a result of the mourner's instinctive censorship of meanings too sacred to profane or too secret to share? Or do the words actually reach the mourner from the other side of silence? If so, Hallam's words may be "silent-speaking" not because they are unspeakable, like the thoughts conveyed in the letters to Hallam that Hallam's father eventually destroyed, but because, like any communication from a ghost, they are inexpressible. In place of proud and knowing irony, the double ironist presents the hesitations and the doubts of uncertainty itself.

When Is a Book or an Idea "Deep"?

What accounts for the "depth" and difficult lucidity of Newman's Oxford sermons? Why do readers grapple in agitation and excitement with the oracular fragments of *In Memoriam*? Why do silences and stoppages bring reading to a halt in *Sartor Resartus?* It is not just that each cryptic stanza of *In Memoriam* is chiseled like an epitaph, or that the aphoristic style of *Sartor Resartus* is both the language of unquestioned authority and the language of probation and inquiry. Such books are "deep" because they mean more than they say. Often their words reach us from the other side of silence. Newman's prose is full of new and deeper silences that hold meaning in reserve. Sometimes Carlyle's prose says nothing but points toward the silence of a "signless Inane." And there are moments of plenitude in *In Memoriam* when, after uttering enigmatic phrases like "Peace" or "The dawn, the dawn," Tennyson finds to his amazement there are no more words to speak, because he is momentarily in possession of all words.

According to Wittgenstein, "deep disquietudes" are rooted in our grammar "and their significance is as great as the importance of our language" (1972, 47e, proposition 111). Unlike Wittgenstein, most Victorians believe it is not just grammatical jokes that are felt to be deep. Something is deep if we can know just so much about it as to know we can never know it all. One of the great crises in representation in Carlyle's prose is his evocation of a "mysterious Mankind" thundering and flaming "in long-drawn, quick-succeeding grandeur, through the unknown Deep" (1:212). His use of "Deep" seems deeply puzzling, for if the "Deep" is as "unknown" as he says it is, how can we know it is "Deep?" It seems as if we can know "Deep" only as a metonymy or part, but never as the whole for which "Deep" stands. If the "unknown Deep" is bottomless, it induces vertigo. But if it has a bottom beyond the reach of our minds, a solid bedrock or *point d'appui*, then it may encourage us to seek more inclusive perspectives. At times Carlyle speaks as if there may be a solid bottom, even though no explorer has ever reached it. At other times he speaks as if the notion of a firm foundation is only a fiction. Is Carlyle's exposer of illusion a heroic quester? Or is he just a doomed and sinking mariner? If ocean floors we can see or reach are felt to be too shallow, then an image of a deep sea—as opposed, say, to a mere black hole or void (or an ocean with trapdoors)—may be used to combine the desire for a ground with the desire for something always out of reach.

Such crises of representation are constantly threatening us with two opposite forms of drowning: we may flounder like Clough's Claude in a dangerous element where bottom is never reached, or we may drown in our own unscrutinized certainties, like Clough's timid shore dweller, who is afraid of taking risks. If we reach bottom prematurely, like the solipsist who can never see beyond the shallows of his own mind, then we perish in our own idolatries. But if we believe, like the realist, that there are always untraveled worlds to explore, whose horizons fade for ever and ever as we move, then the view we are trying to track from outside may begin to assume an uncomfortable resemblance to Tennyson's time-lapse photograph of the earth extending over billions of years.

> There rolls the deep where grew the tree.
> O earth, what changes hast thou seen!
> There where the long street roars, hath been
> The stillness of the central sea.
>
> (*In Memoriam*, 123.1–4)

Only a photographer on a satellite in outer space could take such a picture, and there would never be world enough nor time to develop it. But when the earth is seen from this far out, is it any wonder that a traveler of Carlyle's "unknown Deep" should feel adrift? It is as if the world he was charting has suddenly lost its moorings, and he experiences for the first time the slow catastrophe by which all things "seriously, sadly [run] away," as Robert Frost remarks, "To fill the abyss's void with emptiness" ("West-Running Brook," ll. 48–49).

How Does Literature "Mean"?

In Arnold's definition of "culture," Newman's definition of "faith," or Ruskin's definition of "mystery," we may expect to hear some secret formula, some esoteric doctrine that, once imparted, will increase our understanding of life. But answers to such questions as What is culture? or What is faith? are bound to be as withholding as Socrates' answers. No formula can answer ultimate questions satisfactorily. And it is essential that definitions of these mystery words should never fully resolve the crises of faith and knowledge that give rise to crises in literary representation in the first place. More important than a set of theories about culture, faith, or the scientific method are sets of questions that begin and end in wonder. The delight of such focused questioning and wonder, pursued in a spirit of freedom and playfulness, seems as self-evident to its possessors as any other pleasure.

We have to spend some time with a thinker's syntax and metaphors before we can hope to find profundity in his formulas or point in his definitions. By being responsive to a writer's literary and other values, we come to see that words like "culture" and "faith" mean in different ways. "Meaning" itself is a complex word. For Pater it signifies formal significance and aesthetic value. For Huxley, as for Bentham, "meaning" signifies causal connection. For Arnold the "meaning" of culture is its semantic relation: What are its synonyms? How can neighboring words define it? For Newman "meaning" always includes intention or purpose. What does a believer intend by his faith? What is his purpose?

How can a life exemplify meaning? And how can a poem or novel exemplify it? Nelson Goodman (1968) argues that to exemplify meaning is both to have that meaning and to refer to it. Hopkins sometimes speaks as if God created people as semantic objects to refer to himself. Everyone is a name for God: each person both refers to God and has the property of so referring, like a mirror that flashes back God's face. Often the precise property that a life exemplifies, the quality it both *has* and *refers to* in Goodman's sense is difficult to name. It can best be seen in a figure like Shakespeare, who "led a life of Allegory," as Keats remarked, and whose "works are the comments on it" (letter of Feb. 19, 1819). The life of a great teacher, a Socrates or Christ, resembles a perfect work of art in that it means what it exemplifies. Similarly, an essay like Mill's *On Liberty* becomes a work of art by exemplifying the free enterprise it advocates.

By contrast, Mill's *System of Logic*, like most of Bentham's and Darwin's prose, devotes enormous energy to work in which nothing of the writer's values or important goals is allowed to shine forth. Though something of Bentham's utilitarian rigor may filter through his opaque prose, the truths to be discovered in his *Essay on Government* can be just as readily presented in other people's words, like the conclusions of a scientific report. A social scientist brackets values: he uses quotation marks to fence them off. But even when Arnold tries to achieve a social scientist's objectivity by using quotation marks in *Culture and Anarchy*, his detachment proves illusory. Because Arnold takes elaborate care to view each quotation with reverence or disdain, readers still experience Arnold's own crises of faith and knowing directly.

There is no obvious limit to the complexity of the maneuvers by which authors, in conveying their own responses to value, anticipate readers' responsiveness. In "Before the Curtain" in *Vanity Fair*, Thackeray's portrait of "a man with a reflective turn of mind" dictates the response of an ideal reader. And because Dorothea's response to values in *Middlemarch* encourages readers to respond to her responding, Ladislaw is justified in saying her life is already a "poem," a humanistic work of art (chap. 22).

An inquiry is humanistic if it allows us to respond to values and also to the inquirer's own responsiveness to value. The function of Carlyle's editors and of Browning's silent auditors in his dramatic monologues is to create works of art in which we, the audience, can also respond to values directly. The elaborate nesting structure of *Sartor Resartus* and the infinite recesses that open in the middle of many of Browning's poems mime the complexity of a reader's own crises of faith and knowing. The editor or silent auditor responds in ways we should endorse or reject: it is impossible to remain neutral.

For this reason even science can be carried on in the spirit of the humanities. One commentator wistfully observes that "one of the most glorious achievements of the modern mind, science, seems to leave no room for its own glory; ... the reduced image of man toward which it seems inexorably to lead—a mean and pitiable plaything of forces beyond his control—seems to leave no room even for the creators, and the creation, of science" (Nozick 1981, 627). To recover some portion of that glory is an important function of T. H. Huxley's essays on science. One purpose of humanistic inquiry is to set free our capacity for new experience. New knowledge is not yet knowledge, for we cannot know anything that is wholly unfamiliar to us. But what ought to be continuously new and exciting is the adventure of discovering what scientists like Charles Darwin knew and of relating this knowledge to our experience of life. To recover the sense of boldness and novelty that must have accompanied Darwin's own search for a unifying theory of changes in nature, we turn not to Darwin himself, but to a scientific humanist, Huxley, whose crises of representation in literary prose are continually responding to crises of faith and knowing. Like Lewis Thomas, Huxley realizes that bewilderment is "the family secret of . . . science, and of . . . arts and letters as well. . . . The more we learn, the more we are—or ought to be—dumbfounded" (Thomas 1984, 157). As a disciple of learned ignorance, Huxley is always keen to distinguish between a mathematical proof, which compels assent by rearranging the unknown until the known is fitted into it, and a scientific explanation like his own favored materialist hypothesis, which is more mysterious and unfamiliar than a proof, because it always leaves room for novelties of free assent or doubt.

Are Meaning and Value in Conflict?

Values are threatened in two opposite ways. Since they usually attach themselves to specific ends and goals, values may be eroded from the far side by a search for ever wider contexts of meaning. Alternatively, values may be eroded from the near side by reductive explanations. Mill's rejection of deontological ethics, Huxley's critique of theology, and Pater's deconstruction of Plato's metaphysics all illustrate the process of explaining the complex by the simple. It sometimes seems as if everything has been subject to reductionist explanations except reductionism itself. We explain love of God, the eros that urges Plato's soul toward intellectual contemplation, and even moral intuition, by operations that are not themselves intuitive or "in love."

Values are eroded from the other side by quests for meaning that efface the boundaries to which values tend to adhere. Faced with a conflict between the meaning of her life and its value, George Eliot's Dorothea Brooke is forced to make trade-offs between them. In the end she renounces historical meaning for private value. Though she continues to exercise a diffusive influence, the boundaries of that influence are far more circumscribed than she foresaw in the Prelude. If value is conferred by a value seeker bound indissolubly to a limited point of view, and if meaning is a function of expanding contexts, then even Lydgate reaches a point where the value of his marriage and the meaning of his medical research are in open conflict. Hinting at the darker side of gender relations, the epigraph of the first chapter of *Middlemarch* implies that women are forced to choose value over meaning, whereas men are allowed to conduct experiments in felicity: Lydgate is freer than Dorothea to follow his bliss.

But what is bliss? How does it relate to value and meaning? In a state of bliss value is not bruised to pleasure meaning: the details that confer value do not inhibit an enlargement of the context. Yet how is this possible? Do value and meaning not exist in inverse proportion? Is bliss, like Milton's fame, *not* a plant that grows on mortal soil? Perhaps only the unlimitedness of F. H. Bradley's absolute or Paul Emmanuel's Miltonic god—a "mighty unseen centre incomprehensible, irrealisable" (*Villette*, chap. 36)—can provide a secure stopping place for questions about bliss. Ultimate meaning and bliss are conferred when limits are broken through and a poet like Christina Rossetti, in her search for at-onement with God, reaches something still personal and valuable that has no limit. Her God is just such a boundlessness, because he cannot be stood outside of, even in imagination:

> Our God, Heaven cannot hold Him
>   Nor earth sustain;
> Heaven and earth shall flee away
>   When He comes to reign:
>   ("In the bleak mid-winter," ll. 9–12)

In line 9 God literally escapes the boundaries and bonds of the heaven that would hold him, by becoming the framing word around "Heaven" ("Our God" at the beginning of the line and "Him" at the end) rather than the word we expect "Heaven" and "earth" to "hold" or frame. Another bond that is broken is the boundary we cross when God is allowed to ride freely across the space between lines. In becoming the grammatical object of a second verb, "sustain" (l. 10), God effaces the borderline between heaven and earth, even before that boundary and the two regions it divides are said to dissolve and "flee away" in the following line.

When Rossetti in her union with boundlessness finds all her heart can wish, the question, What is the meaning of such at-onement? cannot arise, because she has reached the place where there is nowhere else to stand. Rossetti acquires meaning through connection with God, but by definition a God who is boundless has nothing outside him with which a worshiper might connect. Unless God is always with her, he cannot be unlimited. But if Christina Rossetti is never, strictly speaking, outside God, why must she strive so strenuously to be at one with him? Can her faith in God survive such crises in knowing?

It seems the wider context that confers meaning on God must be God himself. Perhaps, as Robert Nozick suggests, the self-embedding of an infinite series in mathematics may make this difficult idea more intelligible (1981, 602–3). An infinite series can be put into one-to-one correspondence with a subset of itself, with the result that the set of positive integers, n, appears to contain the same number of terms as the set of even integers, two times n. But even if an unlimited being can survive its greatest crises of representation by simultaneously conferring meaning and bringing that process of conferring meaning to an end, is that any reason for supposing it exists? Scrupulous agnostics like Bradley and Huxley maintain rigorous intellectual standards, uninfluenced by any hope that what they want to believe is true. Such stern integrity in the face of intellectual temptation may be valuable, but can it be an act with any meaning? Meaning is a result of connecting, of placing items in context, and how can even integrity connect meaningfully with a void? Christina Rossetti may be wiser than agnostics like Bradley and Huxley. To find a secure basis for meaning and to survive her crises of faith, she must learn through a discipline of love and prayer to seek at-onement with a God whom "Heaven cannot hold... / Nor earth sustain," a boundlessness to which nothing else can secretly give rise and through which it is impossible to fall to a deeper level of being.

Crises of faith and knowing are most acute in elegiac literature. A weak mourner may utter meaningful catchwords, as Tennyson does in the Prologue of *In Memoriam*. But by violating the silence of reserve, such professions of faith usually lack the authority of more withholding testaments. Both Ulysses' near tautology—"that which we are, we are, — / One equal temper of heroic hearts" ("Ulysses," ll. 67–68)—and Christina Rossetti's barely meaningful repetitions—"That which I chose, I choose; / That which I willed, I will" ("All heaven is blazing yet," ll. 9–10)—become valuable in context only because they voice a stoic, scarcely utterable resolve to gather up and concentrate their life's diminished powers. Instead of affirming prematurely some meaningful credo that has no experienced value for the speaker, a weak mourner may suffer the opposite fate of disintegrating completely. Such is the risk Hopkins runs in "Spelt from Sibyl's Leaves," where his half-hysterical protest that his "night... will end [him]" (l. 8) is the poetic equivalent of hand wringing or of tearing out one's hair. By contrast, Arnold's controlled confrontation with vacancy in "Dover Beach" proves that despair can be bracing rather than defeatist. Weak mourners are incapable of remaining in uncertainty: they must either lapse into premature professions of faith that are meaningful but valueless or else dissolve their identities in the void. Clough shows in *Amours de Voyage* that even the potential strength of double irony—the simultaneous endorsement of two contradictory codes—can be debilitating when it allows a skeptic like Claude to defer decisions indefinitely. The silence that accompanies a meaningful recovery of identity becomes fully valuable only when some speechless mourner like George Eliot's Mrs. Bulstrode learns to build a new life for herself on the ruins of the one that collapses around her. Learning to feel and live her truths without speaking them, the heroine who refuses to violate family silences shrinks from words "as she would have shrunk from flakes of fire." "With one leap of her heart," she finds herself at her disgraced husband's side "in mournful but unreproaching fellowship." "She could not say, 'How much is only slander and false suspicion?' and he did not say, 'I am innocent'" (*Middlemarch*, chap. 74). Most memorable are the unheard words and unspoken thoughts, the conversations in literature that never take place. For "words, after speech, reach / Into the silence" (T. S. Eliot, *Burnt Norton*, 5.3–4). And despite the unavoidable dispossession and loss, the heart of meaning lies in that silence.

Bibliography

Works Cited in the Text

apRoberts, Ruth. 1983. *Arnold and God*. Berkeley: University of California Press.

Austin, J. L. 1975. *How to Do Things with Words*. Cambridge: Harvard University Press.

Bentham, Jeremy. 1838–43. *The Works of Jeremy Bentham*. 11 vols. Edinburgh: William Tait.

Berlin, Isaiah. 1976. *Vico and Herder: Two Studies in the History of Ideas*. New York: Viking Press.

Bloom, Allan. 1987. *The Closing of the American Mind*. New York: Simon and Schuster.

Bradley, F. H. 1874. *The Presuppositions of Critical History*. Oxford: J. Parker. Reprinted, ed. Lionel Rubinoff. Don Mills, Ont.: J. M. Dent, 1968.

———. 1876. *Ethical Studies*. Oxford: Clarendon Press. Reprinted 1970.

———. 1883. *The Principles of Logic*. London: Kegan Paul, Trench.

———. 1893. *Appearance and Reality: A Metaphysical Essay*. Oxford: Clarendon Press.

Buckle, H. T. 1864. *History of Civilization in England*. 2 vols. New York: Appleton. Originally published 1857.

Carlyle, Thomas. 1898. *Two Note Books of Carlyle from 23d March 1822 to 16th May 1832*. Ed. Charles Eliot Norton. New York: Grolier Club.

———. 1899. *The Works of Thomas Carlyle*. Vol. 27. London: Chapman and Hall.

Coleridge, S. T. 1905. *Aids to Reflection*. Ed. Thomas Fenby. Edinburgh: J. Grant.

Culler, Jonathan. 1981. *The Pursuit of Signs: Semiotics, Literature, Deconstruction*. Ithaca, N.Y.: Cornell University Press.

Daniélou, Jean. 1960. *From Shadows to Reality: Studies in the Biblical Typology of the Fathers*. Trans. W. Hibberd. London: Newman Press.

de Man, Paul. 1983. *Blindness and Insight: Essays in the Rhetoric of Contemporary Criticism*. Minneapolis: University of Minnesota Press.

Dickens, Charles. 1987. *Genius in Action: Dickens' Working Notes for His Novels*. Ed. Harry Stone. Chicago: University of Chicago Press.

Eco, Umberto. 1984. *The Name of the Rose*. New York: Warner Books.

349

Eliot, T. S. 1932. "George Herbert": *Spectator* 148: 361.
——. 1951. *Selected Essays*. London: Faber and Faber.
Empson, William. 1984. *Using Biography*. Cambridge: Harvard University Press.
Feuerbach, Ludwig. 1957. *The Essence of Christianity*. Trans. George Eliot. New York: Harper and Row. Originally published 1841.
Fichte, J. G. 1873. *The Vocation of Man*. Trans. William Smith. London: Trübner.
——. 1982. *The Science of Knowledge*. Trans. Peter Heath and John Lachs. New York: Cambridge University Press.
Fish, Stanley. 1980. *Is There a Text in This Class? The Authority of Interpretive Communities*. Cambridge: Harvard University Press.
Foster, Michael B. 1957. *Mystery and Philosophy*. Westport, Conn.: Greenwood Press.
Foucault, Michel. 1972. *The Archaeology of Knowledge and the Discourse on Language*. Trans. A. M. Sheridan Smith. New York: Pantheon.
Fox, W. J. 1831. Review of *Tennyson's Poems, Chiefly Lyrical, Westminster Review* 14. Reprinted in *Victorian Scrutinies*, ed. Isobel Armstrong. London: Athlone Press, 1972.
Frost, Robert. 1968. *Selected Prose of Robert Frost*. Ed. H. Cox and E. C. Lathem. New York: Collier Books.
Frye, Northrop. 1982. *The Great Code: The Bible and Literature*. Toronto: Academic Press.
——. 1986. *Northrop Frye on Shakespeare*. New Haven: Yale University Press.
Gest, J. M. 1925. *The Old Yellow Book, Source of Browning's "The Ring and the Book."* Boston: Chipman Law Publishing Company.
Gibson, Mary Ellis. 1987. *History and the Prism of Art: Browning's Poetic Experiments*. Columbus: Ohio State University Press.
Goffman, Erving. 1959. *The Presentation of Self in Everyday Life*. Garden City, N.Y.: Doubleday.
Goodman, Nelson. 1968. *Languages of Art*. Indianapolis: Bobbs-Merrill.
Hamilton, Sir William. 1829. Review of M. Cousin's *Course of Philosophy Edinburgh Review* 50:196–221.
Hartman, Geoffrey. 1970. *Beyond Formalism: Literary Essays, 1958–1970*. New Haven: Yale University Press.
Hedge, Levi. 1816. *Elements of Logick; or, A Summary of the General Principles and Different Modes of Reasoning*. Cambridge, Mass.: Hillard and Metcalf. Browning owned a copy of this 1816 edition. It was inscribed by R. B., Sr., on the title page, and the father's annotations and underlining occur throughout.
Hegel, G. W. F. 1892. *Hegel's Lectures on the History of Philosophy*. Trans. E. S. Haldane and Frances H. Simson. 3 vols. London: Kegan Paul, Trench, Trübner.
Hirsch, E. D. 1967. *Validity in Interpretation*. New Haven: Yale University Press.
Holloway, John. 1965. *The Victorian Sage: Studies in Argument*. New York: W. W. Norton.
Hopkins, G. M. 1935. *The Letters of G. M. Hopkins to Robert Bridges*. Ed. C. C. Abbott. London: Oxford University Press.
Hume, David. 1896. *A Treatise of Human Nature*. Ed. L. A. Selby-Bigge. 2d ed. Oxford: Clarendon Press.
Jakobson, Roman. 1956. "Two Aspects of Language and Two Types of Linguistic Disturbances." In *Fundamentals of Language*, ed. Roman Jakobson and Morris Halle. The Hague: Mouton.

James, William. 1911. *Pragmatism: A New Name for Some Old Ways of Thinking.* London: Longmans, Green.

——. n.d. *Recollections of Carlyle.* Unpublished Houghton Library MS. 6MS Am 1094.8 (41).

Jowett, Benjamin. 1860. "On the Interpretation of Scripture." In *Essays and Reviews.* London: Longman, Green, Longman, Roberts.

Kant, Immanuel. 1881. *Critique of Pure Reason.* Trans. Max Müller, 2 vols. London: Macmillan.

——. 1923. *Critique of Practical Reason.* Trans. T. K. Abbott. London: Longmans, Green.

Keats, John. 1958. *The Letters of John Keats, 1814–1821.* Ed. H. Rollins. 2 vols. Cambridge: Harvard University Press.

Keble, John. 1833–41. "On the Mysticism Attributed to the Early Fathers of the Church." Tract 89. In *Tracts for the Times.* London: J. G. and F. Rivington, J. H. Parker.

——. 1912. *Lectures on Poetry, 1832–1841.* Trans. E. K. Francis. 2 vols. Oxford: Clarendon Press.

Kermode, Frank. 1979. *The Genesis of Secrecy: On the Interpretation of Narrative.* Cambridge: Harvard University Press.

Kierkegaard, Søren. 1940. *Stages on Life's Way.* Trans. Walter Lowrie. Princeton: Princeton University Press.

——. 1941. *Concluding Unscientific Postscript.* Trans. David F. Svenson and Walter Lowrie. Princeton: Princeton University Press.

——. 1964. *Repetition: An Essay in Experimental Psychology.* Trans. Walter Lowrie. New York: Harper and Row.

——. 1983. *Fear and Trembling.* Trans. and ed. Howard V. Hong and Edna H. Hoy. Princeton: Princeton University Press.

——. 1985. *Philosophical Fragments: Johannes Climacus.* Ed. Howard V. Hong and Edna H. Hoy. Princeton: Princeton University Press.

Lessing, Doris. 1973. *The Golden Notebook.* London: Granada.

Locke, John. 1924. *An Essay concerning Human Understanding.* Ed. A. S. Pringle-Pattison. Oxford: Claredon Press.

Mansel, H. L. 1867. *The Limits of Religious Thought Examined in Eight Lectures.* London: J. Murray.

Melvill, Henry. 1838. *Sermons by Henry Melvill, B.D.* Ed. C. P. McIlvaine. New York: Sword, Stanford. Browning owned the 1833 London edition of Melvill's *Sermons.*

Miller, J. Hillis. 1974. "Narrative and History." *ELH* 41:455–73.

——. 1982. *Fiction and Repetition: Seven English Novels.* Cambridge: Harvard University Press.

——. 1985. *The Linguistic Moment from Wordsworth to Stevens.* Princeton: Princeton University Press.

Nagel, Thomas. 1986. *The View from Nowhere.* New York: Oxford University Press.

Niebuhr, Barthold George. 1831–32. *The History of Rome.* Trans. J. C. Hare and Connop Thirlwall. 2 vols. Cambridge: J. Taylor.

Nietzsche, Friedrich. 1968. *Twilight of the Idols and the Anti-Christ.* Trans. R. J. Hollingdale. Harmondsworth, Middlesex: Penguin.

Nozick, Robert. 1981. *Philosophical Explanations.* Cambridge: Harvard University Press.

Parker, Patricia A. 1983. "Anagogic Metaphor: Breaking down the Wall of Partition." In *Centre and Labyrinth: Essays in Honour of Northrop Frye*, 38–58. Toronto: University of Toronto Press.

Peckham, Morse. 1970. *Victorian Revolutionaries*. New York: George Braziller.
Rawls, John. 1971. *A Theory of Justice*. Cambridge: Harvard University Press.
Ricks, Christopher. 1987. *The Force of Poetry*. Oxford: Oxford University Press.
Royce, Josiah. 1901. *The World and the Individual*. New York: Macmillian.
Schopenhauer, Arthur. 1970. *Schopenhauer: Essays and Aphorisms*. Ed. R. J. Hollingdale. Harmondsworth, Middlesex: Penguin.
———. 1974. *On the Four-fold Root of the Principle of Sufficient Reason*. Trans. E. F. J. Payne. La Salle, Ill.: Open Court Library of Philosophy.
Shaw, W. David. 1987. *The Lucid Veil: Poetic Truth in the Victorian Age*. London: Athlone Press.
Sidgwick, Henry. 1962. *The Methods of Ethics*. London: Macmillian.
Sparshott, Francis. 1982. *The Theory of the Arts*. Princeton: Princeton University Press.
Steiner, George. 1967. *Language and Silence: Essays on Language, Literature, and the Inhuman*. New York: Atheneum.
Stevenson, Charles L. 1944. *Ethics and Language*. New Haven: Yale University Press.
Stoehr, Taylor. 1965. *Dickens: The Dreamer's Stance*. Ithaca, N.Y.: Cornell University Press.
Strauss, David Friedrich. 1845. *The Life of Jesus, Critically Examined*. Trans. George Eliot. 3 vols. London: Chapman.
Thomas, Lewis. 1984. "On Matters of Doubt." In *Late Night Thoughts on Listening to Mahler's Ninth Symphony*. New York: Bantam.
Tillich, Paul. 1951. *Systematic Theology*. Vol 1. Chicago: University of Chicago Press.
Ward, W. G. 1841. Review of Arnold's *Sermons, British Critic and Quarterly Theological Review* 30:298–364.
Weatherby, Harold L. 1975. *The Keen Delight: The Christian Poet in the Modern World*. Athens: University of Georgia Press.
Wittgenstein, Ludwig. 1972. *Philosophical Investigations*. Trans. G. E. M. Anscombe. Oxford: Basil Blackwell.
Wolheim, Richard. 1984. *The Thread of Life*. Cambridge: Harvard University Press.

Editions Used

Arnold, Matthew. 1960–77. *The Complete Prose Works of Matthew Arnold*. Ed. R. H. Super. 11 vols. Ann Arbor: University of Michigan Press.
Austen, Jane. 1971. *Emma*. Ed. David Lodge, notes and bibliography by James Kinsley. London: Oxford University Press.
Borrow, George. 1902. *Lavengro: The Scholar, the Gypsy, the Priest*. London: Oxford University Press.
———. 1902. *The Romany Rye: A Sequel to "Lavengro."* London: J. Lane.
Brontë, Charlotte. 1984. *Villette*. Ed. Herbert Rosengarten and Margaret Smith. Oxford: Clarendon Press.
Brontë, Emily. 1976. *Wuthering Heights*. Ed. Hilda Marsden and Ian Jack. Oxford: Clarendon Press.
Browning, Robert. 1912. *The Works of Robert Browning*. Vols. 5 and 6. London: Smith and Elder. Only quotations from *The Ring and the Book* are taken from this Centenary Edition.
———. 1981. *Robert Browning: The Poems*. Ed. John Pettigrew and Thomas J. Collins. 2 vols. New York: Penguin.
Carlyle, Thomas. 1898–1901. *The Works of Thomas Carlyle*. 30 vols. New York: Scribner's Sons; London: Chapman and Hall.

Clough, A. H. 1974. *The Poems of Arthur Hugh Clough.* Ed. F. L. Mulhauser. 2d ed. Oxford: Clarendon Press.

Collins, Wilkie. 1868. *The Moonstone.* In *The Works of Wilkie Collins,* vols. 6 and 7. New York: Peter Fenelon Collier.

Dickens, Charles. 1973. *Great Expectations.* London: Oxford University Press.

Eliot, George. 1900. *Scenes of Clerical Life.* New York: R. F. Fenno.

———. 1967. *Middlemarch: A Study of Provincial Life.* London: Oxford University Press.

———. 1980. *The Mill on the Floss.* Ed. Gordon S. Haight. Oxford: Clarendon Press.

———. n.d. *Adam Bede.* In *The Works of George Eliot,* vols. 1 and 2. New York: Peter Fenelon Collier.

Hardy, Thomas. 1983. *Tess of the d'Urbervilles.* Ed. Juliet Grindle and Simon Gatrell. New York: Oxford University Press.

Hopkins, G. M. 1967. *Poems.* Ed. W. H. Gardner and N. H. Mackenzie. 4th ed. London: Oxford University Press.

Huxley, T. H. 1909–25. *Collected Essays.* 9 vols. London: Macmillan.

James, Henry. 1907. "Daisy Miller." In *The Novels and Tales of Henry James,* vol. 18 of New York Edition. New York: Scribner.

———. 1966. *The Turn of the Screw: An Authoritative Text, Backgrounds and Sources, Essays in Criticism.* Ed. R. Kimborough. New York: Norton.

Mill, J. S. 1965–. *Collected Works of John Stuart Mill.* Ed. J. M. Robson, Toronto: University of Toronto Press; London: Routledge and Kegan Paul.

Newman, J. H. 1887. *Sermons Preached before the University of Oxford between 1826 and 1843.* London: Rivingtons.

———. 1906. *An Essay on the Development of Christian Doctrine.* New York: Longmans, Green.

———. 1912. *Apologia pro Vita Sua.* London: J. M. Dent.

Pater, Water. 1910. *Plato and Platonism: A Series of Lectures.* London; 1st ed. 1893.

Rossetti, Christina. 1906. *The Poetical Works of Christina Georgina Rossetti.* Memoirs and notes by William Michael Rossetti. London: Macmillian. Referred to in text as *PW.*

———. 1979–. *The Complete Poems of Christina Rossetti.* Ed. Rebecca W. Crump. 2 vols. to date. Baton Rouge: Louisiana State University Press. Quotations are from Crumps' edition whenever poems are available in the volumes already published.

Ruskin, John. 1903–12. *The Works of John Ruskin.* Ed. E. T. Cook and Alexander Wedderburn. London: G. Allen, Longmans, Green.

Tennyson, Alfred. 1987. *The Poems of Tennyson.* Ed. Christopher Ricks, 2d ed. 3 vols. London: Longmans, Green.

Thackeray, W. M. 1963. *Vanity Fair: A Novel without a Hero.* Ed. Geoffrey and Kathleen Tillotson. Boston: Houghton Mifflin.

Trollope, Anthony. 1936. *Barchester Towers* and *The Warden.* New York: Modern Library.

Select Bibliography of Secondary Sources (Works Consulted but Not Cited in the Text)

General Works

Armstrong, Isobel. 1982. *Language as Living Form in Nineteenth-Century Poetry.* Brighton, Sussex: Harvester Press; Totowa, N.J.: Barnes and Noble.

Ball, Patricia M. 1971. *The Science of Aspects: The Changing Role of Fact in the Work of Coleridge, Ruskin, and Hopkins.* London: Athlone Press.

Booth, Wayne. 1961. *The Rhetoric of Fiction.* Chicago: University of Chicago Press.
——. 1974. *A Rhetoric of Irony.* Chicago: University of Chicago Press.
Browning, Robert. 1984. *The Browning Collections: A Reconstruction.* Ed. Philip Kelley and Betty A. Coley. London: Mansell.
Colie, Rosalie L. 1964. "The Rhetoric of Transcendence." *Philological Quarterly* 43: 145–70.
Dale, Peter A. 1977. *The Victorian Critic and the Idea of History: Carlyle, Arnold, Pater.* Cambridge: Harvard University Press.
David, Deirdre. 1987. *Intellectual Women and Victorian Patriarchy: Harriet Martineau, Elizabeth Barrett Browning, George Eliot.* Ithaca, N.Y.: Cornell University Press.
De Laura, David J. 1969. *Hebrew and Hellene in Victorian England: Newman, Arnold, and Pater.* Austin: University of Texas Press.
Foucault, Michel. 1977. *Language, Counter-Memory, Practice.* Trans. Donald F. Bouchard and Sherry Simon. Ithaca, N.Y.: Cornell University Press.
Gilbert, Sandra, and Susan Gubar. 1979. *The Mad Woman in the Attic: The Woman Writer and the Nineteenth-Century Literary Imagination.* New Haven: Yale University Press.
Homans, Margaret. 1986. *Bearing the Word: Language and Female Experience in Nineteenth-Century Women's Writing.* Chicago: University of Chicago Press.
James, D. G. 1937. *Scepticism and Poetry: An Essay on the Poetic Imagination.* London: G. Allen and Unwin.
——. 1948. *The Romantic Comedy.* London: Oxford University Press. See especially part 3, "The Gospel of Heaven."
Kauffman, Linda S. 1986. *Discourses of Desire: Gender, Genre, and Epistolary Fictions.* Ithaca, N.Y.: Cornell University Press.
Knoepflmacher, U. C. 1965. *Religious Humanism and the Victorian Novel: George Eliot, Walter Pater, and Samuel Butler.* Princeton: Princeton University Press.
Landow, George P. 1986. *Elegant Jeremiahs: The Sage from Carlyle to Mailer.* Ithaca, N.Y.: Cornell University Press.
Langbaum, Robert. 1977. *The Mysteries of Identity: A Theme in Modern Literature.* New York: Oxford University Press.
Leavis, F. R. 1963. *The Great Tradition: George Eliot, Henry James, Joseph Conrad.* New York: New York University Press.
Levine, George. 1968. *The Boundaries of Fiction: Carlyle, Macaulay, Newman.* Princeton: Princeton University Press.
——. 1968. *The Art of Victorian Prose.* Ed. George Levine and William Madden. New York: Oxford University Press.
——. 1981. *The Realistic Imagination: English Fiction from Frankenstein to Lady Chatterley.* Chicago: University of Chicago Press.
Loesberg, Jonathan. 1986. *Fictions of Consciousness: Mill, Newman, and the Reading of Victorian Prose.* New Brunswick, N.J.: Rutgers University Press.
Mellor, Anne. 1980. *English Romantic Irony.* Cambridge: Harvard University Press.
Poirier, Richard. 1987. *The Renewal of Literature: Emersonian Reflections.* New York: Random House.
Prickett, Stephen. 1976. *Romanticism and Religion: The Tradition of Coleridge and Wordsworth in the Victorian Church.* Cambridge: Cambridge University Press.
——. 1986. *Words and "The Word": Language, Poetics, and Biblical Interpretation.* New York: Cambridge University Press.
Rader, Ralph W. 1976. "The Dramatic Monologue and Related Literary Forms." *Critical Inquiry* 3:131–51.

Ranke, Leopold von. 1973. *The Theory and Practice of History*. Trans. Wilma A. Iggers, ed. Wilma Iggers and Konrad von Moltke. Indianapolis: Bobbs-Merrill.

Schlegel, Friedrich. 1975. *Lucinde and the Fragments*. Trans. Peter Firchow. Minneapolis: University of Minnesota Press. See especially "On Incomprehensibility," pp. 259–71.

Shaffer, Elinor S. 1975. *"Kubla Khan" and The Fall of Jerusalem: The Mythological School in Biblical Criticism and Secular Literature, 1770–1880*. London: Cambridge University Press.

Wilkinson, Elizabeth M. 1962–63. "The Inexpressible and the Un-speakable: Some Romantic Attitudes to Art and Language." *German Life and Letters* 16:308–20.

Wollheim, Richard. 1973. *On Art and the Mind: Essays and Lectures*. London: Allen Lane.

Works on Individual Authors

Matthew Arnold
Bush, Douglas. 1971. *Matthew Arnold: A Survey of His Poetry and Prose*. New York: Macmillan.

Carroll, Joseph. 1982. *The Cultural Theory of Matthew Arnold*. Berkeley: University of California Press.

———. 1988. "Arnold, Newman, and Cultural Salvation." *Victorian Poetry: Centennial of Matthew Arnold, 1822–88* 26:163–78.

Honan, Park. 1981. *Matthew Arnold: A Life*. New York: McGraw-Hill.

Levine, George. 1988. "Matthew Arnold's Science of Religion: The Uses of Imprecision." *Victorian Poetry: Centennial of Matthew Arnold, 1822–88* 26:143–62.

Robbins, William. 1959. *The Ethical Idealism of Matthew Arnold*. Toronto: University of Toronto Press.

———. 1979. *The Arnoldian Principle of Flexibility*. Monograph Series. Victoria, B. C.: ELS.

Super, R. H. 1970. *The Time-Spirit of Matthew Arnold*. Ann Arbor: University of Michigan Press.

Trilling, Lionel. 1949. *Matthew Arnold*. New York: Columbia University Press.

George Borrow
Collie, Michael. 1982. *George Borrow, Eccentric*. New York: Cambridge University Press.

Herbert, Lucille. 1971. "George Borrow and the Forms of Self-Reflection." *University of Toronto Quarterly* 11:152–67.

Williams, David. 1982. *A World of His Own: The Double Life of George Borrow*. Oxford: Oxford University Press.

Charlotte Brontë
Eagleton, Terence. 1975. *Myths of Power: A Marxist Study of the Brontës*. London: Macmillan.

Gérin, Winifred. 1967. *Charlotte Brontë: The Evolution of Genius*. Oxford: Clarendon Press.

Moglen, Helen. 1984. *Charlotte Brontë: The Self Conceived*. Madison: University of Wisconsin Press.

Peters, Margot. 1973. *Charlotte Brontë: Style in the Novels*. Madison: University of Wisconsin Press.

Tromly, Ann. 1982. *The Cover of the Mask: The Autobiographers in Charlotte Brontë's Fiction*. Monograph Series. Victoria, B.C.: ELS.

Emily Brontë
Chitham, Edward. 1987. *A Life of Emily Brontë*. New York: Blackwell.
Homans, Margaret. 1980. *Women Writers and Poetic Identity: Dorothy Wordsworth, Emily Brontë and Emily Dickinson*. Princeton: Princeton University Press.
Miller, J. Hillis. 1963. "Emily Brontë." In *The Disappearance of God*, pp. 157–211. Cambridge: Harvard University Press.
———. 1981. "Wuthering Heights." In *Fiction and Repetition*, pp. 42–72. Cambridge: Harvard University Press.

Robert Browning
Collins, Thomas J. 1967. *Robert Browning's Moral-Aesthetic Theory: 1833–55*. Lincoln: University of Nebraska Press.
Cook, Eleanor. 1974. *Browning's Lyrics: An Exploration*. Toronto: University of Toronto Press.
Hair, Donald S. 1972. *Browning's Experiments with Genre*. Toronto: University of Toronto Press.
Ryals, Clyde de L. 1975. *Browning's Later Poetry, 1871–1889*. Ithaca, N.Y.: Cornell University Press.
———. 1983. *Becoming Browning: The Poems and Plays of Robert Browning, 1833–1846*. Columbus: Ohio State University Press.
Tucker, Herbert F., Jr. *Browning's Beginnings: The Art of Disclosure*. Minneapolis: University of Minnesota Press, 1980.

Thomas Carlyle
Kaplan, Fred. 1983. *Thomas Carlyle: A Biography*. Ithaca, N.Y.: Cornell University Press.
Le Valley, Albert J. 1968. *Carlyle and the Idea of the Modern*. New Haven: Yale University Press.
Neff, Edward. 1932. *Carlyle*. New York: W. W. Norton.
Rosenberg, John D. 1985. *Carlyle and the Burden of History*. Cambridge: Harvard University Press.
Sanders, Richard, and Clyde de L. Ryals, eds. 1970–. *The Collected Letters of Thomas and Jane Welsh Carlyle*. Durham, N.C.: Duke University Press.
Tennyson, G. B. 1965. *"Sartor" Called "Resartus."* Princeton: Princeton University Press.

Arthur Hugh Clough
Armstrong, Isobel. 1962. *Arthur Hugh Clough*. London: Longmans, Green.
Biswas, R. K. 1972. *Arthur Hugh Clough: Towards a Reconsideration*. Oxford: Clarendon Press.
Greenberger, Evelyn Barish. 1970. *Arthur Hugh Clough: The Growth of a Poet's Mind*. Cambridge: Harvard University Press.
Houghton, Walter E. 1963. *The Poetry of Clough: An Essay in Revaluation*. New Haven: Yale University Press.
Timko, Michael. 1966. *Innocent Victorian: The Satiric Poetry of Arthur Hugh Clough*. Athens: Ohio University Press.

Wilkie Collins
Davis, Neul Pharr. 1956. *The Life of Wilkie Collins*. Urbana: University of Illinois Press.
Eliot, T. S. 1951. "Wilkie Collins and Dickens." In *Selected Essays*, pp. 460–70. London: Faber and Faber.

Hutton, Lawrence, ed. 1892. *Letters of Charles Dickens to Wilkie Collins.* New York: Harper.

Charles Dickens

Bishop, Jonathan. 1972. *Something Else.* New York: Braziller.
Butt, John, and Kathleen Tillotson. 1963. *Dickens at Work.* London: Metheun.
Engel, Monroe. 1967. *The Maturity of Dickens.* Cambridge: Harvard University Press.
Ford, George, and Lauriat Lane, Jr. 1961. *The Dickens Critics.* Ithaca, N.Y.: Cornell University Press.
Garis, Robert. 1965. *The Dickens Theatre: A Reassessment of the Novels.* London: Oxford University Press.
Hardy, Barbara. 1970. *The Moral Art of Dickens: Essays by Barbara Hardy.* London: Athlone Press.
House, Humphrey. 1960. *The Dickens World.* London: Oxford University Press.
Johnson, Edgar. 1952. *Charles Dickens: His Tragedy and Triumph.* New York: Simon and Schuster.
Kaplan, Fred. 1975. *Dickens and Mesmerism: The Hidden Springs of Fiction.* Princeton: Princeton University Press.
Kincaid, James R. 1971. *Dickens and the Rhetoric of Laughter.* Oxford: Clarendon Press.
Leavis, F. R., and Q. D. Leavis. 1970. *Dickens: The Novelist.* London: Chatto and Windus.
Miller, J. Hillis. 1958. *Charles Dickens: The World of His Novels.* Cambridge: Harvard University Press.
Monod, Sylvère. 1968. *Dickens, the Novelist.* Norman: Univeristy of Oklahoma Press.
Poirier, Richard. 1987. *The Renewal of Literature: Emersonian Reflections.* New York: Random House.
Welsh, Alexander. 1971. *The City of Dickens.* Oxford: Clarendon Press.
———. 1987. *From Copyright to Copperfield: The Identity of Dickens.* Cambridge: Harvard University Press.

George Eliot

Beer, Gillian. 1983. *Darwin's Plots: Evolutionary Narrative in Darwin, George Eliot, and Nineteenth-Century Fiction.* London: Routledge and Kegan Paul.
Bennett, Joan. 1948. *George Eliot: Her Mind and Her Art.* Cambridge: Cambridge University Press.
Haight, Gordon. 1968. *George Eliot: A Biography.* Oxford: Clarendon Press.
Hardy, Barbara. 1959. *The Novels of George Eliot: A Study of Form.* London: Athlone Press.
Harvey, William John. 1963. *The Art of George Eliot.* London: Chatto and Windus.
Knoepflmacher, U. 1968. *George Eliot's Early Novels: The Limits of Realism.* Berkeley: University of California Press.
Welsh, Alexander. 1985. *George Eliot and Blackmail.* Cambridge: Harvard University Press.

Thomas Hardy

Bayley, John. 1978. *An Essay on Hardy.* Cambridge: Cambridge University Press.
Gregor, Ian. 1974. *The Great Web; The Form of Hardy's Major Fiction.* London: Faber.

Kramer, Dale. 1975. *Thomas Hardy: The Forms of Tragedy*. Detroit: Wayne State University Press.
Miller, J. Hillis. 1970. *Thomas Hardy: Distance and Desire*. Cambridge: Harvard University Press.
Millgate, Michael. 1971. *Thomas Hardy: His Career as a Novelist*. New York: Random House.
——. 1982. *Thomas Hardy: A Biography*. Oxford: Oxford University Press.

G. M. Hopkins
Harris, Daniel A. 1982. *Inspirations Unbidden, The "Terrible Sonnets" of Gerard Manley Hopkins*. Berkeley: University of California Press.
Hartman, Geoffrey H. 1954. *The Unmediated Vision: An Interpretation of Wordsworth, Hopkins, Rilke, and Valéry*. New Haven: Yale University Press.
Heuser, Alan. 1968. *The Shaping Vision of Gerard Manley Hopkins*. Hamden, Conn.: Archon Books.
Mackenzie, Norman. 1981. *A Reader's Guide to Gerard Manley Hopkins*. London: Thames and Hudson.
Mariani, Paul L. 1970. *A Commentary on the Complete Poems of Gerard Manley Hopkins*. Ithaca, N.Y.: Cornell University Press.
Sprinker, Michael. 1980. *A Counterpoint of Dissonance: The Aesthetics and Poetry of G. M. Hopkins*. Baltimore: Johns Hopkins University Press.
Sulloway, Alison G. 1972. *Gerard Manley Hopkins and the Victorian Temper*. New York: Columbia University Press.

Henry James
Culler, Jonathan. 1975. *Structuralist Poetics*. Ithaca, N.Y.: Cornell University Press.
Edel, Leon, and Lyall H. Powers. 1987. *The Complete Notebooks of Henry James*. New York: Oxford University Press.
Felman, Shoshana. 1977. "Turning the Screw of Interpretation." *Yale French Studies* 55–56:94–207.
Johnson, Warren. 1988. "Parable, Secrecy, and the Form of Fiction: The Example of 'The Figure in the Carpet' and *The Portrait of a Lady*." *JEGP* 87:230–50.
Matthiessen, F. O. 1963. *Henry James: The Major Phase*. London: Oxford University Press.
Poirier, Richard. 1960. *The Comic Sense of Henry James: A Study of the Early Novels*. London: Chatto and Windus.
Sears, Sallie. 1968. *The Negative Imagination: Forms and Perspective in the Novels of Henry James*. Ithaca, N.Y.: Cornell University Press.
Seltzer, Mark. 1984. *Henry James and the Art of Power*. Ithaca, N.Y.: Cornell University Press.
Sicker, Philip. 1980. *Love and the Quest for Identity in the Late Novels of Henry James*. Princeton: Princeton Univeristy Press.
Tanner, Tony. 1979. *Henry James*. Harlow: Longman.
Yeazell, Ruth Bernard. 1976. *Language and Knowledge in the Late Novels of Henry James*. Chicago: University of Chicago Press.

J. S. Mill
Alexander, Edward. 1965. *Matthew Arnold and John Stuart Mill*. New York: Columbia University Press.

Neff, Emery Edward. 1926. *Carlyle and Mill: An Introduction to Victorian Thought.* New York: Columbia University Press.
Rees, J. C. 1985. *John Stuart Mill on Liberty.* New York: Oxford University Press.
Robson, J. M. 1968. *The Improvement of Mankind: The Social and Political Thought of John Stuart Mill.* Toronto: Univeristy of Toronto Press.
Ryan, Alan. 1970. *The Philosophy of John Stuart Mill.* London: Macmillan.

J. H. Newman
Cameron, J. M. 1956. *John Henry Newman.* London: Longmans, Green.
Chadwick, Owen. 1983. *Newman.* Oxford: Oxford University Press.
Culler, A. Dwight. 1955. *The Imperial Intellect: A Study of Newman's Educational Ideal.* New Haven: Yale University Press.
Houghton, W. E. 1970. *The Art of Newman's "Apologia."* Hamden, Conn.: Anchor Books. Originally published 1945.
Vargish, Thomas. 1970. *Newman: The Contemplation of Mind.* Oxford: Clarendon Press.

Christina Rossetti
Harrison, Antony H. 1988. *Christina Rossetti in Context.* Chapel Hill: University of North Carolina Press.
McGann, Jerome J. 1983. "The Religious Poetry of Christina Rossetti." *Critical Inquiry* 10:127–44.
Rosenblum, Dolores. 1986. *Christina Rossetti: The Poetry of Endurance.* Carbondale: Southern Illinois University Press.

Alfred Tennyson
Buckley, Jerome. 1960. *Tennyson: The Growth of a Poet.* Cambridge: Harvard University Press.
Christ, Carol. T. 1975. *The Finer Optic.* New Haven: Yale University Press.
Culler, A. Dwight. 1977. *The Poetry of Tennyson.* New Haven: Yale University Press.
Hair, Donald S. 1981. *Domestic and Heroic in Tennyson's Poetry.* Toronto: University of Toronto Press.
Kincaid, James R. 1975. *Tennyson's Major Poems: The Comic and Ironic Patterns.* New Haven: Yale University Press.
Kolb, Jack. 1981. *The Letters of Arthur Henry Hallam.* Columbus: Ohio State University Press.
Lang, Cecil Y., and Edgar F. Shannon, Jr., eds. 1981, 1987. *The Letters of Alfred Lord Tennyson.* 2 vols. to date. Cambridge: Belknap Press of Harvard University Press.
Martin, Robert Bernard. 1980. *Tennyson: The Unquiet Heart.* New York: Oxford University Press.
Pattison, Robert. 1979. *Tennyson and Tradition.* Cambridge: Harvard University Press.
Priestley, F. E. L. 1973. *Language and Structure in Tennyson's Poetry.* London: Andre Deutsch.
Rosenberg, John D. 1973. *The Fall of Camelot: A Study of Tennyson's "Idylls of the King."* Cambridge: Harvard University Press.
Ryals, Clyde de L. 1967. *From the Great Deep: Essays on "Idylls of the King."* Athens: Ohio University Press.

Sinfield, Alan. 1971. *The Language of Tennyson's "In Memoriam."* New York: Barnes and Noble.
Tucker, Herbert F., Jr. 1988. *Tennyson and the Doom of Romanticism.* Cambridge: Harvard University Press.

W. M. Thackeray
Hardy, Barbara. 1972. *The Exposure of Luxury: Radical Themes in Thackeray.* London: Owen.
Loofbourow, John. 1964. *Thackeray and the Form of Fiction.* Princeton: Princeton University Press.
McMaster, Juliet. 1971. *Thackeray: The Major Novels.* Toronto: University of Toronto Press.
Peters, Catherine. 1987. *Thackeray's Universe: Shifting Worlds of Imagination and Reality.* London: Faber and Faber.
Rawlins, Jack P. 1974. *Thackeray's Novels: A Fiction That Is True.* Berkeley: University of California Press.
Ray, Gordon. 1972. *Thackeray.* New York: Octagon Books.
Sutherland, John A. 1974. *Thackeray at Work.* London: Athlone Press.
Tillotson, Geoffrey. 1954. *Thackeray the Novelist.* Cambridge: Cambridge University Press.

Anthony Trollope
apRoberts, Ruth. 1971. *Trollope: Artist and Moralist.* London: Chatto and Windus.
Cockshutt, A. O. J. 1968. *Anthony Trollope.* London: Methuen.
Herbert, Christopher. 1987. *Trollope and Comic Pleasure.* Chicago: University of Chicago Press.
Kincaid, James R. 1977. *The Novels of Anthony Trollope.* Oxford: Clarendon Press.
McMaster, Juliet. 1978. *Trollope's Palliser Novels: Theme and Pattern.* New York: Oxford University Press.
Wright, Andrew H. 1983. *Anthony Trollope: Dream and Art.* Chicago: University of Chicago Press.

Index

Numerals in italic type indicate the locations of the main discussions.

Aeschylus, 7, 215
Agnosticism, 6–8, 16, 242–43
Allegory, 17, 112, 142, 149, 155, 328; life
  as 78–79, 344
Allusion, 160, 273; allusive mazes, 86;
  Keatsian, 46; Shakespearean, 46
Ambiguity, 70, 91–92, 94, 97–99, 102–3,
  125, 131–40, 144, 168–70, 207–8, 214,
  242, 245, 265–66, 295
Analogy, 59, 249, 280; *Analogy of Religion*
  (Joseph Butler), 105; historical, 14–15,
  246–47, 298, 333
Antigone, 83, 194
Antinomies. *See* Paralogisms and
  antinomies
apRoberts, Ruth, 272
Aristotle, 12, 15, 225, 281, 285; *Ethics*, 105
Arnold, Matthew, 5, 18, 115, 121, 156–57,
  224, 226, 251, 271, 278; *Culture and
  Anarchy*, 224, 226, 228, 230, 234,
  272–75, 286, 329, 335, 343–44; "Dover
  Beach," 235, 348; "The Function
  of Criticism at the Present Time," 9;
  "Palladium," 226, 275
Arnold, Dr. Thomas, 288, 297, 304–5
Assents, 237, 325; notional, 232
Augustine, 13, 78, 324, 331–32
Austen, Jane, 124, 169; *Emma*, 51–52,
  131, 290; *Pride and Prejudice*, 116
Austin, J. L., 23, 199, 218, 239, 280. *See
  also* Language: performative vs.
  descriptive uses of

Babbitt, Irving, 323
Bacon, Francis, 26, 79, 289
Baring the device. *See* Narrator(s):
  method of "baring the device"
Beckett, Samuel, 112, 328
Bede, Venerable, 81
Belief, the problem of, 2, 5, 7
Bentham, Jeremy, 13, 39, 86, 224, 277,
  282, 286, 294, 298, 304, 322, 343; *Essay
  on Government*, 344
Berkeley, Bishop George, 107
Berlin, Isaiah, 327, 331
Bible: Aaron, 73, 201; Abraham, 166,
  184, 200; the Decalogue, 10;
  Ecclesiastes (Koheleth), 160, 164, 271;
  Elisha, 312, Esau, 207; Genesis, 13,
  100, 208, 246, 327, 332; the Gospel
  of John, 223; the Gospel of Mark, 85,
  307, 319, 338; the Gospel of
  Matthew, 59, 319; Isaac, 166, 184;
  Isaiah, 72; Jacob, 207; Jethro, 200;
  Job, 29, 160, 179, 332; Judges, 79;
  Manoah, 79; Moses, 200–201, 209, 214;
  Nebuchadnezzar, 174; Noah, 247;
  Pilate, 83; Saint John the Evangelist,
  307, 318; Saint Paul, 85, 170, 178, 264;
  Saul, 158–59, 160; Scripture, triple
  sense of, 30; Song of Solomon, 70. *See
  also* Typology
Bloom, Allan, 279
Borges, Jorge Luis, 320
Borrow, George, 17, 19, 119, 176;

Borrow, George (cont'd.)
Lavengro, 10, 109, 112, 116, 118–19,
122, 151, 157–67, 171, 174–75, 328–29;
The Romany Rye, 164–65
Bradley, F. H., 228, 346–47; Appearance
and Reality, 107, 326, 330; Ethical Studies,
272, 274, 324, 330, 331; The
Presuppositions of Critical History, 18, 298,
333–34
Bright, John, 274
Brontë, Charlotte, 26, 30, 53, 327;
miniature magazines of, 68; Villette, 3,
22–23, 25–26, 32–33, 61–71, 327, 346
Brontë, Emily, 26, 30, 327; Wuthering
Heights, 3–4, 11, 17, 21–26, 28–29,
53–61, 327, 337
Browning, Elizabeth Barrett, 199, 201–4,
214
Browning, Robert, 5, 9, 16–17, 19, 113,
121, 322, 331; "Abt Vogler," 29, 119,
198, 216, 217–20; "Andrea del Sarto,"
23, 114, 196; "Any Wife to Any
Husband," 211, 212–14; Balaustion's
Adventure, 307; "Bishop Blougram's
Apology," 10, 295; "The Bishop Orders
His Tomb," 196–97, 208–9; "By the
Fire-Side," 45, 113–14, 197–99;
"Caliban upon Setebos," 108–9, 119,
178, 211, 215, 224; "Childe Roland,"
197, 211, 215–16; "Christmas-Eve," 120;
"Cleon," 201; "A Death in the Desert,"
12, 119, 208, 318–20; "Dîs Aliter
Visum," 108, 205, 208, 209–11; "Easter-
Day," 104; "The Englishman in Italy,"
196; "Epilogue" to Ferishtah's Fancies,
214; "An Epistle of Karshish," 30, 201;
Fifine at the Fair, 168; "The Flight of
the Duchess," 204, 206–8; "Fra Lippo
Lippi," 109; his art of the monologue,
121, 196–97, 208, 224, 344; "House
and Shop," 150; "Imperante Augusto
Natus Est," 341; "Johannes Agricola
in Meditation," 8, 119, 196;
"Memorabilia," 211–12; Men and Women,
199, 201–2, 316; "My Last Duchess,"
109, 208; "One Word More," 197,
199–203; Paracelsus, 323, 326;
"Porphyria's Lover," 114, 196;
"Prologue" to Asolando, 211, 214–5, 218,
340; The Ring and the Book, 12, 15, 18,
109, 153, 223, 226–28, 230–33, 288–89,
292–93, 296–98, 300–321, 334–35,
337–38; La Saisiaz, 203–4, 338, 340;
"Saul," 7, 13, 119–20, 216–17, 332;
"Soliloquy of the Spanish Cloister," 215;
Sordello, 298, 316; A Soul's Tragedy, 110;
"The Statue and the Bust," 10, 114,

119, 317; "Two in the Campagna,"
204–6
Buckle, H. T., 227, 228–89, 313, 322
Bunyan, John, 112, 117, 142, 153, 155,
160, 328
Butler, Joseph, 105, 277
Byron, Lord George Gordon, 115, 181,
209–11

Caesura. See Prosody: caesuras
Carlyle, Thomas, 1–4, 7, 9–10, 16–17, 19,
22, 26–28, 72, 163, 272, 298, 302, 316,
322, 326–27, 330, 344; "Characteristics,"
74–76; The French Revolution, 78; "On
History," 297; Past and Present, 83–85,
87, 338; Sartor Resartus, 9–11, 25,
76–83, 86, 223, 326–28, 338, 342–44;
"Signs of the Times," 11, 73–74, 82
Certainty vs. certitude, 88–89, 102–6
Chaucer, Geoffrey, 255–56
Closure, 164, 250, 346–47; arbitary, 231,
338; deferred, 63, 83, 164, 170–71,
250; defiance of, 124, 245; endings that
withhold more meanings than they
promise to disclose, 85, 114; failure to
conclude, 85, 174, 249, 316–17, 337;
fear of, 196, 201, 316; fiction of happy
endings, 70; horror of concluding, 201,
247; opening as disguised closure, 102;
premature, 85, 167, 338; termination
in midsentence, 85
Clough, Arthur Hugh, 8, 10, 17, 19, 78,
121, 251, 275, 326; Amours de Voyage,
10, 109, 111–12, 114, 119, 121, 130,
142, 157, 159, 167–75, 247, 329, 341,
348; Dipsychus, 171–72, 175; Mari
Magno, 174
Coleridge, S. T., 8, 26, 49, 86, 200, 236,
277, 328
Collins, Wilkie, 18; The Moonstone, 108,
112, 223, 226–27, 288–99, 318–19, 334,
337; The Woman in White, 296
Comte, Auguste, 280
Consciousness: and disease, 74, 173; fall
into, 77–78; and language, 11, 21, 53,
63–64, 69, 72, 218; paradoxical
consciousness of the unconscious, 74–
75, 82, 85–87; subliminal, 1, 22, 25,
27–28, 32, 34, 36–38, 40, 42–44, 46,
48, 51–53, 58, 101, 218, 290, 324; three
theories of, 29–30; the unconscious,
3, 4, 22, 25, 34, 73, 80, 294
Continuity vs. discontinuity, 85, 107–8,
110, 113, 139, 147, 159, 162–63, 166,
173, 184, 294–95, 301–4, 307
Cousin, Victor, 326
Crump, R. W., 265, 270

Dallas, E. S., 30
Daniélou, Jean, 323
Dante, 92, 177, 199–200, 202, 235
Darwin, Charles, 2, 6, 107, 221, 276, 286, 344–45
de Beauvoir, Simone, 188
Deconstruction, 218, 230, 273, 300, 302–4, 310–12, 335, 345. *See also* Logic: double binds, logical dilemmas
Definition, problems of, 54, *234–44*. *See also* Mystery: mysteries of contextual definition
Defoe, Daniel, 159, 166
Déjà vu, *40*, 153, 209. *See also* Consciousness: subliminal
Deletions and revisions in manuscripts, 252–58, 260–61, 269–70
de Man, Paul, 64, 198
Derrida, Jacques, 82, 161, 319
Dickens, Charles, 4, 21, 115, 324; *Great Expectations*, 10–11, 16–17, 22, 25–26, 28, *30–43*, 46, 50, 53, 324; *Oliver Twist*, 324
Donne, John, 206
Double binds. *See* Logic: double binds
Dramatic monologue. *See* Browning, Robert: his art of the monologue
Dryden, John, 84

Eco, Umberto, 83
Einstein, Albert, 14
Elegiac literature, 44–46, 57–58, 70–71, 81, 90–96, 153, 182–83, 202–4, 225, 247, 270, 340, 347–48
Eliot, George, 9, 13, 16, 113–15, 120, 174, 322, 330, 332; *Adam Bede*, 5, 12, 113–14,116–18, *176–80*, 332–33; *Amos Barton*, *182–83*; *Middlemarch*, 5, 109, 111–12, 114, 116–18, 120, 122, 176, *183–95*, 225, 298, 333, 344, 346, 348; *The Mill on the Floss*, 12–13, 117, 120, *180–82*
Eliot, T. S., 169, 262, 272, 348
Emerson, Ralph Waldo, 4, 136, 183
Empson, William, 125, 154, 340
Epicurus, 280
Epistemology. *See* Knowledge
Essentialism (categorical living), 6–7, 16, 142, 159, 165, 168, 170, 226, 277, 285, 323, 325, 333
Ethics: Bradley's *Ethical Studies*, 272, 274; deontological, 10, 276–77; ethics of naturalism, 277; four theories of moral value, 119–20; Huxley's *Evolution and Ethics*, 222; Kantian, 9–10, 118, 120, 333; moral intuitionism, 323; neutralizing moral meanings, 144–45;

prescriptive aims of ethics vs. descriptive aims of physical science, 222, 276, 283; the search for moral value as itself a value, 17, 112, 117, 120; Sidgwick's *Methods of Ethics*, 276–77; Spinoza's *Ethics*, 249; Stevenson's *Ethics and Language*, 225; utilitarian, 9, 13, 18, 82, 86, *116–17*, 120, 228, 230, 274, 276–77, 280–82, 285–87, 329, 333, *335–36*, 334
Euripides, 308
Existentialism, 6, 9–10, 16, 111, 113, 142, 159, 168, 170, 322–23, 330–31, 333
Explanations vs. proofs, 15, 120, 225, *228–31*, 238, 248, 325, 345

Fate, meaning of, 4, 16, 35, 41, 43, 324, 337. *See also* Mystery: mystery of a veiled fate
Feminist perspectives, 23, 126, 188–89, 292. *See also* Gender relations
Feuerbach, Ludwig, 9, 12–13, 116, 177–78, 330, 332. *See also* Theology: anthropomorphic
Fichte, J. G., 9–10, 86; *Die Bestimmung des Menschen*, 78, 330; *Wissenschaftslehre*, 77–78
Fictions: of a benign nature, 279; consoling, 324; eroding boundaries between fiction and life, 122; fictions of innocence, 146–47; fictive concords, 273; fictive status of history, 129, 297, 300, 333; fictive theories of matter in Huxley, 14, 222, 229–31, 337; fictive theories of planetary motion, 286; fictive theory of substance, 107; obsessive force of favored fictions, 137; philosophical, 339; protective, 175; rhetorical fictions in Mill, 281; scientific, 313; supreme, 214, 320; symbolic, 82; "unconscious," 339; utilitarian, 286; verbal and poetic, 216, 285. *See also* Gothic fiction
Fish, Stanley, 314
Foster, Michael B., 337
Foucault, Michel, 1, *10–15*
Fox, W. J., 110
Frames: dedicatory, 201–2; frames within frames, 197, 202; framing of one discourse by another, 108; grammatical framing, 217; Miltonic framing of noun by adjectives, 69, 346; switching of picture space and frame, 36, 54, 57, *61–63*, 65, 67–68, 197; triple framing of events, 209–10. *See also* Nesting structures in narrative; Recursive narrative

Free will, the problem of, 2, *21–25*, 111–12, 118–20, 231, 324
Freud, Sigmund, 45
Frost, Robert, 78, 114, 257; "The Home-Stretch," 198; "Nature's first green is gold," 214; "West-Running Brook," 225, 343
Frye, Northrop, 14, 77, 86

Gender relations, 126, 167–68, 346. *See also* Feminist perspectives
Genre: family resemblances in a genre, 232; generic experiments, 61; generic mistakes or uncertainties, 12–13, 113, 181; generic nesting, 162; generic switches, 62, 115, 165, 178, 193–94; literary vs. discursive genres, 224; a novel in search of its own genre, 193–94
Gest, J. M., 302
Gibson, Mary Ellis, 288
Goethe, J. W., 319
Goffman, Erving, 157
Goodman, Nelson, 232, 344
Gothic fiction, 62; "anti-Gothic," 64, 68; "new Gothic," 64
Grammar: apodosis, 63, 207; conditional verbs, 212–13, 217; convergence and diffusion of syntactical units, 217, 268; coupling of pronouns, 268; deictics, 94; double negatives, 130; equivocal grammar, 130, 137; exchange of grammatical subject and object, 185–86, 259; expanding syntactic units, 80, 240, 268; grammar and disquietude, 324; grammar of reserve, 130; grammatical equivalent of infinite regress, 153; grammatical fragmentation, 63, 66, 86, 90, 102, 142, 185, 200, 206, 246, 250; grammatical instability, 265–66; hypotactic syntax, 217; insertion of past participle, 38, 58; mistakes in philosophical grammar, 278, 339; nominative absolute constructions, 64, 66, 265; optatives, 101, 203; paratactic syntax, 66, 98, 101, 208, 213, 217; parentheses, 36, 63, 80, 89, 200, 208, 216, 298; repeated questions, 39, 56; repetitive syntax, 36; shift from finite verbs to timeless infinitives, 99; shift in grammatical moods, 202; solecisms, 95; sundered syntax, 89–90, 96–97, 103, 170, 202, 265; suspended syntax (delayed grammatical completion), 89, 101, 103, 137–38, 202, 209, 212–13, 216–17, 240, 249, 298; syntactic knots, 154, 246; two-way syntax, 5–6, 65, 98,

137, 217, 245; vocatives, 90, 101, 130, 137, 208, 212, 214, 219. *See also* Rhetoric: appositional naming
Green, T. H., 326
Grote, George, 75

Hallam, Arthur, 29, 100, 266
Hamilton, Sir William, 13–14, 69, 79, *82*, 226, *285–86*, 325–26, 328, 337
Hardy, Thomas, 3, 6, 21, 121; poetry of, 8, 49, 279; *Tess of the d'Urbervilles*, 10–11, 16–17, 22, 24, 25–26, 28, 30–32, 34 *43–51*, 53, 69, 112, 118, 324, 337
Harrison, Frederic, 224, 230, 274
Hartman, Geoffrey, 132, 196, 218
Hedge, Levi, 105, 304
Hegel, G. W. F., 4, 7, 13, 80–81, 109, 198, 215, 218, 289, 291, 310, 330, 332
Heisenberg, Werner, 1
Heraclitus, 338
Hermeneutics, 218, 300, *304–9*, 311, 314. *See also* Logic: the hermeneutical circle
Hirsch, E. D., 309
History: cliometricians, 227, 288–89; the historian's empathy with historical agents, 15, 227, 288–89, 291–92, 297–98, 312, 334; historical analogy, 14–15, 246–47, 298, 333; historical criticism, 315–16; history as a self-constituting process, 4, 289, 305; scientific historiography, 4, 289, 305
Holloway, John, 78
Holmes, Sherlock, 226, 295
Homer, 308
Hopkins, G. M., 4, 19, 21–22, 28, 30, 88–89, 97–98, 103, 119, 268, 331, 336, 344; "As kingfishers catch fire," 111; "The Caged Skylark," 4; "No worst, there is none," 198, 235; "Pied Beauty," 29, 111; "Spelt from Sibyl's Leaves," 29, *96–97*, 348; "Thou art indeed just, Lord," 29; *The Wreck of the Deutschland*, 2, 17, 23–24, 27, *90–96*, 104, 223, 332
Humanities. *See* Science: and humanities
Hume, David, 107, 239, 241–43, 286
Huxley, T. H., 1, 5, *13–14*, 222, 224, 228–30, 273, 286, 322, 325–26, 337–38, 343, 345, 347

Idealism. *See* Knowledge: idealist theories
Imagination: Dr. Johnson on, 52, 151, 181, 236; imagination vs. reason in Newman, 236, 241–42; imagination vs. reason in *Villette*, 62–65, 67–68; Ruskin's theories of, 31–32; truth as imagination that succeeds, 295

Incognitos, 162, 166, 187, 294, 301, 303, 340
Inexpressible vs. the unspeakable. *See* Silence: of the inexpressible
Infinite regress, 29, 33, 59, 61, 64, 76–77, 80, 102, 138, 153, 155–56, 161, 197, 209, 231–32, 298, 320, 342, 344, 347
Irony, 32, 73, 114, 124, 126–29, 132–33, 162, 164, 301, 318, 335, 340–41; double, 11, 112–13, *124–25*, 143–46, 150–52, 154, 156, 302, 322–25, 341, 348; ironic double movements, 114, 185–87, 252, 261; mask of, 192; negative, 11, 127, 146; of speaking without saying anything, 114, 166–67, 186–87; *See also* Socrates: Socratic irony
Irving, Edward, 73

Jakobson, Roman, 27, 91, 94, 292. *See also* Language: "contiguity-disorder," "similarity-disorder"
James, Henry, 4, 17, 112, 122–23, 182, 324–25; *The Ambassadors*, 132, 136; *The American*, 132; "Daisy Miller," 112, 122–23, *132–36*; *The Turn of the Screw*, 108, 113, 118, 132, *136–40*, 177, 325
James, William, 9, 26, 72–73, 86
Johnson, Dr. Samuel, 85, 117, 153, 155, 201; on imagination, 52, 151, 181, 236; "The Vanity of Human Wishes," 146, 148–49, 155–56
Jonson, Ben, 324
Jowett, Benjamin, 222, 228, 291, 297, 307–8; "On the Interpretation of Scripture," 311–12
Joyce, James, 86, 205

Kafka, Franz, 178, 206
Kant, Immanuel, 8–9, 47, 61, 79, 82–83, 86, 115, 163, 228, 236, 241, 274, 277, 279, 326, 330
Keats, John, 1, 225, 344; on negative capability, 113, 115, 160, 173, 227, 289; "On Seeing the Elgin Marbles," 89; "This Living Hand," 216
Keble, John, 30, 194, 323, 339; *The Christian Year*, 326; *Tract 89*, 311
Kempis, Thomas à, 12–13, 120, 181–82
Kent, David A., 266
Kermode, Frank, 319
Kierkegaard, Søren, 134, 151, 165–67, 173, 180, 200, 205, 209–11, 301, 340–41
Kingsley, Charles, 230
Knowledge: crises in knowing, 103, 116–17, 137, 223, 230, 250, 255, 334, 340, 343–44, 347; empirical theories, 242–43, 325, 331, 333–34;

heroic theories, 5, 12, 15, 27, 222, 233, 235, 238, 241, 248, 251, 261, 289, 311; idealist theories, 2–3; realist (Platonic) theories, 2–3, 5, 223; reductive theories, 5, 16, 221–23, 233, 304, 338, 341, 345; reflexive knowledge, 108–9, 232; self-knowledge, 107, 298–99; skeptical theories, 5, 16, 104, 222, *230–33*, 241, 243, 248, 310–11, 314–15, 323, 326–27

Langer, Susanne K., 61
Language: "contiguity-disorder," 27, 90–91, 94, 292; contraction of language to the vanishing point, 70–71, 90, 92, 95–97, 103, 262–63; "desynonymizing," 8, 26, 54, 59–60, 94, 106; economy of theological, 244; limits of, 79, 81, 243–44, 251–52, 297; non sequitur, 206, 235, 317–18; partitioning of, 21, 26, 54, 57, 59–*61*; performative vs. descriptive uses of, 13, 17, 23–24, 45, 69, 79, 91, 100, 108, 113–14, 180, 199–200, 202–3, 213–20, 239–40, 312, 322, 331–32; primal word, 59–60, 94, 96–97, 106, 161; semantic stuttering, 91, 94, 207; "similarity-disorder," 27, 90–91, 94, 292; theories of, 16, 26, 218; verbal bewitchment, 18, 276. *See also* Consciousness: and language; Signs; Signs, theories of
Lessing, Doris, 118
Lillo, George, 42
Locke, John, 107, 110, 236, 242–43
Logic: apparent excluders, 228–29, 241, 248; Aristotelian, 225, 237–38, 240–41, 325; disjunctive propositions, 303–4; double binds, 123–24, 214, 237, 240–41, 274–75, 284, 294, 300–304, 310, 314–15, 317–18, 325, 328, 332–34, 336–37, 339; *Elements of Logick* (Levi Hedge), 105, 304; the hermeneutical circle, 12, 15, 18, 334; implicit (undeveloped) inference, 237–38; inductive logic, 12, *221–23*, 226–27, 229, 289; intuitive inferences, 239; law of contradiction, 14, 285, 303; logical dilemmas, 249, 278–79, 293, 303, 308, 324; logical entailment, 228; logical incompatibility, 281, 300; logic of reserve, 97; Occam's razor, 139, 231; presumptive inferences, 238–39; principle of excluded middle, 285; *reductio ad absurdum*, 110; syllogism, 240, 285. *See also* Logical fallacies
Logical fallacies: category mistake, 13, 178, 180–81; fallacy of equivocation, 278; fallacy of limited induction, 104,

Logical fallacies (*cont'd.*)
284; fallacy of misplaced concreteness,
244, 286; genetic fallacy, 282; *petitio
principii*, *15*, 83, 237, 242–43, *285*
Ludlow, J. M., 330

Mansel, H. L., 3, 13, 228, 248, 300, 326,
336–37
Marx, Karl, 280, 310, 323
Masson, David, 30
Maurice, F. D., 330
Maxwell, James Clerk, 13–14
Meaning: the meaning of "meaning," 343;
meaning more than one says, 244, 252,
257–58, 270–73, 275, 283, 335;
"overmeaning," 258; saying all that one
means, 252; saying less than one ought
to mean, 277; saying more than one
means, 181, 244, 257, 273, 277,
285–86, 335; and significance, 309;
source of, 321; and value, 17, 324, 333,
336, *345–47*
Melodrama: debasements of, 144, 180–81,
190; resourceful use of, 176, 186–87,
191
Melvill, Henry, 218–19, 305, 323
Melville, Herman, 300
Metafiction, 15, 338
Mill, James, 277
Mill, J. S., 6, 9, 13, 18, 23, 222–24, 226,
230, 243, 274, *276–87*, 322, 333,
335–36, 345; essays on Bentham and
Coleridge, 277; "Nature," *277–80*; *On
Liberty*, 224, 228, 230, *281–82*, 284, 335,
344; *System of Logic*, 6, 221–23, 229,
239, *285–86*, 344; *Utilitarianism*, *282–84*,
285, 336; "Utility of Religion,"
280–81, 335, 337
Miller, J. Hillis, 97, 164, 192, 206, 218,
300–301
Milton, John, 69, 72, 235; *Lycidas*, 95,
346; Miltonic framing of noun between
adjectives, 171, 346; *Paradise Lost*, 115,
253–54
Mise-en-abîme, 92, 108, 209
Monet, Claude, 178
Montage in cinema, 61, 68, 327
Mystery: definition of, 320; domesticating,
264–65; knowledge as divination (as
revelation of a mystery), 225–26, 232,
322, 325, 335, 339–40; mysteries of
contextual definition, 18, 226, 232, 252,
258–61, 271–75; mysteries of criminal
detection, 18, 136–37, 232, *288–99*;
mysteries of faith, 18, *88–96*, *104–5*,
184–86, *234–50*, 251, 335–36;
mysteries of historical reconstruction,

18, 289, 293–94, 297–99; mysteries of
identity, 2, 15, 17, *107–220*, 320, 322,
335; mysteries of indefinition, 149, 278;
mysteries vs. problems and puzzles, 74,
110, 233, *336–40*; mystery of an
agnostic void, 17, 54, 64, 66, 69, 71,
87, 96, 113, 149; mystery and method,
15, 18, *221–320*, 322; mystery of
a primal word, 17, 59–60, 68, 94,
96, 106, 327, 337; mystery of
self-knowledge, 17, 140, 146, 149,
298–99; mystery of self-making, 17,
175, 215, 272, 323; mystery of a
sublime God, 17, 79, 90, 93–96,
100–101; mystery of an unanalyzable
unity or whole, 198, 218, 334; mystery
and the unconscious, 1, 15, *21–106*,
322; mystery of an unconscious
consciousness, 74–75, 82, 85–87;
mystery of the unlimited vs. mystery
of the merely unknowable, 227;
mystery of a veiled fate, 16–17, 25, 35,
41, 43, 337; mystery words, 234, 251,
258, 261, 271–75, 278, 304, 329;
typological mystery, 265, 311
Mysticism, 11
Myth, 289, 301, 312; Strauss's theory of,
78, 334

Nagel, Thomas, 15, 121, 314
Narrator(s): alignment with a character
inside the fiction, 123, 131, 152;
censorship of edited materials, 138–39;
deflection of inappropriate responses,
46, 57–58; double irony of (*see* Irony:
double); method of "baring the device,"
40–41, 171, 297; multiple, 296–98;
power of sympathetic trespass, 123;
restoration of a reader's ignorance, 124;
unreliable, 139, 155; who forgets as
much as he remebers, 155
Negative capability, 288, 291–92, 298, 312,
320, 329. *See also* Keats: on negative
capability; Role-playing
Nescience vs. ignorance, 2
Nesting structures in narrative, 83–84, 86,
108, 138, 162, 209, 344. *See also*
Frames; Recursive narrative
Newman, J. H., 5, 7, 18–19, 104, 221,
224–26, 228, 230, 251, 271, 278, 282,
322, 324, 336–37; *Apologia pro Vita Sua*,
10–11, 14–15, 224, 230, 243, *244–50*,
273, 298; *Difficulties of Anglicans*, 104;
Essay in Aid of A Grammar of Assent, 88,
104, 232; *Essay on the Development of
Christian Doctrine*, 105, 108, 229–30, 325;
Sermons Preached before the University of

Oxford, 12, 105, 224–25, 230, *234–44*, 247, 251, 325, 329, 341–43
Newton, Sir Isaac, 28, 74, 323
Niebuhr, Barthold, 15, 227–28, 297, 333–34
Nietzsche, Friedrich, 54, 72, 86, 218, 326
Nozick, Robert, 286, 345, 347

Occam, 139, 231
Oedipus, 34–35, 38, 43, 108
Optical illusion, 102–3
Origen, 30

Parabasis, 164
Parables, 206, 235, 317–18
Paralogisms and antinomies, 2–3, 60, 79, 94–95, 104, 171–72, 228, 236, 244, 281, 300, 303, 326
Parker, Patricia, 59
Pater, Walter, 5, 107, 222, 228, 230, 343, 345; *Plato and Platonism*, 223, 300, *338–39*; *Studies in the History of the Renaissance*, 107
Peckham, Morse, 302
Perspectivism, 313–14
Philosophy. *See* Ethics; Knowledge; Logic
Plato, 5–6, 78, 81, 181, 223–24, 278, 291, 324–25, 338–39, 345; doctrine of ideas, 222, 228, 231, 338–39; on "noble lies," 273; Platonism, 77, 228
Pope, Alexander, 124, 127; *Dunciad*, 76
Poststructuralism, 77, 302, 311, 314, 320
Pragmatism, 9–10, 16, 323, 334, 337
Pringle-Pattison, A. S., 9, 116, 330
Probabilities in moral vs. mathematical reasoning, 104–5
Proofs. *See* Explanations vs. proofs
Prosody: anapests, 216–17; caesural pauses and breaks, 80, 89–90, 98, 210, 219, 252, 255–56, 261, 270, 298; caesuras, *89*, 95, 97–98, 169, 200, 204, 206–9, 214, 216–18, 257, 259, 267; crossing the divide between stanzas, 92, 100–101, 170, 240; dimeters, 267; elegiacs, 174; end-line dashes, 93, 204–5, 207; end-stopped lines, 170, 216, 270; enjambement (run-ons), 169–70, 267, 346; extra-stress signs, 96; feminine rhymes, 255; hexameters, 267; hypermetric lines, 216; internal rhymes, 257; multiple rhymes, 257; octaves and sestets in sonnets, 253, 269; pauses filled by words, 267; terminal stress, 171; tetrameters, 267

Rafael, 199–202
Rawls, John, 284, 286
Realism. *See* Knowledge: realist (Platonic) theories

Recollection, 166, 210, 216; vs. remembrance, 211–12
Recursive narrative, 161–62, 209–10
Remaking vs. reinterpreting a character, 108, 116, 122, 124, 127, 130–32, 136
Renan, Ernest, 177
Representation: crises in, 1, 6–7, *10–18*, 46–47, 70, 72, 84, 103, 109–12, 228, 234, 242, 244, 267, 289, 323–25, 327, 331–32, 334–37, 339–40, 342–43, 345, 347; description vs. invention, 115–21; representation vs. presentation, 3–4, 30; representational theory of fiction, *117–18*, 122
Repression, 1, 22–23, 34, *62–64*, 69, 80, 82, 160, 208, 216, 253, 324
Reserve. *See* Logic: logic of reserve; Silence: of reserve; Theology: of reserve
Reynolds, Joshua, 271–72
Rhetoric: acrostic fragments, 83; alliteration, 96, 144, 217, 263, 268; anaphora, 32, 34, 38, 40, 56, 66–67, 80, 144, 253, 269; antithesis, 131; antonymns, 26, 88, 93, 97, 181, 327; aphorisms, 26, 79, 205; aporia, 3, 165, 303; aposiopesis, 93; apostrophe, 62, 91, 96, 101, 153, 202, 204, 208–9, 216; appositional naming, 27, 38, 63, 89, 92, 96, 99–100, 103, 127, 159, 174, 212, 217, 248; assonance, 96, 263; asyndeton, 63, 89, 113, 142, 150, 279; buried metaphor, 203; catachresis, 55, 64, 82–83, 98, 198, 218; chiasmus, 37, 54–55, 66, 99, 127, 133, 158, 219–20, 225–26, 252, 259, 266–67, 270; circumlocution, 130; control of a reader's sympathy, 46, 56, 58; dashes, 95–96, 102–3, 185, 190, 196–98, 204–8, 210–11, 214, 218, 245, 249–50, 252, 258, 261, 298; dilations (amplification), 27, 63, 89–90, 97; double meaning, 132–33, 137–38, 150, 152–53, 158, 187, 203–4, 245, 264; dream rhetoric, 3, 26, 59, 61, 63–68, 161, 164–65; elision, 27, 42, 56, 70, 85, 89, 93, 97, 196–97, 200, 212, 227, 252, 257, 296; ellipsis, 6, 52, 66, 91, 98, 100, 159, 193, 202, 213, 292; etymological links, 76; euphemism, 134, 147, 291; Euphuism, 74; figurative transfer, 70; gnomic words, 34, 43, 50; hyperbaton (wrenching word order), 51, 62–63, 99, 131, 214, 217, 134, 147; hyperbole, 131, 149; literal and metaphoric portraits, 148; metalepsis, 80–81; metaphoric displacement, 70; metaphoric transports, 180–81;

Rhetoric (*cont'd.*)
    metaphors of situation, 4, *30–32, 35–41,*
    43–44, 48, 131, 142–43, 147, 193–94,
    252, 260–61, 324; metonymic chains,
    39; metonymy, 26, 36–37, 81, 91, 94,
    202, 209, 216, 260, 292, 338, 342;
    oracular rhetoric, 26; ostensive
    definitions, 93; oxymoron, 6, 55–56,
    64, 73, 75, 80, 82–83, 88, 95, 102, 105,
    154, 181, 218, 280, 327; paradox, 47,
    56, 74, 82, 95, 160, 185, 190, 214, 234,
    237, 240, 244, 271, 284, 295, 298, 304,
    308, 332, 339; paraleipsis, 148;
    parallelism and antithesis, 89, 295;
    parodic use of like endings, 73, 75,
    150; personification, 62–63; persuasive
    redefinitions (realignment of emotive
    and descriptive meanings), 26, 84, 127,
    133, 135–36, 142–43, 180, 185–86,
    225–26, 230, *235–39,* 272, 283–84, 329,
    333; polysyndeton, 91, 101, 201, 269;
    prophetic fragments, 26; puns (word
    play), 56, 67, 76, 94, 126, 128–29, 135,
    138, 264, 266; restoration of forgotten
    etymology, 177; rhetoric of religion, 14,
    78; rhetorical question, 177; rhetorical
    seesaw, 124; riddles, 34, 43, 83, 254,
    257; simile, 36, 46, 58, 216;
    synecdoche, 80–81, 153, 317;
    synesthesia, 65, 98; tautology, 17, 28,
    35, 56, 60–61, 77, 90, 100, 159, 252,
    261, 264, 266, 270, 327, 347; theory
    of metaphor, 77; tmesis, 21, 25–26, 35,
    38–39, 41, 89–90, 92, 96, 128, 138,
    324; tropes of reserve (and veiling), 4,
    56, 73, 82, 206, 219, 252, 262, 270–71;
    tu quoque argument, 273; verbal
    seduction, 51, 131, 208; verbal
    sleight-of-hand, 101, 263; verbal tennis,
    54–55, 135; zeugma, 201
Richards, I. A., 306
Ricks, Christopher, 16, 196
Role-playing, 109–10, 112–13, 116,
    142–48, 151–52, 155–60, 162–64,
    166–68, 172, 174–75, 328–29; refusal
    to play a role, 189–90
Rossetti, Christina, 4, 18–19, 21–22,
    24–25, 28, 30, 119, 225–26, *251–71,*
    274–75, 325, 347; "Afterward he
    repented, and went," 258–59; "All
    heaven is blazing," *263–64,* 347; "All
    saints," 258; "A bruised reed shall he
    not break," *262–63;* "Cardinal
    Newman," 251; "A Christmas carol"
    ("In the bleak mid-winter"), *258,* 261,
    270, *346–47;* "Dead before death,"
    253–54; "A Fisher-wife," 260; "Have I

not striven, my God?", *268–70;* "A heavy
    heart," 259; "Her seed; it shall bruise
    thy head," *264–66;* "I cannot, Lord,
    lift up my heart to thee," 259; "Judge
    nothing before the time," 251;
    "Listening," 252–53; "Love is strong as
    death," 268; "May," *254–55;* "Praying
    Always," 266; "Seeking Rest," 255–57;
    "Sursam Corda," 259; "Twice," 7,
    259–61, 270; "Up-Hill," 268; "Weary
    in well-doing," *267–68;* "Winter, my
    secret," *257–58*
Rossetti, William Michael, 253
Royce, Josiah, 33
Ruskin, John, 7, 9–10, 30, 178, 224, 226,
    272, 275, 278; *The Elements of Drawing,*
    178; on Imagination Associative, *31–32,*
    226; "The Mystery of Life and Its
    Arts," 234, *271–72,* 330, 343
Russell, Bertrand, 284

Santayana, George, 6
Schiller, F. C. S., 9, 30, 116, 330
Schiller, Friedrich, 26, 81
Schlegel, Friedrich, 164
Schleiermacher, Friedrich, 15, 300, 334
Schopenhauer, Arthur, 6, 8, 43, 47, 315,
    324
Science: evolutionary theory, 221–22;
    family secret of, 345; and humanities,
    2, *345;* scientific method, 5, 222,
    229–30, 343; social science, 344; and
    theological models in Huxley, 13;
    uncertainty principle, 1. *See also*
    Fictions: fictive theories of matter in
    Huxley
Scott, Sir Walter, 181
Self-identity, three thoeries of, 116
Self-making, the doctrine of, 2, 9–10, 13,
    17, 107–11, 329–33
Self-reference, reflexive, 108; three
    theories of, 108–9
Semiotics. *See* Signs; Signs, theories of
Shakespeare, William, 173, 335, 344;
    Hamlet, 37, 41, 141, 171, 173, 247; *King
    Lear,* 46, 72; *Macbeth,* 149; *Romeo and
    Juliet,* 46, 305; *The Tempest,* 1, 81, 156,
    247
Shelley, Percy Bysshe, 7, 26, 49, 68,
    211–12, 251, 323
Sidgwick, Henry, 6, 120, 276–77, 281
Signs: agnostic semiotics, 244, 309, 328;
    extrinsic, 10, 60–61, 79, 198, 243–44,
    327–28; illusion of a grounded sign-
    system, 141, ·155; intrinsic (or iconic),
    10–11, 17, 53, 60–61, 73, 78–79, 101,
    243–44, 327–28; petrified (or

"superannuated"), 73, 84, 314;
self-replicating, 61 (*see also* Infinite
regress); the "signless Inane," 72, 75,
77, 82–83, 86–87, 328, 342; signless
truths, 58, 69, 328; signs without
referents, 117, 142, 243–44, 309, 328;
transparent, 79, 152, 190–92;
"unconsummated," 61, 64. *See also*
Signs, theories of
Signs, theories of, 76–77, 79, 84, 198,
317, 344; agnostic, 10–11, 26, 53–54,
155, 206, 327–28; existential, 10;
Viconian, 10–11, 26, 53–54, 155, 206,
327–28
Silence: of acceptance, 189; of characters
who refuse to play a dramatic part,
189–90, 194–95; Clough's religion of,
78, 251; coy, 184; created by spaces
between dashes, 55–56, 85, 92, 204–5;
and death, 182–83; deceitful, 190; as
a desired state (the goal of discourse),
28–29, 75, 129, 296; of exclusion, 133;
and God, 75, 102, 106; of the
inexpressible, 2–4, 7, 17, 21–22, 26–27,
53–54, 56, 58, 60–61, 63–64, 69, 71,
75, 78, 100, 102, 106, 176, 179–80,
218, 257, 336, *340–41*; of plenitude or
full possession, 26, 106, 130, 189–90,
197, 201, 206, 211–12, 214–18, 270,
342, 348; protective, 183, 192;
remaining silent when one should
speak, 188, 192, 211, 296; of reserve,
7, 16, 21, 49, 84, 112, 123–30, 137–38,
150, 159, 176, 196–204, 206, 218,
244–45, 249, 251, 256–57, 272, 340–41,
347; and secret knowledge, 114; silent
auditors, 114, 196–97; silent censure,
184, 191; "silent-speaking" words, 99,
114, 177, 182, 192, 341; speaking
without saying anything, 134, 184–86;
of stupidity and indifference, 191; three
forms of silence in George Eliot,
192–93; of the unspeakable, 2, 25–27,
78, 100, 136, 186, 189, 195, 201, 206,
218–19, 249, 251–52, 336, *340–41*; of
the void (agnostic silence), 26, 53, 57,
75, 81, 13, 17, 106, 112, 149–50, 158,
189, 197, 204–16, 218, 257, 340
Skepticism. *See* Knowledge: skeptical
theories
Smith, Anne Egerton, 203
Socrates, 75, 77, 80, 159, 166, 278, 282,
294–95, 310, 335, 343–44; Socratic
irony, 268; Socratic questioning, 137;
the Socratic secret, 165
Sophists, 75, 310
Sparshott, Francis, 309

Spencer, Herbert, 8, 14, 326
Spenser, Edmund, 142, 328
Spinoza, Baruch, 23, 249
Split personality, 115, 289, 295
Stanley, A. P., 288
Steiner, George, 251
Stevens, Wallace, 211–12
Stevenson, Charles L., 225
Stevenson, Robert Louis, 115
Stoehr, Taylor, 41
Strauss, David Friedrich, 4, 13, 78–79,
116, 163, 227, 289, 297, 314, 318, 330,
339
Sublimity, 21, 27, 67, 88–89, 94, 96,
100–101, 198; the elliptical sublime, 17,
27; the expansive sublime, 17, 27, 90,
100, 103; the indescribable and the
sublime, 93, 102; the mathematical
sublime, 61; sublime indifference, 208;
"sublime reserve," 86; the sublime and
the subliminal, 89, 95
Subtext, 69
Swift, Jonathan, 77, 149–50, 154, 248,
279, 315
Swinburne, A. C., 251
Symbols. *See* Signs; Signs, theories of
Syntax. *See* Grammar

Taylor, William (of Norwich), 163
Teleology, 221
Tennyson, Lord Alfred, 4, 17, 21–22, 27,
104, 121; "The Ancient Sage," 2; "The
Holy Grail," *101–3*; *Idylls of the King*,
119–20; *In Memoriam*, 1, 7, 10, 12, 23,
29, 81, 90, *97–101*, 104, 110, 121, 223,
225, 266, 326, 331, 341–43, 347; "The
Lotos-Eaters," 25; "The Making of
Man," 331; "The Poet," 68;
"Timbuctoo," 104; "The Two Voices,"
115, 224; "Ulysses," 23, 347; "The
Vision of Sin," 65, 68
Text and intertext, 76
Thackeray, W. M., 11, 17, 176, 323; *Henry
Esmond*, 139, 155; *Vanity Fair*, 28, 108–9,
112, 116–17, 120–22, *141–56*, 160, 174,
176, 225, 328–29, 344
Theology: agnostic, 8, 13–14, 26, 171,
226, 300, 323, 325–28, 347; *agnostos
theos*, 75, 77, 82; anthropomorphic
(religion of humanity), 12, 17, 177–78,
280, 330; Athanasian creed, 159;
biblical, 12; Buddhism, 160, 183;
Calvinist, 8, 324; Clough's religion of
silence vs. religion of work, 8, 78, 171;
Deism, 117, 237, 328; evangelical, 8–9,
25–26, 126, 162, 323, 325–26, 330;
evolutionary, 215; Fichte's "Applied

Theology (*cont'd.*)
Christianity," 77; fideism, 248, 326;
Gnosticism, 337; God the friend, God
the enemy, God the void, 171;
Hegelian, 330–31; the Higher Criticism,
301, 306, 314; Hindu, 329–30;
historical religion, 172, 304–8, 319;
Kantian, 172; Methodism, 177;
Monophysites, 246–47, 298; moral, 119,
171–72; negative, 69, 240; Oxford
Movement (Tractarianism), 273, 323,
339; patristic exegesis, 108, 300;
Pelagian heresy, 323, 325; Protestant
distrust of office and works, 308;
rational, 236, 279–80, 336–37; of
reserve, 27–29, 49, 126, 194, 225, 264,
339; Scholastic, 285; theological models
in science, 13–14; voluntarist, 215,
324–25
Thomas, Lewis, 345
Thucydides, 235
Tillich, Paul, 306
Tooke, Horne, 283
Trollope, Anthony, 4, 11, 17, 169, 323,
325, 335; *Barchester Towers*, 108, 112,
115–16, *122–32*, 152, 290, 325
Tropes. *See* Rhetoric
Turner, J. M. W., 178, 271
Typology, 265, 311, 318–19, 323

Underthought, 95–96
Unspeakable vs. the inexpressible. *See*
Silence: of the unspeakable
Utilitarianism. *See* Ethics: utilitarian

Vaughan, Henry, 251
Vico, G. B., 9, 13, 26, 327, 331–32, 334
View from inside vs. view from outside,
2, 5–6, 25, 110–12, 120–21, 173,
221–25, 334
Virgil, 75, 211, 247, 273
von Ranke, Leopold, 288

Ward, W. G., 305, 326
Weatherby, Harold L., 104
Wesley, John, 178
Whitehead, A. N., 244, 286
Wittgenstein, Ludwig, 226, 276, 342
Wollheim, Richard, 13, 18, 336
Wordsworth, William, 116, 195, 236, 322;
"Elegiac Stanzas," 63, 70, 279; "Ode
to Duty," 25; "Ode on the Intimations
of Immortality," 46, 81; "Tintern
Abbey," 279

Yeats, W. B., 197, 271; "Blood and the
Moon," 291; "The Folly of Being
Comforted," 98

Library of Congress Cataloging-in-Publication Data

Shaw, W. David (William David)
    Victorians and mystery : crises of representation / W. David Shaw.
        p.   cm.
    Includes bibliographical references.
    ISBN 0-8014-2403-8 (alk. paper)
    1. English literature—19th century—History and criticism.   2. Mystery in literature.
3. Subconsciousness in literature.   4. Identity (Psychology) in literature.   5. Knowledge,
Theory of, in literature.   6. Mimesis in literature.   I. Title.
PR468.M87S53   1990
820.9'353—dc20   89-38545